Islam, Politics, Anthropology

ISLAM, POLITICS, ANTHROPOLOGY

EDITED BY FILIPPO OSELLA AND BENJAMIN SOARES

WILEY-BLACKWELL

A John Wiley & Sons, Ltd., Publication

Royal Anthropological
Institute

This edition first published 2010
Originally published as Volume 15, Special Issue May 2009, of *The Journal of the Royal Anthropological Society*
© 2010 Royal Anthropological Institute of Great Britain & Ireland

Blackwell Publishing was acquired by John Wiley & Sons in February 2007. Blackwell's publishing program has been merged with Wiley's global Scientific, Technical, and Medical business to form Wiley-Blackwell.

Registered Office
John Wiley & Sons Ltd, The Atrium, Southern Gate, Chichester, West Sussex, PO19 8SQ, United Kingdom

Editorial Offices
350 Main Street, Malden, MA 02148–5020, USA
9600 Garsington Road, Oxford, OX4 2DQ, UK
The Atrium, Southern Gate, Chichester, West Sussex, PO19 8SQ, UK

For details of our global editorial offices, for customer services, and for information about how to apply for permission to reuse the copyright material in this book please see our website at www.wiley.com/wiley-blackwell.

The rights of Filippo Osella and Benjamin Soares to be identified as the authors of the editorial material in this work has been asserted in accordance with the Copyright, Designs and Patents Act 1988.

Wiley also publishes its books in a variety of electronic formats. Some content that appears in print may not be available in electronic books.

Designations used by companies to distinguish their products are often claimed as trademarks. All brand names and product names used in this book are trade names, service marks, trademarks or registered trademarks of their respective owners. The publisher is not associated with any product or vendor mentioned in this book. This publication is designed to provide accurate and authoritative information in regard to the subject matter covered. It is sold on the understanding that the publisher is not engaged in rendering professional services. If professional advice or other expert assistance is required, the services of a competent professional should be sought.

Library of Congress Cataloging-in-Publication Data

Islam, politics, anthropology / edited by Filippo Osella and Benjamin Soares.
    p. cm.
  Includes bibliographical references and index.
  ISBN 978-1-4443-3295-7 (pbk. : alk. paper) 1. Political anthropology—Islamic countries. 2. Islam and politics. 3. Islam and culture. 4. Politics and culture—Islamic countries. 5. Islamic countries—Politics and government. I. Osella, Filippo. II. Soares, Benjamin F.

  GN641.I75 2010
  306.6'97—dc22

2009041491

A catalogue record for this book is available from the British Library.

Set in 10/12pt Minion by Toppan Best-set Premedia Limited

01 2010

Contents

Notes on contributors

Irfan Ahmad earned his Ph.D. degree in anthropology at the University of Amsterdam. Currently, he is Lecturer in Politics at Monash University, Melbourne, where he is involved in leading the Centre for the Study of Islam and the Modern World. He is author of *Islamism and Democracy in India: the transformation of Jamaat-e-Islami* (Princeton University Press, 2009).

Hatsuki Aishima is a social anthropologist reading Oriental Studies at the University of Oxford. Her doctoral thesis project, which studies Islamic knowledge and intellectuals in contemporary Egypt through the prism of 'Abd al-Halim Mahmud, was awarded the Albert Hourani Graduate Studentship 2008-9 of St Antony's College.

Lara Deeb is Associate Professor in the Department of Anthropology at Scripps College and the author of *An enchanted modern: gender and public piety in Shi'i Lebanon* (Princeton University Press, 2006).

Rosa De Jorio is Associate Professor of Anthropology at the University of North Florida in Jacksonville. Her research focuses on gender, politics, the politics of culture, memory and the historical imagination, Islam and social movements, in Mali. She has guest-edited two special issues for *Polar: The Political and Legal Anthropology Review* (2003) and *Africa Today* (2006). Her book *Representing the nation: the politics of culture in Mali (1960-2002)* will appear in 2010 with the University of Illinois Press.

Maimuna Huq is Assistant Professor of Cultural Anthropology at the University of South Carolina. Her publications include 'From piety to romance: Islam-oriented texts in Bangladesh', in *New media in the Muslim world: the emerging public sphere* (eds) Dale F. Eickelman and Jon W. Anderson (Indiana University Press, 2003).

Kai Kresse is Vice-Director for Research at the Zentrum Moderner Orient (ZMO) in Berlin. He was Lecturer in Social Anthropology at the University of St Andrews (2002-2009) and Evans-Pritchard Lecturer at All Souls College, Oxford, in 2005. His monograph *Philosophising in Mombasa: knowledge, Islam and intellectual practice on the Swahili coast* (Edinburgh University Press, 2007) was a finalist for the African Studies Association's 2008 Melville J. Herskovits Award.

Magnus Marsden is Senior Lecturer in Social Anthropology with reference to South and Central Asia at the School of Oriental and African Studies, University of London. His has conducted research on Muslim thought and identity in the Chitral region of Pakistan, and, most recently, northern Afghanistan.

Julie McBrien is Assistant Professor of Anthropology at the University of Amsterdam. Her current research examines the dreams and disillusions of young women in Kyrgyzstan.

Caroline Osella is Reader in the Department of Anthropology and Sociology at the School of Oriental and African Studies, UK. She has spent twenty years undertaking research work in Kerala and with Malayali migrants in the Gulf states. Her interests revolve around the broad question of how projects of identity crafting are brought back to the body, while socially constructed bodies are differentiated to reflect class, ethnic, and gender differences and to forge social hierarchies.

Filippo Osella is Reader in the Department of Anthropology at the University of Sussex, UK. He has conducted research in Kerala, South India for the last twenty years, and lately in a number of West Asian Gulf countries. His current research focuses on the emergence of Islamic reformist movements and the rise of a new Muslim middle class in Kerala in the context of an intensification of economic, cultural, and religious links between South India and the Gulf region.

Daromir Rudnyckyj is Assistant Professor of Pacific and Asian Studies at the University of Victoria. His research projects examine Islam and globalization in contemporary Indonesia, Malaysia, Singapore, and Brunei. His forthcoming book is entitled *Spiritual economies: Islam and the after life of development*.

Armando Salvatore is Associate Professor, Sociology of Culture and Communication, University of Naples – L'Orientale, and Heisenberg Fellow, Institute of Social Sciences, Humboldt University, Berlin, and Institute for Advanced Study in the Humanities, Essen. His latest book is *The public sphere: liberal modernity, Catholicism, Islam* (Palgrave Macmillan, 2007).

Samuli Schielke received his MA in Islamic studies from the University of Bonn in 2000 and his Ph.D. in social sciences from the University of Amsterdam in 2006. He is currently a research fellow at the Zentrum Moderner Orient (ZMO) in Berlin.

Benjamin Soares is a Senior Research Fellow at the Afrika-Studiecentrum in Leiden, The Netherlands. His publications include *Islam and the prayer economy* (Edinburgh University Press/University of Michigan Press, 2005) and two co-edited volumes, *Islam and Muslim politics in Africa* (Palgrave Macmillan, 2007) and *Islam, Etat et société en Afrique* (Karthala, 2009).

Gregory Starrett is Professor of Anthropology at the University of North Carolina at Charlotte. He is author of *Putting Islam to work* (University of California Press, 1998) and co-editor of *Teaching Islam: textbooks and religion in the Middle East* (Lynne Rienner, 2007).

1

Islam, politics, anthropology

Benjamin Soares *Afrika-Studiecentrum*
Filippo Osella *University of Sussex*

Our main aim in this book is to reflect critically on the study of Islam and politics in anthropology. Islam and politics are, of course, incredibly fraught topics. Anthropology itself has a long and not unproblematic engagement with the study of Islam and Muslim societies, and so first we would like to return to that history before considering ongoing anthropological debates and suggesting new terms of analysis of the relationship between Islam and politics.[1] Our understanding of politics is deliberately broad. We pay attention to the state and formal politics, involving various social actors and organizations. But we are also interested in everyday politics and various kinds of micropolitics, arenas where anthropology proves especially adept. It is at the intersection of these multiple levels – where the field of politics is constituted in practice – that we situate the analytical focus of this book.

While some might claim that the events of September 11, 2001 were among the most central defining moments in the representations of Islam and Muslim societies, stereotypes about Islam and Muslims have actually been remarkably resilient. The figure of the 'mad mullah' who radicalizes the uneducated, naïve, but largely benign Muslim masses in nineteenth-century British accounts of Muslims' anti-colonial politics (see, e.g., Ansari 2005; Edwards 1989; Jalal 2008) and twentieth-century French accounts of allegedly dangerous 'Sufis' and/or 'Wahhabis' who threaten to lead ordinary Muslims in their West African colonies astray (see, e.g., Harrison 1988; Launay & Soares 1999; Triaud 1992) are the genealogical antecedents of contemporary characterizations of 'radical' Islam and Islamism[2] in much Western media and public culture. Meanwhile, images of (veiled) Muslim women have acquired iconic status in the western imaginary as representations of the oppressed and subordinated Other *par excellence*.[3] After the Iranian Revolution in the late 1970s and the widespread recognition of the limitations of the secularization thesis, many questioned the compatibility of Islam and Muslims with modernity. In a countermove, others tried to prove that Islam could indeed be 'modern' and compatible with democracy. As Mahmood Mamdani (2002) has remarked, since September 11, 2001 there has been much 'culture talk' about Muslims and their politics wherever they happen to live in the world. We are, therefore, no longer surprised by many commentators' essentializing impulses when the object of study is Islam or Muslims. Like many other anthropologists, we are also cognizant of and increasingly wary of stepped-up attempts by governments, their militaries, and security apparatuses to appropriate anthropological methods and insights into Islam and Muslim societies for possibly nefarious ends in ongoing wars, including the so-called 'war on terror'.[4] Many of our Muslim research subjects have become well informed and savvy about the images of Muslims (and Muslim women in particular) that circulate, and the kinds of Muslims thought to be 'good' and 'bad' (see Hirschkind & Mahmood 2002; Mamdani 2002). But this is not to assert, as some interpreters of Edward Said's *Orientalism* (1978; cf. Varisco 2007) have seemed to suggest, any facile or inevitable Orientalist trap, which would *a priori* prevent any compelling representations of Islam and Muslim societies. This is not a position which we, or the contributors to this book, are willing to accept.

Let us turn to some of the specific challenges associated with the anthropological study of Islam and Muslim societies. While academic discourse and Western media alike have produced reified views of Islam and Muslims in abundance, such views have also emerged from within Islam itself, via Muslims' interpretations and representations of their own religion as unitary, timeless, and unchanging (see Launay 1992; Parkin 2000). Representations are never simply reflections on or descriptions of reality, of social and religious processes necessarily already 'out there' in the world; they have generative power. In reshaping conceptual categories, they are orientated towards producing something which is given concrete ground, thereby intensifying a reality already alluded to in discourse itself (Callon, Méadel & Rabeharisoa 2002; Mitchell 2005; Navaro-Yashin 2002; Thrift 2005). It is imperative to pay attention to the genealogies of discourses (academic, state, 'official', global, as well as those of our research subjects and interlocutors), which might become authoritative and normative, and through which politics in Muslim societies is comprehended, experienced, legitimated, or contested. We must also remember that seemingly authoritative discourses and disciplinary practices are neither totalizing, nor are their outcomes necessarily easily predictable. Finally, it is also important to heed the warning of those who have argued against automatically privileging religion as the principal – or perhaps unique – foundation for Muslim identity and political practice (see Abu-Lughod 1989; Al-Ali 2000; Grillo 2004; Silverstein 2004).

Social structure, culture, and the conundrums of modernity

It is striking that professional anthropologists who conducted fieldwork in many colonial settings in the twentieth century in Africa and Asia tended to ignore Islam and Muslim societies or simply left the study of Islam and Muslims to historians and/or those trained as Orientalists (see Launay 2006; Soares 2000). Some anthropologists did, however, write about Islam and Muslims at the height of European colonial rule, notably E.E. Evans-Pritchard. His study of the Sanusiyya – a Sufi order – in Libya (Evans-Pritchard 1949) was perhaps the first anthropological study focused on Islam and Muslim society *per se*. At a time when anthropologists were almost exclusively concerned with small-scale societies or those deemed to be somehow more authentically 'African' or 'Asian', the originality of Evans-Pritchard's book was to show how a specifically Muslim institution – the Sufi order – could be established along extensive trans-Saharan trade routes and subsequently used to mobilize 'tribal' groups against the Italian occupation of Libya. Despite Evans-Pritchard's attention to the role of religion and of religious leadership in politics in this book, anthropological research which followed often failed to deal seriously with Islam as an object of study, privileging instead research on 'tribal' societies, particularly in the Middle East, where social structure and kinship were a major focus (see Gilsenan 1990 for an overview).[5]

It was Ernest Gellner who developed Evans-Pritchard's social structural approach furthest.[6] Gellner's work became a key reference-point for many studies of Muslim societies. Although Gellner's model of 'Muslim society' – purposely identified in the singular (1981; see also Gellner 1963; 1968) – posits Islam as resistant to secularization, it is noteworthy that Islam and modernity are not deemed incompatible. In Gellner's neo-Weberian model (cf. Turner 1974), modernity takes the form of progressive rationalization. Gellner argues that Muslim society will over time necessarily eschew the 'traditional' and 'ecstatic' forms of religion associated with the rural (so-called popular or 'low' Islam) for the more modern, puritan, and 'rational' forms of religion (read reformism) associated with the urban and scriptural ('high' Islam). An important element to Gellner's argument is that this will be a permanent break, which occurs as a result of colonial modernization (1981: 56ff.; 159ff.) when 'the pendulum swings more violently and becomes unhinged' (1981: 159). For Gellner, Islamic reformism is indeed perfectly 'compatible' with modernity (see, e.g., Gellner 1981: 170ff.).

In contrast to Gellner's British social-structural model of 'Muslim society' writ large, Clifford Geertz in *Islam observed* (1968) proposed a cultural anthropological reading of 'meaning' and 'culture', which vary according to context in the Muslim world. While Islam here is not, as in Gellner's words, the 'blueprint of a social order' (1981: 1), it nevertheless provides people with enduring 'frames of perception' and 'blueprints for conduct' (Geertz 1968: 98). Geertz contrasted the overall 'cultural styles' of Morocco and Indonesia, in his view much more important than 'social structure'. However, Geertz's attention to 'meaning' was accompanied by a notion of social 'order'. One can see, for example, that both Morocco and Indonesia have undergone what he calls a 'scripturalist interlude' before returning to the dominant – that is, seemingly hegemonic – cultural styles of 'maraboutism' and 'illuminationism', respectively. In other words, Geertz deploys two different understandings of 'religion', firstly, as enduring 'culture', and, secondly, as a set of historically contingent sensibilities and practices. While scripturalism in Indonesia and Morocco emerges as a 'counter-tradition', setting the basis for an engagement with colonial modernity and for the development of nationalist politics, Geertz claims that the logic of a particular 'cultural system' cannot be entirely transcended. Political processes, which might be constrained by 'culture', can engender neither enduring transformations nor historical shifts.[7] Moreover, Geertz's modernity, like Gellner's, is a Western prerogative that spreads with colonialism. While it might be taken up or contested, it will invariably lead to problematic outcomes, such as fledgeling states that have failed to transform themselves into fully modern functioning polities.

Shortcomings notwithstanding, Gellner and Geertz both pointed to the importance of religion in societies undergoing profound social transformations. It is significant that both were writing in the heyday of modernization theory, when the secularization thesis was near-hegemonic in social-scientific thinking about 'modern' societies. They helped counter this by tracing the emergence under colonialism of novel religious and political sensibilities. They understood 'modern' ways of being Muslim – often glossed as 'scripturalism', 'reformism', and so forth – as the articulation of nationalist politics and sought to link these with particular social groups' responses and engagements with colonialism. This is of course a far cry from more recent characterizations of Islam as basically hostile to modernity (see, e.g., Giddens 1999: 4-5; Huntington 1996).

If the Iranian Revolution and the critique of Orientalism spurred many to grapple with the challenges of studying Muslim societies, the post-Cold War era seemed to herald the possibility of new ways of thinking about Islam and Muslim societies. However, commitments to Weberian notions of the progressive rationalization of religion under conditions of modernity have endured. Writing at the intersection of anthropology and political science, Dale Eickelman and James Piscatori (1996) have analysed what they called 'Muslim politics', in a broad synthesis of developments in various settings. They have advanced the argument that, in recent years, Muslims throughout the world have come to 'objectify' their religion. In this process of objectification, which echoes the shift from religiousness to religious-mindedness that Geertz had outlined,[8] Muslims have developed 'heightened self-consciousness' of Islam as a religious 'system' (Eickelman & Piscatori 1996: 39; cf. Deeb 2006 on the 'authentication' of Islam). Eickelman and Piscatori argue that with mass education, increased literacy, and the spread of new media technologies (cf. Anderson 1991; Gellner 1983), there has been an increased fragmentation of authority in Muslim societies. As a result, a greater diversity of people deign to speak about what Islam is. The 'traditional' interpreters of Islam – Muslim scholars or 'ulama – have lost their monopoly and now compete with other Muslims (see also Zaman 2002). This shift away from an assumed dichotomy between 'ulama and the so-called 'popular Islam' of ordinary Muslims opened new possibilities for understanding Islam and Muslim societies.

Focusing on the links between education, literacy, and media and changes in religious authority, Eickelman and Piscatori's analytical turn placed contemporary Muslim politics within epistemological shifts and social processes – reflexivity, increased rationalization, and democratic participation, for instance – ordinarily associated in mainstream social theory with Western modernity (see also Hefner 2005; cf. Soares & Otayek 2007). But for those scholars who have subsequently identified hybrid or alternative modernities in various Muslim societies (e.g. Abu-Lughod 1998; Brenner 1996; Göle 1996; 2002; White 2002; cf. Deeb 2006; Mahmood 2005; Navaro-Yashin 2002), modernity itself remains a specific Northern European or North American intellectual tradition spreading to the rest of the world in the wake of colonialism. In other words, positing the existence of domesticated or indigenized modernities depends on a Eurocentric model implying a lack of authenticity to non-Western modernities and simultaneously denying equal participation of the Muslim Other (Clarence-Smith 2007; cooke & Lawrence 2005: 17ff.; Mitchell 2000; Navaro-Yashin 2002: 9ff.). The arguments of many Muslim intellectuals, oft repeated by our research respondents, attribute this epistemological denial to articulations of colonial and postcolonial power relations (see Clarence-Smith 2007; Washbrook 1997). The consequence of this lopsided model is that Muslims are presented as having to 'engage' with modernity, an external force encroaching on and disrupting their lives. Nilüfer Göle, for example, argues that for many Turkish women, Islamism 'permits a critique of customary Islam and a way to cope with modernity', allowing 'Islamist women to reconcile their social-professional demands with their Islamic identities' (1996: 104). In contradistinction to such perspectives, we want to insist that modernity is necessarily singular and global, always instantiated locally – *in the West as elsewhere* – within wider configurations of social, political, and economic power and historically specific trajectories.

Anthropologists have sidestepped hubristic debates about whether 'modernity' is single or multiple, when it started and possibly ended, and whether it has existed at all. They have instead identified the global regimes of power produced and legitimized by so-called 'modernity-talk' (see, e.g., Mitchell 1991), and they have explored 'modernity' as a folk category, entailing an ambivalent relation with 'tradition' and an orientation towards 'progress' in the present and future (see, e.g., Ferguson 1999; C. Osella & F. Osella 2006). Many scholars have also abandoned the futile task of determining whether Islam might be compatible with 'modernity' and have shifted attention to ways in which Muslims produce themselves as 'modern' in everyday life and have moved to provincialize 'Western' modernity (cf. Salvatore 1997; 2007). This entails explorations of competing, yet overlapping, discourses on what being 'modern' entails, as in Yael Navaro-Yashin's study of Turkey (2002). For the Lebanese Shi'i women whom Lara Deeb has studied, being modern entails 'both material and spiritual progress' (2006: 5). This leads to their self-distancing from what is deemed to be 'tradition' in education, economic activities, and religion (see also Bowen 2003; F. Osella & C. Osella 2008; Otayek & Soares 2007; Soares 2005; Starrett 1998). Everyday experiences of modernity and the diversity of ways of being Muslim and modern have also been taken up in a number of studies on veiling and re-veiling (El Guindi 1999) which both underscore relationships between fashion and piety (e.g. LeBlanc 2000; Meneley 2007; Moors & Tarlo 2007; White 2002) and acknowledge the role of consumption in the production of political subject positions (Navaro-Yashin 2002; cf. Özyürek 2006).

Civil society and the public sphere

Eickelman and Piscatori's *Muslim politics* (1996) undoubtedly went far to show that Muslims and Islam are not inimical to modern democratic politics, and yet it is none the less informed by a rather normative approach to civil society and remains premised on a set of liberal political philosophical assumptions. Indeed, it seems to endorse the universalizing narrative that political liberalism allows for a diversity of views to be expressed in open debate, and that processes of rational deliberation in a marketplace of ideas will eventually, and perhaps even inevitably, lead to pluralism in civil society.[9] Such optimism about and commitment to so-called 'rational' political debate and civil society were perhaps partly a symptom of the immediate post-Cold War era.[10] In the 1990s, many, including anthropologists, hailed the imminent flourishing of 'civil society', often assumed to be the arena of authentic social practice and politics (cf. Comaroff & Comaroff 2000; Hann & Dunn 1996). In anthropology this is best exemplified in the work of Robert Hefner (2000), who identified 'civil Islam' in Indonesia. In Hefner's view, this civil Islam is compatible with democracy, democratic institutions, and pluralism. Certain Muslim organizations in Indonesia have the ability to check state power, and their objective is not necessarily to Islamize the state or to impose Islamic law or sharia (see also Bayat 2007a).

Civil society is often assumed to be the sole space available for democratic civic engagement (cf. Bowen 2003; Peletz 2002). But, in a salutary note, Jenny White warns that civil society 'cannot be assumed to guarantee liberalism' (2002: 27). In her study of Islamist mobilization in Istanbul, she illustrates how 'vernacular politics' are at once based on 'local culture, interpersonal relations, and community networks' (2002: 27), whilst remaining connected to wider party politics (cf. Henkel 2005). Civil society perspectives have subsequently been modified by the introduction of the more malleable notion of the public sphere (see, e.g., Salvatore & Eickelman 2004; Soares 2005). This has had the positive effect of unsettling narrow Eurocentric definitions of civil society and the public sphere as essentially secular and Islam as incompatible with modern democratic processes (cf. Bayat 2007a). Talal Asad's (2003) and Peter van der Veer's (2001) efforts to historicize the 'secular', along with Armando Salvatore's comparative analysis of public spheres in Catholic Europe and Islam (Salvatore 2007; see also Eickelman & Salvatore 2002; Scott & Hirschkind 2006), have contributed to critical assessments of spaces of public debate and confrontation in both 'the West' and Muslim societies. A number of recent studies have looked at the expansion of the public sphere and various new publics, as well as the effects of media technologies in contemporary religious discourse and practices (Edwards 1995; Eickelman & Anderson 1999; Hirschkind 2006; Larkin 2008; Messick 1996; Meyer & Moors 2006; Soares 2005; Turner 2007; Werbner 2002; cf. Coleman 2000).

In his study of those involved in producing and listening to cassette sermons in Cairo, Charles Hirschkind (2006) has shown how the public sphere is not limited to the kinds of deliberative practices that many hail as the hallmarks of rational political debate. Analysing what he calls an Islamic 'counter-public', Hirschkind reveals the equally significant disciplinary mechanisms within the public sphere and cautions us against idealistic and even romantic notions of debate (cf. Starrett 2008). Navaro-Yashin has convincingly argued that rather than 'seeking to isolate an almost ideal-typical picture of an "autonomous" public sphere' (2002: 132; cf. Eickelman & Salvatore 2002), attention should be paid to the political processes and discourses producing 'civil society', in which the state is thoroughly imbricated.[11]

Other commentators offer critical insights into the popular politics of marginalized members of society, whereby participation in 'civil society' presupposes familiarity with specific forms of communication and associational practices, as well as social networks normally associated with, or dominated by, the educated middle classes (see, e.g., Chatterjee 2004).[12] Some underscore the potentially depoliticizing effects of civil society and its linkages to global governance (Ferguson 2006; Ferguson & Gupta 2002; Weiss 2004; West & Sanders 2003) and neoliberal capitalism (Elyachar 2005; Mitchell 2002). Attention to civil society is often unable to account for or analyse 'uncivil' orientations (Harriss-White & White 1996; cf. Appadurai 2006) or outright state control and manipulation of such arenas (Bayat 2007a: 49ff.; Navaro-Yashin 2002: 117ff.). Instances of intolerance, repression, and violence – including state violence – directly shape encounters in civil society and in the public sphere (see Asad 2007; Jasani 2008; Peteet 1994). Finally, the focus on the public sphere naturalizes a hierarchical opposition between 'public' and 'private', which might preclude the exploration of the political within domestic spaces (see, e.g., Khan 2006; Ring 2006). Privileging post-enlightenment styles of reasoned, rational debate can lead us to overlook embodiment, affect, and the ways in which persuasion, debate, and difference-making may proceed by other means.

Gender politics
Anthropologists and feminist scholars have long underscored the centrality of gender in nationalist, secularist, and religious discourses in Muslim societies, and more recently in projects of colonial and neo-colonial governmentality.[13] The latter, informed by Foucauldian and post-Orientalist theory, has substantially transformed

anthropological understandings of power and its articulation with seemingly hegemonic projects of self-fashioning. If earlier literature emphasized patriarchy, subordination of women, and gendered practices such as veiling (see, e.g., Kandiyoti 1991b;
1996; Wikan 1991), in recent years anthropologists have moved towards studying
Muslim women as political actors. These range from activists, including secularists (e.g.
Al-Ali 2000; De Jorio 2001; in press) and Islamists (e.g. Deeb 2006; Göle 1996; Haniffa
2008; Huq 2008; White 2002), to ordinary Muslim women (Brenner 1996; Hegland
1998; Isik 2008; P. Jeffery, R. Jeffery & Jeffrey 2004; Kandiyoti & Saktanber 2002; LeBlanc
2006; Mahmood 2006; Ong 1995; Ring 2006; Schulz 2008). What emerges is that
Muslim women – their bodies, desires, and public and private lives – have been the
object, at least since colonial times, of scrutiny, debate, and intervention, whereby they
are represented, to extend Kandiyoti's insights, simultaneously as 'victims of social
backwardness, icons of modernity or privileged bearers of cultural authenticity' (1991a:
431; see also Abu-Lughod 1998). Women have stood at the centre of political projects
which produce and reproduce (real and imaginary) boundaries between public and
private life (see, e.g., Bayat 2007b; Navaro-Yashin 2002; White 2002), whilst redefining
notions of morality, family life, sexuality, and self-presentation (see, e.g., P. Jeffery et al.
2004), and articulating novel orientations towards education, employment and consumption (Meneley 2007; Moors & Tarlo 2007; Navaro-Yashin 2002; White 2002).

Anthropologists have emphasized Muslim women's active participation in contemporary political processes from a multiplicity of cultural/religious positions and social
locations, whereby instances of resistance (Abu-Lughod 1986; Boddy 1989), overt critique (Al-Ali 2000), pragmatic instrumentalism (Göle 1996; White 2002), or pious
submission (Deeb 2006; Huq 2008; Mahmood 2005) are all expressions of agency
through which complex processes of subjectivation are articulated. Neither feminism
(in secular or Islamic forms) nor pietism is more or less culturally 'authentic' – albeit
sometimes reified as such in discourse. Rather, they represent trajectories of self-
fashioning differentially available to women, all entailing a degree of normativity and
inculcation, whilst opening up possibilities for reflection, deliberation, and expressivity
(see, e.g., Huq 2008; Mahmood 2001). Anthropologists have explored the wider political contexts producing and framing debates between competing understandings of
women and their lives (notably Al-Ali 2000; Navaro-Yashin 2002; White 2002), yet still
little is still known about power relations between women activists within and between
specific movements, how authoritative discourses are produced and who participates in
their elaborations, and how certain categories of women might become the objects of
intervention (for exceptions, see De Jorio 2001; 2002; in press).

The initial overemphasis on 'patriarchy' has not allowed for explorations of masculinities, particularly those emerging within novel forms of political and social engagement. 'Patriarchy' has become a taken-for-granted term which, by constructing men as
an undifferentiated social category, glosses over regimes of power informing men's
everyday lives (cf. Abu-Lughod 1989). Yet, early studies by Barth (1959) in Pakistan and
Bourdieu (1977: 171ff.) in Algeria had explored production and reproduction of power,
leadership, and domination as articulated through patron/client relations and public
performances of masculine values, such as honour, hospitality, and gift-giving, as well
as knowledge, piety, and mystical power. Research on masculinities (see, e.g., Janson
2008; Marsden 2007; Peletz 1994; Walle 2004) and sexuality (e.g. Boellstorff 2005)
notwithstanding, to date transformations of Muslim masculinities – such as those
observed in the context of evangelical Christianity and Hindu nationalism – and their

articulation with women's lives (see, e.g., Amireh 2003; Ring 2006) have eluded inquiry (for exceptions, see Harris 2004; Peteet 1994; Verkaaik 2004).

Politics unbound

Many anthropologists have taken issue with teleological or essentializing analyses of politics among Muslims as an epiphenomenon of Islam (cf. B. Lewis 2002 [1988]). However, some recent work continues to ascribe a degree of exceptionalism to Muslim societies, forestalling possibilities for comparison. Post-Orientalist anthropological scholarship has, unsurprisingly, had little influence beyond the confines of the discipline. Sustained attempts towards comparative understandings of 'fundamentalism' notwithstanding,[14] social scientists – especially those working on Muslim-majority countries – do not engage with ongoing debates about religious 'revivalism' elsewhere, such as Hindu nationalism (Hansen 2001; Verkaaik 2004).

Attempts to de-exoticize Islamism and Islamist movements or challenge Muslim exceptionalism have had, thus far, limited success (see, e.g., Dresch & Haykel 1995; Eickelman & Piscatori 1996; Hirschkind 1997). Some researchers, particularly in sociology and politics, have begun to employ 'social movement theory' to make sense of the emergence and success of novel forms of social activism in various Muslim contexts (see, e.g., Bayat 2005). We want to point out the excessive formalism of such theory, as well as its tendency to downplay (Clark 2004; Wiktorowicz 2001; 2004) or simply take for granted (Bayat 2007a; 2007b; White 2002) differences in motivation and commitment between social actors, for example on the basis of gender and class (see Sen 2007 for a critique). Nevertheless, social movement theory does open up some lines of inquiry. 'New social movements' often share a critique of statism – whether because the state appears too strong or not strong enough – as well as an aversion to the formal politics of political parties, elections, and so forth; meanwhile notions of 'participation' and 'empowerment' as political tools have acquired global currency. All this should lead us towards interrogation of those wider processes and discourses which produce apparent reframings, if not 'depoliticizations', of everyday politics in the context of global capitalism, whereby many expressions of social activism appear as congruent with novel forms of capital accumulation (see Elyachar 2005; cf. Feillard 2004; Haenni 2005; Maurer 2005; Rudnyckyj 2009; Sloane 1999; Tripp 2006). Research on Islamic social activism also opens up novel areas of anthropological inquiry around the transformation and reframing of religious gifting (zakat [mandatory alms] and sadaqa [voluntary alms]) as acts of 'charity' and 'philanthropy' (see, e.g., Benthall & Bellion-Jourdan 2003; cf. Singer 2008) directed towards fostering reform.

Anthropologists have also usefully explored ways in which Muslim societies have been transformed in the wake of increased global interconnections (Ahmed & Donnan 1994; Fischer & Abedi 1990; Manger 1999; F. Osella & C. Osella 2007; Parkin 2000; Simpson & Kresse 2007; Soares 2005), with some envisaging the emergence of an actual (Grillo & Soares 2004) or virtual (Roy 2004 [2002]) 'transnational Islam'. But contemporary circulations of people, religious practices, and political orientations should be located within long-term, historical connections (see cooke & Lawrence 2005; Eickelman & Piscatori 1990) through pilgrimage, circulation of scholars (Laffan 2002; Zaman 2005), as well as trade (Freitag 2003; Freitag & Clarence-Smith 1997; Ho 2006; F. Osella & C. Osella 2007; Simpson 2006) and migration (e.g. Diouf 2002; Riccio 2004; Werbner 2002; 2003). Such linkages have long been crucial to the production of an imagined *umma* – the global community of Muslims – and to the rhetorics of shared interests and goals which sometimes inform politico-religious imaginaries, opening up possi-bilities for building connections between hitherto local groups and for the emergence of transnational Islamic movements such as the worldwide missionary movement, Tablighi Jamaʻat, which originated in colonial India (see, e.g., Horstmann 2007; Janson, 2005; Metcalf 1994; Sikand 2002) and the activist group Jamaat-e Islami with branches in many countries (Ahmad 2008; Huq 2008).

While anthropologists have often pitted an allegedly tolerant and hybrid local Islam – that of Sufism and saint veneration, for example – against the presumably culturally inauthentic, purifying practices of modernist or reformist individuals and groups (see F. Osella & C. Osella 2008; Soares 2000; 2005; 2007a for critiques), historians have underscored the doctrinal continuities and overlap between Sufism and Islamic 'reformism' (see, e.g., Metcalf 1982).[15] But Sufism and Muslim saints have not neces-sarily disappeared with the advent of modernity, the teleological assumptions of many observers notwithstanding. To the contrary, some have proved rather adept at engaging with the demands of modern life and engendering reform (see, e.g., Ewing 1997; Marsden 2005; Schielke 2006; Soares 2005; 2007b; van Bruinessen & Howell 2007; Werbner 2003). At the same time, reformism in some of its organized forms has proved open to substantial transformations, allowing wider socio-political processes to shift its strategies and goals (see, e.g., Ahmad 2009; Bayat 2007a; Metcalf 2001; Shehabuddin 2008).

Islamism, post-Islamism, and questions of piety

Some of the most thought-provoking recent scholarship about Islam and politics comes from outside anthropology. Working within the distinctive tradition of analys-ing Islam and politics that has developed within the social sciences in France, political scientist Olivier Roy (1994; 2004 [2002]) has argued that since Islamists (those for whom an Islamic state is a major objective) have failed to capture state power in most places, a period of post-Islamism is underway. In his way of thinking, 'neo-fundamentalists' – those Muslims concerned with the Islamization of the individual – are now in the ascendancy. Another French political scientist, Gilles Kepel, advances similar ideas and suggests that post-Islamism involves abandoning more radical ideas and adopting such discourses as human rights, sometimes combined with conservative social agendas (see Kepel 2002). Sociologist Asef Bayat (2007a) has also written about post-Islamism, in a somewhat different frame. Like Roy and Kepel, Bayat argues that Islamism seems to have run its course and 'the appeal, energy, and sources of legitimacy of Islamism are exhausted' (2007a: 10-11). However, Bayat emphasizes Islamist engage-ment with rights, democracy, and so forth (2007a: 10-11). Arguably, this formulation of post-Islamism takes a decidedly normative cast, focused largely on those some would call 'progressive' Muslims rather than on a broader range of persons – including those espousing non-liberal views (see Mandaville 2007: 347-8).

In our view, it is premature to hail the advent of post-Islamism. After all, some Muslims might seek to gain state power in the name of Islam and might eventually succeed in doing so. But in any case, the attention to state power and to the formal politics of elections and political parties is entirely too limited from an anthropological perspective. Scholars such as Roy and Kepel fail to take seriously modes and spaces of political action beyond the purview of formal politics and the state; it is precisely in these areas that anthropology has been particularly skilled in applying its tools.

In many ways, Talal Asad's (1986) essay on the anthropology of Islam marked a major turning-point.[16] Rather than treating Islam as blueprint or script for society or even as 'culture', he argued that one should think instead of Islam as a 'discursive tradition'. A discursive tradition is a formation that has produced historically contingent categorizations of doctrine and practice. This contrasts with such categories as 'reformism' and 'scripturalism', which many, including anthropologists, have too often taken for granted as fixed, knowable forms. Asad's influential programmatic statement inspired quite a number of North American anthropologists to focus specifically on the complexity of the discourse of Muslims (see, e.g., Bowen 1993; Lambek 1992; Launay 1992) and such issues as transformations in law (e.g. Bowen 2003; Messick 1993; Peletz 2002) and education (Hefner & Zaman 2007; Starrett 1998).

Drawing on the later works of Michel Foucault and on Talal Asad (1993; 2003), some anthropologists, including Charles Hirschkind (2006) and Saba Mahmood (2005), have analysed modes of ethical self-fashioning among Muslims in so-called 'piety movements'. By focusing on Muslim individuals and activists, these authors directly challenge the state-centric approaches that appeal to political scientists.[17] In her work on women in the Egyptian piety movement, Mahmood has advanced a very compelling critique of Western liberal notions of agency, notions which prevent analysts from taking seriously those Muslim women whom we might gloss as Islamists who do not share the liberatory agendas of Western observers. Mahmood's critique also helps to dispel anthropologists' incomprehension of Muslim participation in Islamist movements and move analysis away from unhelpful deterministic binaries of resistance and subordination (see also Abu-Lughod 1998; Torab 1996). Like Hirschkind, she provides analytical and methodological tools for studying Islamists and the so-called 'piety-minded'.[18] Studies of ethical self-fashioning illustrate the utility of focusing on individual experiences and the importance of fine-tuned ethnography, which helps considerably to de-exoticize the Muslim Other (see also Isik 2008). Arguably, this is anthropology at its best.

However, the focus on individual self-fashioning also has serious drawbacks. With attention on ethical self-fashioning, politics, especially in Mahmood's work, gets reduced to micropolitics. Differences in orientations, which might vary by social location or class, are also glossed over (Bayat 2007a: 158ff.). One advantage of some other studies (e.g. Huq 2008; Navaro-Yashin 2002; White 2002; cf. Mahmood 2001) is that they situate Islamists and/or women involved in piety movements in relation to others, including secularists. Deeb (2006), for example, shows how Shi'i women fashion themselves against images of 'the West', as well as non-Shi'i women in Lebanon. Broader macropolitics also do not get sufficient attention in some recent studies of ethical self-fashioning. Worryingly, inadequate attention is devoted to how the state intervenes to promote, co-opt, thwart, or isolate various forms of Islam and ('good' or 'bad') Muslims, processes which are more acute in the post-9/11 world (cf. Mahmood 2006; Soares & Otayek 2007).

We are also concerned with the totalizing nature of what might be called the 'piety' turn. Indeed, we detect the problematic vestiges of American culturalist approaches, whereby contemporary expressions of religiosity cannot escape overdetermination by deep-rooted cultural orientations. Such post-Orientalist reifications of 'culture', as Navaro-Yashin rightly observes, risk 'reproducing essentialism in leaving a precipitation of cultural authenticity or tradition underneath the layers of European costume, thereby overlapping, by default, with cultural revivalism and nationalism in the contexts studied' (2002: 8; cf. Marsden 2005: 252ff.). In contrast to totalizing pictures of ethical self-fashioning, Magnus Marsden (2005; see also Marsden 2008a; 2008b) has demonstrated how men and women in Pakistan struggle to lead moral lives and to be 'good Muslims'. This requires intense intellectual and emotional engagement, informed by multiple aesthetic and affective values, and is fraught with ambivalence (Marsden 2005).

Elisions of the complexities and contingencies of everyday lives are indeed problematic, and no less so than in the earlier work of Gellner and Geertz. Our own ethnographic research indicates how people move in and out of formal or informal religious groups, often shifting their allegiances, for example, according to the rising popularity of a particular mosque or preacher. They sometimes simply grow bored or lose interest, or domestic and work duties might take a toll on the time at their disposal; life crises, such as illness or a death, might lead some to reconsider religious commitments and orientations. People lead their everyday lives in complex cultural, religious, and political environments, evaluating and responding to different competing local and global media messages, as illustrated by Lila Abu-Lughod (2005) on television-viewing in Egypt. In other words, participation in piety movements and the taking up of specific forms of ethical self-fashioning should be understood within the context of a variety of available, and perhaps competing, styles and practices (cf. Mahmood 2001), as well as a broader field of politics. Struggle, ambivalence, incoherence, and failure must also receive attention in the study of everyday religiosity (see, e.g., Ewing 1997; Marsden 2005; Schielke 2006; Simpson 2008; Soares 2005).

We think it is useful to draw here on some recent work that has attempted to theorize ways of being Muslim in contemporary societies. In contrast to some of the recent work inspired by Foucault, we would like to consider the notion of *islam mondain*. This term, which could be translated as 'Islam in the present world', points to ways of being Muslim in secularizing societies and spheres (see Otayek & Soares 2007: 17-19).[19] Although many Muslims today are engaged in various kinds of ethical self-fashioning and concerned with the correct practice of Islam, this is only one part of what is effectively a new kind of sociality. In many places, Muslims are making efforts to produce themselves as modern religious subjects within contexts of considerable political and economic uncertainty, as well as increased global interconnections. Adeline Masquelier (2007) has shown how marginalized youths in Niger have been refashioning how to be young and Muslim. Such youths' individual self-fashioning involves processes of the affirmation of Islam and being Muslim, which melds hip-hop style and music with less rigid ritual punctiliousness and a striking indifference to the intra-Muslim sectarian divides that frequently preoccupied their elders. The model of Muslim self-fashioning that *islam mondain* seeks to capture is, however, not only compatible with participating in and producing modernity (however defined), but also 'socially and ethically compatible with the neoliberal economy' (Otayek & Soares 2007: 19; cf. Haenni 2005; Hefner 1998; Rudnyckyj 2009; Sloane 1999).

We emphasize that we are not advancing a new version of the anthropological approach that Islam is whatever Muslims in a particular setting say that it is (see note 16 above). Nor, for that matter, are we proposing understandings of Islam as 'culture', or the well-rehearsed argument that Islam varies according to 'cultural' context. The notion of *islam mondain* helps us to think beyond such theoretical impasses, as well as beyond normative categories and unhelpful binarisms – for example, the popular or 'low' Islam of ordinary Muslims versus the 'high' Islam of Muslim scholars (the '*ulama*);

reformism or Islamism versus so-called 'traditionalism' – which have for so long hindered analysis of Islam and Muslim societies. *Islam mondain* also allows us to get past such categories as 'Islamist' or 'piety-minded', or such vague formulations as 'Islamic resurgence' (or 'revival' or 'renewal', for that matter) to apprehend some of the complex ways of being Muslim in the contemporary world in which Muslims reflect upon being Muslim, upon politics, morality, family, consumption, employment, media, entertainment, and so forth (see also Marsden 2009). *Islam mondain* does not privilege Islam over anything else, emphasizing instead the actual world in which Muslims find themselves. This allows us to avoid, on the one hand, narrowly instrumentalist analyses of the relation between Islam and politics, and, on the other, analyses that reduce the politics of Muslims to an epiphenomenon of Islam or the micropolitics of ethical self-fashioning. The chapters in this book explore some of these contemporary ways of 'being Muslim' and the complex politics of Muslim self-fashioning, including debates about religious practice, the nature of the state, citizenship, and efforts to simply get by in the current historical conjuncture.

Islam and politics today

The contributors to this volume follow time-honoured anthropological traditions of emphasizing the heterogeneity of experience, and the complexity and contingencies of everyday Muslim lives. But they do not stop there. The authors are attentive to the interplay of religion and politics without ever reducing one to the other, as often happens in the social sciences. In this way, this set of chapters attempts to chart new terms for analysis.

As we have suggested, in stressing the uniqueness of Muslim experience – a position that sometimes verges close to cultural determinism – some recent studies overprivilege the coherence and disciplinary power of Islam. We learn here about the ambiguities in young Egyptian men's lives and everyday practice, with all its contradictions and imperfections (Schielke this volume). While young men give up drink, drugs, and other illicit activities during Ramadan, they often enough return to these pleasurable practices once the 'holy month' is over. This is not to suggest that they are not concerned with questions of morality or ethical self-fashioning, as those involved in piety movements no doubt are. However, the study of religious and moral subjectivity and the affirmation of Islam (the so-called 'Islamic resurgence') in a place like Egypt can be usefully broadened further. Aishima and Salvatore (this volume) show the importance of considering the careers and trajectories of some leading Muslim public figures and their various publics in Cairo. As they argue, 'doubt', rather than certainty, was of central importance in the making of the careers of two Muslim media stars, one a member of the Islamic university al-Azhar establishment, Sufi shaykh, and radio personality, and the other a lay thinker, medical doctor-turned television star, both with aspirations to attain the not unambiguous status of recognized 'Islamic intellectual' in the context of the considerable uncertainties of the post-colonial period. With their attention to questions of knowledge, ethics, and morality, such public figures play important intermediary roles between the ever-present Egyptian state and individual Muslims.

We also learn about how young Chitrali Muslims in rural Pakistan 'cultivate an appreciation for the heterogeneity' of life through their leisure activities, including village tours in their region (Marsden this volume, p. 57). Such tours foster 'a modality of understanding and perceiving the wider world founded not on the active cultivation of embodied ethical dispositions but in the appreciation of a mindful, if often sceptical, curiosity about heterogeneity' (p. 68). Focusing on rural Muslims, Marsden shows how they are cosmopolitan *avant la lettre* and clearly not 'traditional' Muslims in the Gellnerian sense. Such ethnographic cases help us to understand the complexity and diversity of Muslim experiences of and responses to modernity, which should not be limited to urban piety movements that have been receiving so much attention. Kenyan coastal Muslims, in similar fashion, draw on their experience of double marginality – within a Christian-dominated state, but also as Muslims living in a place considered to be at the 'periphery' of Islam – to develop an orientation towards 'patience' and 'endurance', but also a self-critical and conscious independence of mind. This provides them with the intellectual tools necessary to deal with the political contingencies and predicaments of everyday life as a marginalized minority (Kresse this volume).

While we recognize the importance of studying textual traditions in Islam, an overemphasis on theological debates and religious milieus has sometimes produced a re-exoticization effect, which sets certain modalities of religious expression as a uniquely 'Muslim' way to be modern. As a result, little attention gets paid to the historical processes through which practices and discourse are produced, taken up, or contested within specific (economic, political, and social) contexts by particular actors. In Mali, a country that is overwhelmingly Muslim, recent heated debates over women's rights and modern emancipatory projects in the public sphere show the importance of shifting the analytical focus towards reflexive forms of religiosity. Women activists have increasingly had to position themselves *vis-à-vis* certain readings of Islam and pre-sumed 'correct' Muslim practice, including the comportment of women. In the process, many Malian women are, 'more vocal in questioning public readings of Islam that reinforce male hegemony' and have become more reflexive and outspoken on religious matters (De Jorio this volume, p. 93). Beirut's pious Shi'i Muslim gender activists taking part in a seminar on 'public participation', sponsored by the Hizbullah Women's Committee, debate their political location and experiences on the basis of reflections which bring together wider 'transnationally constituted discourses about Muslim women and about Western women' (Deeb this volume, p. 109). The relationship between piety and politics in such a context is very complex and connects the local with the national and the global. Islam itself can also become the means through which to explore relationships with – and commitment to – secular modernity in the very different context of post-Soviet Kyrgyzstan. Here, debates regarding the adoption of the veil as an expression of religious piety lead to nostalgic interrogations of past, present, and future engagements with the modern, ultimately suggesting that modernity is neither linear nor predictable (McBrien this volume).

In his contribution, Ahmad engages with some classical debates in political anthro-pology to reflect on the nature of the state and the relationship of religion and politics in India. Many assume that in Islam there can be no functional differentiation between these spheres. The well-rehearsed argument is that for Muslims religion and politics are fused and inseparable. In an original rereading of Maududi's writings, Ahmad argues that the very conditions of the colonial state in India, with its unprecedented reach into the lives of colonial subjects, propelled Maududi to theorize the need for an Islamic state. While the influence of Maududi's ideas on Muslim intellectuals and Islamist movements in the twentieth century is well known, Ahmad's genealogy of 'the Islamic state' also helps us to understand the Shi'i women in Lebanon who are the subject of Deeb's contribution, as well as the Muslim women activists in Bangladesh (Huq this volume). In other words, orientations towards the 'Islamization' of the state are not simply self-generated within Islam itself, but emerge within the context of wider political events and debates.

Given all of the recent attention to piety movements and questions of moral reform, there has been insufficient sustained attention to the question of politics, including political actors, who might seek to take control of state power and to Islamize society, as well as those involved in everyday politics. The claim that all Islamist political projects are doomed to failure seems rather premature. In her ethnography of the Bangladesh Islami Chatri Sangstha (BICSa; Women Students' Islamic Association of Bangladesh), Huq considers the female-student wing of the dominant Islamic political party (Jamaat-e Islami) in the country. Although these Muslim women activists are certainly concerned with questions of moral reform and the cultivation of an appropriately Muslim subjectivity, they are also deeply involved in politics and endeavour to advance a political programme that seeks to Islamize society and state. The BICSa women emphasize that their activism is part of their *jihad*, which should remain non-violent. Such activism has tangible personal, as well as political, effects, widespread popular and scholarly caricatures of violent Islamic *jihad*, apolitical liberal or progressive Muslims, and peaceful Sufis notwithstanding.

At the same time, the Osellas and Rudnyckyj alert us to novel articulations between religious and economic practice, whereby economic development and success in the global economy become linked to the cultivation of specific ethical dispositions. Rudnyckyj deploys the notion of 'market Islam' to foreground ways through which 'spiritual reform' is mobilized in conjunction with mainstream business management strategies to address what are perceived to be obstacles to effective participation in an increasingly competitive free market, namely a widespread moral and religious crisis within Indonesian society. Self-styled business management consultants are thus employed by private and public corporations to instil a new and Islamic work ethic amongst their employees, stressing self-discipline, commitment, and honesty. Work, in other words, is reframed as religious and moral duty. Moving away from Weberian theory, Rudnyckyj argues that while market Islam can sustain both Islam and neoliberal capitalism, it cannot be reduced as an epiphenomenon of either.

The Osellas discuss the practices of a number of wealthy Gulf-based South Indian Muslim businessmen who project themselves as 'community leaders' through participation in and promotion of charitable activities, especially in education. While they seek ways of embedding their business practices within an 'Islamic' framework of ethics and moral responsibilities, they are also committed towards re-orientating local Muslim subjectivities and practices towards the requirements of neoliberal capitalism and the opportunities it affords them. The Osellas argue, though, that while orientations towards ethical self-transformation are mobilized to sustain novel forms of capital accumulation, reformist Islam might be equally called upon to set moral boundaries for engagement with the neoliberal economy.

The unfolding of post-9/11 politics in Euro-America provides the background to Starrett's contribution. Islam and Muslims have become not simply objects of public scrutiny and debate, but, as Starrett argues, also 'objects of imagination' with 'implications for politics and for experiences of the modern by non-Muslims, even in places where Muslims are nearly absent' (Starrett this volume, p. S222). Controversies regarding teaching and learning about Islam in American state schools – with schools alleged to have coerced children into Islam – have entered not only the public sphere, but also the judicial system. And it is through such debates that a number of social actors – schools, courts, parents, activists – redefine wider relationships between 'knowledge' and 'belief', between 'religion' and society. Paradoxically, '[b]y encouraging public education as a response to political and cultural tensions, educators may in fact be heightening the public's concerns about Islam as a comprehensive threat' (Starrett this volume, p. S221).

Together, the contributors to this book help to challenge the dominance of formalist definitions and models of political participation in the social sciences, whilst also rejecting widespread assumptions about Muslim exceptionalism. Rather than privileging 'religion' or reducing contemporary politics to an epiphenomenon of Islam, they identify multiple orientations and strands in Muslims' lives and stress complexities, contingencies, and contradictions in the political engagements of Muslims. Although formal organized politics and state interventions are articulated through and certainly help to frame various projects of ethical self-fashioning, the chapters in this book show how in generating debates about the value or morality of social action, everyday politics allow for participation, reproduction, or contestation of broader social and political projects.

ACKNOWLEDGMENTS

Most of the chapters in this book were first presented in a double panel at the American Anthropological Association annual meeting in San Jose in November 2006 organized by Rosa De Jorio and Benjamin Soares. We are most grateful to Rosa De Jorio for her invaluable input, the panel discussants, John Bowen and Dale Eickelman, for their commentary, and the individual authors. A special thanks to Marloes Janson for assistance with references and to Jonathan Benthall, Richard Fardon, Kai Kresse, Magnus Marsden, Simon Coleman, Jonathan Spencer, Kamran Matin, and Laura Menin for commenting on a draft of this chapter. Above all, we thank Caroline Osella.

NOTES

[1] We cannot present here an exhaustive overview of the debates about the production of Islam, Muslim societies, and 'religion' more generally as objects of anthropological inquiry. On the anthropology of Islam, see Abu-Lughod (1989); Asad (1986); Launay (1992); Lindholm (2002); Soares (2000); and Starrett (1997). On religion as a category, see Asad (1993).

[2] Our definitions of Islamism and Islamist are simple and restrictive. Islamists are those for whom an Islamic state is often a major objective (hence Islamism) and who might self-designate as such.

[3] For a discussion see Abu-Lughod (2002); Grewal (1996); and/or who might self-designate as such and Hirschkind & Mahmood (2002).

[4] See, e.g, the recent and ongoing debates in the pages of *Anthropology Today* and *Anthropology News*. See also Assayag (2008).

[5] For this reason, it is not surprising that as late as 1983 Akbar Ahmed was chiding his fellow anthropologists for continuing to 'study Muslim groups without reference to the Islamic framework' (1983: 139).

[6] Space limitations do not allow us to discuss the extensive literature in political anthropology that focused on various Muslim societies that followed Evans-Pritchard's study of the Nuer (1940), including Frederik Barth's study of the Pukhtun (1959), I.M. Lewis's work on Somalia (e.g. I.M. Lewis 1961), and Ernest Gellner's book on 'tribal' Morocco (e.g. Gellner 1969). Moreover, in our review of some of the vast bodies of literature related to Islam and politics that follows, we will of necessity be selective and focus primarily, though not exclusively, on anthropology.

[7] For a more recent example of such a cultural approach, see Hammoudi's book on 'culture' and authoritarianism (Hammoudi 1997).

[8] See Geertz's notion of ideologization as 'the movement from religiousness to religious-mindedness' (1968: 107).

[9] This is, however, not always unequivocal in their text. When they write, for example, about the fragmentation of authority in Muslim societies, they point out that this might lead to 'an Islamic-tinged authoritarianism' in the medium term, but 'may well precipitate a civic pluralism' (Eickelman & Piscatori 1996: 159) in the long run.

[10] These views are substantially different from the dystopic predictions on the future of Muslims' politics of Ahmed & Donnan (1994) and Ahmed (1992).

[11] We are reminded here of a number of anthropological studies which have added complexity and nuance to the understanding of people's imagination of and actual relations with the state and its modern practices (see, e.g., Das & Poole 2004; Ferguson & Gupta 2002; Gupta 1995; Hansen & Stepputat 2001; Messick 1993; F. Osella & C. Osella 2000; Ruud 1996; Trouillot 2001; West & Sanders 2003).

[12] Bayat (2007*b*) and White (2002) both note differences between Islamist politics – associated with educated, urbanized middle or lower classes – and the 'politics of the poor'. The latter are ostensibly informed by pragmatism and driven by the necessity to secure jobs, housing, and education (cf. Ismail 2000).

[13] Space limitations prevent us from engaging fully with the vast literature on gender and Islam. For reviews of some of that literature from an anthropological perspective, see Abu-Lughod (1998; 2001) and Kandiyoti (1991*a*; 1991*b*).

[14] See, e.g., the five volumes published in the 1990s as a result of the 'Fundamentalism Project' directed by Martin Marty and R. Scott Appleby.

[15] 'Reformism' is particularly troublesome as a term, in that it covers broad trends – from 'Islamic modernism' to 'Islamism' – stretching back at least one hundred years (and arguably much further), and encompassing a variety of positions which lay more or less stress upon specific aspects of processes of renewal. It is nevertheless useful for identifying the differences between such projects and other such contemporary preoccupations such as 'political Islam', 'Islamic fundamentalism', and so on.

[16] In characteristic fashion, Asad took both Gellner and Geertz to task, rejecting both social structural and cultural approaches to Islam. He also directed harsh criticism towards those such as Abdul Hamid el-Zein (1977) and Michael Gilsenan (1982), who asserted that Islam was whatever one's informants said that it was. This is the so-called 'Islams' approach, in which Islam varies by context, and anthropologists talk about various Islams with geographic qualifiers – Moroccan, Egyptian, Indonesian, and African Islam. This is a trend that is not entirely out of fashion even within anthropology.

[17] In a related argument, Faisal Devji (2005; cf. Asad 2007) has tried to shift attention to the question of 'ethics' in understanding those involved in *jihad*.

[18] 'Piety-minded' is a term that Marshall Hodgson used (see Hodgson 1977: *passim*), though anthropologists writing about piety among contemporary Muslims do not usually cite Hodgson's work.

[19] Cf. Bayat (2007*a*) on the 'Islamization' of everyday life in Egypt and Iran; and R. Jeffery, P. Jeffery & Jeffrey (2006) on 'banal Hinduism'.

REFERENCES

ABU-LUGHOD, L. 1986. *Veiled sentiments: honor and poetry in a Bedouin society.* Berkeley: University of California Press.

——— 1989. Zones of theory in the anthropology of the Arab world. *Annual Review of Anthropology* **18**, 267-306.

——— 1998. Introduction: feminist longings and postcolonial conditions. In *Remaking women: feminism and modernity in the Middle East* (ed.) L. Abu-Lughod, 3-31. Princeton: University Press.

——— 2001. Orientalism and Middle East feminist studies. *Feminist Studies* **27**, 101-13.

——— 2002. Do Muslim women really need saving? Anthropological reflections on cultural relativism and its others. *American Anthropologist* **104**, 783-90.

——— 2005. *Dramas of nationhood: the politics of television in Egypt.* Chicago: University Press.

AHMAD, I. 2008. Cracks in the 'mightiest fortress': Jamaat-e-Islami's changing discourse on women. *Modern Asian Studies* **42**, 549-75.

——— 2009. *Islamism and democracy in India: the transformation of Jamaat-e-Islami.* Princeton: University Press.

AHMED A.S. 1983. *Religion and politics in Muslim society: order and conflict in Pakistan.* London: Routledge & Kegan Paul.

——— 1992. *Postmodernism and Islam: predicament and promise.* London: Routledge.

——— & H. DONNAN (eds) 1994. *Islam, globalization and postmodernity.* London: Routledge.

AL-ALI, N.S. 2000. *Secularism, gender, and the state in the Middle East: the Egyptian women's movement.* Cambridge: University Press.

AMIREH, A. 2003. Between complicity and subversion: body politics in Palestinian national narrative. *South Atlantic Quarterly* **102**, 747-72.

ANDERSON, B.R.O. 1991. *Imagined communities: reflections on the origin and spread of nationalism.* London: Verso.

ANSARI, M.T. 2005. Refiguring the fanatic: Malabar 1836-1922. In *Subaltern Studies XII* (eds) S. Mayaram, M.S.S. Pandian & A. Skaria, 36-77. New Delhi: Permanent Black.

APPADURAI, A. 2006. *Fear of small numbers: an essay on the geography of anger*. Durham, N.C.: Duke University Press.

ASAD, T. 1986. *The idea of the anthropology of Islam*. Washington, D.C.: Center for Contemporary Arab Studies.

——— 1993. *Genealogies of religion: discipline and reasons of power in Christianity and Islam*. Baltimore: Johns Hopkins University Press.

——— 2003. *Formations of the secular: Christianity, Islam, modernity*. Stanford: University Press.

——— 2007. *On suicide bombing*. New York: Columbia University Press.

ASSAYAG, J. 2008. L'anthropologie en guerre: les anthropologues sont-ils tous des espions? *L'Homme* **187-8**, 135-68.

BARTH F. 1959. *Political leadership among Swat Pathans*. London: Athlone.

BAYAT, A. 2005. Islamism and social movement theory. *Third World Quarterly* **26**, 891-908.

——— 2007a. *Making Islam democratic: social movements and the post-Islamist turn*. Stanford: University Press.

——— 2007b. Radical religion and the habitus of the dispossessed: does Islamic militancy have an urban ecology? *International Journal of Urban and Regional Research* **31**, 579-90.

BENTHALL, J. & J. BELLION-JOURDAN 2003. *The charitable crescent: politics of aid in the Muslim world*. London: I.B. Tauris.

BODDY, J. 1989. *Wombs and alien spirits: women, men, and the Zar cult in Northern Sudan*. Madison: University of Wisconsin Press.

BOELLSTORFF, T. 2005. *The gay archipelago: sexuality and nation in Indonesia*. Princeton: University Press.

BOURDIEU, P. 1977. *Outline of a theory of practice*. Cambridge: University Press.

BOWEN, J.R. 1993. *Muslims through discourse: religion and ritual in Gayo society*. Princeton: University Press.

——— 2003. *Islam, law and equality in Indonesia*. Cambridge: University Press.

BRENNER, S. 1996. Reconstructing self and society: Javanese Muslim women and 'the veil'. *American Ethnologist* **23**, 673-97.

CALLON, M., C. MÉADEL & V. RABEHARISOA 2002. The economy of qualities. *Economy & Society* **31**, 194-217.

CHATTERJEE, P. 2004. *The politics of the governed: reflections on popular politics in most of the world*. New York: Columbia University Press.

CLARENCE-SMITH, W.G. 2007. Scientific and technological interchanges between the Islamic world and Europe, c. 1450-c. 1800. In *Relazioni economiche tra Europa e mondo islamico, secc. XIII-XVIII/Europe's economic relations with the Islamic world, 13th-18th centuries* (ed.) S. Cavaciocchi, 719-37. Prato: Le Monnier.

CLARK, J. 2004. *Islam, charity and activism: middle-class networks in Egypt, Jordan and Yemen*. Bloomington: Indiana University Press.

COLEMAN, S. 2000. *The globalisation of Charismatic Christianity: spreading the gospel of prosperity*. Cambridge: University Press.

COMAROFF, J.L. & J. COMAROFF (eds) 2000. *Civil society and the political imagination in Africa: critical perspectives*. Chicago: University Press.

COOKE, M. & B. LAWRENCE (eds) 2005. *Muslim networks from hajj to hip hop*. Chapel Hill: University of North Carolina Press.

DAS, V. & D. POOLE (eds) 2004. *Anthropology in the margins of the state*. Santa Fe: School of American Research Press; Oxford: James Currey.

DE JORIO, R. 2001. Women's organization, the ideology of kinship, and the state in postindependence Mali. In *New directions in anthropological kinship* (ed.) L. Stone, 322-40. Lanham, Md.: Rowman & Littlefield.

——— 2002. Gendered museum, guided he(tour)topias: women and social memory in Mali. *Polar: The Political and Legal Anthropology Review* **25**, 50-72.

——— in press. *Representing the nation: the politics of culture in Mali*. Urbana: University of Illinois Press.

DEEB, L. 2006. *An enchanted modern: gender and public piety in Shi'i Lebanon*. Princeton: University Press.

DEVJI, F. 2005. *Landscapes of the jihad: militancy, morality, modernity*. London: Hurst.

DIOUF, M. 2002. The Senegalese Murid trade diaspora and the making of a vernacular cosmopolitanism. In *Cosmopolitanism* (eds) C. Breckenridge, S. Pollock, H.K. Bhabha & D. Chakrabarty, 111-38. Durham, N.C.: Duke University Press.

DRESCH, P. & B. HAYKEL 1995. Stereotypes and political styles: Islamists and tribesfolk in Yemen. *International Journal of Middle East Studies* **27**, 405-31.

Edwards, D.B. 1989. Mad mullahs and Englishmen: discourse in the colonial encounter. *Comparative Studies in Society and History* **31**, 649-70.

———— 1995. Print Islam: media and religious revolution in Afghanistan. *Anthropological Quarterly* **68**, 171-84.

Eickelman, D.F. & J.W. Anderson (eds) 1999. *New media in the Muslim world: the emerging public sphere.* Bloomington: Indiana University Press.

———— & J.P. Piscatori (eds) 1990. *Muslim travellers: pilgrimage, migration, and the religious imagination.* Berkeley: University of California Press.

———— & ———— 1996. *Muslim politics.* Princeton: University Press.

———— & A. Salvatore. 2002. The public sphere and Muslim identities. *European Journal of Sociology* **43**, 92-115.

Elyachar, J. 2005. *Markets of dispossession: NGOs, economic development and the state in Cairo.* Durham, N.C.: Duke University Press.

Evans-Pritchard, E.E. 1940. *The Nuer.* Oxford: Clarendon.

———— 1949. *The Sanusi of Cyrenaica.* Oxford: Clarendon.

Ewing, K. 1997. *Arguing sainthood: modernity, psychoanalysis and Islam.* Durham, N.C.: Duke University Press.

Feillard, G. 2004. Insuffler l'esprit du capitalisme à l'Umma: la formation d'une éthique islamique du travail en Indonesie. *Critique Internationale* **25**, 93-116.

Ferguson, J. 1999. *Expectations of modernity: myths and meanings of urban life on the Zambian Copperbelt.* Berkeley: University of California Press.

———— 2006. Transnational topographies of power: beyond 'the state' and 'civil society' in the study of Africa. In *Global shadows: Africa in the neoliberal order*, J. Ferguson, 89-112. Durham, N.C.: Duke University Press.

———— & A. Gupta 2002. Spatializing states: toward an ethnography of neoliberal governmentality. *American Ethnologist* **29**, 981-1002.

Fischer, M.J. & M. Abedi 1990. *Debating Muslims.* Madison: University of Wisconsin Press.

Freitag, U. 2003. *Indian Ocean migrants and state formation in Hadhramaut.* Leiden: Brill.

———— & W. Clarence-Smith (eds) 1997. *Hadhrami traders, scholars and statesmen in the Indian Ocean, 1750s-1960s.* Leiden: Brill.

Geertz, C. 1968. *Islam observed.* Chicago: University Press.

Gellner, E. 1963. Sanctity, puritanism, secularisation and nationalism in North Africa. *Archives de Sociologie des Religions* **15**, 71-86.

———— 1968. A pendulum swing theory of Islam. *Archives Marocaines de Sociologie* **1**, 5-14.

———— 1969. *Saints of the Atlas.* Chicago: University Press.

———— 1981. *Muslim society.* Cambridge: University Press.

———— 1983. *Nations and nationalism.* Ithaca, N.Y.: Cornell University Press.

Giddens, A. 1999. *Consequences of modernity.* Cambridge: Polity.

Gilsenan, M. 1982. *Recognising Islam: an anthropologist's introduction.* London: Croom Helm.

———— 1990. Very like a camel: the appearance of an anthropologist's Middle East. In *Localizing strategies: regional traditions of ethnographic writing* (ed.) R. Fardon, 220-39. Edinburgh: Scottish Academic Press; Washington, D.C.: Smithsonian Institution Press.

Göle, N. 1996. *The forbidden modern: civilization and veiling.* Ann Arbor: University of Michigan Press.

———— 2002. Islam in public: new visibilities and new imaginaries. *Public Culture* **14**, 173-90.

Grewal, I. 1996. *Home and harem: nation, gender, empire and the cultures of travel.* Durham, N.C.: Duke University Press.

Grillo, R.D. 2004. Islam and transnationalism. *Journal of Ethnic and Migration Studies* **30**, 861-78.

———— & B.F. Soares (eds) 2004. Special issue: *Islam, transnationalism and the public sphere in Western Europe. Journal of Ethnic and Migration Studies* **30**: 5, 861-1031.

El Guindi, F. 1999. *Veil: modesty, privacy and resistance.* Oxford: Berg.

Gupta, A. 1995. Blurred boundaries: the discourse of corruption, the culture of politics and the imagined state. *American Ethnologist* **22**, 375-402.

Haenni, P. 2005. *L'islam de marché: l'autre révolution conservatrice.* Paris: Seuil.

Hammoudi, A. 1997. *Master and disciple: the cultural foundations of Moroccan authoritarianism.* Chicago: University Press.

Haniffa, F. 2008. Piety as politics amongst Muslim women in contemporary Sri Lanka. *Modern Asian Studies* **42**, 347-75.

Hann, C. & E. Dunn (eds) 1996. *Civil society: challenging Western models.* London: Routledge.

Hansen, T.B. 2001. *Wages of violence: naming and identity in postcolonial Bombay.* Princeton: University Press.

——— & F. STEPPUTAT (eds). 2001. *States of imagination: ethnographic explorations of the postcolonial state.* Durham, N.C.: Duke University Press.

HARRIS, C. 2004. *Control and subversion: gender relations in Tajikistan.* London: Pluto.

HARRISON, C. 1988. *France and Islam in West Africa, 1860-1960.* Cambridge: University Press.

HARRISS-WHITE, B. & G. WHITE 1996. Corruption, liberalization and democracy: editorial introduction. *IDS Bulletin* **27**, 1-5.

HEFNER, R. (ed.) 1998. *Market cultures: society and morality in the new Asian capitalisms.* Boulder, Colo.: Westview.

——— 2000. *Civil Islam: Muslims and democratization in Indonesia.* Princeton: University Press.

——— (ed.) 2005. *Remaking Muslim politics: pluralism, contestation, democratization.* Princeton: University Press.

——— & M.Q. ZAMAN (eds) 2007. *Schooling Islam: modern Muslim education.* Princeton: University Press.

HEGLAND, M.E. 1998. Flagellation and fundamentalism: (trans)forming meaning, identity, and gender through Pakistani women's rituals of mourning. *American Ethnologist* **25**, 240-66.

HENKEL, H. 2005. 'Between belief and unbelief lies the performance of *salāt*': meaning and efficacy of a Muslim ritual. *Journal of the Royal Anthropological Institute* (N.S.) **11**, 487-507.

HIRSCHKIND, C. 1997. What is political Islam? *Middle East Report* **27**: **4**, 12-15.

——— 2006. *The ethical soundscape: cassette sermons and Islamic counterpublics.* New York: Columbia University Press.

——— & S. MAHMOOD 2002. Feminism, the Taliban, and politics of counter-insurgency. *Anthropological Quarterly* **75**, 339-54.

HO, E. 2006. *Graves of Tarim: genealogy and mobility across the Indian Ocean.* Berkeley: University of California Press.

HODGSON, M. 1977. *The venture of Islam,* vol. I: *The classical age of Islam.* Chicago: University Press.

HORSTMANN, A. 2007. The Tablighi Jama'at, transnational Islam, and the transformation of the self between southern Thailand and South Asia. *Comparative Studies of South Asia, Africa and the Middle East* **27**, 26-40.

HUNTINGTON, S. 1996. *The clash of civilizations and the remaking of world order.* New York: Simon & Schuster.

HUQ, M. 2008. Reading the Qur'an in Bangladesh: the politics of 'belief' among Islamist women. *Modern Asian Studies* **42**, 457-88.

ISIK, D. 2008. On *sabir* and agency: the politics of pious practice in Konya's weaving industry. *International Feminist Journal of Politics* **10**, 439-54.

ISMAIL, S. 2000. The popular movement dimensions of contemporary militant Islamism: socio-spatial determinants in the Cairo urban setting. *Comparative Studies in Society and History* **42**, 363-93.

JALAL, A. 2008. *Partisans of Allah: jihad in South Asia.* Cambridge, Mass.: Harvard University Press.

JANSON, M. 2005. Roaming about for God's sake: the upsurge of the Tablīgh Jamā'at in The Gambia. *Journal of Religion in Africa* **35**, 450-81.

——— 2008. Renegotiating gender: changing moral practice in the Tablighi Jama'at in The Gambia. *Journal for Islamic Studies* **28**, 9-36.

JASANI, R. 2008. Violence, reconstruction and Islamic reform: stories from the Muslim 'ghetto'. *Modern Asian Studies,* **42**, 431-56.

JEFFERY, P., R. JEFFERY & C. JEFFREY 2004. Islamization, gentrification and domestication: a girls' 'Islamic course' and rural Muslims in western Uttar Pradesh. *Modern Asian Studies* **38**, 1-53.

JEFFERY, R., P. JEFFERY & C. JEFFREY 2006. Parhai ka mahaul? An educational environment in Bijnor, Uttar Pradesh. In *The meaning of the local: politics of place in urban India* (eds) G. de Neve & H. Donner, 116-40. London: Routledge.

KANDIYOTI, D. 1991a. Identity and its discontents: women and the nation. *Millennium* **20**, 429-43.

——— 1991b. Islam and patriarchy: a comparative perspective. In *Women in Middle Eastern history: shifting boundaries in sex and gender* (eds) N.R. Keddie & B. Baron, 23-42. New Haven: Yale University Press.

——— 1996. *Gendering the Middle East.* London: I.B. Tauris.

——— & A. SAKTANBER (eds) 2002. *Fragments of culture: the everyday of modern Turkey.* New Brunswick, N.J.: Rutgers University Press.

KEPEL, G. 2002. *Jihad: the trail of political Islam.* London: I.B. Tauris.

KHAN, N. 2006. Of children and *jinn*: an inquiry into an unexpected friendship during uncertain times. *Cultural Anthropology* **21**, 234-64.

LAFFAN, M. 2002. *Islamic nationhood and colonial Indonesia: the umma below the winds.* London: RoutledgeCurzon.

LAMBEK, M. 1992. *Knowledge and practice in Mayotte: local discourses of Islam, sorcery, and spirit possession.* Toronto: University Press.

LARKIN, B. 2008. *Signal and noise: media, infrastructure, and urban culture in Nigeria.* Durham, N.C.: Duke University Press.

LAUNAY, R. 1992. *Beyond the stream: Islam and society in a West African town.* Berkeley: University of California Press.

———— 2006. An invisible religion? Anthropology's avoidance of Islam in Africa. In *African anthropologies: history, critique, and practice* (eds) D. Mills, M. Babiker & M. Ntarangwi, 188-203. Dakar: CODESRIA; London: Zed.

———— & B.F. SOARES. 1999. The formation of an 'Islamic sphere' in French colonial West Africa. *Economy & Society* **28**, 497-519.

LEBLANC, M.N. 2000. Fashion and the politics of identity: versioning womanhood and Muslimhood in the face of tradition and modernity. *Africa* **70**, 443-81.

———— 2006. Proclaiming individual piety: pilgrims and religious renewal in Côte d'Ivoire. In *Claiming individuality: the cultural politics of distinction* (eds) V. Amit & N. Dyck, 173-200. London: Pluto.

LEWIS, B. 2002 [1988]. *The political language of Islam.* Karachi: Oxford University Press.

LEWIS, I.M. 1961. *A pastoral democracy: a study of pastoralism and politics among the Northern Somali of the Horn of Africa.* New York: Oxford University Press.

LINDHOLM, C. 2002. Kissing cousins: anthropologists on Islam. In *Interpreting Islam* (ed.) H. Donnan, 110-30. London: Sage.

MAHMOOD, S. 2001. Rehearsed spontaneity and the conventionality of ritual: disciplines of ṣalāt. *American Ethnologist* **28**, 827-53.

———— 2005. *Politics of piety: the Islamic revival and the feminist subject.* Princeton: University Press.

———— 2006. Secularism, hermeneutics, and empire: the politics of Islamic reformation. *Public Culture* **18**, 323-47.

MAMDANI, M. 2002. Good Muslim, bad Muslim: a political perspective on culture and terrorism. *American Anthropologist* **104**, 766-75.

MANDAVILLE, P. 2007. *Global political Islam.* London: Routledge.

MANGER, L. (ed.) 1999. *Muslim diversity: local Islam in global contexts.* Richmond, Surrey: Curzon.

MARSDEN, M. 2005. *Living Islam: Muslim religious experience in Pakistan's North-West Frontier.* Cambridge: University Press.

———— 2007. All-male sonic gatherings, Islamic reform, and masculinity in northern Pakistan. *American Ethnologist* **34**, 473-90.

———— 2008*a*. Women, politics, Islamism. *Modern Asian Studies* **42**, 405-29.

———— 2008*b*. Muslim cosmopolitans? Transnational life in Northern Pakistan. *Journal of Asian Studies* **67**, 213-47.

———— 2009. Debating debate in northern Afghanistan. *Anthropology Today* **25**: 2, 20-4.

MASQUELIER, A. 2007. Negotiating futures: Islam, youth, and the state in Niger. In *Islam and Muslim politics in Africa* (eds) B.F. Soares & R. Otayek, 243-62. New York: Palgrave Macmillan.

MAURER, B. 2005. *Mutual life, limited: Islamic banking, alternative currencies, lateral reason.* Princeton: University Press.

MENELEY, A. 2007. Fashions and fundamentalisms in fin-de-siècle Yemen: chador Barbie and Islamic socks. *Cultural Anthropology* **22**, 214-43.

MESSICK, B. 1993. *The calligraphic state: textual domination and history in a Muslim society.* Berkeley: University of California Press.

———— 1996. Media muftis: radio fatwas in Yemen. In *Islamic legal interpretation: muftis and their fatwas* (eds) K. Masud, B. Messick & D. Powers, 310-20. Cambridge, Mass.: Harvard University Press.

METCALF, B. 1982. *Islamic revival in British India.* Berkeley: University of California Press.

———— 1994. 'Remaking ourselves': Islamic self-fashioning in a global movement of spiritual renewal. In *Accounting for fundamentalisms* (eds) M.E. Marty & R.S. Appleby, 706-25. Chicago: University Press.

———— 2001. 'Traditionalist' Islamic activism: Deoband, Tablighis, and Talibs. In *Understanding September 11* (eds) C. Calhoun, P. Price & A. Timmer, 53-66. New York: New Press.

MEYER, B. & A. MOORS (eds) 2006. *Religion, media and the public sphere.* Bloomington: Indiana University Press.

MITCHELL, T. 1991. *Colonizing Egypt.* Berkeley: University of California Press.

———— 2000. The stage of modernity. In *Questions of modernity* (ed.) T. Mitchell, 1-34. Minneapolis: University of Minnesota Press.

———— 2002. *Rule of experts: Egypt, techno-politics, modernity*. Berkeley: University of California Press.

———— 2005. The work of economics: how a discipline makes its world. *European Journal of Sociology* **46**, 297-320.

Moors, A. & E. Tarlo. 2007. Introduction. *Fashion Theory* **11**, 133-42.

Navaro-Yashin, Y. 2002. *Faces of the state: secularism and public life in Turkey*. Princeton: University Press.

Ong, A. 1995. State versus Islam: Malay families, women's bodies, and the body politic in Malaysia. In *Bewitching women and pious men: gender and body politics in Southeast Asia* (eds) A. Ong & M.G. Peletz, 159-94. Berkeley: University of California Press.

Osella, C. & F. Osella 2006. Once upon a time in the West? Stories of migration and modernity from Kerala, South India. *Journal of the Royal Anthropological Institute* (N.S.) **12**, 569-88.

Osella F. & C. Osella 2000. The return of King Mahabali: the politics of morality in Kerala. In *The everyday state and society in modern India* (eds) C. Fuller & V. Benei, 137-62. New Delhi: Social Science Press.

———— & ———— 2007. 'I am Gulf': the production of cosmopolitanism in Kozhikode, Kerala, India. In *Struggling with history: Islam and cosmopolitanism in the Western Indian Ocean* (eds) E. Simpson & K. Kress, 323-56. London: Hurst.

———— & ———— 2008. Islamism and social reform in Kerala, South India. *Modern Asian Studies*, **42**, 317-46.

Otayek R. & B.F. Soares 2007. Introduction: Islam and Muslim politics in Africa. In *Islam and Muslim Politics in Africa* (eds) B.F. Soares & R. Otayek, 1-24. New York: Palgrave Macmillan.

Özyürek, E. 2006. *Nostalgia for the modern: state secularism and everyday politics in Turkey*. Durham, N.C.: Duke University Press.

Parkin, D.J. 2000. Inside and outside the mosque: a master trope. In *Islamic prayer across the Indian Ocean: inside and outside the mosque* (eds) D.J. Parkin & S.C. Headley, 1-22. Richmond, Surrey: Curzon.

Peletz, M.G. 1994. Neither reasonable nor responsible: contrasting representations of masculinity in a Malay society. *Cultural Anthropology* **9**, 135-78.

———— 2002. *Islamic modern*. Princeton: University Press.

Peteet, J. 1994. Male gender and rituals of resistance in the Palestinian 'intifada': a cultural politics of violence. *American Ethnologist* **21**, 31-49.

Riccio, B. 2004. Transnational Mouridism and the Afro-Muslim critique of Italy. *Journal of Ethnic and Migration Studies* **30**, 929-44.

Ring, L. 2006. *Zenana: everyday peace in a Karachi apartment building*. Bloomington: Indiana University Press.

Roy, O. 1994. *The failure of political Islam* (trans. C. Volk). Cambridge, Mass.: Harvard University Press.

———— 2004 [2002]. *Globalised Islam: the search for a new ummah*. London: Hurst.

Rudnyckyj, D. 2009. Spiritual economies: Islam and neoliberalism in contemporary Indonesia. *Cultural Anthropology* **24**, 104-41.

Ruud, A.E. 1996. State and civil society interaction: without a 'civil society' or a 'public sphere'? Some suggestions from rural India. *Forum for Development Studies*, **2**, 259-87.

Said, E. 1978. *Orientalism*. New York: Pantheon.

Salvatore, A. 1997. *Islam and the political discourse of modernity*. Reading: Ithaca Press.

———— 2007. *The public sphere: liberal modernity, Catholicism, Islam*. New York: Palgrave Macmillan.

———— & D.F. Eickelman (eds) 2004. *Public Islam and the common good*. Leiden: Brill.

Schielke, S. 2006. Snacks and saints: mawlid festivals and the politics of festivity, piety, and modernity in contemporary Egypt. Unpublished Ph.D. thesis, University of Amsterdam.

Schulz, D.E. 2008. Piety's manifold embodiments: Muslim women's quest for moral renewal in urban Mali. *Journal for Islamic Studies* **28**, 66-93.

Scott, D. & C. Hirschkind (eds) 2006. *Powers of the secular modern: Talal Asad and his interlocutors*. Stanford: University Press.

Sen, A. 2007. *Shiv Sena women: violence and communalism in a Bombay slum*. London: Hurst.

Shehabuddin, E. 2008. *Reshaping the holy: women, Islam, and democracy in Bangladesh*. New York: Columbia University Press.

Sikand, Y. 2002. *The origins and development of the Tablighi-Jama'at (1920-2000)*. New Delhi: Orient Longman.

Silverstein, P.A. 2004. *Algeria in France: transpolitics, race, and nation*. Bloomington: Indiana University Press.

Simpson, E. 2006. *Muslim society and the Western Indian Ocean: the seafarers of Kachchh*. London: Routledge.

———— 2008. The changing perspectives on three Muslim men on the question of saint worship over a 10-year period in Gujarat, western India. *Modern Asian Studies* **42**, 377-403.

———— & K. KRESSE (eds) 2007. *Struggling with history: Islam and cosmopolitanism in the Western Indian Ocean*. London: Hurst.

SINGER, A. 2008. *Charity in Islamic societies*. Cambridge: University Press.

SLOANE P. 1999. *Islam, modernity and entrepreneurship among the Malays*. New York: St Martin's Press.

SOARES, B.F. 2000. Notes on the anthropological study of Islam and Muslim societies in Africa. *Culture and Religion* 1, 277-85.

———— 2005. *Islam and the prayer economy: history and authority in a Malian town*. Edinburgh: University Press for the International African Institute; Ann Arbor: University of Michigan Press.

———— 2007*a*. Rethinking Islam and Muslim societies in Africa. *African Affairs* 106, 319-26.

———— 2007*b*. Saint and Sufi in contemporary Mali. In *Sufism and the 'modern' in Islam* (eds) M. van Bruinessen & J. Day Howell, 76-91. London: I.B. Tauris.

———— & R. OTAYEK (eds) 2007. *Islam and Muslim politics in Africa*. New York: Palgrave Macmillan.

STARRETT, G. 1997. The anthropology of Islam. In *The anthropology of religion: a handbook* (ed.) S.D. Glazier, 279-303. Westport, Conn.: Greenwood.

———— 1998. *Putting Islam to work: education, politics, and religious transformation in Egypt*. Berkeley: University of California Press.

———— 2008. Authentication and affect: why the Turks don't like enchanted counterpublics, a review essay. *Comparative Studies in Society and History* 50, 1036-46.

THRIFT, N. 2005. *Knowing capitalism*. London: Sage.

TORAB, A. 1996. Piety as gendered agency: a study of Jalaseh ritual discourse in an urban neighbourhood in Iran. *Journal of the Royal Anthropological Institute* (N.S.) 2, 235-52.

TRIAUD, J.-L. 1992. L'Islam sous le régime colonial. In *L'Afrique occidentale au temps des Français (colonisateur et colonisés, c. 1860-1960)* (ed.) C. Coquery-Vidrovitch, 141-55. Paris: Découverte.

TRIPP, C. 2006. *Islam and the moral economy: the challenge of capitalism*. Cambridge: University Press.

TROUILLOT, M.-R. 2001. The anthropology of the state in the age of globalization: close encounters of the deceptive kind. *Current Anthropology* 42, 126-38.

TURNER, B.S. 1974. *Weber and Islam*. London: Routledge & Kegan Paul.

———— 2007. Religious authority and the new media. *Theory, Culture & Society* 24, 117-34.

VAN BRUINESSEN, M. & J.D. HOWELL (eds) 2007. *Sufism and the 'modern' in Islam*. London: I.B. Tauris.

VAN DER VEER, P. 2001. *Imperial encounters: religion and modernity in India and Britain*. Princeton: University Press.

VARISCO, D.M. 2007. *Reading Orientalism: Said and the unsaid*. Seattle: University of Washington Press.

VERKAAIK, O. 2004. *Migrants and militants: fun and urban violence in Pakistan*. Princeton: University Press.

WALLE, T.M. 2004. Virginity vs decency: continuity and change in Pakistani men's perception of sexuality and women. In *South Asian masculinities: context of change, sites of continuity* (eds) R. Chopra, C. Osella & F. Osella, 96-130. New Delhi: Women Unlimited.

WASHBROOK, D. 1997. From comparative sociology to global history: Britain and India in the pre-history of modernity. *Journal of the Social and Economic History of the Orient* 40, 410-43.

WEISS, B. (ed.) 2004. *Producing African futures: ritual and reproduction in a neoliberal age*. Leiden: Brill.

WERBNER, P.J. 2002. *Imagined diasporas among Manchester Muslims*. Oxford: James Currey; Santa Fe: School of American Research Press.

———— 2003. *Pilgrims of love: the anthropology of a global Sufi cult*. Bloomington: Indiana University Press.

WEST H. & T. SANDERS (eds) 2003. *Transparency and conspiracy: ethnographies of suspicion in the new world order*. Durham, N.C.: Duke University Press.

WHITE, J.B. 2002. *Islamist mobilization in Turkey: a study in vernacular politics*. Seattle: University of Washington Press.

WIKAN, U. 1991. *Behind the veil in Arabia: women in Oman*. Chicago: University Press.

WIKTOROWICZ, Q. 2001. *The management of Islamic activism: Salafis, the Muslim Brotherhood, and state power in Jordan*. Albany: State University of New York Press.

———— (ed.) 2004. *Islamic activism: a social movement theory approach*. Bloomington: Indiana University Press.

ZAMAN, M.Q. 2002. *The ulama in contemporary Islam: custodians of change*. Princeton: University Press.

———— 2005. The scope and limits of Islamic cosmopolitanism and the discursive language of the 'ulama'. In *Muslim networks from hajj to hip hop* (eds) m. cooke & B. Lawrence, 84-106. Chapel Hill: University of North Carolina Press.

EL-ZEIN, A.H. 1977. Beyond ideology and theology: the search for the anthropology of Islam. *Annual Review of Anthropology* 6, 227-54.

2

Being good in Ramadan: ambivalence, fragmentation, and the moral self in the lives of young Egyptians

SAMULI SCHIELKE *Zentrum Moderner Orient*

For young men in the northern Egyptian village of Nazlat al-Rayyis,[1] the holy month of Ramadan is a privileged time for football. Every afternoon before fast-breaking time, youths gather to play at schoolyards or other open spaces. At the secondary school, a Ramadan tournament of local amateur clubs attracts up to a hundred spectators, who sit from early afternoon until shortly before sunset in the shade, watching the usually two or three consecutive matches that take place in an afternoon. I was amazed at first by this display of what seemed to me an extreme exercise of physical endurance in face of a fasting that involves complete abstinence from food, drink, smoking, and sex from dawn to sunset. But when I discussed the subject with the young men, they said that playing football during the hours before fast-breaking is not very arduous at all. On the contrary, concentrating on the game makes one forget the feelings of hunger and thirst.[2] The hours before the fast-breaking can be long, and male students and civil servants especially often have a lot of free time in Ramadan.

Football is not only about killing time, however. It is also seen as a form of the sociality (*lamma*) and amusement (*tasliya*) that characterize Ramadan in Egypt as much as fasting and praying do. Despite the ascetic character of fasting, Ramadan in Egypt is surrounded by a festive atmosphere. Streets are decorated with flags, colourful strips of paper, lights, and lanterns. In the evenings – especially towards the end of Ramadan – people invite friends and relatives, the cafés are full, and in the cities a veritable season of cultural events characterizes the second half of the month. But festive as they may be, Ramadan gatherings nevertheless express a spirit of religious and moral discipline. Forms of entertainment deemed immoral or un-Islamic – flirting and making out, consumption of alcohol and cannabis, pornography – largely stop during the holy month. In the cities, bars are closed. In the villages, internet cafés are empty. The trade in cannabis that otherwise flourishes in cities and villages alike reaches a seasonal low. Other forms of entertainment that are not seen as immoral as such are suspended in Ramadan because they have no place in the rigid schedule of fasting. Popular celebrations such as saints-day festivals (*mûlids*) and weddings are not celebrated at this time.[3] These forms of entertainment, temporarily unavailable during the holy month, are partly replaced by football. 'The football matches', a friend of mine argued, 'are for the youths a way to compensate for not being able to go after girls, smoke marijuana and drink beer. It's a way to fill the emptiness that they otherwise fill with immoral entertainment'.

Ramadan football is an ambivalent exercise. It is one of the gatherings so characteristic of the sense of community that prevails in the month of fasting, and a way to kill time that is not deemed immoral or un-Islamic. But at the same time it shows a very complex understanding of religion and morality. Not only does it mix ascetic discipline with fun and entertainment, it is also part of a time of exceptional morality that, by its nature, will only last as long as Ramadan lasts, and that by virtue of its temporally limited nature indirectly legitimizes less consistent approaches to religion and morality for the rest of the year.

Since the Islamic revival of the 1970s, rigid religious moralism has become a leading tone of the debates in Egypt on norms and values. Daily life, however, continues to be characterized by the ambiguity between and an uneasy coexistence of religious morality and discipline, communal respect and reputation, the expectations and promises of consumerism and romantic love, and the limitations of practical circumstances. This tension is most strongly present among the youth, whose life experience has become (or perhaps has always been) highly fragmented, characterized by contradictory values and expectations, and often by strong crises and shifts in lifestyle and attitudes.

While subjectivity, religiosity, and morality have become a central topic of the anthropology of Muslim societies, the issues of ambivalence and fragmentation have so far been given relatively little attention. Notably Talal Asad (1993), Michael Lambek (2000), Charles Hirschkind (2001; 2006a; 2006b) and Saba Mahmood (2005) have – with somewhat different emphases – argued for an anthropology of morality that, rather than focusing on codes, commands, and prohibitions, should have as its focus the ways in which moral personhood and responsibility are created and practised. Morality, in this sense, is about the conscious cultivation of virtues with the aim of developing a virtuous self. The problem of these approaches is that although they give considerable attention to practical judgement in the face of conflict, debate, and contestation, they look at the practice of morality and religion primarily from the perspective of coherence. In the work of Mahmood and Hirschkind, this is especially evident in the way they juxtapose the ideals of the Islamic revival with an equally idealized secular liberal position, and most crucially in the way they focus on the declared aim of a pious discipline rather than its actual outcomes. Lambek's approach with its emphasis on practical judgement (*phronesis*) is more nuanced, but it remains grounded in the Aristotelian notion of moral action as a search for an ideal middle way. Yet if we are to understand the ambiguity of Ramadan football, we must find a way to account for views that are neither clearly nor consistently in line with any grand ideology, and lives that are full of ambivalence – not only between moral and amoral aims, but also between different, at times mutually hostile, moral aims.

Other scholars in the field have given more consideration to ambiguity. Katherine Ewing (1990) and Gary Gregg (1998; 2007) demonstrate that while people may present their identity, aims, and trajectory as clear and coherent at a given moment, they routinely shift between conflicting self-representations, and are regularly torn between conflicting self-ideals and aims (see also van Meijl 2006; Masquelier 2007). Lila Abu-Lughod (1996 [1986]: 255-8) makes a similar point in her study of Bedouin oral poetry, showing that neither the public face of honour nor the more intimate face of love poetry can be taken as the more true expression of people's sensibilities. More recently, Magnus Marsden has argued that approaches with an emphasis on self-discipline 'are unable to confront the ways in which Muslims are called upon to face, explain and contend with inconsistencies and complexities in their attempts to live virtuous lives' (2005: 261). Benjamin Soares (2006) argues that rather than producing hybrids and compromises, the various normative registers and ideals present in modern Muslim societies often stand in strong juxtaposition to each other in the public sphere and in people's lives. My own research on Muslim saints-day festivals (Schielke 2006) indicates that while in earlier, more mystical traditions of Islam ambivalence was accommodated as part of a normative order that did not require a comprehensive and universalizing discipline, modernist and reformist approaches that emphasize rationality and purity often take the abolition of ambivalence as a key task. Their attempt to do so, however, actually leads not to more clarity but to more fragmentation.

In this chapter, I argue that moral subjectivity is a very important issue indeed, but there is a risk – especially when morality and piety come together – of favouring the complete, the consistent, and the perfect in a way that does not do justice to the complex and often contradictory nature of everyday experience. To develop this theoretical critique, I shall depart somewhat from the conventions of academic writing: I will present my empirical case first and only afterwards conclude with a detailed critical discussion, informed by my empirical argument, of current research in the field. For the sake of clarity, I single out one particularly influential and good example of the study of piety and subjectivity – Saba Mahmood's *Politics of piety* (2005) – which, I believe, offers inspiring directions for the anthropological study of religion, but falls into the trap of what Katherine Ewing (1990) has called 'the illusion of wholeness'.

Ramadan morality

Ramadan, in Muslim belief, is a blessed, holy month which constitutes a special period of piety that involves much more than just fasting. There is a general sense of increased social, moral, and pious commitment during Ramadan. In the evenings, the mosques are often packed with believers participating in the voluntarily *tarâwîh* prayers, in addition to canonical ritual daily prayers that can extend over more than an hour after the evening (*'ishâ*) prayer. In the streets of the cities, wealthy citizens offer large-scale services of free food at fast-breaking time, known as 'tables of the Merciful' (*mawâ'id ar-Rahmân*).

Arduous to maintain especially in summer heat, fasting is seen by many as a spiritual exercise in disciplining carnal desires. Furthermore, many people ascribe to the feeling of hunger a strong power in facilitating social responsibility towards the poor. The central and most important motivation for fasting, however, is the prospect of Paradise. Ramadan is a time when God rewards believers most generously and forgives their sins. For the duration of Ramadan, 'the gates of Paradise are open and the gates of Hell are closed'.[4] According to a *hadith* (authoritative tradition) of the Prophet Muhammad, distributed as a poster by the local Branch of the Muslim Brotherhood,

> Whoever fasts and stands for prayer in the month of Ramadan with faith and entrusting God with counting the reward, the sins he has previously committed are forgiven. And whoever stands for prayer in the Night of Destiny (*Laylat al-Qadr*)[5] with faith and entrusting God with counting the reward, the sins he has previously committed are forgiven.[6]

Other traditions state that the obligatory prayer counts seventy times its value during Ramadan, that voluntary prayer gains the same reward as an obligatory one, and that a prayer in *Laylat al-Qadr* is better than that of a thousand months. On the other hand, the consequences of not observing Ramadan are severe. Intentionally breaking the fast without a legitimate reason cannot be recalled or equalled out by anything, and both good and bad deeds count their double in reward and punishment during Ramadan.[7]

Not surprisingly, then, Ramadan is 'the season of worship' (*mûsim al-'ibâda*), a time when people try to be good – that is, observe religious commandments and moral virtues more rigorously than they usually do. People who otherwise rarely pray try to fulfil this obligation during the holy month, especially in the beginning and around *Laylat al-Qadr*. Since it is believed that anger, curses, and insults break the fast, people attempt to avoid them during Ramadan, and in arguments and fights (which are numerous in Ramadan as people often have short tempers due to fasting), people often use the phrase 'Oh God, I'm fasting!' (*Allâhumma ana sâyim*)[8] to avoid using foul language but also to call oneself and others to calm down.

During the holy month, one must abstain from all the other minor and major misdeeds that may be forgivable at other times. If God's reward and blessings are very close during Ramadan, so are His wrath and punishment. This belief involves not only practices deemed as immoral and sinful, such as drinking, flirting, adultery, watching pornography, lying, stealing, and violence. It also implies restrictions upon practices with more ambiguous status, notably cinema, music, and dress. Many women opt for a more conservative dress during Ramadan (by not using make-up, for example), and some people abstain from listening to pop music and watching movies, arguing that 'they are *harâm* (forbidden) during Ramadan'.

This focus on reward and piety is framed, however, by the general sense of gathering, joy, and entertainment of which the afternoon football matches are only one example. A month of fasting, Ramadan is also a privileged time of eating as people compensate for the fasting in daytime with special delicacies in the evening. The consumption of meat and sugar skyrockets. Special television programmes and, in the cities, cultural events in theatres and tents offer a wide range of Ramadan entertainment. At night, cafés, promenades, and parks are packed with people, including many more women and families than usually. People generally spend more money in Ramadan, and towards the end of the month, with *'îd al-fitr* (the feast of breaking the fast) approaching, consumption reaches an intensity similar to that of Christmas in the West.

This 'Christmasization of Ramadan', as it has been called by Walter Armbrust (2002), and the character of Ramadan as a time of exceptional morality have been regularly subjected to criticism both from religious authorities and from ordinary citizens who feel that the 'true' spirit of Ramadan is lost in the midst of all this. They argue that Ramadan should be a time of spirituality and discipline that helps to create a 'committed' (*multazim*) Muslim character and society free of vices and unnecessary spending, orientated to the purpose of individual and collective self-improvement (Abû l-Ma'âtî 2006: 7; al-Khashshâb 2006: 7; Matar 2006: 23-4; Sha'bân 2006: 4; al-Shurbâsî 2006: 1428-31).

The popular practice of Ramadan, both in its ascetic and festive variations, does not focus on progressive improvement of society and self. Firmly based on the authoritative sources of Islam but with a different emphasis than offered by established religious discourse, its focus is explicitly on reward (*thawâb*), the forgiving of sins, and the ultimate aim of entering Paradise in the afterlife. During Ramadan, people frequently discuss in detail the correct form of voluntary prayers and the exact details of fasting in order to maximize the reward of praying and fasting. This is a highly utilitarian understanding of religion that implicitly allows Ramadan to be established as a moral and pious exception from not so perfect everyday life. If Ramadan is a time of exceptional reward when God forgives one's previous sins, one may commit some sins and slip a little from one's obligations during the rest of the year – in a year's time, after all, it is Ramadan again.

The ways in which most people practise Ramadan do not require an ethical subjectivity that aims at the perfection of a purified, God-fearing self capable of keeping right and wrong clearly apart in one's judgement of one's own and others' conduct. This is, however, the ideal promoted by the Salafi reformist movement and, to a less radical extent, established public-sector religious functionaries. It is, more importantly, closely connected with the (for the time being) hegemonic ideology of developmentalist nationalism, which, despite some severe compromises it has undergone in the process of economic liberalization, continues to posit the ideal of a rational, committed, and disciplined citizen who, much like the ideal Salafi believer, has 'awareness' (*wa'y*), that is, clear and authoritative knowledge and a correspondingly sound ethical disposition. This is a notion of society, religion, and the subject which, in its secular and Islamist varieties alike, centres on discipline, clarity, and consistency in service of a grand purpose (Schielke 2006; 2007). What the modern citizen or believer (or, most commonly, both in the same person) should not have are ambivalent states of mind and contradictory values. This, however, is not the case with Ramadan morality, which is based not on progressive discipline and perfection but on a temporal and contextual hierarchy of different norms, motivations, aims, and pressures. The moral subject in this practice of and vernacular discourse on morality is one who acts appropriately according to the time and the occasion in order to find a more or less acceptable temporary balance between God's commands, social customs and values, personal desires, and economic pressures, a balance in which the weight of different constituents can change depending on the social context of a practice, the time of the year, and one's personal biography. For such a notion of moral subjectivity, norms and boundaries are not absolute; on the contrary, they are subject to temporal and contextual shifts, as is stated in the colloquial proverb: 'There is an hour for your heart and an hour for your Lord' (*sâ'a l-qalbak w-sâ'a l-rabbak*), in other words: there are times to follow your desires, and there are times to follow the commandments of religion. Ramadan as a time of exceptional morality demonstrates and enforces the supremacy of God's commands by constituting a time in which morality is not situational but strict and in which religious obligations *must* be fulfilled. But in the end it is precisely the temporary rigour of the holy month that establishes and legitimizes the flexible nature of norms and ethics for the rest of the year.

This can be best seen in the time of *'îd al-fitr*, the feast of breaking the fast that marks the end of Ramadan. In line with the established traditions of ritual Law, Muslims take the Feast as an occasion to reward themselves for withstanding the trial of fasting. But the extent and ways in which they do so can significantly depart from individual and collective self-improvement and reform. The Feast marks not only a reward for fasting, but also the return to a normal order of affairs. On the first Friday after Ramadan, at the congregational Friday noon (*gum'a*) prayer, the sermons invariably circle around one issue: reminding the believers that they must follow the commandments of their creed not only during Ramadan, but for all of the year, that the Feast does not mean that one is allowed to revert to one's bad habits. And yet every year when Ramadan football gives way to other forms of entertainment, the same young men who pray and fast during Ramadan now celebrate in ways that would have been out of the question a few days earlier. The sales of hashish skyrocket, cafés with satellite dishes start showing porn again, and, most visibly and dramatically, youths gather in parks, promenades, and public places to celebrate in an excited and tense atmosphere that often leads to outbreaks of sexual harassment with young men aggressively touching and grabbing women passing by (Malek 2006).

But the power of the moral shift of the Feast lies not simply in the reversion to bad habits. More importantly, it marks the shift from a period of observance during which the sins of the previous year are erased, to a more complex order of morality. Sexuality is a strong case in point. While, according to Islamic rituals, sexual intercourse is allowed in the night during Ramadan, the rigorous and often tiring schedule imposed by fasting leaves little time and energy for sex. On the first evening of the Feast in 2004, I met with young men from the village in a café. They were sitting outside in the alley, while inside, behind mostly closed doors, middle-aged family fathers were watching porn on a French satellite channel.[9] The youths explained that the married men were 'warming up' to go home and have sex with their wives after a month's abstinence. Since the young unmarried men did not have wives waiting for them at home, they were doing their best to annoy and make fun of the older men, who were slightly but not very uncomfortable with the situation, exposed, on the one hand, confirmed in their striving for potency, a very important male virtue, on the other. But also for the young men the Feast meant a return to male virtues based on virility and sexuality after temporarily devoting themselves to the more ascetic virtues of piety and sportsmanship during Ramadan. Many of them had girlfriends and prospective brides whom they were courting, and those who did not were nevertheless busy with romantic and erotic fantasies, as well as attempts to make contacts with girls, with strategies ranging from flirting to aggressive harassment. The end of Ramadan meant that they were free to resume 'going after girls' (*yimshi wara l-banât*), a practice deemed morally questionable but all the same essential for their male self-esteem and their expectations of romantic love.

Moral registers

The moral universe in which Ramadan morality is embedded is characterized by a profound ambivalence that is not only a coincidental result of circumstances but actually provides the foundation of situational moral action and an ethical subjectivity that is based on a coexistence of various motivations, aims, and identities that can and often do conflict but do not constitute exclusive opposites.

Young people in the village, often strongly influenced by Salafis and Muslim Brothers in their religious beliefs, generally share a literalist understanding of religion as a clear, exact set of commandments and prohibitions that leave little or no space for different interpretations or negotiation. In their everyday practice, however, they also express other ideals that may more or less clearly contradict their religious discourse.

The life experiences and expectations of the young men of Nazlat al-Rayyis are characterized by several moments of ambivalence that consider not only others' expectations of them but also, as far as I can tell on the basis of their accounts, their own expectations of themselves. Ideals of rigid sexual morality coexist and compete with the imaginaries and experiments of romance and sex, wishes of self-realization with the aspirations for social status, ideals of moral integrity with the drive for material well-being. In fact, people often speak in very different tone and with very different arguments and style about different topics. While young men often ridicule Salafi activists with their long beards, short-hemmed *gallâbiyas* (long loose gowns worn by men), and painstakingly precise ritualism, at the same time their idea of a profoundly religious person is usually identical with the image of the Salafi. A talk, very critical and satirical, about social values can turn suddenly very serious and dogmatic when the subject of religion crops up. On the other hand, people can argue for very conservative and strict standards of gender relations at one time, but express rather liberal ideals of romantic love at other times. In short, morality is not a coherent system, but an incoherent and unsystematic conglomerate of different moral registers that exist in parallel and often contradict each other. There are several key moral registers, each with values, terminologies, discourses, and fields of their own, that play a role in the lives and discourses of the young men with whom I did fieldwork. The most important among them are as follows:

- Religion, understood as a set of clear norms, often referred to as 'Qur'an and the Sunna', that is, the two central sources of Islam. Religion, in this understanding, is essentially a normative system that defines all acts as either permitted (*halâl*) or prohibited (*harâm*) on the base of evidence from the Scripture.
- Social justice, generally with a clear socialist overtone problematizing issues such as corruption, privatization of public-sector enterprises and public services, nepotism, authoritarian rule, economic exploitation, the lack of opportunities of people with state education, and the ridiculously low salaries of civil servants.
- Community and family obligations, usually referred to with 'respect' (*ihtirâm*), including one's social standing in the community, good behaviour, responsibility for one's family, recognition of authorities and hierarchies, and wealth.
- Good character (*tîba, gadaʿâna*), based on the readiness to help friends, avoidance of conflicts, and a general sense of joviality and sympathy. Good character is often seen by young men as a more 'true' virtue than respect, which, in their view, often is based purely on money and can conceal an essentially vicious character.
- Romance and love, celebrating passion and emotional commitment and describing 'pure love' as an all-sacrificing obsession that disregards both self-interest and other moral ideals.
- Self-realization, expressed in the aim of finding a well-paid job and a place in life and, to a lesser degree, of widening one's horizon of experience.

Morality in this sense is not only unsystematic and ambiguous, it is also accompanied by declaredly amoral aims and strategies that people deem necessary to fill the 'emptiness' of the everyday and to reach material well-being. Some of the most important amoral registers are money and the necessity of earning an income (which, for example, force a respectable and God-fearing civil servant to live on bribes), sex and desire, and fun and excitement, including the consumption of alcohol and drugs. On the other side, there are also recurring topoi which in a moralizing tone at once establish a moral register and offer an excuse – most notably so a critique of materialism which consists of claiming that 'in this village' or 'in our society' all that really counts is money and that true moral values have no importance anymore. By insinuating that if it were not for all this money and materialism, people really would be able to live happy, spiritual lives in justice and harmony, the critique of materialism at once establishes the registers of religion and social justice and explains why it is not possible to live according to them.

Romantic love and sexuality, to stay with an example that is deemed crucially important by the young men I have followed in my fieldwork, form an ethical discourse with specific virtues and teleologies of the subject, that is, ways to become and be a good human being (see Foucault 1990: chap. 3). Romance is strongly present not only in everyday experience, but also in the public media in the form of love songs, films, soap operas, and so on. While the plots and the kinds of problems that the heroes of love songs and stories face certainly move within a moral universe that makes them meaningful and understandable to their audiences, they definitely cannot be reduced to the religious discourse of legitimate and illegitimate relationships, the vernacular ethics of patriarchal family, or the forms of double morality that measure different actions on different scales depending on gender, social status, and the context of the action. Love represents an ethics of desire and commitment (which can reach the degree of obsession) that stands in stark contrast to the religious discourse on chastity and the social practice of parental control over marriages.[10] But committed to the ideals of romance as the young men are, they can simultaneously be very convinced about the necessity of gender segregation and the absolute prohibition of adultery (zinâ) in Islam. The interesting point here is not just the fact that despite the religious discourse on chastity premarital sex does take place quite often, but the ambivalent coexistence of partly opposing teleologies of the subject, on one level striving for a sinless and pure disposition that excludes erotic relationships before marriage, on another level aiming for a romantic and erotic relationship that in the end (not at the beginning) may lead to marriage, while on a further level committed to ideals of family hierarchies and respect that exclude girlfriends from the role of potential wives exactly because their participation in romantic affairs makes them 'bad' (wihsha) and unrespectable.[11]

The practice of all these contradictory and conflicting expectations and ideals is necessarily situational and inconsequent. Love stands in a continuous tension to the register of gender segregation and sexual morality and the register of family responsibilities. The communal quality of respect is often seen as a mere mask based on material values and detached from the virtue of good character. The ideal of social justice stands in a striking juxtaposition to a reality where nepotism, bribes, and illegal trade are often the only and usually the most lucrative way to make a living. The over-arching normativity of religion, finally, is continuously relativized by references to other registers that, rather than questioning or subverting religious norms, circumvent them.

Ramadan, in this mosaic of a moral universe, is a site of higher order, a moral exception which through the exercise of fasting establishes a clear hierarchy and a clear teleology: the commands of God and the prospect of Paradise. By the logic of its exceptional nature, it cannot and need not be a permanent state of affairs. My point here is that this is not merely a compromise that allows for amoral practices for the sake of material necessity. Romantic love, social respect, good character, and self-realization constitute moral registers and ethical teleologies of the subject that are by no means amoral; on the contrary, they imply normative expectations in their own right. While during Ramadan they can be temporarily subordinated to the superior normativity of religion, in the everyday their relationship is one of competitive coexistence.

Living according to the book

This coexistence is increasingly troubled – but not replaced – by the current turn of many young people towards a Salafi revivalist understanding of religion as an all-encompassing ritual and moral discipline that has as its declared aim the abolition of ambivalence and the imposition of clarity (see also Lincoln 2006: 56-60). Good life, in this understanding, must and can only be based on full and comprehensive application of *al-kitâb wa-s-sunna*, that is, the Qur'an and the Prophet's tradition *qua* definitive manuals of moral action. This, however, does not mean that people would actually live in this way, and therein lies both the power and the fundamental trouble of the Salafi ideal of religiosity. On the one hand, people can hold to it without actually having fully to realize it, and its being unrealized allows it to remain pure and simple while life is messy and complex. On the other hand, however, it can become a serious obstacle in people's lives, a debate-killing argument that can lead people into serious crises and dead ends.

Many researchers have convincingly argued that the Islamic revival is not simply an expression of dogmatic fundamentalist obscurantism, but in fact very dynamic and open for a great degree of debate and difference (Ahmad 2008; Hirschkind 2006a; Osella & Osella 2008). But we should be careful not to over-state the possibilities of debate and deliberation opened by the democratization of religious interpretation that has accompanied the spread and popularization of Islamic reformism (see Eickelman 1992). With its emphasis on direct knowledge and application of religious 'facts', Islamic reformism opens up powerful possibilities of critique while excluding or marginalizing others by positing them beyond discussion. Other styles of being religious exist, but they are increasingly stigmatized as incomplete or erroneous. Spaces of ambiguity are increasingly dependent on silence, double standards, and cognitive dissonance. While values can be debated, declaring them religious often ends the debate. All other moral registers have either to accept or ignore the supremacy of religion, but they cannot openly contest it.

What makes this troubling for young men is the way the current wave of religiosity often leaves people hanging in a situation where they accept the promise of religion for a better life both in this world and the Hereafter, but cannot measure the promise in any legitimate way, or search for alternative solutions should the reality fall short of the promise. The problems this causes are best seen in the fragmentation of people's biographies. Young age is often characterized by strong changes in beliefs and attitudes, and it is usually at young age that people choose to become 'committed' (*multazim*) Salafis who not only meticulously fulfil religious obligations such as praying and fasting, but also apply a wider pious discipline to all aspects of their lives, changing their style of dress, giving up smoking,[12] starting to socialize primarily with other Salafis, and adapting a distinctive jargon. Becoming an active Salafi with the corresponding comprehensive discipline is usually marked by a strong break between a 'sinful' ('*âsî*) past and a 'committed' present – therefore disqualifying the more ambivalent forms of morality. But we must be careful not to take the way from ambivalence and imperfection to clarity and commitment as the regular and typical one. The perfectionist nature of the piety movement produces much starker contrasts between commitment and deviance than the temporal relativism of Ramadan morality. The result is not necessarily a general shift from Ramadan piety to comprehensive piety, but rather the increasing intensity of the juxtapositions and shifts. People always live complex lives; a person's identity is in practice dialogical, made up of different voices and experiences

(Gregg 2007; van Meijl 2006). In consequence, people commonly shift between different roles and identities. This can become a problematic and troublesome experience, however, when one or some of the ideologies of the self a person holds to are based on a demand for strict and exclusive perfection – as the Salafi revivalist notion of subjectivity based on 'commitment' (*iltizâm*) is.

Salafis, just like everybody else, live everyday lives loaded with ambiguities and contradictions. To a certain degree Salafi discourse allows for pragmatic solutions legitimized by the Islamic legal category of necessity (*darûra*). Shaving one's beard for conscription is a common case of such compromises for the sake of necessity that young Salafi men face. The problem, however, is that this by no means lessens the pressure on pious self-perfection. On the level of emotional and spiritual commitment, there is little space for negotiation. The rigour of Salafi piety that makes it so attractive in the mess of the everyday also makes it difficult to maintain in the face of ambivalent feelings. Take, for example, the story of Mustafa (a pseudonym), a man in his early twenties who after a period of excessive consumption of hashish and a lifestyle deemed irresponsible and unrespectable by his friends and family turned to Salafi religiosity in order to find a clear distinction between right and wrong.

I first met Mustafa some time before his military service and shortly after he had given up his practice of Salafi piety. While he continues to hold to Salafi ideas on religion when asked, he now regularly shaves, has returned to smoking, prays irregularly, and maintains contact with female friends in a way which Salafis would consider unacceptable (but which is considered well within the limits of respectable behaviour by his friends). It has not been an easy shift for him: he frequently reports intense feelings of guilt and failure because of the temporary suspension of his commitment (he does indicate that he hopes to return to a more pious lifestyle after the end of his military service). Neither his move from deviation to commitment, nor his slip (as he describes it) from commitment to ambivalence are in any way unusual. I know people who have gone through periods as a Muslim Brotherhood activist at school, a left-wing atheist as a university student, and a liberal believer attached to ideas of Nasr Abû Zayd[13] as a family father. There are some women whom I came to know as veiled and conservative young students but who have since given up veiling and have grown increasingly critical of what they see as misguided religious moralism, without, however, turning against religion as such. Others again have begun to wear a more covering dress and adopted a more 'committed' (*multazima*) lifestyle after completing their studies, seeing this not as a break, however, but rather as a ripening process. Some men I know have become radical and strictly committed Salafis who make a clear break with their past, grow their beards, and (try to) stop smoking after spending wild student years with girlfriends, alcohol, and drugs. Some among them remain Salafis, while others later shave their beards again and return to an ambiguous, 'ordinary' lifestyle.

It is for the people for whom pious commitment is only a period in their life that the Salafi aim of comprehensive purity is most troubling. They often tell of having experienced a period of intense happiness and satisfaction as active Salafis but then losing the drive, facing everyday problems at work or with state authorities (who view Salafis with great suspicion), and reverting to their old habits. In the following period, they often report a feeling of failure and guilt. With their earlier standards and norms no longer sufficient or legitimate in their eyes, they are nevertheless not able to hold the drive for purity so central for Salafi piety. Troubled by the loss of his earlier almost euphoric sense of piety and commitment, Mustafa says:

> Yesterday I heard a sermon on the computer that made me think about my priorities. You have to be self-vigilant and repent every day to our sublime and exalted Lord, and renew your promises to our Lord. I felt a state of lethargy. When I heard the same tape earlier I cried. So why didn't I cry yesterday? Because my heart is black. Why am I like this? I remember an example Shaykh Salâh told me: Let's assume that next to the chimney of an oven there is a freshly painted wall. What will happen to that wall? On the first day it blackens a little. On the next day it blackens more. On the third day it blackens more, and so on. The same thing in the heart, which stays polished and clean with the obedience to sublime and exalted God. When you give up worship ('ibâdât) the heart keeps being blackened by dirt.

For one thing, this account describes pious commitment as a fragile form of continuous self-suggestion rather than as cumulative self-perfection. Furthermore, it pinpoints how the Salafi discourse of piety with its tremendous emphasis on purity makes it very difficult to find a balance with different desires if the drive of self-suggestion recedes – as it often does. There is neither return to the relative comfort of the negotiated ambiguity of living for God in Ramadan and for oneself for the rest of the year, nor comfort in the rigid understanding of religion. Since religion stands totally beyond critique, people can only search for faults in themselves. And since the Salafi interpretation of religion insists that there are no interpretations of religion, only plain objective Religion on the one side and erroneous deviations on the other, rural young people rarely have access to other interpretations of religion that would allow them to reconcile their ambivalent experiences with their religious faith.

As a consequence, the wave of Salafi religiosity with its insistence on purity and perfection actually intensifies the fragmentation and contradictions in young people's lives. While wishing to be good Muslims living by the Qur'an and the Sunna and going to Paradise in the Hereafter, the young men in the village still also wish to fall in love, to be excited, to get high, to be wealthy, to get abroad, to have sex, and many other things. Some of these aims do not contradict the young men's religious convictions. But those that do are becoming more and more difficult to include as legitimate elements of a necessarily ambiguous and complex life. Instead, they become increasingly separate and mutually antagonistic.

Flaws of perfection

With football as a paradigmatic case of Ramadan piety and morality, we reach rather different conclusions than we would have with, say, the practice of prayer (see, e.g., Henkel 2005; Möller 2005: 380). Of course, Ramadan is about prayer as much as it is about football, and, if given the choice, most Muslims would certainly name prayer as the more important part (although the most important, undoubtedly, would be fasting, which gives both prayer and football their special 'taste' during Ramadan). But my point is that in looking at what may seem a marginal practice and a way to kill time instead of focusing on a core ritual, we may actually learn more about the moral and religious world to which both belong. A focus on key religious practices and the attempt to fulfil them is likely to produce analyses that highlight the moment of perfection. A focus on the margins of these practices, on the contrary, is likely to shed more light on the much less perfect social experiences and personal trajectories that all too easily remain obscured by the strong tendency of religious discourse – both in first and third person – to describe the normative as the normal.

Before closing, the final part of this chapter is devoted to a critical theoretical discussion of some of the current research on religion and morality, especially in the fields of Islam and the Middle East. Much of the recent research on morality, piety, and subjectivity is characterized by what I see as a problematic tendency to privilege the aim of ethical perfection. Here I single out the currently perhaps most prominent example of such a tendency: Saba Mahmood's (2003; 2005) work on the piety movement in Egypt, which, closely aligned with the work of Talal Asad (1986; 1993; 2003) and Charles Hirschkind (2001; 2006a; 2006b), has gained great (and for a large part deserved) acclaim within the anthropology of Islam (see, e.g., Bautista 2008).

Mahmood argues that rather than positing a liberal autonomous subject as a natural starting-point of the study of religious and moral subjects, we need to look at the creation of an ethical self through embodied religious practices and accept that there are religiously and culturally preconditioned moral subjectivities that differ from those prescribed by liberal and feminist theory. This research programme owes allegiance, on the one hand, to the later work of Michel Foucault (1990: chap. 3), who, in his *History of sexuality*, shifted his focus towards the techniques of forming the self, and, on the other hand, to communitarian moral philosophers, most notably Charles Taylor (1989), who, critical of the abstract rationalism of Kantian ethics, have turned towards the Aristotelian tradition. Aristotle (2002 [350 BC]), in his *Nicomachean ethics*, develops a theory of ethics that is based on the habituation of virtues: virtue does not exist before practice; it is developed by the power of habit that enables one to live a good life.

Critical of both the denunciatory tone of many studies on Islamist piety movements, on the one hand, and of the search for moments of resistance and subversion, on the other, Mahmood refers to Aristotle to call for a focus upon the way people attempt to learn and live moral dispositions. Acting within a moral universe that provides certain kinds of legitimate arguments and forms of action, the women active in the piety movement consciously attempt to develop a docile and pious character. In doing so, Mahmood argues, they are neither making free choices of the autonomous, liberal kind, nor are they passive objects of manipulation. To avoid such simple oppositions and the ideological weight they carry, we should look at the kind of actions and arguments that are available to people and the ways they relate individual dispositions to ethical practice.

A key category in Mahmood's study of the piety movement is habitus; however, in a very different sense from that popularized by Pierre Bourdieu (1984: 168-77). Mahmood criticizes Bourdieu for missing the Aristotelian point of *habituation*, the active acquiring of an ethical disposition by the means of bodily habit. Habitus, according to Mahmood, involves the active capacity of forming and transforming the self through bodily practice:

> [T]he Aristotelian notion of habitus forces us to problematize how specific kinds of bodily practice come to articulate different conceptions of the ethical subject, and how bodily form does not simply express the social structure but also endows the self with particular capacities through which the subject comes to enact the world (Mahmood 2005: 139).

Mahmood's emphasis on practice, at once formative and expressive of ethical disposition – and the way she relates practice to the discursive imagination of the world providing people a framework for action – offers significant advantages for the study of morality both as a socially negotiated collective order and as individual practice. She is also right, in my judgement, in criticizing attempts to find moments of resistance and subversion in the women's piety movement. Such attempts, she argues, are guided by a romantic search for empowerment that may distract our attention from the power of authoritative religious discourses which the women of the piety movement, firmly convinced of their Truth, attempt to realize in their life. But there is a problem: Mahmood actually tells us very little about practice and life. She does tell that the path of piety can lead to conflicts, most notably between the task to serve God and the obligation to obey one's husband. But the cases she discusses, and the solutions the women in her ethnography find, are success stories of piety. They tell of women who work to develop a docile pious disposition, and of wives who, in the end, manage to persuade their not so religious husbands of the necessity of their pious commitment without questioning the husbands' authority (Mahmood 2005: 174-88). While there is no doubt that stories like these do exist and that they make a strong point against the quest of resistance and subversion, they offer only one part of a much more complex story. What we, given the scope of her ethnography, do not hear are the stories of people who at some point in their life experienced a period of strong religiosity which they, however, later gave up in favour of a more ambivalent relation to religion, nor do we hear about the more profound contradictions of different urges and wishes which even the most pious are likely to experience (see, e.g., Gregg 2007: 189-225). The image of ethics that Mahmood draws on the basis of the Salafi piety movement is too perfect.

Mahmood's analysis, as important as it is in many ways, is flawed in three respects: firstly, in its taking committed religious activists as paradigmatic representatives of religiosity; secondly, in its focus on the *attempt* to realize a docile, God-fearing ideal which leaves out the actual consequences of that attempt; and, thirdly, in its hermetic approach to 'culture' and 'tradition'. The first is a limitation which *Politics of piety* (Mahmood 2005) shares with many other studies on religious practice, especially in the context of Islam, where perhaps too many works have been devoted to religious activists, on the one hand, and intellectuals who attempt to revise the very basics of religious morality, on the other. The problem of such studies is that by limiting the scope of religious expression either to a strive towards perfection or a fundamental critique of religious norms, they unintentionally reproduce the bias of the committed groups they study. If we are to understand the ambiguous logic of Ramadan morality and the fragmentary outcome of the Salafi project of perfection, we will have to look at that majority of people who are not actively committed to religious or political activism, who do share a recognition of the supreme authority of religion but do not practise it as an over-arching teleological project of ethical self-improvement (see Marsden 2005: 251-61; Masquelier 2007; Otayek & Soares 2007: 17-19).

More importantly, we will have to avoid Mahmood's second and perhaps more profound flaw of looking at the declared attempt, but overlooking its outcome. In a way, Mahmood offers us an analysis that takes practice as a central category but does not tell us much about actual practice itself. 'Practice' in Mahmood's usage is primarily a conceptual category describing 'the relationships [people] establish between the various constituent elements of the self (body, reason, volition, and so on) and a particular moral code or norm' (2003: 846). As a result, she can tell us much about the intended outcomes of the project of piety, but only little about its actual consequences. As Gary Gregg points out, the fact that a person has fashioned a perfect pious identity 'does not predict how consistently his or her experience will conform to its contours' (2007: 297-8). What happens when claims and ideals such as those formulated by the women of the piety movement come to be practised as guidelines in a life that has other, competing orientations and is characterized not by the primary purpose of perfection but rather by a struggle to find one's place in life?

Piety does not proceed along a unilinear path. It is an ambivalent practice that is often related to specific periods in life, especially those marked by crises. While it does not leave one unchanged, the endeavour of pious self-suggestion does not seem to build such strong dispositions that they would simply override other parts of an individual's personality. This is, of course, common knowledge in Egypt, as it is probably everywhere. But when we try to conceptualize the constitution of moral selves, we are easily tempted to take the more perfect and consistent life-stories as the more paradigmatic ones. I posit that it is precisely the fragmented nature of people's biographies which, together with the ambivalent nature of most moral subjectivities, should be taken as the starting-point when setting out to study moral discourse and ethical practice.

A third flaw in Mahmood's argumentation is that she too easily identifies the moral universe of the pious women with that of an Islamic discursive tradition that offers a set of references to the Scripture and ways of argumentation and reasoning (see Asad 1986). While there is no doubt that a such discursive tradition exists – or, more accurately, is produced and imagined by the people who as Muslims talk about Islam (Schielke 2007) – the problem is that a focus on 'discursive tradition' makes it very easy to view religion as if it were a coherent entity, dynamic within but clearly demarcated to the outside. The focus on the inner dynamics and traditions of Islam easily insinuates a determining force of 'culture' that is contradicted by those often highly idiosyncratic ways of positing oneself in the world that I have encountered among the young men of Nazlat al-Rayyis. To state that people are primarily acting within their discursive traditions understates the complexity, reflectivity, and openness of their worldviews and life experiences, especially so in a globalizing world characterized by the registers of consumerism, nationalism, human rights, and romance just as much as it is articulated by the striving for pious discipline and communal respect (Gregg 2007; Marsden 2005).

Developing her concept of ethics and self-formation, Mahmood notes in brackets that as far as specific conceptions of the self are concerned, 'there may be different kinds that inhabit the space of a single culture' (2005: 139). The short exploration of moral subjectivities among the young men of Nazlat al-Rayyis that I have undertaken in this chapter suggests that while this statement clearly is true (although it is very unlikely that such a clearly demarcated thing as 'a single culture' exists), it does not go far enough. Not only do different conceptions of the self inhabit the space of a single culture, they are also present in the life experience of a single individual, to some extent simultaneously, to some extent periodically. An anthropological study of morality and ethical subjectivity has to take this inherent ambivalence as a starting-point. Rather than searching for moments of perfection, we have to look at the conflicts, ambiguities, double standards, fractures, and shifts as the constitutive moments of the practice of norms.

ACKNOWLEDGMENTS

An earlier version of this chapter was presented to the conference 'Youth and the Global South: Religion, Politics and the Making of Youth in Africa, Asia and the Middle East' in Dakar on 15 October 2006. I am indebted to the people of Nazlat al-Rayyis for their help, hospitality, and friendship, Omnia Mehanna for research assistance, and Rijk van Dijk, Sindre Bangstad, Jan Beek, Benjamin Soares, and Filippo Osella, and last but not least the anonymous reviewers of *JRAI*, for comments that assisted the revision of the chapter into its current shape.

NOTES

[1] Nazlat al-Rayyis, where I have conducted a large part of my fieldwork for this chapter, is a large village between the Rosetta branch of the Nile and Lake Burullus, some 30 kilometres from the Mediterranean coast. A centre of schools and services for surrounding hamlets, it is nevertheless clearly rural in character, unlike

many other villages of similar size. The population is entirely Muslim and divided into two economic groups of approximately equal size: farmers and fishermen who earn their living on Lake Burullus. This economic distinction is also an important base for identity, especially for the fisher families, who identify themselves as such even when they earn their living as workers, civil servants, and so on. By rural standards, Nazlat al-Rayyis appears to have relatively high levels of literacy and education. The village also has a long history of political activism. In the colonial period, it was a Wafdist stronghold, and in the republican period it has had a high level of leftist and communist activism. Today it has a strong and active branch of the Muslim Brotherhood.

The people with whom I conducted the fieldwork for this chapter mostly come from fishermen families but aim for careers in trade or the public sector. They have middle or high education, but their actual work and careers often fall short of their qualifications and expectations.

[2] Trying it out myself, I found out that fasting and football indeed do go well together, to the degree that I once almost missed fast-breaking because of a match. The bigger problem for me was the absolutely superior level of the youths compared to my very modest skills and condition.

[3] While there is no provision in Islamic rites against celebrating weddings in Ramadan, it is unusual to do so. This, like so many religious sensibilities, derives less from any specific textual traditions than a common sense that designates practices and times with specific qualities which, while not mutually exclusive, don't harmonize well.

[4] Al-Bukhârî: *Sahîh*, book of fasting (as-sawm), chapter 5; at-Tirmidhî: *al-Jami' as-sahîh*, book of fasting (as-sawm), chapter 1, hadith 682. (Because of the great variety of different printed and electronic editions of the Sunnite *hadith* collections, I refer to the *hadiths* by chapters rather than page numbers. References to canonical *hadith* collections are by editor, short title, and chapter.)

[5] One of the last ten nights of Ramadan, when according to Islamic belief the revelation of the Qur'an to Muhammad began. The exact date of *Laylat al-Qadr* is not known, but it is commonly celebrated on the night before the 27th of Ramadan.

[6] Reported in slightly different versions by ad-Dârimî: *Sunan*, book of fasting (as-sawm), chapter 54 (Fadl qiyâm shahr Ramadân); at-Tirmidhî: *al-Jami' as-sahîh*, book of fasting (as-sawm), chapter 1, hadith 683; al-Bukhârî: *Sahîh*, book of fasting (as-sawm), chapter 6.

[7] For *Laylat al-Qadr*, see Mâlik ibn Anâs: *al-Muwatta'*, book of retreat in the mosque (al-i'tikâf), chapter 6 (mâ jâ' fî laylat al-qadr), hadith 15; for intentionally breaking the fast, Bukhârî: *Sahîh*, book of fasting (as-sawm): chapter 29; for double reward, Muslim: *Sahîh*, book of fasting (as-siyâm): chapter of the merit of fasting (fadl as-siyâm), hadith 164.

[8] Similarly, bystanders can also appeal to people involved in an argument with the phrase 'Because you're fasting' ('ashân inta sâyim).

[9] Owing to the exposed character of cafés and the recent spread of internet in the countryside, pornography has largely disappeared from regular cafés and moved to internet cafés and private homes.

[10] It is often difficult to draw a clear line between arranged and love marriages because a degree of negotiation is at play in most cases (see Hart 2007).

[11] While men can more easily employ common standards of double morality to manoeuvre between different ethical ideals, women experience much more pressure to fulfil conflicting ideals of chastity and attractiveness.

[12] While smoking cigarettes is not seen as a vice in Egyptian society, the Salafi movement makes a strong point about smoking being *harâm*.

[13] The hermeneutic approach to the study of the Qur'an employed by the Egyptian academic Nasr Abû Zayd, which caused a scandal that forced him to emigrate to Europe, has significant popularity among people searching for alternatives to what they deem a narrow-minded, fundamentalist interpretation of their religion.

REFERENCES

ABÛ L-MAʿÂTÎ, ʿÂ. 2006. Min khawâtir ash-Shaʿrâwî ar-ramadanîya: hikmat as-siyâm fî ramadan (Al-Shaʿrâwî on Ramadan: the wisdom of fasting in Ramadan). *al-Akhbâr*, 28 September, 7.

ABU-LUGHOD, L. 1996 [1986]. *Veiled sentiments: honour and poetry in a Bedouin society.* Cairo: American University of Cairo Press.

AHMAD, I. 2008. Cracks in the 'mightiest fortress': Jamaat-e Islami's changing discourse on women. *Modern Asian Studies* **42**, 549-75.

ARISTOTLE 2002 [350 BC]. *Nicomachean ethics* (trans. C. Rowe, intro. and commentary S. Broadie). Oxford: University Press.

ARMBRUST, W. 2002. The riddle of Ramadan: media, consumer culture, and the 'Christmasization' of a Muslim holiday. In *Everyday life in the Middle East* (eds) D. Bowen & E. Early, 335-48. (Revised edition). Bloomington: Indiana University Press.

ASAD, T. 1986. *The idea of an anthropology of Islam*. (Occasional Papers Series). Washington, D.C.: Center for Contemporary Arab Studies, Georgetown University.

———— 1993. *Genealogies of religion: discipline and reasons of power in Christianity and Islam*. Baltimore: Johns Hopkins University Press.

———— 2003. *Formations of the secular: Christianity, Islam, modernity*. Stanford: University Press.

BAUTISTA, J. 2008. The meta-theory of piety: reflections on the work of Saba Mahmood. *Contemporary Islam* **2**, 75-83.

BOURDIEU, P. 1984. *Distinction: a social critique of the judgement of taste* (trans. R. Nice). London: Routledge.

EICKELMAN, D. 1992. Mass higher education and the religious imagination in contemporary Arab societies. *American Ethnologist* **9**, 643-55.

EWING, K. 1990. The illusion of wholeness: culture, self, and the experience of inconsistency. *Ethos* **18**, 251-78.

FOUCAULT, M. 1990. *The history of sexuality*, vol. 2, *The use of pleasure* (trans. R. Hurley). New York: Vintage.

GREGG, G. 1998. Culture, personality, and the multiplicity of identity: evidence from North African life narratives. *Ethos* **26**, 120-52.

———— 2007. *Culture and identity in a Muslim society*. Oxford: University Press.

HART, K. 2007. Love by arrangement: the ambiguity of 'spousal choice' in a Turkish village. *Journal of the Royal Anthropological Institute* (N.S.) **13**, 345-62.

HENKEL, H. 2005. 'Between belief and unbelief lies the performance of *salât*': meaning and efficacy of a Muslim ritual. *Journal of the Royal Anthropological Institute* (N.S.) **11**, 487-507.

HIRSCHKIND, C. 2001. The ethics of listening: cassette sermon audition in contemporary Cairo. *American Ethnologist* **28**, 623-49.

———— 2006*a*. Cassette ethics: public piety and popular media in Egypt. In *Religion, media, and the public sphere* (eds) B. Meyer and A. Moors, 29-52. Bloomington: Indiana University Press.

———— 2006*b*. *The ethical soundscape: cassette sermons and Islamic counter-publics*. New York: Columbia University Press.

AL-KHASHSHÂB, U. 2006. Fî multaqâ l-fikr al-islâmî: al-intisâr 'alâ shahawât an-nafs tadrîb lil-intisâr fî ma'ârik al-hayât (At the podium of Islamic thought: the victory over desires of the lower soul is a training for victory in the battles of life). *al-Akhbâr*, 28 September, 7.

LAMBEK, M. 2000. The anthropology of religion and the quarrel between poetry and philosophy. *Current Anthropology* **41**, 309-20.

LINCOLN, B. 2006. *Holy terrors: thinking about religion after September 11*. Chicago: University Press.

MAHMOOD, S. 2003. Ethical formation and politics of individual autonomy in contemporary Egypt. *Social Research* **70**, 837-66.

———— 2005. *Politics of piety: the Islamic revival and the feminist subject*. Princeton: University Press.

MALEK 2006. Su'âr Wasat al-Madîna al-jinsî (Downtown sexual harassment) (available online: *http://malek-x.net/node/268*, accessed 25 June 2007).

MARSDEN, M. 2005. *Living Islam: Muslim religious experience in Pakistan's North-West frontier*. Cambridge: University Press.

MASQUELIER, A. 2007. Negotiating futures: Islam, youth, and the state in Niger. In *Islam and Muslim politics in Africa* (eds) B. Soares & R. Otayek, 243-62. New York: Palgrave Macmillan.

MATAR, I. 2006. Okaziyôn al-maghfara (Discount redemption). *Rúz al-Yúsuf*, 29 September, 23-4.

MÖLLER, A. 2005. *Ramadan in Java: the joy and jihad of ritual fasting.* (Lund Studies in History of Religions **20**). Stockholm: Almqvist & Wiksell.

OSELLA, F. & OSELLA, C. 2008. Introduction: Islamic reformism in South Asia. *Modern Asian Studies* **42**, 247-57.

OTAYEK, R. & SOARES, B. 2007. Introduction: Islam and Muslim politics in Africa. In *Islam and Muslim politics in Africa* (eds) B. Soares & R. Otayek, 1-24. New York: Palgrave Macmillan.

SCHIELKE, S. 2006. Snacks and saints: mawlid festivals and the politics of festivity, piety, and modernity in contemporary Egypt. Ph.D. thesis, University of Amsterdam.

———— 2007. Hegemonic encounters: Criticism of saints-day festivals and the formation of modern Islam in late 19th- and early 20th-century Egypt. *Die Welt des Islams* **47**, 319-55.

SHA'BÂN, K. 2006. as-Siyâm wa-sh-shabâb (Fasting and the youth). *al-Akhbâr*, 9 October, 4.

AL-SHURBÂSÎ, A. 2006. as-Sawm madrasat tahdhîb (Fasting is the school of cultivation). *al-Azhar* **79**, 1428-31.

SOARES, B. 2006. Islam in Mali in the neo-liberal era. *African Affairs* **105**, 77-95.

TAYLOR, C. 1989. *Sources of the self: the making of the modern identity*. Cambridge, Mass.: Harvard University Press.

VAN MEIJL, T. 2006. Multiple identifications and the dialogical self: urban Maori youngsters and the cultural renaissance. *Journal of the Royal Anthropological Institute* (N.S.) **12**, 917-33.

3

Doubt, faith, and knowledge: the reconfiguration of the intellectual field in post-Nasserist Cairo

Hatsuki Aishima *University of Oxford*
Armando Salvatore *University of Naples – L'Orientale*

The Naqshibandis suit me since I don't have much time.

Mustafa Mahmud

The pattern of 'state Islam' facing 'radical Islam', which has dominated socio-political and journalistic analyses since the late 1970s, has been matched since the 1990s by a growing socio-anthropological interest in examining shifts in media authority based on Islamic credentials and supported by Islamic discourses (Eickelman & Anderson 2003 [1999]; Hirschkind 2006). This approach has often opposed small and allegedly authentic to big and governmental media (Sreberny-Mohammadi & Mohammadi 1994). More generally, and often on the back of a wave of interest in civil society as the key to the opening of authoritarian systems, scholars have shifted their attention to emerging public-sphere dynamics (Burgat & Esposito 2003; Salvatore & Eickelman 2004).

These ways of framing the research question have supported – though mostly unintentionally – the view that Islam's intellectual framework is *per se* subject to a limited set of variations: Islamic ideas can surely nest in different places and institutions, inspire various and even new practices – yet the shared repertoires of argumentation, modes of piety, and patterns of life conduct that the message of Islam is able to instil in the faithful are taken as variations on basically fixed schemes. In the prevailing approach, what creates the new is the way of its communication or 'staging' (e.g. Salvatore 1998). While emphasis is given to the power of the media in 'fragmenting' the authority to define Islam, it seems that media might either help new types of intellectuals to participate in the Islamic discourse, or alter and curtail the traditional systems of knowledge (Eickelman & Piscatori 1996).

The study of Islamic Resurgence in the Muslim world has probably overestimated the media-mediated mechanisms of 'public Islam' and underestimated the importance of the intellectual trials and tribulations that some leading public personalities underwent at a crucial stage of post-colonial crisis. In particular, it has neglected markers of disorientation, factors of disappointment, and sources of individual imagination, all dismissed as the inevitable by-products of overwhelming processes of transformation that are largely outside the control of the intellectual elite themselves. Perhaps by reacting against an overly text-centred approach to the work on Muslim thinkers by an older generation of Western scholars, research has privileged the power of the media to the detriment of a detailed analysis of the relation between media scripts and the way these narratives are appropriated by larger, often heterogeneous, audiences.

Apart from this problem, even the most sophisticated type of political analysis has tended to explain the impetus of the Islamic Resurgence as the result of a plain disappointment with the capacity of Nasserist policies to deliver what they promised (see Wickham 2002: 21-62). The Nasserist momentum had been intimately wedded to the promise of producing and disseminating a type of knowledge facilitating not only communal welfare but also individual growth – if not of the entire population, at least among the expanding middle classes and especially their educated fractions. Nasser's reforms, including the nationalization of the Azhar mosque-university complex (the historically most prominent centre of Islamic learning world-wide) in 1960, were framed by the rationale of diverting the social dimension of Islam from dependence either on a repetitive transmission of knowledge or on charitable activity, projecting it instead towards the goal of educating the masses. The revival of Islamic associational life during the 1970s, which represented the hard kernel of the Islamic Resurgence much more than did its overtly political manifestations, cannot be subsumed under the banner of a one-sided anti-Nasserist ethos (Ben Néfissa-Paris 1992). The thinkers of the Islamic Resurgence had to confront both the strengths and the limitations of the postcolonial state to capture the imagination, fulfil the normative legitimacy, and satisfy the welfare needs of the middle and popular classes.

The Islamic Resurgence did not reject the potentially democratic idea of an emancipating type of knowledge. It intended to reframe its rationale in terms of faith (*iman*). What is often neglected, as we will try to show in some detail, is that in the new context characterized by recurring frustrations and upcoming uncertainties about the future, faith was not only the engine of a new politics of piety based on the Islamic discourse (Mahmood 2005), but also depended on its purported opposite, that is, doubt (*shakk*), acting as the insidious yet ubiquitous flip-side of processes of change: *shakk* being itself an important key-word within the Islamic discourse and the theological corpus on which it ultimately relies. Earlier on, doubt in the progressive path of Nasserism was trivialized and equated with political subversion. In the new era, bridging faith and doubt required the imagination of the lonely thinker and a capacity to exploit the new media to convey a refreshed Islamic message. The tribulations and trials of the epoch became a potential resource to reconstruct a type of media authority investing in the resurging strength 'faith', while retrieving the unsuppressed potential of 'doubt'.

How did doubt and imagination relate to the question of authority and guidance? Were they also connected to the power of creativity, originality, and criticism as alleged prerogatives of intellectuals and their public role? The Nasser regime had attempted to control Sufi orders as an important channel of transmission of authority: stigmatized as the bulwark of tradition by several generations of Muslim reformers, Sufism represented a significant source of consensus within the emerging mass politics of postcolonial societies. While the post-Nasserist state was no less eager to exploit this channel to pinpoint its vacillating legitimacy, in the new era mass-mediated Sufism penetrated the public sphere no longer as the backward-looking side of Islam, but as an alternative arena of self-disciplining for the politically disillusioned middle classes and as a reservoir of meaning that could be freely elaborated and put to use in public discourse.

Many of the key issues that characterized the reconfiguration of the intellectual field surrounding the Islamic Resurgence have been formulated in this climate of upheaval, via the activities of the myriad associations, media and public personalities, mainly located in Cairo. The fact that Cairo had not only been a major focal point of post-colonial hopes on a world scale but had also been for a millennium a centre of Islamic learning was reflected in the ways public knowledge was reconfigured, and contributed to the popularity of some of the leaders of the Islamic Resurgence.

We will analyse the combined role of doubt and faith in the public redefinition of Islamic knowledge on the basis of the trajectories of two intellectual leaders of the Islamic Resurgence of the 1970s, whose legacy continues to be eagerly discussed among educated and popular audiences alike within the current adjustments to a neoliberal global order. The Sufi scholar and Shaykh al-Azhar 'Abd al-Halim Mahmud (1910-78) and the media-savvy lay thinker Mustafa Mahmud (b. 1921) are two different personalities who equally impacted not only on the Egyptian public sphere but also on the realms of politics and civil society – while also enjoying a considerable degree of popularity outside of Egypt. The ambivalence of their public teaching and their intricate relationships with the Egyptian elite (including Sufi circles) reflect many of the quandaries of the post-Nasserist order and the troubled search for a new ideological balance by the shrinking Egyptian middle classes. In particular, we will show how educated members of these classes (muta'allimun, muthaqqafun) contribute to the reconfiguration of the intellectual field by providing key words and ideas to wider public debates. This process also facilitates a redefinition of what it means to be an intellectual (mufakkir) in the Islamically influenced dimension of the public sphere. Clearly, being an intellectual can no longer reflect the vanguard idea of the middle-class radicalism of the Nasserist era, but has to fit into a much more complex picture fraught with ambiguities, anxieties, and the need to reposition Islam-based knowledge – also via the effects of doubt – vis-à-vis a variety of contradictory demands coming from the West as well as in relation to the aspirations of the educated middle classes of Cairo. The social strata who build the bulk of the audiences we are going to analyse have been in search for a rationale to defend their eagerly cultivated and often carefully displayed piety, while maintaining a comfortable lifestyle and an adequate class status.

As a generating source of the awakening, it cannot be disputed that faith occupied an important place in post-Nasserist public discourse. This change was also engineered by Nasser's successor, Anwar al-Sadat, who fabricated for himself the image of the 'faithful president'. It was also because of this excess of public emphasis and overt political instrumentalization that faith appeared soon as a rather unmarked – and therefore discursively weak – source of consensus. Against this top-down view that intends to identify faith with an increasingly unpopular president, the narrative of the awakening depended on the challenge of recuperating iman after the secular hubris of the Nasserist era. The aspirations of the middle classes nurtured by Nasserism were left unsettled, and a space was opened for attempts to match such hopes via ideas more tightly fitting an Islamic discourse. This discourse was propped up by the spread of audiocassettes, but was also supported by radio programmes and then by a new style of edifying entertainment on TV screens. The narrative of the awakening needed not only conceptual markers but also charismatic signposts that could be recognized by the growing audiences of electronic media, the bulk of them consisting of the middle classes. The new forms of media authority facilitated sometimes reflexive, sometimes resentment-filled, reactive processes consisting in repositioning faith in the context of a society in which the discourse and the authority of science occupy an important place. It is by a public acknowledgement of the impact that public personalities such as 'Abd al-Halim Mahmud and Mustafa Mahmud had on these processes that they have managed to compete for the contested status of *mufakkir* ('intellectual') or for the even more problematic fame of *mufakkir islami* ('Islamic intellectual').

'Abd al-Halim Mahmud: Ghazali of the twentieth century and radio pioneer

'Abd al-Halim Mahmud, as many other *'ulama* of his generation and rank, had been outraged by Nasser's policies that eroded the autonomy of al-Azhar. Yet he selectively appropriated the Nasserist rationale of reinvesting Islamic principles into an activist stance for the reform of society (see Zeghal 1996; 1999). Among a number of public personalities who taught Islam through mass media, 'Abd al-Halim was one of the first actively to incorporate a consciously public role and the methods of self-presentation associated with it. In 1964 he contributed to founding the national radio station Idha'at al-Qur'an al-Karim (the Noble Qur'an Radio), which specializes in Islamic programmes.[1] He spoke regularly on radio, including on the Morning Talk (*Hadith al-Sabah*), the first programme on the Noble Qur'an Radio. Although it was a daily talk show of only 5-7 minutes, it succeeded in having renowned scholars go on air to give simple lectures on Islamic subjects. The radio station staff selected the guest speakers and topics; scholars prepared their talks accordingly. In spite of such a restricted setting, the individuality of the speakers emerged through the style rather than the content of their speeches and thus allowed for the fashioning of radio 'stars'.[2] This was a steep learning process for the scholars themselves, who had to get accustomed to the studio recording and to acquiring a partly new language and performance skills in order to address larger audiences. 'Abd al-Halim Mahmud's appearance on radio broadcasts steadily increased and peaked as he became Shaykh al-Azhar, the Grand Imam of the al-Azhar mosque-university complex, in 1973. While occupying the pinnacle of the hierarchy of Islamic authority, he also instituted a committee for planning TV programmes specializing in teaching Islam to the general public (Shalabi 1982: 535-43).

Since 'Abd al-Halim Mahmud was a prolific writer on Sufism (Aishima 2005), the back covers of his books from the leading Cairo-based, public-sector publishing house Dar al-Ma'arif introduce him as 'a father of Sufism in the modern age'. In his publications and radio programmes 'Abd al-Halim spoke openly about his Sufi experiences in order to provide knowledge on Sufism to the general public. He entwined a formal level of teaching with a rather informal reference to his personal experiences, thus earning the fame of being a unique *'alim mutasawwif* (Sufi scholar). While there were several leading Sufi shaykhs among government officials and high-ranking *'ulama*, they usually did not speak about their experiences to mass media. ('Abd al-Halim was aware of the controversial images of Sufism within Egyptian society and in the wider Islamic world – often associated with stereotypes of superstition and 'backwardness' – but he was also eager to take advantage of the newly developing media for transmitting Sufi knowledge, by taking into account the socio-cultural conditions and needs of his respective audiences.)

Decades after his death, 'Abd al-Halim Mahmud continues to appear in popular magazines like *Nisf al-Dunya*, an Egyptian weekly targeting educated classes of female professionals, as 'the Ghazali of the Twentieth Century'.[3] Associating 'Abd al-Halim with al-Ghazali[4] is the combined result of 'Abd al-Halim's endeavours at self-representation and of the mechanisms of mass-mediated image production. 'Abd al-Halim's autobiography, *Praise be to God, this is my life* (2001 [1976]), is narrated in the same form as al-Ghazali's best-known work, *Deliverance from error*. In his autobiography 'Abd al-Halim claimed to have been saved from an intellectual crisis threatening the edifice of his Islamic knowledge by discovering the intellectual tradition of Sufism, and thus regaining complete confidence in God. At the same time, the radio programmes featuring 'Abd al-Halim contributed to create his image of a great *'alim* (scholar), up to the point that he could even be credited to be a *wali* (saint). These programmes opened with classical music (a sure marker of 'high cultured' standing), followed by an extended narration of 'Abd al-Halim's brilliant academic career as a French-trained Azharite *'alim*. The elaborate introduction reminded listeners of the speaker's credentials. After that, 'Abd al-Halim started speaking with a gentle voice in a type of *fusha* (the standard Arabic use in writing and official speeches) catering to an educated public, in the name of God the Merciful, thus producing the notion of him as an *'alim salih* (authentic scholar).[5] His efforts to revitalize the Sufi tradition by popularizing the scholarly knowledge of *tasawwuf* (Sufism) were well accepted by his audiences because he re-narrated this intellectual tradition within the framework of – and *vis-à-vis* – Western modernity.

In the life narrative of 'Abd al-Halim Mahmud, 'Western sciences' played an important role. He single-handedly decided to go to study in France in 1932, after he received a first education at al-Azhar. He was soon enchanted with the cleanliness and the efficiency of French cities, like many other modern Egyptians who travelled to Europe for the first time. However, as time passed, doubts about the value system that underpinned Western civilization surfaced in his mind. He fell into a state of scepticism, torn between purportedly Western and Islamic values. These had appeared equally important to him upon his arrival in France, but now he feared that the spread of scepticism, materialism and atheism, which he regarded as the basis of Western sciences, might destroy the fundaments of social values.

Initially, after studying sociology, comparative religion and psychology for his *licence* at the Faculty of Letters, 'Abd al-Halim wanted to specialize in psychology or aesthetics for his doctoral studies (A.H. Mahmud 2001 [1976]: 125). However, he was advised by his professors to change his topic because he was not qualified enough to write a doctoral dissertation in either of those fields. In the end, the French Orientalist Louis Massignon (1883-1962) took him under his wing. 'Abd al-Halim recalled in some radio programmes how he felt relieved to meet Massignon and was able to overcome his sense of cultural alienation.

'Abd al-Halim Mahmud presents Sufism as the only scientific method to reach the metaphysical truth. While other disciplines, including rational sciences, are bound to the sensory perceptions, which only lead to doubt and uncertainty, Sufism guides one's heart to the affirmation of faith and certainty (*yaqin*). However, although the scepticism inherent in the methods of Western sciences produces doubts without end, doubt complemented by faith can bring one to certainty. Surprisingly perhaps, 'Abd al-Halim used the vocabulary of reformist Islam, such as *'ilm*, sharia, and *jihad*, in a Sufi context, in order to market his Sufism to audiences both inside and outside Sufi circles. His strategy to present the Sufi tradition as integral to the Sunna often consisted – also in radio programmes – in quoting verses of Qur'an and *hadith* that were familiar to non-scholarly audiences. For instance, he emphasized *'ilm* (knowledge of Islamic law) over *ma'rifa* (mystical knowledge) in order to refute the stereotypical image of Sufism as a set of deviant practices performed by Muslims who are ignorant of the fundaments of Islam. Furthermore, in order to combat the perception of Sufi orders as puppets of authoritarian regimes and indifferent to socio-political affairs, he provided historical examples of *jihad* performed by great Sufis, such as 'Abd al-Qadir al-Jaza'iri (1807-83), who struggled in defence of Algeria against the French colonial occupation. In this sense, Sufis are distinguished from 'mystics' – who live in seclusion and practise asceticism in order to attain unity with God.

Though 'Abd al-Halim Mahmud reached the status of a celebrity who appeared on TV with President Sadat, gave lectures on radio, and wrote articles in magazines and newspapers, he continued to live in a modest flat in Zaytun, a lower middle-class neighbourhood in Cairo. This choice contributed to promote his fame as an exemplarily 'good Muslim' committed not only to a pious lifestyle, but also to social values of modesty and solidarity with the less affluent segments of the population. Most importantly, his life conduct is contrasted with the widespread images of Azharites as opportunists who purchase expensive real estate while ignoring the social grievances that their fellow Muslims are facing. In this way, 'Abd al-Halim is presented as an ideal model of how a learned man with public responsibilities ought to be.

The construction of this public image, which endures to the present day, becomes particularly relevant in the context of the thriving of a teach-yourself cultural market, which encourages Muslims privately to acquire a knowledge of their faith without having to rely directly on authority figures. 'Abd al-Halim's success in expanding the market for Sufism to non-Sufi audiences stems from the channels through which he chose to communicate with them. By using mass media, he managed to generate the notion of 'Sufism as culture'. This idea became a publishing project with the book series which 'Abd al-Halim edited with the publisher al-Maktaba al-Misriyya during the 1960s and which was entitled *al-Maktaba al-Thaqafiyya* ('the cultural library'). In the form of books, Sufism became a cultural commodity, which could be purchased and acquired independently from the mediations of spiritual masters with Sufi credentials.

There are several people in Egypt who claim to know about 'Abd al-Halim Mahmud, though it is more rare to find individuals who had any personal interactions with him or even read his books. He was never the shaykh of a particular Sufi brotherhood and took only a handful of disciples (Schleifer 1991: 203). Although the memory of 'Abd al-Halim has left sediments in wide sections of the Egyptian popular public and seems to be well rooted, it is much more difficult to locate those roots with precision. Conversations with his former students suggest that 'Abd al-Halim was a celebrity to whom people were eager to claim connections. Most of them did not have more information about him than could be acquired from magazine articles, yet they often asserted that they recognized in him the original station of their own personal *silsila* (intellectual genealogy).

Replying to a question regarding the place of 'Abd al-Halim in contemporary Egyptian society, a blind Azharite *'alim* who studied with him said: 'Dr 'Abd al-Halim was a social phenomenon, on a par with Muhammad al-Ghazali (1917-1996) and Shaykh al-Sha'rawi (1911-1998)'.[6] What these three men have in common is that they are leading public personalities whose fame is sustained by their constant presence in the mass media – quite apart from any concrete specialist knowledge or direct experience of them that a given individual might have. Yet while it would be difficult to find Egyptians who ascribe to al-Ghazali or al-Sha'rawi the status of a *mufakkir* (intellectual), surprisingly perhaps the opposite can be true with 'Abd al-Halim Mahmud.

In a conversation with a young representative of an internet provider and with his in-laws, the young man stated that a *mufakkir* cannot be an *'alim* because the former is credited with thinking freely, whereas the latter's mind is entrapped in institutional knowledge. Thus Mustafa Mahmud or also Jamal al-Ghitani (b. 1945),[7] two famous writers and public figures who studied Islam independently, are prime examples of a *mufakkir islami*, while 'Abd al-Halim Mahmud, who came out of an establishment like al-Azhar, could be nothing more than an *'alim*. Yet according to the young man's brothers-in-law, who were Azharite preachers with beards grown in the Sunni way, a *mufakkir islami* had to be a professional scholar trained in Islamic sciences, such as Ibn Taymiyya (1258-1356). For them, while Mustafa Mahmud can be an *'alim* in medical sciences, he cannot be a *mufakkir islami* because his understanding of Islamic sources is necessarily limited. In any case, from their viewpoint, 'Abd al-Halim's credentials as a *mufakkir islami* were diminished by his Sufi background.

'Video killed the radio star': a doctor goes on TV

During the period when 'Abd al-Halim Mahmud was first lecturing on radio and then became Shaykh al-Azhar – between the late 1960s and early 1970s – another character reached public fame through a path even less conventional and more enmeshed in the trials and tensions of the passage from the Nasserist epoch to the post-Nasserist 'opening'. While 'Abd al-Halim had tried to subdue the doubt that insinuated the consciousness of the Egyptian educated public through Western sciences and the upheavals of the era, Mustafa Mahmud, a medical doctor, put the same doubt squarely at the centre of his tribulations and made it the hard kernel of an elaborate script that became the key to his public success. It is symptomatic that in the single major instance when the trajectories of these two men crossed, 'Abd al-Halim appeared much more supportive of Mustafa than were the rest of the establishment of Azharite scholars. 'Abd al-Halim introduced the emir of Qatar to Mustafa Mahmud in 1974. The emir soon became the main funder of Mustafa Mahmud's ambitious project to build a mosque with an integrated *markaz islami* (Islamic centre) attached to it, providing a wide range of health and educational services; both intended to be based on *'ilm* (science), put at the service of social welfare and cultural progress (Salvatore 2000; 2001). The mosque and the centre were built in the upper-middle-class district of Muhandisin (engineers), which was built in the 1950s and 1960s in the Giza governorate, within Greater Cairo, with the great pride of the Nasserist elite, some of whom chose to take residence there (Abaza 2006: 98-9).

During a period when 'Abd al-Halim Mahmud managed to organize the supervision of al-Azhar on the production of TV programmes of Islamic teaching – at a time when TV was becoming ubiquitous in middle-class households – Mustafa Mahmud produced independently and broadcast a documentary programme of 'edifying entertainment' by purchasing foreign-produced documentaries and commenting on them in person. In the new programme, *al-'ilm wa-l-iman* (Science and Faith), which he ran for more than two decades and which met with unexpected success, Mustafa Mahmud presented the wonders of the cosmos, awesome phenomena and peculiar creatures, whose existence and shape only the power of God the creator could help explain; the patterns of explanation came close to a diluted Aristotelianism, repackaged for a growing mass media audience.

The twin achievement of the TV programme and of the Islamic association was the smooth outcome of a tormented personal trajectory that was deeply ingrained in the potentials and contradictions of the Nasserist project and of its underlying promise of an emancipating knowledge. A medicine graduate, since the late 1940s Mustafa Mahmud had written short stories, novels, and plays as well as essays, many of which appeared in popular Egyptian weeklies and dailies, like *Akhir Sa'ah*, *al-Tahrir*, *Akhbar al-Yaum*, and *Ruz Al-Yusuf*. After Egypt's defeat in the June War of 1967, at the end of an intellectual journey during which he studied and confronted a variety of philosophies, religions, and paths of spiritual liberation, Mustafa Mahmud proclaimed Islam the best of all religions and philosophies (M. Mahmud 1987 [1970]).

Between December 1969 and the beginning of 1970, during the last months of Nasser's era, Mustafa published a *tafsir* (commentary of the Qur'an), first in successive issues of a popular magazine (*Sabah al-Khayr*), and then in a book. Several critics questioned his knowledge credentials due to his insufficient skills in grammar, rhetoric, jurisprudence, and so on, traditionally considered requisite for commenting on the Qur'an. Yet, as later for his TV programme, he managed to reach a composite middle-class public via a smart combination of the vocabulary of natural sciences and the vernacular of everyday experience.

Unlike most other leftist intellectuals, who had to find some accommodation with Nasserism in the name of national interest, anti-colonialism, and development, Mustafa Mahmud had been uncompromising in his critique of Nasserist authoritarianism. He considered it not the cause but the reflex of the crisis of Egyptian society, of the impossibility to attain people's welfare via the production and dissemination of adequate knowledge or 'science' (*'ilm*). Mustafa's approach was in tune, though not identical, with the viewpoint of the *'ulama*, such as 'Abd al-Halim Mahmud, who had opposed Nasser's socialization of Islam, to the extent that they saw in the project a domestication of the teachings of Islam with the function of preserving the president's personal power.

Yet, at a deeper level the stake was knowledge itself more than Islam *per se*. In the crisis that preceded his redemption, Mustafa Mahmud's confrontation with religion overlapped with his frustration with the medical profession. He became disillusioned with materialist schemes of understanding society and healing humanity. Interestingly enough, his response to the crisis proved to be a practical failure: his association grew to a certain extent, but the dream of a multi-functional 'Islamic centre' based on a reformed idea of knowledge and science remained a chimera. Mustafa's public presence, though, has since made history and set standards for 'public Islam'.

Three main axes have supported the script publicly enacted by Mustafa Mahmud: the first, and the main one, has been his own life, 'journey', and conversion, *min al-shakk ila-l-iman* (from doubt to faith: M. Mahmud 1987 [1970]); the second is his intellectual discourse and media message of reconciliation between *al-'ilm wa-l-iman* (science and faith) inaugurated by his *tafsir*; the third is a social project of religious, educational, and medical services. There is no necessary coherence between these three elements, but the public does not see a contradiction. Mustafa has been able to suggest that the intellectual discourse and the social project are emanations of his personal life experience, revolving around the motif of doubt (*shakk*).

In conversations with some hundred people met in public spaces around Mustafa Mahmud's mosque in Muhandisin, the book kiosks of the 'Azbakiyya gardens in central Cairo, and in other random places of Greater Cairo, it emerged that Mustafa's *shakk* was not perceived as a residue from a difficult past, and could therefore not be equated with error or derailment from the straight path (being an atheist), but was accepted as a permanent generating force of *iman* – as if in the burgeoning metropolis of Cairo the embattled members of the shrinking Egyptian middle classes would themselves make the journey from doubt to faith every day. The ubiquity of this media star allows virtually everybody in the Egyptian public to articulate a judgement about him.

Since reaching the shores of *iman*, Mustafa Mahmud has always thought of himself as an Islamic thinker (*mufakkir islami*). Publishing networks which supported his self narrative and shared in the underlying stakes, as well as the personnel working for his association, strongly endorsed this self-identification. On the other hand, most interviewees belonging to his wider public were eager to stress that he is not a man of religion. In other words, the general public acclaims him for being a committed Muslim who spreads knowledge and helps people. Yet this view does not, in itself, accrue to his image as a leading *mufakkir islami*. People on the street who discussed the image and self narrative of Mustafa Mahmud were more interested to comment on the unpredictable elements of his personality and message and on the rifts created by his journey through doubt. They preferred to discuss the creative side of his intellectual production rather than to promote him as an 'Islamic intellectual'.

For a larger part of his public, the foothold of Mustafa Mahmud's authority is doubtless *'ilm*, as distinguished from *din* (religion) or *iman*. Most of the people described him as a scientist who has been capable of making morally acceptable and socially viable his scientific knowledge and practice as a physician. The word for scientist, *'alim*, has become for Western Orientalists the epithet of certified religious personnel (the *'ulama*, plural of *'alim*). Yet from elementary school Egyptians learn that *'ilm* is primarily the science of nature and that the *'alim* is the 'scientist' who studies it. Religious personnel are mostly identified by the public through the designation of *rijal al-din* (men of religion). Their *'ilm* is also a highly specialized one.

'An Islamic thinker and scientist who ties up science with religion, and has also a sound political position'. This type of characterization of Mustafa Mahmud occurred rarely among his audiences, though it is the only type of portrayal that neatly matches the image that he and the networks of production of his public image have tried to produce and spread. The promotion of his persona as a *mufakkir islami* would require a widespread acceptance, in Egyptian society, of the creation of an autonomous knowledge field based on the capacity of the purported 'Islamic intellectual' to communicate to wider audiences, the social dimension of the fundamental values inspired by Islam in isolation from Islamic institutions of learning. To date, this acceptance is probably not (or not yet) currency among educated Egyptian Muslims. Judging on the basis of the specific case of Mustafa Mahmud, the recognition of his status as a *mufakkir islami* by his public is cautiously approached when people are ready to acknowledge him as having shown, in practice and in theory, that science confirms faith, and that faith makes science socially accessible and vital, through turning it into public services. An explicit recognition of Mustafa Mahmud as an 'Islamic thinker' can be attained – though only seldomly – by deepening a conversation and reflection on his public impact. Yet it is not so much his status of *mufakkir* that seems to escape the public consensus, but its qualification as a *mufakkir islami*.

If we dig further into Mustafa Mahmud's networks, new elements emerge that complicate the picture, raising the question as to the type of authority underpinning his public charisma. For a professor of Arabic literature at the University of Helwan in

Greater Cairo, Mustafa is primarily a *mufakkir* because in his novels, short stories, and plays – through which he gained some public fame long before the *rihla* (journey) and the *markaz islami* (Islamic centre) – he cares less for art and more for conveying key ideas drawn from his personal experience and from his own reading of social reality.[8] A senior editor at Dar al-Ma'arif who was Mustafa's main publishing contact said that his readership embraced all ages and that his complex and somewhat contradictory personality was a key to his success and status of a public intellectual.[9]

An employee at the weekly *Uktubar*, who claimed to have met Mustafa Mahmud several times, went as far as to recognize in him the charisma of one of *awliya' Allah*, so basically naming him a 'saint', due to his modesty and a spirit of service informed by Sufism. For him, this was what made Mustafa a model for people of different ages and degrees of education. For Ahmad Kamal al-Jazzar, who wrote a book titled *Dr Mustafa Mahmud and Sufism* (al-Jazzar 1997), the sum of his combined skills made him capable of addressing a growing public not in order to entertain them, but to reconstruct their values. Al-Jazzar added that Mustafa Mahmud sharply refused to be called a Sufi and insisted that he was just an admirer and reader of Sufi authors. In spite of that, al-Jazzar remained convinced that Mustafa Mahmud belonged to *ahl Allah al-salikin*, the privileged people of God, that is, the Sufi elite of knowledge.

Although we have no particular reasons to question the sincerity of al-Jazzar in characterizing Mustafa Mahmud's charisma in this way, by the time the book was published, Mustafa had become a leading author of the daily newspaper, *Akhbar al-Yawm*. This was also the time when the dream of a comprehensive *markaz islami* had started to fade and the wave of success of subsequent cycles of the TV programme was on the wane. At that time, Mustafa's presence in public discussions could no longer rely on the combined solidity of his wider programme. He became more resolute in practising an approach to knowledge nurtured by doubt and in applying it to key issues of faith. In the late 1990s he argued in some newspaper articles against the principle of *shafa'a*, according to which on the Day of Judgment the Prophet Muhammad can intercede on behalf of sinners. Based on some *hadiths*, Mustafa claimes, this article of faith contradicts the basic Qur'anic principle according to which sinners will be punished by God. This argument attracted the hostility of several people, both within the puritan/Islamist camp and among Sufi circles.

A tense conversation on the issue started when Khalid, at the time a 34-year-old worker in a car repair shop, and Hasan, 22, a shop seller,[10] questioned Mustafa Mahmud's lucidity for daring to attack the Prophet Muhammad. They argued that in old age the once pious thinker had crossed a red line. Khalid stressed that while it is still admissible for a lay thinker like him to come up with a new *tafsir* of the Qur'an, questioning *hadith* that are considered authentic by the consensus of the *'ulama* is crazy. Ahmad, a 27-year-old state employee with a degree in administration, retorted that Mustafa Mahmud was not denying anything but just showing contradictions between some *hadith* and specific Qur'an verses. Khalid responded that the issue at stake was not limited to the issue of *shafa'a*. He warned that by reading carefully one of the articles dedicated to the topic one could see that Mustafa Mahmud was denying the authority of *hadith* itself as a reliable source, and doubting *hadith* might soon spill over to some verses of the Qur'an as well – God forbid.

Apparently the cultivation of *shakk* – which Mustafa Mahmud had turned into a methodological approach and even into an educational tool, and which he continued to see as integral to his personality even after embracing faith as a born-again Muslim

– was stirring up sharp controversies among his audiences. Ahmad insisted that he had also read the article quite carefully and that there was some logic in it. 'How can a sinner end up in heaven just because he invokes the Messenger of God's intercession by simply saying *la ilah illa Allah wa Muhammad rasul Allah*? [this is the Islamic profession of faith according to which "there is no god but God/Allah and Muhammad is God's messenger"]'. Khalid burst out: 'Logic?? What logic are you talking about? Logic is fine at school or at the university, but not with the words of the Messenger, whom God mentioned as the one who speaks nothing but the truth'. Hassan interrupted with a smile: 'Take it easy oh Shaykh Khalid, logic is from the Qur'an too'. At which point Khalid retorted: 'OK I will talk to you about logic: if your son does something wrong, it is logical to punish him, yet if your wife intercedes and asks you, for her sake, not to punish him for once, isn't it logical to accept her intercession?' Ahmad hesitated a bit, then said that they were not talking about ordinary situations but about Allah, who unequivocally stated in the Qur'an that sinners will go to hell and will never escape it. Then he added: 'I did not say that I completely agree with what Mustafa Mahmud wrote, I just said there is some logic in what he said – that's it!'

Clearly, Mustafa Mahmud had been effective in insinuating doubts and triggering a collective reasoning via arguments and counter-arguments. At this point Samir, 29, a computer expert who aspired to a career in journalism, and whose immediate goal was to know more about what other people thought of Mustafa Mahmud, asked his companions: 'So what do you think was the real motive for Mustafa Mahmud to write all this?' Hasan, smiling, suggested that Mustafa was smart enough to realize that what he writes is eventually repeated by many people: 'So he sat down and thought about a new topic that might be exciting'. Hasan ended the sentence with a loud laugh. At that point Khalid warned that if Mustafa Mahmud really did that, then he was not a true Muslim, since such topics are so serious and must not be used to provoke public excitement or to achieve fame. Ahmad asked then: 'Do you think that Mustafa Mahmud is lacking fame or searching for it? He is one of the most famous and popular writers in Egypt. He is even more famous than Naguib Mahfuz, even if he did not get a Nobel prize'. Khalid answered that Mustafa Mahmud is only famous because of his TV programmes and newspaper articles; if it were for his books, he would not have been famous at all. Samir suggested that Khalid had forgotten to mention Mustafa Mahmud's association. Khalid retorted that it was unremarkable and did not make him famous at all. On the contrary, it was Mustafa's fame that had made the association successful and this eventually accrued to his fame. He concluded: 'Look, you're taking this as a funny topic but it's a very serious one. It's very dangerous. Now you don't rely on *hadith* and later you'll forget about the sharia and finally *goodbye* [he said it in English] to Islam. They want Islam to be like Christianity in the West. Just a decoration'.

Three decades of Mustafa Mahmud's public deployment of doubt to inculcate a more self-conscious faith had resulted in a lively and critical, yet at times vicious, discussion on one of the most sensible topics of Islamic teaching, the status of the Qur'an and its relation to *hadith*. Clearly, such a critical discussion was also nourished by suspicions and clichés. The net result was, though, that the controversial image of Mustafa Mahmud was far from earning the status of an uncontroversial *mufakkir islami*, even for Ahmad and Samir who were quite sympathetic with his critical approach to the specific issue and more generally to his public role.

Conclusion: the status of *mufakkir* ('intellectual') between social commitment and originality in knowledge production

As Kate Zebiri mentions in her work on the former Shaykh al-Azhar Mahmud Shaltut (1893-1963), one of the reasons why the value of studying the thought of an *'alim* used to be underestimated was the presupposition that 'any original, creative thinking is far more likely to come from outside the ranks of the *'ulama'* (Zebiri 1993: 2). More recently, this search for originality in the prevailing Western sense of the term has been linked to a key category of Islamic jurisprudence which featured prominently among Muslim reformers like Muhammad 'Abduh (1849-1905) and Rashid Rida (1865-1935), namely *ijtihad*. Traditionally designating the faculty of exerting efforts in finding solutions to unprecedented legal issues, *ijtihad* was propagated by reformers no longer as a juridical skill of excellence or as a device for updating legal norms (Johansen 1993: 29-30), but as a largely super-legal method to channel the participation of all Muslims in discussions on issues of public interest. Rashid Rida went so far in the redefinition of *ijtihad* as to affirm that each Muslim should be a *mujtahid*, a practitioner of *ijtihad* (Rida 1988 [1922]: 115-16).

'Abd al-Halim Mahmud tried to restore a traditional understanding of *ijtihad*. He admired the *mujtahids* as those who rendered distinguished services to Islamic history, but criticized Muslims who practise *ijtihad* without a proper qualification in the authentic Islamic sciences. Malika Zeghal reports that 'in a letter sent to the president of Parliament in 1976, he claimed that "no *ijtihad* is allowed to any human if a *shar'i* text (a legal text deriving from revelation) exists" ' (Zeghal 1999: 383). *Ijtihad* was intended by him as a supplemental aid, reserved for the gifted people of knowledge, on the path first trod by the Prophet and his companions, representing the peak of the ceaseless endeavour to reach as far as they once had (Aishima 2005).

Significantly, on the back cover of several of his books, 'Abd al-Halim Mahmud is not presented as a *mujtahid* but as a high-ranking scholar who performs discrete *ijtihadat* (in the plural) with rigour, providing answers to various questions related to Islam. The logic of this presentation seems to be that a confidence with scholarly established knowledge based on a solid understanding of core texts can bring flexibility, and so originality, to one's knowledge production. Commenting on this presentation of 'Abd al-Halim Mahmud, some readers observed that 'originality' which is not derived from scholarly established texts may turn out to be mere imagination (*khayal*). In this perception, *ijtihad* is an intellectual effort to illuminate the deeper meanings of the textual sources transmitted through scholarly chains. Surprisingly perhaps, from among the audience of Mustafa Mahmud it was sometimes asserted that he was a *mujtahid* (a qualification he rarely claimed for himself), but that being a *mujtahid* does not require specific qualifications in the sciences of religion or a deep knowledge of the foundational texts. Being a *mujtahid* is then contrasted to being an *'alim*.

Accordingly, performing discrete operations of *ijtihad* can be seen as a practice of individual reasoning conforming to the rules of tradition and so contributing to the progress of knowledge via a deep understanding of the sources, while, on the contrary, acquiring the identity of a fully fledged *mujtahid* might enfeeble the knowledge credentials of the speaker and make him into a sort of lay generalist, a commoner striving to do his best out of a basic lack of familiarity with fundamental knowledge tools (not to forget, the primary meaning of *mujtahid* in common parlance in Egypt is 'diligent', and is frequently used for schoolchildren).

This combined, and not fully coherent, notion of the merits of *ijtihad* and the shortcomings inherent in being a *mujtahid* might sound surprising, because of the customary praising of *ijtihad* as a tool of social development by Muslim reformers and as a symbol of intellectual creativity by Western observers. Yet the status of *ijtihad* cannot be isolated from more complex, ongoing processes of cultural production in contemporary Egypt. These processes seem to create a bifurcation between what is understood as general culture and what is appreciated as specialized knowledge. It is often the case that mass media, rather than school education, are regarded as the source of 'culture'. Thus, the characters of the *muthaqqaf* (cultured) and of the *muta'allim* (educated) may overlap, but are not necessarily synonymous. While some *muta'allimun* are also *muthaqqafun*, there are *muthaqqafun* who did not attend school. Literacy acquired through schooling is certainly valued, but schools are not expected to provide *thaqafa* ('culture' intended as the cultivation of one's personality). Rather, 'culture' is something one actively seeks through reading books, listening to radio, or watching television. The above-mentioned dispute on Mustafa Mahmud's notion of *shafa'a* is clearly a conversation among *muthaqqafun*, not all of whom are *muta'allimun*, and who try hard not to disqualify their position by arguing as mere *mujtahidun*, intended in a slightly derogatory sense.

A popular definition of *muthaqqaf* met in our conversations is 'somebody who knows something about everything'. *Muta'allim* and *muthaqqaf* overlap but do not coincide, since there are many university graduates who are unaware of current affairs, having stopped reading after they left school. While the *muthaqqafun* build the public that the *mufakkirun* aim to reach and impact upon, a *mufakkir* does not have to be a *muta'allim* either. Salwa, a 27-year-old Arabic teacher, nominated 'Abbas al-'Aqqad (1889-1964), a leading Egyptian poet and writer, as an example of a self-educated intellectual. She stressed that al-'Aqqad didn't even finish elementary school but trained his mind through intensive reading and produced a number of insightful books.

The status of a *mufakkir* is attained by a sustained effort at producing a type of knowledge that can be consumed as 'culture' by an audience of *muthaqqafun* – a public that is far from a merely passive receptor and, as we have seen, can be sharply critical. Unlike the public construction of a *mufakkir*, an *'alim* is trained in one discipline to produce works of 'science'. In this sense, 'Abd al-Halim Mahmud is an *'alim* in the field of religious sciences and Mustafa Mahmud is an *'alim* within the natural sciences. Some creations of a *mufakkir* can be as valuable as those produced by a trained *'alim*, but this depends not on the assessment of peers, but on the judgement of the public.

If being a *mufakkir* is associated with some degree of originality and innovation, Egyptians respect an *'alim* for his ability to illuminate the deeper meanings of his predecessors' works. The product of a *mufakkir*'s activity does not exceed the realm of 'personal opinion', which can be correct or incorrect, while the work of an *'alim* pertains to the domain of truth because the origins of his knowledge can be identified with certainty. Referring to 'Abd al-Halim Mahmud's autobiography, *Praise be to God, this is my life*, some people called him a *mufakkir islami* because he starts with his own ideas and then develops his thoughts by relating them to the Qur'an and *hadith*. While his Sufi knowledge, which is communicated in a simplified *fusha*, addresses the sensibilities of a wider audience, his credibility as an 'authentic' scholar is questioned by some members of the scholarly community. However, when 'Abd al-Halim chose the mass media as a channel to promote Sufism, his intended audiences were not experts on Sufism but members of the general public with a secular educational background. Thus, it might be safe to conclude that it was a wider public who attributed to him credibility as an 'authentic' scholar and – though less frequently – a *mufakkir islami*.

Mustafa Mahmud's public message and status as a *mufakkir* appeared quite uncontested as long as his public relied on the three main axes of his schema and more specifically on his prerogatives as an *'alim* who was successful in his field (medicine, or more generally the natural sciences). Yet it could create controversies in cases where he applied the motif of doubt as a key to shift the consensus in his society on controversial issues concerning Islam: a type of action that is usually associated with the authority of the modern critical intellectual in a Western context. The work and message of 'Abd al-Halim Mahmud could be more reassuring in terms of truth value because his ideas are supported by unquestioned sources such as the Qur'an and *hadith*. For him, carrying the double insignia of being an *'alim* and a *mufakkir* was an easier task: paradoxically perhaps, his specifically religious legitimacy provided him a more solid footing for gaining recognition as an intellectual. In the context of the Cairo-centred Islamic Resurgence discussed here, the types of authority that we tend to associate with modernity and tradition, respectively, do not relate to each other in the expected way. The publicly accepted role of a *mufakkir* becomes problematic on issues related to Islam, because the raising of controversial issues clashing with established orthodoxy can be suspected of serving the goal not of enlightening the public but of attaining a facile, personal fame.

Moreover, the audience's reflection on the legacies of the two Mahmuds relativizes the hierarchy of importance of the electronic media (in the era during which TV overlapped with radio) and resuscitates the fame of the 'killed' radio star 'Abd al-Halim Mahmud as a kind of media authority more capable, in the longer term, of attaining the fame of a comprehensive *mufakkir islami*. Yet, the wider public's perception is partly contradicted by more educated people. While they easily agreed that 'Abd al-Halim Mahmud was an *'alim*, since he worked for al-Azhar, they differed greatly on whether he was a *mufakkir*. For more religious persons, an *'alim* of his rank ought to be a *mufakkir*, hence 'Abd al-Halim was both; but for those who take some distance from religion, the *mufakkir*'s place occupies a higher rank than a simple *'alim*. Here the TV star Mustafa Mahmud has a chance to regain a higher place in the hierarchy, yet always at the price of being exposed to the suspicion of aiming at self-promotion. The screen of tradition, even when it encompasses the ever-controversial teachings of Sufism, seems at times to provide a protection against this suspicion.

ACKNOWLEDGMENTS

Our research data are based on several field research trips to Egypt that took place between 1998 and 2008. Our thanks go to Walter Armbrust for his comments on earlier drafts of the part on 'Abd al-Halim Mahmud and to our interlocutors in Egypt. Special thanks go to Dr Mani' 'Abd al-Halim and his family for their support since 2001.

NOTES

[1] Mani' 'Abd al-Halim, pers. comm., 26 September 2001. He is the son of 'Abd al-Halim and professor at the College of Religious Fundaments, al-Azhar.

[2] The Arabic word for 'stars', *nujum*, is ubiquitous in writing and talking about public personalities in Egypt well beyond show business.

[3] This article appeared in January 2001, introducing 'Abd al-Halim as a rare imam who reconciles Western sciences and Eastern cultures, religious sciences and philosophy.

[4] In the history of Islamic thought, Abu Hamid al-Ghazali (1058-1111) is distinguished for theoretically bridging the gap between *tasawwuf* (Sufism) and *fiqh* (Islamic jurisprudence) as distinctive genres of knowledge.

[5] While such a recognition of 'Abd al-Halim Mahmud as an *'alim* with high-ranking knowledge is widespread among a mass audience, it appears much more problematic among Egyptian scholars. They are often suspicious of his public success and sometimes claim that his books are only suitable for a 'popular' audience and have no scholarly value.

[6] Taha Habeyshi, pers. comm., 13 March 2007. He is the head of the Department of Philosophy and Dogmatics of the College of Religious Fundaments, al-Azhar.

[7] Editor in chief of *Akhbar al-Adab*, writer. His latest novel, *Kitab al-tajalliyat* (The book of illumination) (1983-6), is an autobiography narrated through his spiritual interactions with Sufi celebrities.

[8] Pers. comm., 18 May 1999.

[9] Pers. comm., 15 May 1999.

[10] All informants' names are pseudonyms.

REFERENCES

ABAZA, M. 2006. *The changing consumer cultures of modern Egypt: Cairo's urban reshaping*. Leiden: Brill.

AISHIMA, H. 2005. A Sufi-'alim intellectual in contemporary Egypt: 'Al-Ghazali of 14th century A.H.,' Shaykh 'Abd al-Halim Mahmud. In *Une voie soufie dans le monde: la Shâdhiliyya* (ed.) E. Geoffroy, 319-32. Paris: Maisonneuve et Larose.

BEN NÉFISSA-PARIS, S. 1992. Le mouvement associatif égyptien et l'islam. *Élèments d'une problématique, Monde Arabe – Maghreb-Machrek* **135**, 19-36.

BURGAT, F. & J. ESPOSITO (eds) 2003. *Modernizing Islam: religion and the public sphere in the Middle East and Europe*. New Brunswick, N.J.: Rutgers University Press.

EICKELMAN, D.F. & J.W. ANDERSON (eds) 2003 [1999]. *New media in the Muslim world: the emerging public sphere*. Bloomington: Indiana University Press.

———— & J. PISCATORI 1996. *Muslim politics*. Princeton: University Press.

AL-GHITANI, J. 1983-6. *Kitab al-tajalliyat* (The book of illuminations) (3 vols). Cairo: Dar Al-Mustaqbal Al-'Arabi.

HIRSCHKIND, C. 2006. *The ethical soundscape: cassette sermons and Islamic counterpublics*. New York: Columbia University Press.

AL-JAZZAR, A.K. 1997. *Dr Mustafa Mahmud wa-l-tasawwuf* (Dr Mustafa Mahmud and Sufism). Cairo: Akhbar al-Yawm.

JOHANSEN, B. 1993. Legal literature and the problem of change: the case of land rent. In *Islam and public law: classical and contemporary studies* (ed.) C. Mallat, 29-47. London: Graham & Trotman.

MAHMOOD, S. 2005. *Politics of piety: the Islamic revival and the feminist subject*. Princeton: University Press.

MAHMUD, A.H. 2001 [1976]. *Al-hamdu li-llah hadhihi hayati* (Praise be to God, this is my life). Cairo: Dar al-Ma'arif.

MAHMUD, M. 1987 [1970]. *Rihlati min al-shakk ila-l-iman* (My journey from doubt to faith). Cairo: Dar al-Ma'arif.

RIDA, R.M. 1988 [1922]. *Al-khilafa aw al-imama al-'uzma* (The Caliphate or the supreme Imamate). Cairo: al-Zahra' li-l-I'lam al-'Arabi.

SALVATORE, A. 1998. Staging virtue: the disembodiment of self-correctness and the making of Islam as public norm. In *Islam – motor or challenge of modernity* (ed.) G. Stauth, 87-12. (Yearbook of the sociology of Islam 1). Hamburg: Lit; New Brunswick, N.J.: Transaction.

———— 2000. Social differentiation, moral authority and public Islam in Egypt: The path of Mustafa Mahmud. *Anthropology Today* **16**: 2, 12-15.

———— 2001. Mustafa Mahmud: a paradigm of public Islamic entrepreneurship? In *Muslim traditions and modern techniques of power* (ed.) A. Salvatore, 213-25. (Yearbook of the sociology of Islam 3). Hamburg: Lit; New Brunswick, N.J.: Transaction.

———— & D.F. EICKELMAN (eds) 2004. *Public Islam and the common good*. Leiden: Brill.

SCHLEIFER, A. 1991. Sufism in Egypt and the Arab East. In *Islamic spirituality: manifestations* (ed.) S.H. Nasr, 194-205. New York: Crossroad.

SHALABI, R. 1982. *Shaykh al-Islam al-Imam 'Abd al-Halim Mahmud* (The Shaykh of Islam Imam 'Abd al-Halim Mahmud). Kuwait: Dar al-Qalam.

SREBERNY-MOHAMMADI, A. & A. MOHAMMADI 1994. *Small media, big revolution: communication, culture, and the Iranian revolution*. Minneapolis: University of Minnesota Press.

WICKHAM, C.R. 2002. *Mobilizing Islam: religion, activism, and political change in Egypt*. New York: Columbia University Press.

ZEBIRI, K. 1993. *Mahmud Shaltut and Islamic modernism*. Oxford: Clarendon Press.

ZEGHAL, M. 1996. *Gardiens de l'islam: les oulémas d'Al Azhar dans l'Égypte contemporaine*. Paris: Presses de Sciences Po.

———— 1999. Religion and politics in Egypt: the ulema of Al-Azhar, radical Islam, and the state (1952-94). *International Journal of Middle East Studies* **31**, 371-99.

4

A tour not so grand: mobile Muslims in northern Pakistan

MAGNUS MARSDEN *School of Oriental and African Studies*

Whan that Aprill with his shoures soote
The droughte of March hath perced to the roote,
And bathed every veyne in swich licour
Of which vertu engendered is the flour; ...
Thaan longen folk to go on pilgrimages,
And palmeres for to seken straunge strondes.

Geoffrey Chaucer, 'Prologue' to *The Canterbury Tales*

A great deal of my time conducting fieldwork amongst Khowar-speaking Muslims living in the mountainous Chitral region of northern Pakistan is spent travelling between the region's many and dispersed villages and valleys. Chitral is made up of verdant villages sited on alluvial fans located within high mountain valleys flanked by snow-capped peaks and fast-flowing rivers. The beauty of Chitral's landscape is the focus of extensive present-day Khowar poetic composition, much of which describes the feeling of 'freedom' (*azadi*) to be had from travelling through the region in spring – a season when many Chitralis follow the sweet scent of Russian olive tree blossom up valley as the summer months progress. Yet Chitralis also say that they are 'mice-like' 'prisoners of the mountains' who live in the 'darkest corner' of the world; and they make inter-regional distinctions between 'open' (*kulao*) and 'narrow' (*trang*) village life. Life in narrow villages, as well as small towns with busy bazaars, is said to cause people to feel 'heart explosion' (*hardi phat*) and put them at constant danger from mental '*collapse*' (they use the English term). To offset these dangers, groups of young Chitrali men visit villages that are known for being old-fashioned and distinctive places full of 'wonders and marvels' (*aja'ibo ghara'ib*), or that have earned a reputation for the beauty, hospitality, and 'life-loving' (*zindadil*) dispositions of their inhabitants. Referred to using the English term '*tours*', these are mostly short trips that involve a one-night stay in the house of a friend. They may also be more expedition-like journeys (*safar*) that see the travellers walking over high mountain passes and staying in the guesthouses of strangers. Tour-going is an important practice through which Chitralis encounter, perceive, and seek to understand their region's valleys and villages, investing them as well as themselves with significance (Gray 2006: 225, 227). At the same time, Chitralis talk about tours as providing complex opportunities to hone their capacity to enact and cultivate diverse modes of sociality and moral, aesthetic, and intellectual sensibilities, notably those connected to a complex performative nexus of wit, humour, and mockery.

As school-leaver and undergraduate visitor to Chitral, I was frequently whisked off in the darkness of night by boys of my age on the eve of annual wheat harvests on week-long excursions to distant valleys. My friends only returned when they knew that the 'noisy threshers' had left their homes, and the 'polluting wheat-chaff' had long since left its diarrhoea-inducing dust on the village's ripened apricots. The groups of young men with whom I travelled were mostly studying in higher education colleges, and told me that they yearned to break free from the 'era of speed' that had come to characterize life in their 'developed' and 'city-like' village. In particular, they talked about the ways in which the expansion of their village's bazaar over the last twenty years had led its people to become *bazaaris* who no longer took pride in being hospitable but instead spent their lives 'running' after 'pieces of work' in the bazaar and its government offices. To escape all this *tensien*, they often decided to travel to 'remote' and 'backward' villages where bazaars are minuscule, guests are respected, and home-produced foods continue to be cultivated and prepared. Sometimes they stay with their Chitrali relatives, but often they say that being the guest in 'relative-houses' is painfully 'boring'. Instead, they invest great energy into choosing a house where they are likely to be treated as guests and not relatives. In Chitral's dispersed yet intimate and interconnected villages, being offered hospitality as a friend (*dost*), kin (*rishtadar*), or work-mate (*korumo malgiri*) is a relatively simple task; being honoured as a respectable 'outsider' and achieving the desired aim of experiencing a break from everyday village reality requires more sustained displays of trickery and creative performance. Thus, my young village friends pursued a range of strategies to assume the honoured status as 'guest' (*mehrman*) in a stranger's house for the evening. The enactment of identities very different from those performed during the course of everyday village life was a favourite strategy to adopt – they presented themselves as the sons of important local government officials and visiting religious preachers from elsewhere in Pakistan and as far away as Canada. These strategies were, however, rarely entirely persuasive – names, bodily comportment, and slips in performative standards frequently alerted hosts' attention to the family, village, and religious backgrounds of my companions.

Much recent anthropological work on travel focuses on the insights that ethnographic explorations of mobility afford into understanding the effects of globalizing modernity, ranging from the emergence of exclusive forms of transnational identities to cosmopolitan 'openness' (e.g. Augé 1995; Clifford 1997; Hannerz 1996). As Enseng Ho has noted, however, there is tendency for this writing to be 'obsessed with speed', to the extent that it fails to consider the ways in which older 'experiences of mobility' involved 'tactile, visual, auditory, affective, aesthetic, textual, and mystical' dimensions (2006: 10; cf. Tsing 1993). Travel, indeed, has long been an important dimension of Muslim life (e.g. Eickelman & Piscatori 1990; Euben 2006). In particular, historians have documented the importance of travelogues for understanding 'pre-modern' forms of Muslim subjectivity, notably in the Indian subcontinent (e.g. Alam & Subrahmanyam 2007). Alam and Subrahmanyam explore the ways in which Indian scribes of the Mughal court wrote Persian-language accounts of their seventeenth-century journeys within and beyond their realm, which emphasized the scribes' ability to 'comfortably straddle' (Alam & Subrahmanyam 2004: 70) starkly different social milieus. Historians have also documented the role played by concepts of travel in Indian political thought. Majeed's study of the twentieth-century Islamic thinker Alama Iqbal argues that Iqbal 'defined himself against ethnographic representations of the "native" in which Indians were represented as being incapable of individual growth through travel' (Majeed 2007: 5), instead emphasizing a 'restless self' (2007: 25) constantly reconstituted during a metaphysical inner journey. This work emphasizes travel's role in the production of unfinished conceptions of self, which challenged the fixity of Indians as depicted in colonial accounts as well as bounded ideas of the modern nation (cf. Pratt 1992). Likewise, Ho's study of mobile Yemeni Sayyids and their role in the creation of an Indian Ocean Islamic ecumene shows that these men integrated into diverse societies across the Indian Ocean. What distinguishes Ho's work, however, is his emphasis on the way in which these peoples' experiences of their wider world contributed to rather than attenuated their sense of 'resolute localism'.[1]

In the light of this expanding body of anthropological and historical work on the relationship between mobility and identity, this chapter has two major aims. Firstly, it explores the ways in which local practices of mobility are important to everyday life in Chitral because they are seen to cultivate in young village minds a sense of curiosity about their region and the diverse influences found therein. In so doing, it challenges the notion that the most important forms of mobility today are global and the harbingers of transnational 'cosmopolitanism'. Secondly, exploring the ways in which Muslims perceive and interact with their worlds also furnishes broader insights into the complexity of collective and personal forms of Muslim self-understanding. Mahmood (2005) has documented the ways in which 'piety-minded' Muslims in Cairo fashion themselves as good Muslims through the habituation of norms formulated according to the Islamic tradition and in response to Egyptian expressions of secular modernity. Through an analysis of ethnographic material that points to 'submission to certain forms of "external authority" ' as being 'a condition for the self to achieve its potentiality' (Mahmood 2003: 857), she challenges the cross-cultural relevance of 'Western modes of subjectivity that associate agency exclusively with an inner ego, constituted as thought and desire as independent of the body, nature, society and other extrinsic conditions' (Waggoner 2005: 248).[2] In a similar vein, Henkel focuses on the ways in which piety-minded Muslims in Istanbul seek to overcome local manifestations of modernity's 'heterogeneous lifeworlds' in order to live coherent Muslim lives, by visiting felicitous Muslim spaces and 'designating certain elements' of the city as 'significant and others as unimportant' (Henkel 2007: 57-8). Recent anthropological works, however, have paid less attention to the ways in which rural Muslims act within, perceive, and invest with relevance their worlds. As a result, the assumption that village Muslim life is static, bucolic, and of little relevance for anthropological debates concerning wider trends currently affecting life in the Muslim world remains largely uncontested.

In what follows, I document the practices though which Chitralis invest their region, its places and landscapes, with complex forms of personal and collective significance (Gray 2006). Yet what I also seek to emphasize is that the wider significance of these forms of 'place-making' assume importance within a landscape already deeply 'enshrined' (Gilsenan 1996) with contested forms of power and memory and animated by 'energies' that 'pervade' their everyday lives (Hirsch 1995; Humphrey 1995: 135).

All the Chitralis I know are aware that travelling to 'felicitous Muslim' spaces is important to their being Muslim (Henkel 2007: 58) – many of them undertake the pilgrimage to Mecca, embark on more local 'religious journeys' (see Marsden 2005), and debate amongst themselves the relevance of these for being virtuous Muslims.[3] Tours, however, are inspired by a complex combination of both sacred and non-sacred motivations.[4] Visiting sacred sites, acquiring knowledge about Chitral and its people, escaping the moralizing constraints of daily village life, evading social claims placed upon them by their fellow villagers, and 'relaxing' are amongst the most important motivations for tours. At one level, these diverse motivations for touring illuminate the ways in which Chitralis Muslims experience their region thorough a complex bundle of thoughts and desires, which reflect more complex concerns than their knowledge of Islamic doctrinal standards. More significantly, many Chitralis associate movement outside the confines of their villages with a complex nexus of performance, curiosity in difference, the display of wit, and what they refer to as a fleeting sensation of freedom (*azadi*) from the constraints (*pabandi*) of daily village life. More than simply offering a monetary release from Chitrali village life, tours furnish Chitralis with possibilities to both recognize and point beyond the 'inescapability' of the conditions that shape their everyday lives (Waggoner 2005: 238); understanding such events in their full complexity requires a consideration of the moments of 'self-reflection, self-interrogation [and] openness to the unforseeable' (Waggoner 2005: 239) which they stimulate.[5]

Importantly, when Chitralis do seek to cultivate an appreciation for the heterogeneity of their region and its people or think out loud about questions of sameness and difference, they do so in a region of Pakistan that is profoundly 'Islamized'. At first glance, Chitral's landscape suggests the hegemony of political Islamists who have sought to fashion Muslim life in the region according to reform-minded Islamic doctrinal precepts. Over the past twenty years there has been a notable increase in the construction of large mosques with domes and towering minarets – architectural styles which reflect Middle Eastern funding.[6] Chitral, moreover, is home to Sunni and Shi'a Ismai'li Khowar-speaking Muslims.[7] Today, the shimmering tin roofs of Sunni mosques and Ismai'li places of worship face off another across Chitral's doctrinally mixed villages, graphically illustrating the importance of emergent 'sectarian geographies' (Makdisi 2000: 134) to everyday Chitrali Muslim life. Yet in the context of this world of prescribed faith, many Sunni and Shi'a Ismai'li Chitralis do not simply or without regard to their particular circumstances interpret heterogeneity – old or new – as an obstacle to living a coherent Muslim life or as a threat to their society's truly Muslim nature. The appreciation of Chitral's diversity, rather, adds another dimension to local understandings of their region's uniqueness and wider significance. Tracking Chitralis who circulate through their region and noting their performances during the course of these journeys illuminates the ongoing importance of dimensions of rural Muslim life long noted by anthropologists. It also demonstrates the ways in which wit, irony, and humour are important intellectual resources deployed by Chitralis who actively seek to evaluate the changing conditions that are currently shaping their daily lives.

Travel in the Indo-Persian world

It would be tempting to assume that Muslims living in a remote and rural region of Pakistan travel primarily to visit kin, seek out labour, or make pilgrimages. People also travel for leisure, however; and this is a constant source of planning, expenditure, and discussion in Chitral. Ethnographically, the form of mobility explored here – mundane forms of intra-regional travel motivated by the desire to experience a break from the constraints of everyday village life – is rarely considered important in relationship to the burgeoning body of work on long-distance or transnational mobility. Given current anthropological concerns with globalization and cosmopolitan 'serial migrants' (Ossman 2007), the paucity of studies on local practices of travel and the notion that the world is made up of transnational labour migrants and elite cosmopolitans, on the one hand, and the immobile entrapped at home, on the other, are hardly surprising. Travel in Chitral today has been stimulated by modern developments – metalled roads, jeeps, and minibuses are all important for Chitrali modes of everyday travel. Yet the tours that Chitralis make bear the ongoing influence of forms of travel that derive from the region's past; and Chitralis seek to mark the difference between fast and purposeful journeys and slow and leisurely tours.

Many Chitralis do live and work in the hyper-modern cities of the Persian Gulf; even more are employed as labourers in Pakistan's cities. Yet Chitralis who are not active participators in long-distance forms of labour migration do not simply live stagnant lives confined to their villages. Indeed, having heard tales of Gulf life from their relatives, they often contrast their ability to travel with the camp-bound existences of Chitrali living in the 'outside world' (*berieo duniya*).[8] And, as I now explore, they discuss the ability to travel as something that animated contentious political debates in their region's past and continues to do so amongst different categories of Chitralis today.[9]

The entire region that is now Chitral was an independent monarchical state until 1895, when the British negotiated a forced treaty with its hereditary ruler, the Mehtar, under which Chitral became a semi-autonomous princely state within the Indian empire. Chitral retained this status after its accession to Pakistan in 1947, only being made an administrative district in Pakistan's North-West Frontier province in 1969. Chitral inherited traditions of status, politeness, and etiquette, which were characteristic of the Mughal-Timurid states and khanates of South and Central Asia, despite the fact that Chitral was never fully integrated into the Mughal realm (e.g. Parkes 2001; Marsden 2008).

Since the region's incorporation within Pakistan's North-West Frontier province, Chitral society has undergone profound social transformations: notably the dissolution of the social estates of the region's gentry landlords (Staley 1982), and the emergence of a new class of state-employed bureaucrats and NGO employees (Parkes 1996). Chitral's political culture has also been influenced by wider political trends associated with the Frontier's predominantly Pukhtun-speaking people. In October 2002 a coalition of Islamist parties (the Muttahida Majlis-e Amal), the leadership of which is predominantly Pukhtun (Nasr 2005), was elected to government in the Frontier and Chitral (Marsden 2007a). The Islamist legislators quickly set to the task of 'Islamizing' Chitral, by, for example, openly 'speaking against' the region's one-time princes and seeking to ban 'traditional' Chitrali music events.

Yet the ongoing legacy of older court-derived forms of status and hierarchy and a rich 'high culture' – defined by its diverse and vibrant poetic and musical tradition – have meant that Indo-Persian cultural influence continues to be a dynamic source of shared identification in Chitral (Marsden 2008). Historians conceptualize the Persianate realm as defined by the importance of Persian as a language of political authority and high culture, and in terms of the shared literary and cultural traditions that were important in diverse 'Persianate' settings (e.g. Cole 2002). Much recent work has explored the role played by travel and travel writing in the cultural and political life of pre-modern Indian societies (Alam & Subrahmanyam 1996; 2004; 2007). These works are descriptions of journeys made to 'exotic' places, such as holy Islamic cities, but also to more 'familiar' settings within northern India. Such travel accounts were not simply frivolous literary excursions for Mughal India's scribes – travel writing was a vehicle used by court officials in order to demonstrate their 'command over the art of description' and 'allusion and comparison' (Alam & Subrahmanyam 2004: 65, 66).

The cultivation of skills for the acquisition and sharing of knowledge about both familiar and more 'wondrous' (aja'ib) places forms an important dimension of Chitralis' experiences of travel in their region today. Chitralis often richly inject even their most mundane journeys with meaning by reciting stories about the significance of particular places for their region's history, as well as anecdotes concerning the current character of Chitrali people. On the main road between Rowshan and Markaz there is a narrow area of flat land in a small village through which the road passes. Whilst speeding in minibuses through this village, my friends often tell me and their travelling companions a story about an early British visitor to the region. This 'britisher' was said to have been riding on horse-back through the village when he came across a gathering of thin and shoddily dressed Chitralis. 'What are you doing?' he is said to have asked. 'We are the prisoners of the Mehtar', the people replied, 'our jailer is in a house having a lunch and a cup of tea'. After much laughter, the significance of this story is expressed in terms of the inherent inability of Chitralis actively to seek out 'freedom' (azadi). 'We', they say, 'don't know how to be free – is it surprising that we remain prisoners of the mountains?' Many Chitralis contrast their ability to move with the immobility of their forefathers; they also talk about the ongoing influence of past experiences of confinement on their thinking and behaviour.

The constraints imposed upon mobility by Chitral's Mehtar are often talked about in even more explicit ways. In the 'era of the Mehtar', Chitralis often say, a man who left the boundaries of Chitral was never allowed to return, whilst no man's land or family was safe from the ruling family's ceaseless greed to occupy Chitral's most beautiful places and marry its prettiest girls. Reflecting on the Mehtar's rule is something Chitralis often do as they travel by places associated with their region's courtly past. The excitement of 'embodied memories' (Stoller 1994), reflective processes, and movement form an important nexus that powerfully shapes these articulations of viewpoints about the region's history.

Many of Chitral's old forts continue to be inhabited by the descendants of Chitral's one-time princely family. These (today crumbling) forts are often located in scenic spots overlooking fast-flowing rivers. In the summer of 1998, I travelled with some Chitrali friends to a valley where the Mehtar had built a summer house in which he stayed whilst hunting ibex in the mountains. The two men with whom I travelled were in their mid-twenties, unemployed, and studying privately for BA degrees in the social sciences. Both were descended from Seyyid families who claim descent from the Prophet, and they often told me how the Chitral's Mehtars had feared their grandfather so greatly that they had forced him into exile into a neighbouring province of Afghanistan, Badakshan (Marsden 2008). Having nowhere to stay in the village, my friends decided that we should visit the Mehtar's summer palace and ask the princes if we could pass the night in their home. In order to persuade these young princes (at the time studying in expensive private schools in Karachi and Lahore) of our worthiness of being accorded hospitality, my friends pretended to be tahsildars (local government officials); I was told to act out the part of a British Embassy official. The tactic worked:

the young princes chatted with us, and later presented us with a prized meal of ibex meat curry. Yet rather than giving us a room in their guesthouse, they arranged for us to sleep on carpets in its garden. This caused great irritation to my Seyyid friends, who told me during the night that the land on which we were sleeping had once belonged to their forefathers before it was usurped by the Mehtar. Visits to the old seats of courtly authority and fleeting interactions with the region's princes stimulate Chitralis to cunningly repudiate the continuing importance of the old courtly order to life in the region today. Thus, whilst few Chitralis may fully escape the 'immanence of the conditions' shaping their daily lives, the forms of wit and irony that are enacted during tours do give rise to 'moments of self-reflection, self-interrogation, [and] openness to the unforseeable' (Waggoner 2005: 239).

Concerns over the types of vision associated with high land vividly illustrate the extent to which Chitral's landscape is 'enshrined' (Gilsenan 1996) with older and newer conceptions of social order and power. Visiting, buying land, or building houses on 'high places' with views over villages, houses, and hamlets is a source of great contestation in Chitral's villages. One man from Rowshan who hailed from a one-time lordly family, for example, told an elderly man, purportedly a one-time 'serf' (chermuzh) yet recently elected as a local government councillor, that he should not allow his recent political success to go to his head. 'Whenever I want', said the lord (lal) to his neighbour, 'I can look down from my veranda and gaze at your daughters'. The local councillor's reply mocked the lord's attack and sought to demonstrate that his thinking was locked in a bygone era. 'That may be the case', he responded, 'but then you should remember that all I have to do is stare up my chimney and see deep inside the vagina of your wife'. Chitral's landscape is experienced as being 'enshrined' with older forms of status distinction, exclusion, extraction, and violence, thus filling it with cross-cutting sentiments of 'anger, sorrow and jubilation' (Makdisi & Silverstein 2007: 9). The 'embodied memories' stimulated by movement through Chitral's landscape produce modes of social critique that contest but also re-inscribe the importance of the old courtly order for present-day Chitrali identity.

Memories of courtly power, colonial expansion, and newer conflicts over the validity of older forms of social distinction to modern life are 'anchored' within connected places (Tilly 2006: 25), which constitutes a distinct 'landscape of powers' (Hirsch 2006: 154), embedded with overlapping tensions that Chitralis experience, reflect upon, and discuss during their travels. This overlaying of places with different forms of historical significance ensures that the memories of 'later generations do not displace earlier ones but perdure alongside them', thereby 'allowing each period to serve as a commentary on the others' (Lambek 1998: 108). Rather than conceptualizing Chitral's heterogeneity as a problem to living a coherent Muslim life, for many Chitrali villagers negotiating the complexities of conducting life 'with respect to distinctive epochs' that stimulate 're-occurring' senses of both modernity and tradition (Hirsch 2001: 133) involves complex reflective processes, during the course of which Chitralis simultaneously challenge and reaffirm both the older and newer influences on their lives.

Divine love and sexual flirtation

The multiply layered significances of Chitral's landscape are not, however, confined alone to the differential ways in which it has become embedded with older values, conflicts, and embodied memories of violence. The landscape is also actively filled with different forms of moral and sacred significance by Chitralis; these afford complex opportunities for them to think and act in overlapping spaces according to different moral registers.

As in much Persianate Sufic composition, metaphors of travel are widely deployed by Chitrali poets in order to evoke the experience of ecstatic forms of love, or *'ishq* (e.g. Majeed 2007). The experience of ecstatic love is a key theme in the Persianate Sufi canon, often also connected to ways in which the poet's self is fashioned as he makes a complex inner spiritual journey (Majeed 2007: 24). In much Khowar-language poetry, for example, 'lovers' describe being left to wander alone in barren plains (*biyaban*) whilst searching in a maddened state for their 'beloved' (Marsden 2007*b*). These poems often invoke mountain pastures and passes, which invest Chitral's own landscapes with abstract religious concepts. 'Lovers' are depicted in these poems as world-renouncing Sufi mendicants walking for time immemorial over high mountain passes, with only a begging bowl (*kishti*) strung around their neck and an oboe (*surnai*) in their mouth. Performed by musical groups in village houses, these poems invest both travel and the landscape with the powerful imprint of Sufi concepts. What I now document are the ways in which during the course of their tours Chitralis also acquire and exchange intimate knowledge about their region's sacred landscape.

There is usually a set pattern to the activities undertaken by Chitralis when staying in a friend's house for the evening. Having taken tea and fruit at home, the host suggests taking a stroll (*chaker*) to a beautiful place in the village – usually a high riverbank or water channel. These places are often the host's *nishini* – the place where a man sits in the evening alone or with friends, contemplates expansive views (*nazria*) of his village, listens to the radio, composes poetry, or relaxes and smokes a cigarette, occasionally 'filled' with hashish.

Farid[10] is a well-known Chitrali singer, who lives in the region's district headquarters, Markaz, where he works as a medical technician, yet tries to visit his home village as often as possible. I visited him there in May 2001 with two other Rowshan men; he took us to the water channel on the mountain overlooking his house where, he told us, he had learned to sing as a 'boy' (*daq*). In his early teenage years, his father and other village elders (*lilotan*) had told Farid not to sing – it would distract him from his studies, lead him to make friends with 'bad' hashish-smoking village boys, and might also mean that respectable men would refuse to give their daughters in marriage to him. The *nishini* was out of earshot of the village, however, and had expansive views of the valley below. Distant although not detached from villages, *nishinis*, as do sacred places elsewhere, offer the potential for the momentary experience of abstract 'emptiness' (Hirsch 1995: 4).

The landscape that this high water channel overlooks is richly invested with sacred and poetic histories. On the opposite side of the valley from Farid's *nishini* is the village and small dusty shrine of Chitral's most famous Sufi poet: Baba Seyar. Most Chitralis know Baba Seyar's love poetry, written after he fell in love with a married woman. So besotted with this woman was he that on meeting her whilst crossing the bridge that linked their two villages, he jumped into the fast-flowing river below so as to avoid both immorally crossing her path and rudely turning his back. Farid often recites Baba Sayar's poems from his *nishini*. These poems compare the distinctive 'red land' of Sayar's beloved's village to her 'ruby red lips'. On the one hand filled with 'anger, sorrow, and jubilation', Chitral's landscape is also injected with abstract religious concepts that posit the possibility of experiencing moral, selfless, and devotional-like feelings of love to one's beloved – human or divine. Whilst not being pilgrimages in any simple sense, travelling to the *nishini* of a friend plays an active role in investing Chitral's landscape with personal yet abstract forms of significance.

Such sacred spaces embody the possibility of experiencing things beyond the everyday because of their connectedness to the quotidian world (Hirsch 1995: 4). *Nishini*s do not merely transcend the everyday, but are invested with the possibility of experiencing more bodily forms of action and emotion as well. As I have documented above, high land is a source of considerable moral and emotional contestation in Chitral; a man's *nishini* does not simply exist in a geographical realm beyond this. Often sited on high land, *nishini*s are exactly the type of place where village boys may be able to view the houses, bodies, and brightly coloured clothing of their beloved ones below. Their visionary potential does not escape the attention of village elders – fathers scream at young men sitting on hillocks, accusing them of loitering solely in order to 'look at' the village girls. Visitors to villages are also aware of these dangers, and always ask their friends if other villagers will object to them sitting on high places.

Village girls, too, are actively involved in these disputes; they become angry with young men whom they accuse of looking at them with 'immoral eyes'. On one occasion a young man in his late teens took me to a 'high place' where, he told me, we would have expansive views of the valley below. As we sat atop the crest, a young woman approached from below with a flock of sheep, and I soon realized that my young host's interest in the 'view' had a distinctly carnal dimension. The young woman was also aware – shouting at the boy to go away, and asking him why he brought his guests to this place exactly at the time she returned with her sheep.

Sites of personal significance are often richly injected with sacred dimensions, yet they also signify the possibility of enacting categories of thought, emotions, and sociality, which should ideally be abstract, moral, and other-worldly, yet, on the limits of the village, have the potential of assuming more direct and bodily forms. Abstract and Sufi-derived conceptions of other-worldly love sit jaggedly alongside feelings of lust, desire, and love that are widely considered as being illicit and posing a threat to the order of everyday village life. This all takes place, moreover, in a setting where politically influential mullahs have sought to 'Islamize' society both from the top down and from the bottom up, and where reform-minded forms of Islam hostile to Sufi-influenced ways of being Muslim are currently all-powerful (e.g. Zaman 2002). In this setting, few Chitrali Muslims simply designate some spaces as being 'significant' and 'Muslim' and others as being 'unimportant'. Nor is it helpful to understand these dimensions of Chitrali Muslim subjectivity by drawing rigid distinctions between Islamist-derived conceptions of 'pious pleasure' and, presumably more authentic, forms of pleasure involving 'expressions of individuality, spontaneity and lightness, in which joy is the central element' (Bayat 2007: 434). Anthropological work on sacred spaces allows a better understanding of this complexity because it emphasizes the ways in which 'fragmented quotidian existence' (Hirsch 1995: 5) and the experience of abstract 'emptiness' are two related, rather than opposing, 'poles of experience' (1995: 4; cf. Parkin 1991).

The morality of mobility
Negotiating this multiply configured historical, moral, and sacred landscape is a complex process, which is often of intense personal significance, yet also fraught with conflict, tensions, and moral ambiguities. These processes of negotiation are not

something that Chitralis unthinkingly or automatically do. Rather, as youngsters they are trained to learn the correct emotional and moral dispositions that are attached to particular places. During tours, young Chitrali men hone their capacity to enact contrasting modes of performance in relationship to their region's heterogeneously constituted landscape. At the same time, tours ensure that young village minds are injected with curiosity about their region, and, thus, are central to the production of structures of emotional and intellectual attachment to Chitral as an interconnected regional locality.

Chitralis discuss both the negative and positive dimensions of travel as a recurrent feature of village life. At one level, villagers question one another's morality by making assertions about the motives of their journeys. Young men in particular told me that they were 'compelled' to listen repeatedly to the complaints of their parents (*naan-taat*), who accused them of being 'loafers' (*baghola*) and 'wanderers' (*kosak*) who travelled in order to avoid doing hard agricultural work at home. The terms *baghola* and *kosak* imply very serious forms of immoral behaviour. *Baghola* refers to a young man who 'walks' freely, is known to drink alcohol, smoke hashish, not study, and 'lead on' or even have illicit sexual relations with village girls. The term *kosak* is used to talk about young women who frequently move unaccompanied beyond the confines of their home, visit neighbours, and/or even make trips to other villages to visit their friends and relatives – such forms of mobility in excess are assumed to be an important indicator that a woman is sexually *free* (an English term often used in Khowar) or lax.

At another level, villagers emphasize the role played by travel in contributing to the healthy and moral development of young village minds. Travel ensures that the wider 'village environment' fosters 'high thoughts' and not 'low' and 'immoral' conversations, notably back-stabbing and gossiping. Villagers contrast the 'impoverished thoughts' of men whose lives are confined to their villages with the 'life-loving' attitudes of elderly men who, despite their advancing age, frequently leave their villages in order to travel across the region. Men and, despite proscriptions on their social mobility, women who 'sit in their homes' and 'make work' of becoming old risk 'going mad'. In particular, the noises (*hawaza*) associated with the repetitive experience of village life are said to pose a very serious threat to a person's mental health: family arguments, children crying, fights with villagers over the supply of irrigation water, and repeatedly listening to village gossip, it is said, make 'the brain crazy' (*kak aspah*).[11] In contrast, village 'lovers of life' (*zindadil insanan*) who travel widely earn both 'value' and 'position' in society: they become known personalities (*shaksiyat*) in villages across the region, and spend time sitting in the peaceful guesthouses and gardens of their friends rather than amongst their screaming children at home.[12] Villagers today, thus, are deeply concerned about the negative effects of unbalanced forms of thought and emotion on the behaviour of village people and the collective morality of the village as a whole. These are dangers they often connect to the pressures of life in the 'era of speed' in which they say they are currently living, and they talk widely about the need to do things to promote balance (*barra bari*) in their daily lives; travelling is one of the most important ways in which they seek to do this. Living a mobile Muslim life simultaneously enriches and impoverishes the properly moral nature of Chitrali society. Yet mobility is held as being central to a person's proper moral and intellectual development, which is something that is activated in youth, but should ideally be carried through adulthood into elderly life.

In the light of these complex attitudes towards travel, Rowshan villagers invest great efforts into ensuring that morally appropriate forms of travel are an important dimension of village life. Village children (*tsetsek*) are taught the benefits of travel from a very young age. When I travel, for example, from Rowshan to a nearby village, the elder brother and sisters in the house in which I stay often encourage me to take their children with me. They tell me that they are anxious that their children are excessively shy and bored; one of the best ways of ensuring that children grow into 'social' adults is by taking them on *tours*. Travel, they say, affords children with the opportunity to sit with 'different types of people'. Alongside being educated in schools that encourage 'critical thinking', attending musical programmes, and spending time in the company of jokers and story-tellers, travel is a practice through which Chitrali Muslims invest the minds of village youngsters with a curiosity about their their region, and the capacity to understand the joys and virtues of living creative intellectual lives.

As village children mature, however, their travelling often becomes a focus of family conflict and contestation. Parents worry that their once 'rose-like' children are now growing into excessively polite (*sharif*) or dumb (*ghot*) automatons, who will be 'useless' (*faltu*) individuals, unable 'to do anything', and, thus, in constant danger of being tricked and deceived by less scrupulous villagers when they grow older. At the same time, however, parents must also ensure that their children become 'active' young adults and not immoral loafers who prowl the region's villages in search of pretty girls and, thus, pose a constant threat to the reputation of the family, hamlet, and the 'sectarian community' to which they adhere.

Village youth develop a wide range of strategies to travel widely despite the contradictory messages emerging from their parents, who encourage them to be social but also emphasize the moral dangers of excessive time spent outside the home. Occasionally, they leave the houses in the darkness of night in order to avoid being asked by their parents the detested question 'Where are you going and why?' On a day-to-day basis they walk along hidden village paths mostly used by women in order to ensure that they are not seen loitering in the bazaar and reported to their parents by its suspicious shopkeepers. Twice a year or so, young village male youths (*nau juan*) embark on tours to other villages, telling their parents that they are going to visit their relatives. During the course of these tours, usually in groups of two or three friends, young men, instead, often avoid staying with their relatives, and present themselves to the strangers in whose houses they stay in a distinctly performative mode.

Rowshan's male youth mainly embark on tours to nearby villages and valleys. Yet far from being a homogeneous ethnic or linguistic space in any simple sense, Chitral is characterized by a great deal of internal heterogeneity and is seen by Chitralis as offering numerous possibilities for experiencing difference. There are three major valleys near Rowshan, all of which are known for being home to Chitralis who exhibit contrasting collective qualities. The villages to the south of Rowshan are said to be home to carefree people with a taste for luxury (*ayashi*) – the outdoor performances of music and dance in these villages are said to be especially 'hot' and 'enjoyable'; Rowshan's youths often travel to attend such events together. In contrast, the valley running parallel to Rowshan's is said to be home to 'hardened' Muslims – who are also a touch mean. Finally, five hours' drive to the north of Rowshan is a valley known for being old-fashioned. Its people are said to be simpletons whose lives have been barely touched by the modernizing changes affecting life in places such as Rowshan – purdah in this valley's villages, for example, is said to be less strict, making chances of glimpsing an unveiled 'girl' with rosy red cheeks a real possibility.

Tour-goers often decide not to wait for a jeep on the side of the dusty road, but, instead, walk to the village they intend to visit. Walking is considered safer than travelling in an overcrowded jeep; more importantly, it makes meeting people during the course of the journey easier. Chitralis actively seek to invest tours with slowness, thereby distinguishing them from other types of travel that see travellers sitting in jeeps in order quickly to accomplish a piece of work or visit their relatives. Tour-goers often walk until they see a house that appears sufficiently plush to suggest that its owner can provide a decent meal: a freshly slaughtered chicken and plates of home-grown rice are what my friends mostly hanker for. The ability to extract a rich evening meal, indeed, is a talent greatly valued in Chitral, and young Chitrali villagers deploy a wide range of strategies in order to fill their stomachs as best they can.

These strategies of extraction can often be distinctly self-edifying for tour-goers, who take pleasure in demonstrating their precocious wit at the expense of less-educated hapless villagers. Yet they also have a particular history in the region's past, and this points towards the ways in which new forms of recreational travel interact with older forms of mobility and self-understanding associated with Chitral's courtly past. In order to persuade the strangers with whom they are staying to feed them, my friends sometimes claim that they are government or NGO officials. As elsewhere in South Asia, the tours of princes and latterly colonial as well as post-colonial officals (Pouchepadass 2003; Sauli 2003) around their realm was one important strategy through which authority was enacted in Chitral. The Mehtar often travelled around the region with his courtly retinue, and, during such tours, it was the duty of particular noble status groups who were exempt from the paying of land tax to provide him with cooked food (*ashimat*) (e.g. Murtaza 1982). Today, fierce contests erupt regarding whose privilege it is to invite the visiting Chief Examiner to dinner at their home. Yet people from lower-status backgrounds mock the ways in which the elders of the *ashimat* families are proud to remind villagers that they had once cooked food for the Mehtar.

The tours that Chitrali men and boys make are not always short three-day affairs that involve visiting relatives, friends, or strangers in nearby valleys – sometimes they travel much further. Thus, I have been with groups of men to visit a remote village in the far south of Chitral (approximately an eight-hour jeep drive from Rowshan) which is home to a community of Persian-speaking people who were brought to Chitral 'many years ago' in order to make matchlock rifles for the Mehtar. I have also made numerous trips to three valleys that are home to Chitral's non-Muslim Kalasha community with both Sunni and Shi'i Ismai'li Chitral friends.[13] Strikingly, these valleys, rather than being seen as posing a one-dimensional threat to the truly Muslim nature of Chitrali society, are frequently visited by groups of Chitrali men, who form friendships with Kalasha people, and take the opportunity to drink their home-distilled wine. At the same time, when Chitralis visit these familiarly exotic places, they also seek to acquire knowledge about the places visited, asking questions about village history, agricultural practices, culinary traditions, and language, and they share the information gathered with friends, relatives, and neighbours on return to their homes.[14]

There is an important ethnographic dimension to Chitrali tours. This goes beyond merely encountering exotic others within their realm. Chitralis, rather, as anthropologists have been recently encouraged to do, recognize how 'heterogeneous people, things, processes are "thrown" together' in ways that challenge the 'completeness of the "cultural formations" to which one might be tempted to think they belong' (Candea 2007: 179). The emphasis they place on the pleasures of searching out knowledge about Chitral indicates the dangers of assuming that a pre-existing 'community of knowledge' lies behind Chitrali self-understanding (Markovits, Pouchepadass & Subrahmanyam 2003b: 20). Rather, Chitral's diversity is considered of local importance because it renders the region worthy of ceaseless exploration.

Many of the tours on which I have embarked have been with groups of young men in their early and mid-twenties; these groups were often made up of both Sunni and Shi'i Ismai'lis. In the context of village life, some tour-goers were known to hold hardened sectarian ideas – one of my Sunni companions, for example, went through a period of refusing to eat meat killed by Ismai'ls on the grounds that it was unlawful or *haram*. Yet during tours, these mixed Sunni-Ismai'li groups stayed in the houses of families belonging to religious communities other than their own, and shared food with one another (Sökefeld 1999). Not only long-distance labour migrants or elite cosmopolitan Muslims 'develop an increased capacity to recognise, account for and debate difference within their religion' (Mandaville 2004: 179). Chitrali tours are an everyday social practice that are often purposefully deployed by people – albeit temporarily – to distance themselves from the concerns of sectarian difference and status distinction that permeate everyday village life.

When travelling, thus, my friends pretended to be English tourists, Canadian Ismai'lis preachers, and Punjabi visitors from 'down Pakistan'. The shared experience of high-intensity performances which called upon people to enact identities very different from those associated with everyday village life was an especially memorable dimension of these tours. Their performances were often not particularly convincing: on one tour we made to a very remote Chitrali valley, my travelling companions told our countless hosts that their group was made up of two English-speaking Canadian Ismai'li preachers – their faces smeared with whitening cream – and one Chitrali man who was employed as their translator; I was told to play the son of a Pakistan Army General, and had to spend several minutes persuading my friends that it would be better if I told our hosts the truth – that I was a visiting student from Cambridge University. One morning, however, our supposedly Canadian Ismai'li missionary colleague woke up and asked his host in fluent Khowar if he would give his permission for them to leave. In one fell swoop the night's performance had been rendered an embarrassing farce. One of the group's quick-thinking members, acting out the role of the missionaries' translator, made a stab at saving the situating: 'Well done, well done, your Khowar is coming on very well', he said to his friend, before confidently turning to the host and saying, "See how quickly he's learned Khowar; how fast their minds work – we'll never learn English in a hundred years" '.

Village youths talk about these secret tours as proof of their capacity to outwit their parents and evade doing hard agricultural work at home. At the same time, they also demonstrate the uneducated simplicity (*sadahagi*) of villagers living in more 'backward' (*pasmanedah*) villages than their own. Nevertheless, parents appear to tolerate and even encourage such forms of behaviour as indicators that their children are witty (*namakeen*), independent-minded 'lovers of life'. The tales of extravagant youthful tours become an important way in which villagers remember their own childhood and applaud the cunningness (*chalaki*) of their fellow villagers. Tours are often recorded for memory on video cassettes that are shown repeatedly in the houses of villagers – these cassettes stand both as testament to the ways in which young village men endured unthinking hardships during their journeys; and as proof of their ability to have fun, outwit, and make fools of the people they met.

In his work on rural Lebanon, Michael Gilsenan (1996) has documented the ways in which 'the youth' constantly tested one another and 'young men' in their rhetorical and performative ability by engaging in 'contests of mockery', for example; artfully engaging in these contests allowed youths to stake their claim to being considered as young men. Embarking on physically testing tours, during which young men also demonstrate their capacity to trick, outwit, and deceive fellow Chitralis, is one such important way that Chitral's youth (*nau juan*) stake their claims to manhood (*moshigari*). At the same time, touring is about more than contests of trickery alone. Tours an important way in which young Chitralis forge complex 'structures' (Das 2007: 158) of emotional attachment to their locality; they are also a social practice that cultivates young village minds with curiosity as to their wider world whilst also developing locally valued skills for the acquisition and sharing of knowledge.

Conclusion

By exploring the role played by tours in the constitution of Chitral as a regional totality defined not by its homogeneous ethnic, religious, or linguistic identity, but as a socially heterogeneous place that offers the potential for being Chitrali Muslim according to very different performative registers, this chapter has sought to contribute to debate concerning the relationship between Islam, modernity, and politics in two major ways. Firstly, it has focused on local practices of mobility that build on a long-standing culture of Persianate travel whilst also reflecting newer anxieties about mental and emotional balance that villagers express as being a product of the 'era of speed' in which they say they are now living. Far from Chitral being a dead space of immobile villagers who inhabit sub-proletarian habituses (e.g. Derluguian 2005), mobility is central to the ways in which its young men are trained in locally valued modes of inhabiting, understanding, and perceiving their world. Through tours, young Chitrali Muslims hone their capacity to be witty, funny, clever, and strategic adults capable of evading the multiple claims that will forever be placed upon them by fellow village people; and enacting forms of sociality that are appropriate to particular places and social contexts.

Many Chitralis see tours as playing an important role in ensuring that village life does not become intellectually stagnant or morally corrupt, notable because Chitral is a mountainous region of Pakistan's North-West Frontier where unemployment, migration to Pakistan's cities as well as the Persian Gulf, and support for Islamist political parties are all important features of daily life. It is tempting to imagine that radical and deeply sectarian forms of Muslim self-understanding would be a focus for enthusiastic support amongst village youth living in such a setting. What I have emphasized, however, is not simply that the coherence of reform-minded forms of Islam are contested by Muslims living in this politically volatile setting, but also that many Chitralis seek to nurture and sustain very different strands of Muslim life alongside them. Prominent amongst these are the forms of work they invest into cultivating complex forms of emotional and intellectual attachment to their region and a curiosity about its heterogeneity.

Secondly, a number of recent studies have highlighted the role played by Muslim religious habits, practices, and modes of expression in shaping the ethical dispositions of piety-minded Muslims living in cities such as Cairo, Istanbul, and Beirut (Deeb 2006;

Henkel 2005; Hirschkind 2006; Mahmood 2005). Chitrali touring, in contrast, cultivates a modality of understanding and perceiving the wider world founded not on the
active cultivation of embodied ethical dispositions but in the appreciation of a mindful,
if often sceptical, curiosity about heterogeneity. As Chitralis move through their region,
they continually invest it with different types of significance and meaning. They talk
about contrasting emotional and moral qualities and memories as adhering to different
types of spaces and places: the cruelty of the region's courtly past, the significance of its
rich tradition of Persianate Sufic poetry, and opportunities for romance and sexual
flirtation, for example. These different spaces sit jaggedly alongside one another. Yet
they are connected by people who move within and between them and reflect on what
they say, do and, importantly, see as they do so. In spite of the pressures placed upon
Chitrali Muslims to conform to Islamic doctrinal standards, during the course of their
tours Chitralis expect one another to question, reflect upon, and interrogate the conditions of their everyday lives.

The cultivation of such modes of critically perceiving the world stand in contrast not
only to anthropological depictions of Islamic ethical selfhood amongst piety-minded
Muslims in urban settings, but also to the emphasis that young men in Karachi place on
'somatic' (Verkaaik 2004: 7) forms of masculinity within which personal dignity is
achieved above all else through displays of 'physical strength and courage' (2004: 6).
Drawing monolithic distinctions between 'rural' and 'urban' Islam has been rightly
discredited in recent years (notably Mundy 1995). Nevertheless, considering comparisons of contrasting yet interactive forms of Muslim self-understanding as enacted in
cities, small towns, and villages illuminates much about the complexity of the Muslim
world today. Above all else, making such comparisons raises important questions about
the extent to which the expectation that people should question and think critically
about the conditions of their everyday lives necessarily reflects the engraftment of
liberal secular standards onto unsuspecting non-liberal subjects. In Chitral's villages,
religious knowledge, far from being marginalized under the conditions of secular
governance (Mahmood 2005), has expanded in strength and political importance in
recent years. In this world of increasingly prescribed faith, many Chitralis cultivate
other strands of mindful existence alongside those associated with the need to live
virtuous pious Muslim lives, and these build upon complex local traditions, such as
travel. The expectations that Chitralis have of one another to live questioning and
thoughtful lives are not, in short, reducible to a model that contrasts Western notions
of secular-liberal autonomy with those associated with Islamic traditions of discipline
and piety. Instead, they ask for careful attention to be paid to the everyday factors that
lead people to cultivate or problematize the claims of reflexive, independent, and
critical selfhood at shifting political, religious, moral, historical, and personal junctures,
and in particular places.

ACKNOWLEDGMENTS

This chapter would not have been possible without the friendship and support of many people in Chitral.
Among the most helpful of my fellow travellers there include: Hazar Baig, Sher Hussain, Shamsul Haq
Qamar, Mir Hussain Shah, Muzafar Hussain Shah, and Shamsudin. I have conducted fieldwork in Chitral
since 1999 with the generous support of Trinity College, Cambridge, an Economic and Social Research
Council research studentship, and grants from the British Academy Society for South Asian Studies and the
Nuffield Foundation. This chapter has benefited from insightful comment and criticism from Filippo Osella,
Benjamin Soares, Diana Ibañez Tirado, Lucilla Marsden, and Mathew Carey.

NOTES

[1] On the pilgrimage to Mecca, see Delaney (1990) and Hammoudi (2005). For work on shrine visitation, see Tapper (1990) and Werbner (2004). Metcalf (1993) explores the significance of preaching tours organized by worldwide movements of 'Islamic reform', such as the Tablighi Jama'at.

[2] See also: Deeb (2006); Henkel (2007); and Hirschkind (2006). Henkel (2007) brings a consideration of place-making to the constitution of Muslim subjectivity in Istanbul.

[3] The hajj has long formed an important dimension of the 'religious imagination' (Eickelman & Piscatori 1990) of Chitrali Muslims – Chitral was located on important overland pilgrimage routes used by Central Asian Muslims travelling to Mecca. Elderly Chitrali people continue to talk about Chinese 'Turks' passing through their villages, staying in their houses, and sometimes also taking wives in the region. Today, some Chitralis complain that the expansion of state-organized mass pilgrimages has cheapened the hajj's importance for the region's Muslims.

[4] Anthropologists have noted the ways in which pilgrimage shapes personal and collective experiences of space at different scales. In the case of Hinduism, these scales may include those of India and the village (Gold 1988) or involve complex modes of time-space compression as Hindu diasporic communities map India's sacred landscape elsewhere (Eisenlohr 2007).

[5] See Willerslev for a comparable debate in the anthropology of hunter gatherers concerning the degree to which 'indigenous animism ... represent[s] a basic affinity between the world and other beings that Western society has lost' (2007: 187). As Willerslev illustrates in his monograph on the Siberian Yukaghirs, 'we can only have an experience of a world if we are conscious subjects of experience who can distinguish ourselves as subjects and an external world that transcends our subjective experience of it' (2007: 187).

[6] Such mosques stand in contrast to older, mud-brick, flat-roofed village mosques decorated with Chitrali wooden carvings.

[7] Shi'a Ismai'lis are taught to believe in the spiritual leadership of the Aga Khan (e.g. Daftary 1990); there have been moments of communal sectarian violence between the region's two communities.

[8] Chitralis living and working in labour camps in the Gulf often talk about yearning to visit villages on their return home. They say that they find life in Gulf labour camps more difficult than their fellow workers: 'We are accustomed to travel and freedom', I am often told, 'and this makes life in the camp very difficult'.

[9] For scholarly debates on the role played by circulatory forms of mobility in the historical constitution of Indian society, see Markovits, Pouchepadass & Subrahmanyam (2003a).

[10] All names are pseudonyms.

[11] On the importance of sound and listening to Muslims' subjectivity in Cairo, see Hirschkind (2006).

[12] Villages also make distinctions between men whose status allows them to spend their days in leisurely travel and others whose tours are a reckless 'waste of expenses' (*fuzul kharj*); these distinctions about the appropriateness of travel are often made on the basis of a person's status and genealogy.

[13] On Kalasha society, see Parkes (2001).

[14] Many Kalasha people complain about the intrusive curiosity of Chitralis, who are accused of disturbing the peace of life in their remote valleys, staring at their unveiled women, and pestering them to sell bottles of 'grape water' made for important ceremonial gatherings.

REFERENCES

ALAM, M. & S. SUBRAHMANYAM 1996. Discovering the familiar: notes on the travel account of Ananad Ram Mukhlis. *South Asia Research* **16**, 131-54.

———— & ———— 2004. The making of a Munshi. *Comparative Studies of South Asia, Africa and the Middle East* **24**: **2**, 61-72

———— & ———— 2007. *Indo-Persian travels in the age of discoveries, 1400-1800.* Cambridge: University Press.

AUGÉ, M. 1995. *Non-places: introduction to an anthropology of supermoderntity* (trans. J. Howe). London: Verso.

BAYAT, A. 2007. Islamism and the politics of fun. *Public Culture* **19**, 433-59.

CANDEA, M. 2007. Arbitrary locations: in defence of the bounded field site. *Journal of the Royal Anthropological Institute* (N.S.) **13**, 167-84.

CLIFFORD, J. 1997. *Routes: travel and translation in the late twentieth century.* Cambridge, Mass.: Harvard University Press.

COLE, J. 2002. Iranian culture and South Asia, 1500-1900. In *Iran and the surrounding world: interactions in culture and cultural politics* (eds) N. Keddie & R. Matthee, 15-35. Seattle: University of Washington Press.

DAFTARY, F. 1990. *The Ismailis: their history and doctrines*. Cambridge: University Press.

DAS, V. 2007. *Life and worlds: violence and the descent into the ordinary*. Berkeley: University of California Press.

DEEB, L. 2006. *An enchanted modern: gender and public piety in Shi'i Lebanon*. Princeton: University Press.

DELANEY, C. 1990. The hajj: sacred and secular. *American Ethnologist* **17**, 513-30.

DERLUGUIAN, G. 2005. *Bourdieu's secret admirer in the Caucasus: a world-system biography*. Chicago: University Press.

EICKELMAN, D. & J. PISCATORI (eds) 1990. *Muslim travellers: pilgrimage, migration, and the religious imagination*. Berkeley: University of California Press.

EISENLOHR, P. 2007. *Little India: diaspora, time and ethno-linguistic belonging in Hindu Mauritius*. Berkeley: University of California Press.

EUBEN, R. 2006. *Journeys to the other shore: Muslim and western travellers in search of knowledge*. Princeton: University Press.

GILSENAN, M. 1996. *Lords of the Lebanese marches: violence and narrative in an Arab society*. London: I.B. Tauris.

GOLD, A. 1988. *Fruitful journeys: the ways of Rajasthani pilgrims*. Berkeley: University of California Press.

GRAY, J. 2006. Open spaces and dwelling places: being at home on hill farms in the Scottish borders. In *The anthropology of space and place: locating culture* (eds) S.M. Low & D. Lawrence-Zúñinga, 224-44. Oxford: Blackwell.

HAMMOUDI, A. 2005. *A season in Mecca: narrative of a pilgrimage*. Cambrige: Polity.

HANNERZ, U. 1996. *Transnational connections: culture, people, places*. London: Routledge.

HENKEL, H. 2005. 'Between belief and unbelief lies the performance of *salāt*': meaning and efficacy of a Muslim ritual. *Journal of the Royal Anthropological Institute* (N.S.) **11**, 487-507.

——— 2007. The location of Islam: inhabiting Istanbul in a Muslim way. *American Ethnologist* **34**, 57-70.

HIRSCH, E. 1995. Landscape: between place and space. In *The anthropology of landscape: perspectives on place and space* (eds) E. Hirsch & M. O'Hanlon, 1-30. Oxford: University Press.

——— 2001. When was modernity in Melanesia? *Social Anthropology* **9**, 131-46.

——— 2006. Landscape, myth and time. *Journal of Material Culture* **11**, 151-65.

HIRSCHKIND, C. 2006. *The ethical soundscape: cassette sermons and Islamic counterpublics*. New York: Columbia University Press.

HO, E. 2006. *The graves of Tarim: genealogy and mobility across the Indian Ocean*. Berkeley: University of California Press.

HUMPHREY, C. 1995. Chiefly and shamanist landscapes in Mongolia. In *The anthropology of landscape: perspectives on place and space* (eds) E. Hirsch & M. O'Hanlon, 135-62. Oxford: University Press.

LAMBEK, M. 1998. The Sakalava poiesis of history: realizing the past through spirit possession in Madagascar. *American Ethnologist* **25**: 2, 106-27.

MAHMOOD, S. 2003. Ethical formation and the politics of individual autonomy in contemporary Egypt. *Social Research* **70**, 837-66.

——— 2005. *Politics of piety: the Islamic revival and the feminist subject*. Princeton: University Press.

MAJEED, J. 2007. *Autobiography, travel and postcolonial national identity: Gandhi, Nehru and Iqbal*. Basingstoke: Palgrave Macmillan.

MAKDISI, U. 2000. *The culture of sectarianism: community, history and violence in nineteenth-century Ottoman Lebanon*. Berkeley: University of California Press.

——— & P. SILVERSTEIN 2007. Introduction: memory and violence in the Middle East and North Africa. In *Memory and violence in the Middle East and North Africa* (eds) U. Makdisi & P. Silverstein, 1-24. Bloomington: Indiana University Press.

MANDAVILLE, P. 2004. *Transnational Muslim politics: reimagining the umma*. London: Routledge.

MARKOVITS, C., J. POUCHEPADASS & S. SUBRAHMANYAM 2003a. *Society and circulation: mobile people and itinerant cultures in South Asia, 1750-1950*. New Delhi: Permanent Black.

———, ——— & ——— 2003b. Introduction. In *Society and circulation: mobile people and itinerant cultures in south Asia, 1750-1950* (eds) C. Markovits, J. Pouchepadass & S. Subrahmanyam, 1-22. New Delhi: Permanent Black.

MARSDEN, M. 2005. *Living Islam: Muslim religious experience in Pakistan's North-West Frontier province*. Cambridge: University Press.

———— 2007a. Islam, political authority and emotion in northern Pakistan. *Contributions to Indian Sociology* **41**, 41-80.

———— 2007b. Love and elopement in northern Pakistan. *Journal of the Royal Anthropological Institute* (N.S.) **13**, 91-108.

———— 2008. Muslim cosmopolitans? Transnational life in northern Pakistan. *Journal of Asian Studies* **67**, 213-48.

METCALF, B. 1993. Living hadith in the Tabligh-i Jamaat. *Journal of Asian Studies* **52**: 584-608.

MUNDY, M. 1995. *Domestic government: kinship, community and polity in north Yemen.* London: I.B. Tauris.

MURTAZA, M. 1982. *New history of Chitral* (based on the original Persian text of Mirza Muhammad Ghufran; revised and enlarged with additional research of Late His Highness Sir Nasir-ul-Mulk by Mirza Ghulam Murtaza; trans. from the Urdu version into English by Wazir Ali Shah). Chitral.

NASR, S.V.R. 2005. National identities and the India-Pakistan conflict. In *The India-Pakistan conflict: an enduring rivalry* (ed.) T.V. Paul, 178–201. Cambridge: University Press.

OSSMAN, S. 2007. Introduction. In *Places we share: migration, subjectivity and global mobility,* S. Ossman, 1-16. Lanham, Md.: Lexington Books.

PARKES, P. 1996. Indigenous polo and the politics of regional identity. In *Sport, identity and ethnicity* (ed.) J. MacClancy, 43-57. Oxford: Berg.

———— 2001. Unwrapping rudeness: inverted etiquette in an egalitarian enclave. In *An anthropology of indirect communication* (eds) J. Hendry & C.W. Watson, 232-51. London: Routledge.

PARKIN, D. 1991. *Sacred void: spatial images of work and ritual amongst the Giriama.* Cambridge: University Press.

POUCHEPADASS, J. 2003. Itinerant kings and touring officials: circulation and a modality of power in India, 1700-1947. In *Society and circulation: mobile people and itinerant cultures in south Asia, 1750-1950* (eds) C. Markovits, J. Pouchepadass & S. Subrahmanyam, 240-74. New Delhi: Permanent Black.

PRATT, M. 1992. *Imperial eyes: travel writing and transculturation.* London: Routledge.

SAULI, A. 2003. Circulation and authority: police, public space and territorial control in the Punjab, 1861-1920. In *Society and circulation: mobile people and itinerant cultures in south Asia, 1750-1950* (eds) C. Markovits, J. Pouchepadass & S. Subrahmanyam, 215-39. New Delhi: Permanent Black.

SÖKEFELD, M. 1999. Debating self, identity, and culture in anthropology. *Current Anthropology* **40**, 417-47.

STALEY, J. 1982. *Words for my brother: travels between the Hindu Kush and the Himalayas.* Karachi: Oxford University Press.

STOLLER, P. 1994. Embodying colonial memories. *American Anthropologist* **96**, 634-48.

TAPPER, N. 1990. *Ziyaret:* gender, movement, and exchange in a Turkish community. In *Muslim travellers: pilgrimage, migration, and the religious imagination* (eds) D. Eickelman & J. Piscatori, 236-55. London: Routledge.

TILLY, C. 2006. Introduction: identity, place and landscape. *Journal of Material Culture* **11**, 7-32.

TSING, A. 1993. *In the realm of a diamond queen: marginality in an out-of-the-way place.* Princeton: University Press.

VERKAAIK, O. 2004. *Migrants and militants: fun and urban violence in Karachi.* Princeton: University Press.

WAGGONER, M. 2005. Irony, embodiment, and the 'critical attitude': engaging Saba Mahmood's critique of secular morality. *Culture and Religion* **6**, 237-61.

WERBNER, P. 2004. *Pilgrims of love: ethnography of a global Sufi cult.* London: Hurst.

WILLERSLEV, R. 2007. *Soul hunters: hunting, animism and personhood among the Siberian Yukaghirs.* Berkeley: University of California Press.

ZAMAN, Q. 2002. *The ulama in contemporary Islam: custodians of change.* Princeton: University Press.

5

Muslim politics in postcolonial Kenya: negotiating knowledge on the double-periphery

KAI KRESSE *Zentrum Moderner Orient*

Muslim politics, according to Eickelman and Piscatori, 'constitutes the field on which an intricate pattern of cooperation and contest over form, practice, and interpretation takes place' (1996: 21). The distinctiveness of Muslim politics, then, is linked to 'the specific, if evolving, values, symbols, ideas, and traditions that constitute "Islam" ' (1996: 21) in particular places, and research should consider the multiple contexts of such politics. It follows that the distinct character of regional Muslim politics evolves out of mediation and negotiation processes that constitute Islam in specific geographical and historical contexts. Here, I explore Muslim politics in a particular postcolonial setting, the Kenyan coast. Drawing from Asad's approach to Islam as a 'discursive tradition' (1986), I investigate how regional practices and interpretations of everyday life in sociality and language make reference to, 'knowledge', and how they overlap, intersect, and feed into (or alter) the negotiation of Islam in coastal Kenya.

History and power constitute two fundamental axes underpinning a proper understanding of Muslim politics. As Zaman has argued, Islam is shaped not just by a continuous interactive link between the present and the past, 'but also by the manner in which relations of power and other forms of contestation and conflict impinge on any definition of what it is to be a Muslim' (2002: 6). Here, I examine internal negotiations of difference and sameness among Muslims in coastal Kenya. I also consider how these processes are influenced by (and may in turn have to be balanced out against) external, non-Muslim forces and pressures, like those generated by the state. In order to reflect upon the specific postcolonial dynamics of Kenyan politics, I use Chabal and Daloz's paradigm for postcolonial African politics, 'the political instrumentalization of disorder' (1999: 13, 155).

Muslims in coastal Kenya
Since Independence from Britain in 1963, when upcountry Christians under President Jomo Kenyatta took over the rule of the Coast province and implemented 'Africanization' policies on all administrative levels, coastal Kenyan Muslims have been on the

receiving end of postcolonial politics.[1] Many of them were regarded as 'less Kenyan' by the new rulers, and made to feel as outsiders, due to their Swahili, Arab, South Asian, or Persian descent. Political tensions were not surprising, since before Independence many coastal Muslims had resisted the political integration of the Coastal Strip, the so-called 'Mwambao' (which belonged to the Sultanate of Zanzibar and was administered by the British), into Kenya. Instead, they had campaigned for Coastal Independence (Brennan 2008; Salim 1970). Bitter memories of this failed endeavour live on in vivid discussions in coastal towns today. During postcolonial rule, Kenyan Muslims have increasingly organized themselves more assertively as 'Muslims' in the public arena, partly in response to the discrimination they saw themselves facing as a neglected minority.[2] Mutual suspicions between Muslims and the state have continued, with tensions and anxieties flaring up after each of the terrorist attacks that affected Kenya as well as the wider world: on the US embassy in Nairobi in August 1998; the events of September 11, 2001 in the United States; and on a beach hotel and aeroplane near Mombasa in 2002 (see Seesemann 2007b). These were condemned by Muslim communities and their representatives.

As elsewhere in the Muslim world, a different kind of pressure towards more assertive public engagement 'as Muslims' has come from within the Muslim community itself, through the growing ideological impact of Islamic trans-local networks on local Muslim discourse and practice. Especially since the 1980s, with the return of students who had studied in the Middle East, ideological confrontations between different groups of Islamic 'reformists' and their others have become more agitated (see Bakari 1995). This is visible, for instance, in the emphatic rejection of regionally established Muslim practices, like the celebration of the birthday of Prophet Muhammad (*maulidi*), the visit to graves of deceased pious people (*ziyara*), and other Sufi-related practices by so-called 'Wahhabi'[3] reformists. Islamic reformism in East Africa, initiated and shouldered from within the region since the 1930s, displays liberating as well as dogmatic features in a kind of 'dialectic', opening social debate on some issues while closing it on others (see Kresse 2003; for South Asia, see Osella & Osella 2008a). Contrary to simplifying descriptions in popular and academic writing, Islamic 'reformism' in Africa as elsewhere comes in different shapes and forms and is ambivalent in character (a potentially creative as well as destructive force).[4] The increase of public attention on Muslim identity through reformist debates pushed coastal Kenyan Muslims to deliberate their stances more consciously.

Taking these aspects into account, we can say that there is a two-way front on which 'Muslim identity' is negotiated by coastal Muslims: an external one, *vis-à-vis* the post-colonial state; and an internal one, within the *umma* (the community of believers) itself. The internal differences and divisions are most significant since this is where the real negotiation of paradigms of interpretation takes place, the contest about what really counts and is publicly acceptable as Islamic practice. Yet the framework conditions of the postcolonial setting also influence and affect these internal dynamics.

I argue that two aspects shaping the everyday life experience of coastal Muslims should be considered when seeking to understand postcolonial Muslim politics: first, the setting of a 'double-periphery' on the Kenyan coast; and, second, the social dynamics around a 'knowledge economy' within the Muslim community. I use 'double-periphery' to refer to coastal Muslims as situated on two peripheries at the same time, namely the postcolonial state and the *umma*. For coastal Muslims, life on the Kenyan periphery – *vis-à-vis* a state governed and administered by upcountry Christians –

reflects the continuation of historical tensions between coast and upcountry (*pwani* and *bara*) which has also involved channels of serfdom and slavery (*utumwa*). These tensions are also expressed in religious and ethnic ideologies which have pitted coastal people (*wapwani*) against those from upcountry (*wabara*), Muslims against Christians (and others), or, in the simplifying language of ethnicity, 'Arabs' or 'Swahili' against 'Africans'. These basic oppositions are somewhat distorting (as there are no clear boundaries between these groups) yet they are used in political discourse, both among coastal Muslims and between them and others (see also McIntosh 2009).

The double-periphery
Throughout the postcolonial era, coastal Muslims have been ruled by upcountry Christians and, as I heard on many occasions, felt treated like second-class citizens. The most common complaints against upcountry governance included the following: the revenues of Kilindini Harbour in Mombasa (the biggest in East Africa) being channelled upcountry and not invested in the coast; lucrative fishing and mangrove-pole trade being restricted; no significant investments benefiting the coastal community being made; education being deliberately kept at a low level (with, for example, the worst teachers sent to the coast); difficulty for Muslims in obtaining identity cards and passports, or other legal documents (like title deeds); drug trafficking and abuse in coastal towns[5] not being controlled but seemingly being condoned by the authorities. In short, it is a common sentiment among coastal Muslims that consecutive upcountry governments have worked to decrease their economic prosperity, diminish their educational perspectives, and undermine their chances for the future (see Ali A. Mazrui 1993; A. Mazrui 1994; A.M. Mazrui & Shariff 1994; Hoorweg, Foeken & Obudho 2000). Thus for many coastal Muslims, national politics *are* upcountry politics which seek to keep the coast weak and internally divided, echoing the colonial *divide et impera*. In the same vein, comments contrasting an often mythically romanticized 'golden' (colonial) past with the bleak (postcolonial) present are not infrequently made, mostly, but not exclusively, by older people. These features characterize one side of the double-periphery within which Kenyan coastal Muslims are situated.

The other side of the double-periphery refers to the position of coastal Muslims within the Muslim world. Here, too, a sense of living on the 'periphery' can sometimes be observed *vis-à-vis* the Middle East. However, we have to differentiate very carefully since the Swahili coast has been part of Muslim networks for a very long period. Islam was present from around 800 CE (Horton & Middleton 2000; Pouwels 1987). Reliable climatic conditions facilitated sailboat travel across the Western Indian Ocean, pilgrimage to Mecca, and thus social, economic, and religious interaction and exchange within the *umma* from an early stage. The Swahili coast is not a Muslim periphery in a strong historical and geographical sense of 'distance' in time or space. Yet in everyday life, there are ways in which 'felt distance' brings a sense of being on the periphery into play, as Lambek (1990: 25) has noted for Mayotte. While arguments against a simple division between an Arab Islamic heartland and a lesser periphery (e.g. Reese 2004; Seesemann 2007a: 38) are analytically compelling, such simple oppositions are at times appropriated and deployed by local actors.

Next to their pride in the long history of Islam on the Swahili coast, Muslims also harbour insecurities about their standing within the *umma*. They are conscious of their limited ability to use Arabic, the language of the Qur'an. They also feel economically disadvantaged, especially in comparison to wealthy Gulf and Middle Eastern countries where many youths aspire to work. Educationally, established institutions of Islamic scholarship (of different sectarian orientation) based in countries like Saudi Arabia, Egypt, Pakistan, Iran, or Sudan offer scholarships and funding opportunities through their respective networks, thus further increasing a sense of unequal charity-based relationships. Generally, coastal Muslims may see themselves as situated on the receiving side of patron-client relationships within the Muslim world (of Islamic knowledge, of economic and moral support). Considering that they feel treated as second-class citizens in their own country, the question arises whether they are also regarded as second-class citizens within the *umma*. These tensions are present in social discourse and practice and feed into the framework within which Muslim politics on the Kenyan coast have to be understood. Kenyan Muslims seem 'marginalized both within the national context of Kenya and within the international context of the Muslim *umma*' (Seesemann 2007a: 38).

The knowledge economy

Michael Lambek has used knowledge 'as an analytic tool' (1993: 10; cf. 1990) for the study of a Muslim community in Mayotte. Following a hermeneutical approach to ethnography, he explores how knowledge in different ways and on different levels shapes social practice. He also addresses the social relevance of knowledge in Islam generally, especially for the moral task of being a good Muslim. Muslims have an obligation to acquire knowledge: the Qur'an as God's word and the accounts of the role model of Prophet Muhammad (*hadith*) should be known in order to feel sure about what is right and wrong. Thus knowledge provides guidance, orientation, and justification for practice, through knowledgeable people who teach others. Knowledge is involved in granting authority and leadership yet also in challenging or undermining it, by those who know the sources and how to present them. From this perspective, knowledge is a kind of organizing principle. A wealth of complex sub-fields of social interaction become visible where knowledge is central to exchange relationships among social actors. I use the term 'knowledge economy' for such dynamics, and I will show more concretely how this applies to the Swahili coast, where references to knowledge are variously embedded in social interaction among Muslims.

The term 'knowledge economy' also draws from Benjamin Soares' elaborations upon a 'prayer economy' in a West African context with strong Sufi traditions (Soares 1996; 2005). Soares uses this term – after Murray Last (1988) – to discuss how exchange relationships of commodities and services for prayer are ranked around 'saints' and their networks, thus marking the wider field of social relationships more generally. Here, I argue that reciprocal patterns and obligations exist also in the ways in which knowledge, and particularly Islamic knowledge, is used, sought, passed on, and exchanged among Kenyan Muslims. In this sense, the term 'knowledge economy' indicates an explicit interest in knowledge (and practices related to it), as part of a social economy of exchange. When investigating this further, it is not always possible to distinguish clearly between knowledge and claims to it. Within the social contestation and negotiation of knowledge, the intertwined nature of the relationship between knowledge and rhetoric is observeable in the way speakers or writers seek to win over or capture their audiences. They often tend to present their own position as a valid normative interpretation supported by a majority consensus (see Kresse 2007b).

Being Muslim in Mombasa

Let me introduce the scenario of Muslims in Mombasa by means of a fictional vignette, written in 1929 by the Islamic scholar Sheikh al-Amin Mazrui (d. 1947), the initiator of Salafi-inspired Islamic reformism on the Swahili coast. Influenced by Muhammad Abduh and Rashid Rida and his journal *al-Manar*, from which he acquired a sense of the importance of journalism to bring about change, he wrote, 'Among the modern things that show people good ways, and that bring good thoughts into their heads, and that wake up their hearts, and that even make them stand up and go forward, there is nothing like the newspaper'.[6] He subsequently published two Swahili Islamic newspapers, *Sahifa* (literally 'page') and *al-Islah* ('reform'), that combined social commentary and critique with Islamic education. The dialogue below was first published in *Sahifa*, a weekly paper written by Sheikh al-Amin himself (see M.K. Mazrui 1980) of which about a hundred copies were distributed every Friday. The text was reprinted in 1978, on the front page of the Swahili Islamic quarterly *Sauti ya Haki* (Sound of Justice), edited by Sheikh Muhammad Kasim Mazrui (d. 1982), al-Amin's student and relative.

The scene was presented under the heading 'An educational conversation: truth in a joke, and a joke in truth ...' (*Mazungumzo ya ilmu: kweli katika mzaha na mzaha katika kweli*). Readers should imagine – as local readers would – the five speakers involved sitting on a stone bench in front of a house (or mosque), thus creating an informal gathering, or *baraza*.[7] For a more concrete and vivid picture, readers should imagine the speakers as elderly men – those who are supposedly well versed in jokes as well as truths – wearing white gowns (*kanzu*) and white embroidered caps (*kofia*):

> *Abdulla*: I hear that according to Imam Hanbali it is forbidden to eat a chicken that has eaten dirt, and even to eat its eggs.
>
> *Ali*: What! If that is true, then all chickens would be forbidden to eat, as well as their eggs, because there is no chicken that does not eat any dirt. [Hanbali's] *madhhab* [legal school of Islam] is a difficult one, and not measured!
>
> *Swaleh*: You remind me, Abdulla; I have heard that for Imam Malik it is permitted to eat a cat.
>
> *Hemed*: Sallaala [expression of surprise or wonder]! That's not a real *madhhab*, that. That's like French people! They indeed eat every little creature!
>
> *Swaleh*: You! And a pig is not unclean for him [Imam Malik]; yet it is forbidden to eat it.
>
> *Hemed*: That is surprising, a pig is not dirty, so if a dog eats a pig, what does that mean?
>
> *Swaleh*: And even a dog is not considered dirty by him.
>
> *Hemed*: What's that – aah, ah! I can't agree with that. What's that with that Malik *madhhab* of yours!
>
> *Nassir*: I have heard something even more strange about the *madhhab* of Imam Hanafi.
>
> *All*: Oh – well, spill the news!
>
> *Nassir*: I hear that for Abu Hanafi if someone marries, and he stays here and his wife is somewhere in Arabia, if the wife bears a child six months after the marriage, then the child is considered the child of that husband here, even if he has not gone to Arabia at all, nor has his wife come here!
>
> *Hemed*: Mama! Mama! Sallala! Those are no real *madhhabs*, those. That doesn't even go into the head of a human being. The Banyani [Hindu Indians] are usually known for such things!
>
> *Ali*: But those three *madhhabs* are heavy! One tells us to eat chicken, one of them feeds us cats, and another one makes permissible what the others forbid! There is just no *madhhab* like Shafii [most common *madhhab* in East Africa], bwana! That *madhhab* is centred and well balanced.
>
> [...]
>
> *Ali*: Have you heard that a *mganga* [traditional healer] is considered an infidel by those (other) three *madhhabs*?
>
> *Hemed*: La-ilaha-illa-alla! We have never heard that from any of our sheikhs, ever, that a *mganga* should be an infidel; and all the people who went to a *mganga* for consultation were never ever told that that is an act of heresy.

Nasir: If it were really true that such matters were not permitted, our scholars would not have failed to inform us, and would have prohibited us from that. Ah! Here these imams have got it even more wrong.

Abdalla: There is some even more extraordinary news.

Ali: Ok, let's hear.

Abdalla: Well, [the scholars] Subky and Adhrai, and Ibn Swaleh and Ibn Hajar have said that to play the *matwari* and *zumari* [small hand-held drums] is forbidden by Islamic law, and that even to play the *matwari* during *maulidi* and to 'dance' or move rhythmically with it is like Hindu worship! And Ibn Hajar said that to pray to/for the Prophet Muhammad (i.e. to stand up while his birth is being praised) during *maulidi* is *bida* [an unacceptable religious innovation].

Hemed: Is that right! That really sounds like the Wahhabi *madhhab*! Our sheikhs and *masharifu* [descendants of the Prophet] play the drums, and they 'dance' – if that was worship, would they do that?!! And to give special praises to the Prophet is now *bida*? By the repentance of the Lord! We are hearing strange things these days!

(commentator:)

Khulasa: And this is indeed how the people of Mombasa are. We do not follow something because it is right, nor because it is supported by the majority of scholars; nor do we follow that or this particular person – but we follow our own people only. May God forgive us (al-Amin Mazrui 1978 [1929]).

'This is indeed how the people of Mombasa are', says the author of this humorous, yet bitingly self-critical text in 1929, a statement endorsed by the editor of *Sauti ya Haki* by reprinting it in 1978. There are indeed commonalities with recent discussions that allow us to use this text as an entry-point to contemporary Muslim politics. Some of the prominent contested issues in current ideological disputes are mentioned here. As elsewhere in the Muslim world, these are ranked around the so-called '*bida* debate' (about unacceptable innovation in Islamic practice); the celebration of *maulidi* and ritual behaviour associated with *maulidi*; local healing practices (*uganga*); and the status of *sheikhs* (traditional scholars) and *sharifs* (descendants of the Prophet Muhammad) (see, e.g., Kresse 2003; 2006).

There are several important features in the *baraza* vignette that illustrate crucial aspects of sociality, interaction, and the perception of how the world is (and should be) among urban Muslims in Mombasa. Among them are:

- the *baraza* conversation with its typical elements of humour and teasing;
- the insistence on a supposedly unquestionable and clearly defined group identity (Shafii, with local traditions of ritual practice, healing, and Islamic knowledge) – which is pointedly questioned and ridiculed in the commentator's concluding remarks;
- the way 'knowledge' and its invocation, negotiation, interrogation, and its relevance for practice are major underlying themes – even though satirically portrayed.

The commentator's remark at the end of the dialogue is revealing. His plea to God, to 'forgive us', expresses criticism of his own community, 'the people of Mombasa'. As he says, they follow 'their own people only', irrespective of what they say or do or, more precisely, irrespective of whether their position is based on correct Islamic knowledge. This is a sin, the comment implies (despite the obvious touch), for which forgiveness is required. The wrongdoing is in blindly following others, not simply in one's lack of proper Islamic knowledge as such. What is criticized is that no serious interest in such knowledge is expressed, nor any sincere attempt made to seek guidance. This violates the principal demand to put effort into the acquisition of Islamic knowledge, to ascertain that one's actions are acceptable and in accordance with Islam proper. This responsibility, it is implied, all believers have for themselves (and *can* only have for themselves). What is flagged as reprehensible is ignoring one's obligation to act responsibly and with reference to proper knowledge, for the common good. This includes monitoring one's peers, 'commanding good and forbidding wrong' of them – a principle that characterizes the central ethical task for all Muslims across historical and sectarian divisions (see Cook 2000). The criticism of the five fictional Swahili elders of the *baraza* voiced in *Sauti ya Haki* is linked to this assumption of a basic obligation for all Muslims to act according to their best knowledge of Islam. Here, as in many other places in the Muslim world, there exists an implicit social hierarchy wherein those with greater degrees of Islamic knowledge are seen as closer to God and ascribed higher status. Likewise, they shoulder the responsibility to transmit this knowledge to others (e.g. Bowen 1993; Eickelman 1985; Lambek 1990; 1993; Loeffler 1988; Salvatore & Eickelman 2004).

In contrast, the attitude that the vignette's final comments reject can be coined in local Swahili terminology as one of *ukabila* (tribalism). As many Kenyans and analysts agree, this has long been an obstacle for the cultivation of a democracy that is truly national in outlook, and the adverse effects of *ukabila* are lamented upon by both Muslims and non-Muslims. During my fieldwork, I heard many such complaints by local Muslims who were also critical of their own community (see Kresse 2007a). For instance, I noted an Islamic scholar's characterization of the troubling disunity within the Kenyan Muslim community. He stated that 'today, we do not know our religion (*leo, sisi hatujui dini yetu*; see Kresse 2007b: 241) – and, 'Islam for us is tribalism' (*Uislamu kwetu ni ukabila*). This criticism of one's own group almost echoes Sheikh al-Amin's comments above. Here, too, the need for knowledge about Islam was expressed, now in order to cope with the challenges as a minority group in a 'Christian state', and contrasted with the frustrating reality of currently dominant Muslim practice, which often meant blindly following 'one's own' without any true concern for knowledge.

Sheikh al-Amin's efforts as an Islamic reformist were explicitly directed against such self-congratulatory rhetoric. Instead, he sought to raise Muslims' awareness about what happens around them, to develop and nurture a critical consciousness, and to use knowledge and education (secular and religious) as means to social liberation and self-determination. In this way, he was engaged in anti-colonial politics as well as efforts to unite East African Muslims, advocating the use of 'modernization' to them, so that they might not lose their educational advantage and political privileges to the upcountry people (see also Farsy 1989; Kresse 2003; Lacunza Balda 1993; Pouwels 1981). Particularly with a view to knowledge and education, he warned his Muslim peers of a future 'black danger' (*khatari nyeusi*), prophesying that 'us coastal people' (*sisi watu wa pwani*) would become 'the ignorant people' (*wajinga*), due to their rejection of secular education (al-Amin Mazrui 1955 [1944]: 33). Overall, he pushed towards an Islamically shaped modernity that is both regional and trans-regional in outlook and inspiration. His ideas became popular among East African Muslims because they addressed specific local issues and problems such as colonialism, education, and development with a view to wider contexts and frameworks (for similar visions of Islamic modernities in South Asia, see Osella & Osella 2008b; Robinson 2008; for Lebanon, see Deeb 2006).

His prophetic vision, of coastal Muslims becoming 'backward' in comparison to their compatriots, became real in postcolonial Kenya, and as the coastal region came to lag behind educationally, Sheikh al-Amin's political and social agenda remained pressing. This must have influenced the decision to reprint the dialogue above in 1978 in *Sauti ya Haki*. As the editor Sheikh Muhammad Kasim Mazrui commented, 'The goal of this article is clear, it is to show that the state of being of people during times when they are ruled by others is foolish admiration (*hawaa*), which then becomes their guide'. Foolish self-admiration among the men at the *baraza* was indeed at the centre of the narrative and the author's criticism. His critique of the lack of engagement with Islamic knowledge also castigates coastal Muslims for political and social inactivity. They are, he implies, not following the demands of Islam, but instead are self-righteously secluding themselves from the problems actually facing them.

The reprint of this dialogue also draws attention to the continuities between the colonial and postcolonial experience of coastal Muslims. Indeed, 1978 was also the year when Daniel arap Moi became Kenya's second president. He embarked on a long period of autocratic rule (1978-2002) under the mantle of the so-called *nyayo*-politics of 'peace, love, and unity', ultimately demanding blind obedience of all citizens.

National politics: the Moi era

In 1981, Moi turned Kenya into a *de jure* one-party state by prohibiting all parties other than the ruling KANU through constitutional change. In 1991, Kenya re-introduced multi-party democracy in reaction to international political pressure. Not cowed by this challenge and adept at making divide-and-rule politics or 'political tribalism' (the ugly side of ethnicity, see Lonsdale 1992) work for himself in multi-ethnic Kenya, Moi was re-elected twice (1992 and 1997). Yet, it is regarded as an open secret that before both elections the government was involved in orchestrated so-called 'ethnic clashes', armed conflicts between ethnically defined groups competing for land and other resources around the country (most prominently the Rift Valley). This fuelled existing social fears and tensions between neighbouring groups. Thus the government used the spectre of 'tribalism' (*ukabila*) to realign and rally political support behind itself, promising to be the only party able to safeguard peace, stability, and national unity.

In the pre-election months of 1997, 'ethnic clashes' also haunted the coast. South and north of Mombasa, armed vigilante groups of coastal Mijikenda youths targeted and attacked people of upcountry origin, demanding them to leave (Kenyan Human Rights Committee 1997; 1998). While urban Muslims of Swahili and Arab descent were hardly directly involved or affected by this (cf. McIntosh 2009), the rhetoric of clashes drew from the historical antagonisms between coastal and upcountry people (*wapwani* and *wabara*). Many coastal Muslims continue to view the Christian *wabara* as foreign rulers over their territory, and their task has been called 'coping with Christians' (Cruise O'Brien 1995). Whereas they resented upcountry rule in general, many preferred Moi as president, as a known entity ('the devil they know'), to any other potential upcountry ruler who could shift the political imbalance even further to their disadvantage.

As president, Moi coined a political ideology called '*nyayo*' (Swahili for 'footsteps'), or '*nyayoism*'. The word itself became a euphemism for the followership he demanded of all Kenyans: faithful, trusting, and unquestioning – just like he claimed he himself had followed the footsteps of the mighty Kenyatta (see Ngūgi 1981: 86). In return, Moi promised 'peace, love, and unity' to the people through *nyayo* politics. Without discussing the exclusively Christian bias of the *nyayo* PR campaign (A. Mazrui 1994: 196) or academically dressed versions explaining and justifying *nyayo* as 'philosophy' (Moi 1986), the implicit message to all citizens should be underscored: as long as one follows the supreme ruler unquestioningly, one will live in peace. How coastal Muslims responded to and dealt with this is beyond the scope of this chapter. However, they were in general conscious and wary of the limits within which they could operate. Yet when the government threatened to abolish the constitutionally granted authority of Islamic courts for Muslim family and inheritance law in the early 1980s, Muslims unified and protested successfully. Among coastal Muslims (like among other groups), there were some who played along and prospered under the regime. Some made it to high administrative positions, though even in the Coast province itself most such jobs were given to people of upcountry origin.

With the reinstatement of multi-party politics in 1991, a coast-based political movement of Muslims sought to be registered as a national party and stand for election, the Islamic Party of Kenya (IPK). The IPK was denied registration on the grounds that the constitution forbade the formation of religiously defined parties. This sparked off a string of public protests by coastal Muslims (see A.M. Mazrui & Shariff 1994; Oded 1996), who expressed frustration about treatement as second-class citizens. This was a rare public scenario of (coastal) Muslims being pitted against the (upcountry) state, and the national media eagerly picked up on this. Still remembered vividly in Old Town Mombasa today, the street-fights and skirmishes back then made public the long-harboured resentments that had been kept in check for decades. However diverse and internally complex the local Muslim community, the events around IPK activism document Muslim solidarity *vis-à-vis* the postcolonial Kenyan state – which again sought to undermine this solidarity by divide-and-rule politics.[8] While some former IPK activists continue their civic engagement within regional politics, some IPK grafitti is still visible in Mombasa.

In some ways, the recent climate of a 'war on terror' in which the Kenyan government submits to US policies exhibits similar features to this earlier period. The Kibaki government has not seemed to care about the rights of Muslim citizens and has cast general suspicion over the Muslim community, which, in response, has again demonstrated solidarity (see Seesemann 2007*b*). Muslim representatives have spoken out against this latest wave of discrimination of Muslims in Kenya as the violation of their basic human rights as citizens in their own country.

The other side of the double-periphery

On the other side of the double-periphery, within the Muslim *umma*, the 1980s saw rising external influence in the ways Islamic ideologies were presented and negotiated in public. Most prominently, Saudi-funded Salafi-orientated reformists and Iranian-funded Shi'ite organizations established visible networks of Islamization. At the same time, they fought out ideological battles with each other, for instance in Islamic pamphlets (written in or translated into Swahili) distributed in large numbers. Thus factional tensions from elsewhere in the Muslim world, in this case between state-funded reformism from Saudi Arabia and Iran, had an impact on Kenyan Muslims in a novel manner (such hostility had not existed here before, according to my interlocutors). A few representative quotations from Islamic pamphlets below indicate the scale of the rhetorical attacks. They also show an invocation of knowledge as a criterion of judgement that Muslim readers should learn to employ to find the right path of Islam. First an excerpt from a Saudi-sponsored pamphlet:

> This is a very surprising phenomenon, our African brothers who have left us and converted to Shi'ism. But until now I have not heard of even one of them asking *their Iranian masters* where those books are that they have been told about? And in which belief have they been written? And what for?? *Earthly desires* [for money] have confused them, and if it were not so would they have agreed to Shi'ism? Through which *argument or truth* or which books? (Anon. n.d.: 25-6, my translation, emphasis added).

This pamphlet is entitled *Mashia na maimamu waliobuniwa* (The Shi'as and the imams who were invented by them) and was written by someone of Swahili background. The reproach of African converts to Shi'ism here is that they have been fooled into following their material desires instead of seeking knowledge and truth. The pamphlet restates the point and appeals to the converts to return to their senses and evaluate the arguments and truth claims made by the Shi'as – who are repeatedly sketched as insincere and racist 'white' foreigners taking advantage of lesser educated Africans – in order to return to the right path of the Qur'an and the Sunna. Once they have done so, the author claims, God will forgive and accept them again into his community. The author warns readers that 'Shi'as are progressing to delude those people who have little education' (Anon n.d.: 27). Thus not only do we witness an explicit invocation of claims to knowledge and truth by rhetorical means, but we can also see a picture of the East African region portrayed as a peripheral stage of the Muslim world. Shi'a converts are pictured as innocent and un-educated Africans who are susceptible to the trickeries of the Iranians, who are not only foreigners but also racists who represent 'Shi'a religion', not Islam.

Corresponding Shi'a pamphlets are readily available. The title of the following one does not mince its words: *Upotovu wa madhehebu ya 'Mawahhabi' na hatari zake* (The perversion of the Wahhabi *madhhab* and its dangers). Written originally in Swahili, it was published in Dar es Salaam in a first edition of 3,000 copies, with 10,000 copies reprinted the following year. This text responds in kind to the Wahhabi attacks on Shi'as. Here, it is no less than the destruction of Islam and the sowing of disunity among Muslims that is repeatedly said to top the agenda of the Wahhabi, who are said to 'wage a war against Islam, with all their means and resources' (Khalifa 1988 [1987]: introduction). In a mirror image of the anti-Shi'a attacks, the Wahhabi are called the 'enemies of Islam' and accused of luring the lesser educated and financially needy Africans away from the true faith. The author writes:

> These youths [of the Wahhabi faction who have entered previously peaceful and unified Muslim communities] have not only been given *sufficient training to confuse people who have little education*, they are also given *huge salaries* to pursue their work of division. For what reasons, do you think, has the Saudi government agreed to pay a lot of foreign money to divide Muslims? (Khalifa 1988 [1987]: 6-7, my translation, emphasis added).

'Cunning strategies' of the 'enemy' are assumed to be at work to divide the Muslim community. Along with alleged large sums of money, there is again a clear reference to the importance of knowledge: supposedly only 'people who have little education' can be won over by such strategies. This implies that properly educated Muslims could not be tempted; their knowledge would let them see through such tricks and stay on the right path. Reason is invoked to protect the supposedly true faith against Wahhabi attacks, whereby knowledge is rhetorically claimed by the writer.[9]

Looking at the way both 'Wahhabi' and Shi'a authors portray those whom they actually want to missionize speaks volumes on their views of ordinary East African Muslims. In both cases these are characterized as unequal and inferior within an inherently hierarchical model that places Arabs and Iranians as superior actors on top. The writers of these ideological Islamic pamphlets, even Swahili-speakers, seem to have internalized a perspective that regards East Africa on the lower end of a centre-periphery axis in the Muslim world. Africans appear as passive objects of Islamization, as lesser Muslims who can be 'saved' by the right doctrine from the Islamic heartland (either Saudi Arabia or Iran). This is similar to the colonial view of supposedly ignorant African souls waiting to be saved by Christian missionaries (see Tempels 1959) and can be related to the self-perception of coastal Muslims. I witnessed passionate rejection of such paternalism (and apparent racism) by self-confident and well-educated people. But I also noticed lingering insecurities and a tendency to submit to the powerful and supposedly more promising positions from elsewhere.

This raises questions about the claims to knowledge expressed in the pamphlets, and about the messages actually conveyed. East Africans, the presumed reading public, were not addressed by a reasoned argument seeking to convince them. Rather, the pamphlets are mostly concerned with proving their own given position *vis-à-vis* their ideological arch-enemies. Ultimately, the medium of religious pamphlets is used here as a stage for the re-enactment of existent hostilities. While engaged in the missionary project of transmitting knowledge to potential converts, writers from both sides were mainly engaged in a struggle for ideological hegemony in the Muslim world.

What can be said, then, about the effects on the self-perception of coastal Muslims? If they were regarded as ignorant, needy, and dependent by outsiders, they have also presented themselves as such, for instance to secure educational and financial aid, regular salaries, new mosques, and political support. These processes within the Muslim community have significantly re-shaped regional Muslim identities and increased the tendency towards the internal rejection of historically established positions and practices that Islamic reformism of the 'Wahhabi' kind does not tolerate. By demanding the rejection of practices that had long shaped Islam and the self-image of coastal Muslims, this had a major impact. Indirectly, it was conducive to the spread of Shi'ism in the region. Since Shi'a doctrine commonly justifies and defends practices like *maulidi* and *ziyara*, alliances between Sufi-orientated groups and Shi'as (*vis-à-vis* Wahhabi criticism) became possible. If by linking themselves to recently enforced networks of Islamic ideology local Muslims could have greater self-realization (e.g. liberation from Islam as customary practice), this might also lead to a kind of self-negation. This points to a fundamental ambivalence with regard to their agency and to the role of 'knowledge' and its rhetorical invocation as a guiding principle. Islamic ideological pressures affected coastal Muslims individually and socially, and these pressures were linked to the public revision of parameters of what it meant to be a good Muslim.

The Swahili knowledge economy

In Muslim societies across the world, seeking knowledge, and particularly Islamic knowledge, plays a central role in shaping society, as it is through knowledge of the Qur'an (and the *hadith*) that Muslims acquire guidelines for their orientation and practical behaviour (see also Deeb 2006: 27; Hefner 2007: 4). In a sense, then, there is an implicit social hierarchy linked to the possession of Islamic knowledge which entails an obligation to transmit it to the less educated. In general terms, this applies to Muslim communities around the world, and to 'traditional' Islamic scholars (the *'ulama*) as much as to 'modernizers' or 'Islamic reformists' (see Bowen 1993; Eickelman 1985; Lambek 1993; Marsden 2005; Zaman 2002). I now want to show how this basic principle operates and plays out in social interaction among coastal Muslims in Kenya and how it underpins and informs what people say and do.

In the Swahili language, a whole host of verbal expressions exist that denote activities of mutuality or reciprocity. This meaning is expressed by adding the suffix '–na' (or '–ana') to the verb, so that, for instance, the verb 'to love' (*kupenda*) can be turned into 'to love each other' (*kupendana*), or 'to leave' (*kuacha*) into 'to leave each other' (*kuachana*). Such expressions of mutuality that mark social relationships and imply knowledge-related obligations should be considered when describing and analysing sociality in the Swahili context. Five important ones that come to mind are: 'to know each other' (*kujuana*), 'to interact with each other' (*kuwasiliana*), 'to educate each other' (*kuelimishana*), 'to observe each other' (*kuangaliana*), and 'to remind each other' (*kukumbushana*). Together, through their meaningful interconnections and overlaps, they illustrate the field of social interaction in terms of mutual obligations and expectations that infer (or are linked to) knowledge, norms of Islamic behaviour, and morality. These terms are used and invoked in social discourse – in discussions, speeches, or in didactic poetry, for instance – and it seems to me that they reflect some of the general implications of Islam and Islamic knowledge for social interaction in everyday life. The social institution of the *baraza*, as a semi-public regular meeting-point for men mentioned above, illustrates these principles in social interaction.

Sociality is most basically delineated by the terms *kujuana* (to know each other) and *kuwasiliana* (to interact with each other, or to communicate). The former makes reference to the knowledge of each other with which we begin or which we end up with at the end of communication processes (as the basic axis of communication that is constantly expanded through communication). The latter refers to the activities of communicative exchange in social interaction: being connected to, involved with, 'in touch' with others is what is pronounced here. There is already a hint of obligation to social interaction and knowing about each other implied in these terms: people should communicate, should know their neighbours and others in their community and interact regularly with them, in short, be social. This is well illustrated by the Swahili saying '*mtu ni watu*' (a human being is human beings), which explicitly marks and acknowledges human beings as social beings for whom it is not only natural but also necessary to interact and live with others. Another expression indicating this is a common remark to those whom one has not seen for a while but whom one expects to see regularly (e.g. neighbours or friends): 'you have got lost' (*umepotea*), or 'where did you get lost?' (*umepotea wapi?*).

If *kujuana* and *kuwasiliana*, then, shape a basic axis for social communication and interaction, the other three terms mentioned above, *kuelimishana* (to educate each other), *kuangaliana* (to observe each other, or, better: to look out for each other), and *kukumbushana* (to remind each other), refer more explicitly to the idea of a moral community where people have the obligation to care and look out for each other. Ultimately, the community imagined here can be as wide as the global *umma*, or even the whole of humanity itself (see Kresse 2007a: chap. 5). The social implications of each term are interlinked and refer back to the Islamic obligations of looking out for one's fellow Muslims, making sure they adhere to proper standards of behaviour. As I heard many times during fieldwork, Muslims should make sure they pass on their knowledge to those who have less; they should be observant of their social peers and assist them if necessary; and they should remind them of the proper ways and standards of doing things whenever they would observe a lack of commitment or a violation of the proper guidelines. These Swahili expressions of mutuality would often be used and invoked in public speeches, in didactic poetry (*tenzi*), or in discussions among peers.

Thus social awareness, knowledge, and sensitivity about one's neighbours and peers, and a pro-active attitude to monitor people and possible wrongdoing, are implicitly inscribed as features of a model of proper social Muslim conduct. Yet these features have also become part and parcel of a normative notion of Swahili sociality itself. Clearly, reference to knowledge – and, implicitly, Islamic knowledge setting normative standards – is present here. Still, it is important to note that we are dealing with a particular Muslim community, and one should relate these reciprocal features of a 'knowledge economy' embedded in society back to the discussion of Muslim politics in postcolonial Kenya. One can better understand some of the internal social dynamics and tensions between Muslim factions within the *umma* (in Kenya), and also the degree of their mutual ideological accusations, if we keep in mind the features and principles above as being at work within the discourses of difference and disunity that currently mark much of public Islamic discourse.

Since the 1980s, the ideological and social divisions within the Muslim community in East Africa have been accentuated in public, when external ideological pressures have became more prevalent. This accompanied a dwindling sense of being part of the same social and religious community with shared social and moral underpinnings. Once it became possible to qualify other local Muslims of different Islamic orientations no longer just as misguided peers who should be redirected toward the right path but as 'unbelievers' and 'enemies of Islam', the sense of common sociality and mutual obligations inherent in Muslim sociality had obviously broken down. At the same time, the combative rhetoric that was adopted treated the factional frontlines as irreversible, as the examples above suggested. Socially, the lack of concern for a common basic platform for negotiating disputes led to awkward instances of confusion that reflected disunity. This happened, for instance, on major Islamic festivals like Id-el-fitri, which ideally should also celebrate and reflect Muslim unity. Because of disagreements over the correct methods of sighting the moon to determine the exact date, it has become common for different groups of Muslims to begin and end their fasting period on different days (see Kresse 2007*a*; 2007*b*; van der Bruinhorst 2007).

Increased engagement with different and competing factions of the wider Muslim *umma* during the postcolonial period has helped to undermine and destabilize the unity of coastal Muslims on the whole. At the same time, some individuals have benefited for themselves, and various groups are more imbricated in transnational networks. On the other side of the double-periphery, this points to an interesting role of the postcolonial state in the minds of Kenyan Muslims. Little else is able to unify Kenyan Muslims – or at least able to create an impression of unity among them – more than the opposition to apparent discrimination by the upcountry Christian government. Here, the opponent is by definition a religious and social outsider, and there is no pre-conceived common framework of socially binding knowledge that is referred to, nor of reciprocal obligations that members of a community commonly recognize and act upon (however different from each other they feel). Common membership in the nation (Kenya) does not automatically invoke such sentiments, in contrast to common membership of religion (Islam). Despite their frequent violations, these principles are acknowledged to be operative and adherence to them is accepted as desirable, if not obligatory.

In the end, there are two sides, or levels, of the knowledge economy and its social use and potential. If, on the one hand, it underpins common sociality among Muslims, and for each Muslim community is embedded in particular social practices in terms of care and mutual obligations, on the other hand it consists of rhetorical invocations of the knowledge of the discursive tradition that marks it as Islam. The latter characterizes a partial and instrumental use, for instance (as we have seen) as part of a strategy against Muslim 'opponents'.

Conclusion

If the two major axes of investigation of the situatedness of Kenyan coastal Muslims are marked, firstly, by Kenya as a postcolonial African state and, secondly, by the wider Muslim world and the variety of changing, developing, and transforming Islamic networks, a better understanding of the internal dynamics of Muslim identity in postcolonial Mombasa can be gained by reflecting further on the two axes, as I have tried to show here. Within Kenya, 'under postcolonial rule', coastal Muslims have often felt neglected, exploited, or even oppressed. As a cultural and religious minority *vis-à-vis* upcountry Christians dominating national politics, they are regarded as 'backward' in terms of economic development and secular education, socially disadvantaged but also dependent, as well as patient in endurance. The more this picture becomes part of their self-perception, the more peripheral coastal Muslims may think they are, and eventually might become. This suggests a kind of vicious circle at work in the post-colonial scenario in which they find themselves.

In other words, within the Muslim community, along and in parallel with a sense of 'suppression of the self' (on the axis of Islamic interaction *vis-à-vis* reformist pressures) goes a sense of 'oppression by the Other', here the upcountry Christian government (on the axis of postcoloniality). In relation to both axes, the Kenyan coastal Muslim community has experienced processes of transformation that have significantly reshaped their everyday life. From both directions strong forces negating the Muslim community and its way of life had to be absorbed. While this has led to a kind of 'dialectic' in the social formation of Muslim identity – the negation of their negation, leading to a positive re-assertion of themselves as Muslims – this scenario of a double-burden or double-challenge may also have positive effects. Being under pressure from both sides, individual Muslims grow up in a social environment that may be challenging but also ultimately rewarding once the challenges have been mastered. They experience these pressures but are also compelled to accept – and choose from – offers of outside support and alliance. In this sense, the double-periphery may be providing a 'privileged locus' (Lambek 1990: 26). Accustomed to dealing with such social, political, and ideo-logical pressures in their everyday lives, those who do not resign and give in may acquire valuable skills in the process. Among these are patience, endurance, and a broader scope of knowledge and experience based on the variety of available perspec-tives on society and on Islam.

Because of the position they are in, facing two fronts – an external and an internal antagonism – those persistent to struggle through become adept at negotiating the different demands and offers from various directions. They may be able to work themselves through several available options of Islamic ideologies, and by dealing with such challenges develop the potential to become more independently minded and (self-)critical than otherwise. By training the intellect, endurance, sensitivity, and per-suasiveness of individual Muslims living in this setting, being situated on a 'double-periphery' sensitizes and prepares them for quotidian struggles different from those in more socially homogeneous Muslim contexts (see also Marsden 2005).

I have in mind the example of a young man 'trained' in such a manner. Saidi (a pseudonym) is a self-educated religious layman and civic activist who has for some time and with moderate success been giving public speeches about the need for Kenyan Muslims to unify and assert common positions as a political force. At the same time, he criticized the Muslim establishment for its long-term failure to work for the good of the community (Kresse 2007a: chap. 7). When the post-Moi government began to liberalize the media and he was offered the chance of moderating his own weekly radio pro-gramme for a new local Islamic radio station, he became far more influential within the community. On air, he facilitates public discussions about pressing and contentious issues for the wider urban community (e.g. addressing the need to improve water supplies, the coastal economy, co-operation between citizens and the town council, or speaking out against violence and 'terrorism' in the name of Islam). For this, the medium of a live radio phone-in programme can be seen as a kind of extended *baraza* – the *baraza* being the historically established and culturally distinct setting of discur-sive negotiation of social or political issues that affect the coastal Muslim community. Issues of social and religious relevance are again discussed on the basis of common frameworks and standards of knowledge. Through efforts and initiatives like these, the *baraza* neighbourhood setting has become projected into the wider virtual space reached by the transistor, and from there continues to mediate and negotiate public disputes, common opinions, and private convictions within a group of listeners and participants that are part of a dynamic discursive community.

If Islam as discursive tradition is constituted by 'an ongoing interaction between the present and the past' and the ways in which 'relations of power and other forms of contestation and conflict impinge upon any definition of what it means to be a Muslim' (Zaman 2002: 6), both these aspects are at work here. When considering the relation-ship between the postcolonial and the colonial order in contemporary Kenya (admin-istration, political structure, etc.), core elements of the colonial are still inherent in the postcolonial sphere – often in the pragmatic sense that existent structures that 'work', or were made to 'work', in a social context continue to be used. This leads us to Chabal and Daloz's reflections about postcolonial African politics. Africa 'works' after all, they say, by means of disorder as a political instrument: 'In contemporary Africa, politics turn on the instrumentalization of disorder' (1999: 155). Yet, importantly, they also empha-size that to understand the political processes in postcolonial Africa, 'the disorder of which we speak is in fact a different "order", the outcome of different rationalities and causalities' (1999: 155). How this 'order' is created and 'works' in specific African soci-eties follows a different paradigm from the one which political science usually assumes. It is rooted in cultural traditions, social practices, or religious conceptions that were operative in African communities before, during, and after colonial rule. The formula of 'disorder as a political instrument' is also at work in postcolonial Kenya, on the scale of national politics and, in a structurally similar manner, within the realm of Muslim politics (though both aspects still need to be investigated further).

Particularly during the Moi era, the government seemed to have used and steered political disorder in the country to secure and guard its own position of power. The coastal region was affected by some aspects of this disorder much like other Kenyan regions (in terms of 'ethnic clashes', for instance). While popular discourse among coastal Muslims may exaggerate their status as victims, the structural neglect of the Kenyan coast (economic, educational, etc.) is one feature of such 'disorder' (an inverse 'order') – understandably leading to the common complaint among Muslims of being second-class citizens in their own home region. The foundations for this kind of 'order' that is locally seen as having furthered the grip of the upcountry government on the coastal population were laid during colonial times. In a sense, then, the postcolonial government has reaped what the British colonial administration had sown.

On the stage of Muslim politics, disorder was, in a way, useful to the regional impact of the transnational Islamic reformist ideologies discussed above. The frailty of the existing socio-religious order with its shaken-up fundamentals gave reformists a chance to offer a new one, and thus to make their ideology – which was markedly different and at times hostile to the previously established Muslim 'order' on the coast – a more likely and acceptable candidate than it otherwise might have been. If this is true, the post-colonial conditions of political disorder in Kenya also enhanced the possibilities for Islamic reform (in various shapes and forms) within the Muslim community more than has been hitherto addressed.

ACKNOWLEDGMENTS

This chapter draws on about twenty months of fieldwork conducted since 1998 and is part of a larger project. I am grateful to John Davis and David Parkin at All Souls College, Oxford, for hospitality and feedback in November 2005 when I presented the Evans-Pritchard Lectures dealing with some of these issues. Funding for fieldwork, from the Deutscher Akademischer Austauschdienst, the School of Oriental and African Studies, the University of St Andrews, the Deutsche Forschungsgemeinschaft, and the Bundesministerium für Bildung und Forschung, is gratefully acknowledged. I also thank my friends and interlocutors in Kenya. Earlier versions of this chapter were presented in Berlin, Münster, Leiden, and Vienna in 2007. In particular, I thank Thomas Fillitz, Benjamin Soares, Filippo Osella, Joy Adapon, and my colleagues at the Zentrum Moderner Orient for their comments, especially Hassan Mwakimako, Roman Loimeier, and Knut Graw.

NOTES

[1] The term 'coastal Muslims' includes Muslims of African (particularly Mijikenda and Swahili, also Somali), South Asian (Bohora, Ismaili, Shia Ithnaashari, Memon, Badala, Kokni), and Arab (especially Hadrami and Omani) background. Using it, I draw from common parlance in Kenya, whereby 'upcountry Christians' and 'coastal Muslims' are frequently contrasted. But the generic character of the term should not detract from the considerable internal diversity of coastal Muslims (see, e.g., Bakari 1995; Faulkner 2006; Fuglesang 1994; McIntosh 2009; Parkin 1970; 1984; 2000; Seesemann 2006), the majority of whom are Sunni Shafii.

[2] There is no shortage of reliable data on the proportion of Muslims in Kenya. Estimates range between 6 and 35 per cent, with 20-5 per cent seeming to be a reasonable estimate (see Ayubi & Mohyuddin 1994: 147; Cruise O'Brien 1995: 201; Seesemann 2007b: 158; Sperling 2000: 159).

[3] This term is commonly used (mostly by opponents, but sometimes also by adherents – see M.K. Mazrui 1971; Msallam 1991) to refer to supporters of Islamic reformism of the Salafi or Wahhabi kind, who usually call themselves 'people of the Sunna' (watu wa sunna or ahlul sunna).

[4] For more global political context and a view of Africa within the Muslim world see Hunwick (1997) and Otayek and Soares (2007). For patterns and varieties of Islamic reform in Africa, see Loimeier (2003; 2009).

[5] See Beckerleg (1995), who presents young males in an economically and socially frustrating environment facing the alternatives of drug-taking or Islamic activism.

[6] Sheikh al-Amin bin Ali Mazrui, 4 June 1944, in the introduction to Uwongozi (Leadership), a selection of texts from Sahifa: http://www.swahilionline.com/features/articles/islam/alamin.htm (last accessed 6 June 2007); my translation.

[7] A baraza is a prototypical institution of male sociality in the street-life on the Swahili coast. See also Kresse (2005) and Loimeier (2007). NB: the stone bench in front of a house is also called a baraza.

[8] A counter-organization was formed, supposedly representing 'African' Muslims. These were government-friendly and attacked IPK supporters viciously in word and deed, as 'Arab foreigners' whom they threatened with death (see, e.g., Oded 2000: 182).

[9] See Alam (2008) on similar enmities in South Asia.

REFERENCES

Alam, A. 2008. The enemy within: madrasa and Muslim identity in North India. *Modern Asian Studies* **42**, 605-27.

Anon. n.d. *Mashia na maimamu waliobuniwa* (The Shi'as and the imams who were invented by them). No author, place, or date of publication identifiable.

Asad, T. 1986. *The idea of an anthropology of Islam.* (Occasional paper series). Center for Contemporary Arab Studies. Washington, D.C.: Georgetown University.

Ayubi, S. & S. Mohyuddin 1994. Muslims in Kenya: an overview. *Journal of Muslim Minority Affairs* **15**, 144-56.

Bakari, M. 1995. The new *'ulama* in Kenya. In *Islam in Kenya* (eds) M. Bakari & S.S. Yahya, 168-93. Nairobi: MEWA.

Beckerleg, S. 1995. 'Brown sugar' or Friday prayers: youth choices and community building in coastal Kenya. *African Affairs* **94**, 23-38.

Bowen, J. 1993. *Muslims through discourse: religion and ritual in Gayo society.* Princeton: University Press.

Brennan, J. 2008. Lowering the Sultan's flag: sovereignty and decolonization in coastal Kenya. *Comparative Studies in Society and History* **4**, 831-61.

Chabal, P. & J.-P. Daloz 1999. *Africa works: disorder as political instrument.* Oxford: James Currey.

Cook, M. 2000. *Commanding right and forbidding wrong in Islam.* Princeton: University Press.

Cruise O'Brien, D.B. 1995. Coping with the Christians: the Muslim predicament in Kenya. In *Religion and politics in East Africa* (eds) H.B. Hansen & M. Twaddle, 200-19. London: James Currey.

Deeb, L. 2006. *An enchanted modern: gender and public piety in Shi'i Lebanon.* Princeton: University Press.

Eickelman, D.F. 1985. *Knowledge and power in Morocco.* Princeton: University Press.

——— & J. Piscatori 1996. *Muslim politics.* Princeton: University Press.

Farsy, A.S. 1989. *The Shafii ulamaa of East Africa, c. 1830-1970: a hagiographic account* (ed., trans., and annotated by R.L. Pouwels). Wisconsin: University of Wisconsin-Madison, African Studies Program.

Faulkner, M. 2006. *Overtly Muslim, covertly Boni: competing calls of religious alliance on the Kenyan coast.* Leiden: Brill.

Fuglesang, M. 1994. *Veils and videos: female youth culture on the Kenyan coast.* Stockholm: Gotab.

Hefner, R. 2007. Introduction: the culture, politics, and future of Muslim education. In *Schooling Islam: the culture and politics of Muslim education* (eds) R. Hefner & M.Q. Zaman, 1-39. Princeton: University Press.

Hoorweg, J., D. Foeken & R.A. Obudho (eds) 2000. *Kenya Coast handbook.* Hamburg: Lit-Verlag.

Horton, M. & J. Middleton 2000. *The Swahili: the social landscape of a mercantile society.* Oxford: Blackwell.

Hunwick, J. 1997. Sub-Saharan Africa and the wider world of Islam. In *African Islam and Islam in Africa* (eds) D. Westerlund & E.E. Rosander, 28-54. London: Hurst.

Kenyan Human Rights Committee 1997. *Kayas of deprivation, kayas of blood.* Mombasa.

——— 1998. *Kayas revisited: a post-election balance sheet.* Mombasa.

Khalifa M. Hamisi Mohammed 1988 [1987]. *Upotovu wa madhehebu ya 'Mawahhabi' na hatari zake* (The perversion of the Wahhabi *madhhab* and its dangers). Dar es Salaam: Sherman Islamic Book Stall. Publisher: Umoja wa Wahubiri wa Kiislamu wa Mlingano wa DINI (UWAMDI).

Kresse, K. 2003. 'Swahili Enlightenment?' East African reformist discourse at the turning point: the example of Sheikh Muhammad Kasim Mazrui. *Journal of Religion in Africa* **33**, 279-309.

——— 2005. At the *baraza*: socializing and intellectual practice at the Swahili coast. In *Christianity and social change in Africa: essays in honor of J.D.Y. Peel* (ed.) T. Falola, 613-31. Durham, N.C.: Carolina Academic Press.

——— 2006. Debating *maulidi*: ambiguities and transformation of Muslim identity along the Kenyan Swahili coast. In *The global worlds of the Swahili: interfaces of Islam, identity and space in 19th- and 20th-century East Africa* (eds) R. Loimeier & R. Seesemann, 211-30. Berlin: Lit-Verlag.

——— 2007a. *Philosophising in Mombasa: knowledge, Islam, and intellectual practice on the Swahili coast.* Edinburgh: University Press.

——— 2007b. The uses of history: rhetorics of Muslim unity and difference on the Kenyan Swahili coast. In *Struggling with history: Islam and cosmopolitanism in the Western Indian Ocean* (eds) E. Simpson & K. Kresse, 223-60. London: Hurst.

Lacunza Balda, J. 1993. The role of Kiswahili in East African Islam. In *Muslim identity and social change in Sub-Saharan Africa* (ed.) L. Brenner, 226-38. London: Hurst.

LAMBEK, M. 1990. Certain knowledge, contestable authority: power and practice on the Islamic periphery. *American Ethnologist* **17**, 23-40.

———— 1993. *Knowledge and practice in Mayotte: local discourses of Islam, sorcery, and spirit possession.* Toronto: University Press.

LAST, M. 1988. Charisma and medicine in northern Nigeria. In *Charisma and brotherhood in African Islam* (eds) D.B. Cruise O'Brien & C. Coulon, 188-201. Oxford: Clarendon.

LOEFFLER, R. 1988. *Islam in practice: religious beliefs in a Persian village.* Albany: SUNY Press.

LOIMEIER, R. 2003. Patterns and particularities of Islamic reform in Africa. *Journal of Religion in Africa* **33**, 237-62.

———— 2007. Sit local, think global: the *baraza* in Zanzibar. *Journal of Islamic Studies* **27**, 1-15.

———— 2009. Traditions of reform, reforms of tradition: case studies from Senegal and Zanzibar/Tanzania. In *Diversity and pluralism in Islam* (ed.) Z. Hirji. London: Institute of Ismaili Studies/I.B. Tauris.

LONSDALE, J. 1992. The moral economy of Mau Mau. In *Unhappy valley: conflict in Kenya and Africa*, B. Berman & J. Lonsdale, 265-314. London: James Currey.

McINTOSH, J. 2009. *The edge of Islam: power, personhood, and ethnoreligious boundaries on the Kenya coast.* Durham, N.C.: Duke University Press.

MARSDEN, M. 2005. *Living Islam: Muslim religious experience in Pakistan's North-West Frontier.* Cambridge: University Press.

MAZRUI, AL-AMIN 1955 [1944]. *Uwongozi* (Guidance). Mombasa: EAMWS.

———— 1978 [1929]. Mazungumzo ya ilmu (An educational conversation). *Sauti ya Haki* **3**, 1, 7

MAZRUI, ALI A. 1993. The black intifadah? Religion and rage at the Kenyan coast. *Journal of Asian and African Affairs* **4**, 87-93.

MAZRUI, A. 1994. Ethnicity and pluralism: the politicization of religion in Kenya. *Journal Institute of Muslim Minority Affairs* **14**, 191-201.

MAZRUI, A.M. & I.N. SHARIFF 1994. *The Swahili: idiom and identity of an African people.* Trenton, N.J.: Africa World Press.

MAZRUI, M.K. 1971. *Hukumu za sharia (sehemu ya pili)* (Judgements according to Islamic law (part two)). Mombasa: The City Bookshop.

———— 1980. Dibaji (Preface). In *Tafsiri ya Qur'ani Tukufu. Al-Faatihah – Al Baqarah* (Translation of the Holy Qur'an), al-Amin Mazrui, ix-xii. Nairobi: Shungwaya Publishers.

MOI, D.A.T. 1986. *Kenyan African nationalism: Nyayo philosophy and principles.* Nairobi: Macmillan.

MSALLAM, A. 1991. *Huo ndio uwahabi* (This is Wahhabism). (Second edition). Nairobi: Mtendaji kheri.

NGŨGĨ WA THIONG'O 1981. *Decolonising the mind.* London: James Currey.

ODED, A. 1996. Islamic extremism in Kenya: the rise and fall of Sheikh Khalid Balala. *Journal of Religion in Africa* **26**, 406-15.

———— 2000. *Islam and politics in Kenya.* London: Lynne Rienner.

OSELLA, F. & C. OSELLA 2008a. Introduction: Islamic reformism in South Asia. *Modern Asian Studies* **42**, 247-57.

———— 2008b. Islamism and social reform in Kerala, South India. *Modern Asian Studies* **42**, 317-46.

OTAYEK, R. & B.F. SOARES 2007. Introduction: Islam and Muslim politics in Africa. In *Islam and Muslim politics in Africa* (eds) B.F. Soares & R. Otayek, 1-24. New York: Palgrave Macmillan.

PARKIN, D. 1970. Politics of ritual syncretism: Islam among the non-Muslim Giriama of Kenya. *Africa* **XL**, 217-33.

———— 1984. Being and selfhood among intermediary Swahili. In *Swahili language and society* (eds) J. Maw & D. Parkin, 247-60. Vienna: Afro-Pub.

———— 2000. Invocation: *salaa, dua, sadaka* and the question of self-determination. In *Islamic prayers across the Indian Ocean: inside and outside the mosque* (eds) D. Parkin & C. Headley, 137-68. Richmond, Surrey: Curzon.

POUWELS, R. 1981. Sheikh al-Amin b. Ali Mazrui and Islamic modernism in East Africa, 1875-1947. *International Journal of Middle Eastern Studies* **13**, 329-45.

———— 1987. *Horn and crescent: cultural change and traditional Islam on the East African coast, 800-1900.* Cambridge: University Press.

REESE, S. 2004. Introduction: Islam in Africa – challenging the perceived wisdom. In *The transmission of learning in Islamic Africa* (ed.) S. Reese, 1-14. Leiden: Brill.

ROBINSON, F. 2008. Islamic reform and modernities in South Asia. *Modern Asian Studies* **42**, 259-81.

SALIM, A.I. 1970. The movement for 'Mwambao' or coast autonomy in Kenya, 1956-63. In *Hadith 2* (ed.) B.A. Ogot, 212-28. Nairobi: East African Publishing House.

Salvatore, A. & D.F. Eickelman (eds) 2004. *Public Islam and the common good*. Leiden: Brill.

Seesemann, R. 2006. African Islam or Islam in Africa? Evidence from Kenya. In *The global worlds of the Swahili: interfaces of Islam, identity and space in 19th- and 20th-century East Africa* (eds) R. Loimeier & R. Seesemann, 229-50. Berlin: Lit-Verlag.

——— 2007a. Between tradition and reform: the Hadrami model of Islamic learning in 20th-century Kenya. In *Bildungsformen und Bildungstraeger zwischen Tradition und Moderne* (eds) S. Leder & H. Schoenig, 37-59. Halle: Orientwissenschaftliche Hefte.

——— 2007b. Kenyan Muslims, the aftermath of 9/11, and the 'war on terror'. In *Islam and Muslim politics in Africa* (eds) B.F. Soares & R. Otayek, 157-76. New York: Palgrave Macmillan.

Soares, B.F. 1996.The prayer economy in a Malian town. *Cahiers d'Etudes Africaines* **36**, 739-53.

——— 2005. *Islam and the prayer economy: history and authority in a Malian town*. Edinburgh: University Press for the International African Institute.

Sperling, D.C. 2000. Religion and society. In *Kenya Coast handbook* (eds) J. Hoorweg, D. Foeken & R.A. Obudho, 157-71. Hamburg: Lit-Verlag.

Tempels, P. 1959. *Bantu philosophy*. Paris: Présence Africaine.

van der Bruinhorst, G. 2007. *'Raise your voices and kill your animals': Islamic discourses on the Idd el-Hajj and sacrifices in Tanga (Tanzania)*. Amsterdam: University Press.

Zaman, M.Q. 2002. *The ulama in contemporary Islam: custodians of change*. Princeton: University Press.

6

Between dialogue and contestation: gender, Islam, and the challenges of a Malian public sphere

Rosa De Jorio *University of North Florida*

This chapter focuses on gender debates in Mali in the neoliberal era as one privileged arena for the articulation of conflicting ideas of the social order. It centres on a five-day conference on women's issues I attended in Bamako, 11-15 December 2004. During the conference, both male and female participants expressed a variety of views on gender relations to account for gender disparities or to address society's problems. While reflecting on the subject of women's responsibilities and prerogatives as citizens, several participants attempted to reconcile or problematize the relationship between religiously informed normative orders and women's modernist emancipatory agendas. The political liberalization in Mali has created an environment conducive to the public expression of more diversified voices on gender relationships, in particular with regard to the rights and responsibilities of women as modern citizens. This has coincided perhaps unexpectedly with the further blurring of the French-derived boundaries between church and state (*laïcité*) formally espoused by the Malian political and intellectual elites. References to Islam have increasingly become an authoritative idiom used to reflect publicly upon women's and men's relationships and to articulate often conflicting constructs of the ideal social order.[1]

The nature and modalities of such gender debates allow me to reflect more broadly on the Malian public sphere. Several scholars of Mali have observed how the democratization of the country's political apparatus has opened new civic opportunities for its people (1991-present), commenting upon the proliferation of media and news organizations and often interpreting this trend as an expression of the increased vitality of Malian civil society. The expansion and diversification of public participation have affected not only secular organizations such as women's groups and parties but also religious organizations, so some scholars have talked of the widening of Mali's religious sphere (Launay & Soares 1999; Soares 2005; more generally on the Muslim public sphere, see, e.g., work by Salvatore 2007a; 2007b; 2007c; Salvatore & Eickelman 2004). Muslim intellectuals and clerics have become more vocal and often influential in public politics (Soares 2006). They have effectively managed public media and imposed themselves as important and critical reference-points in a number of national debates (Otayek & Soares 2007; Schulz 2006; Soares 2009). Furthermore, ordinary Malian Muslims are increasingly engaging in critical reflections on religious texts and participating in religious and political debates. This is particularly the case for debates on issues affecting people's everyday lives such as women's status, women's relations with men, and the relationship between Malian households and the state.

Challenging Habermas's early conception of the public sphere as inclusive and eminently rational, a number of studies have thus highlighted the role of religion in contributing to the articulation of spaces for debate (e.g. Salvatore 2007a; Salvatore & Eickelman 2004). Part of this literature has identified in the common good the driving force orientating debates within the public sphere (Salvatore 2007a). Differing from such a perspective, the present analysis suggests that the understanding of religious debates may be aided by feminist analysis and, in general, scholarship foregrounding the ways in which power and discourse intertwine in public contexts (e.g. Fraser 1992; Kögler 1999). Indeed, interventions at the conference were significantly affected in terms of both content and form by power differentials among attendees; speakers' gender identities (Gal 1991), political affiliations, and transnational connections had significant implications for their discursive practices. Accordingly, this chapter examines the modalities of reference to the religious as well as the power dynamics between counter-publics in the context of a gender conference (Fraser 1992; 2007; Kögler 1999; 2005).

The analysis of gender discourses in public contexts also allows me to reflect on women's modalities of participation in the religious domain. In particular, it enables me to shift the attention from women's embodied forms of religiosity towards women's reflexive forms. Recent approaches rethink the forms of female agency and religious participation in the context of non-liberal movements (e.g. Mahmood 2005). They represent an important corrective to a tendency on the part of the anthropological literature (and particularly within the tradition of feminist anthropology) to describe their interlocutors' everyday life as expressions of resistance and thus 'to impose a theology of progressive politics' onto otherwise defined subjects (Mahmood 2005: 9). In contrast, Mahmood's work seeks to address the question of how we 'analyze operations of power that construct different kinds of bodies, knowledges, and subjectivities whose trajectories do not follow the entelechy of liberatory politics' (2005: 14). However, Mahmood's compelling study of the piety movement in Egypt with its focus on 'the cultivation of those bodily aptitudes, virtues, habits, and desires that serve to ground Islamic principles within the practice of everyday living' (2005: 45) certainly does not exhaust the multiplicity of women's engagements with the religious. If generalized, her approach would prove problematic. Indeed, I would argue that it would reduce the study of subjectivity to the mere analysis of the mode of subjectivation of the self under a certain regime of power, leaving out other, more critical forms of engagement as demonstrated, for instance, by Deeb's analysis (in this volume) of some Lebanese Muslim women's 'engagements with transnationally constituted discourses about Muslim women and about Western women' (p. 109).

I also submit that resistance and, more generally, critical reflexivity are forms of engagement intimately connected to the project of the social sciences, which cannot be content with a mere description of existing power as such. According to Foucault, the analysis of power relations begins by 'taking the forms of resistance against different forms of power as a starting point' (1982: 211). Its ultimate purpose, however, is 'to liberate us both from the state and from the type of individualization which is linked to the state' (1982: 216). For Foucault, power analyses are thus not resolved in the study of modes of subjectivation but should retain a critical orientation: 'the task of philosophy as a critical analysis of our world is something which is more and more important' (1982: 216). Furthermore, this reflexive view is not superimposed by the critical analyst onto the field, but exists in the discursive and political practices of the subjects themselves. Under conditions of globalization, people's religious engagements are more or less consciously framed in relation to a multiplicity of different forms of being, grounded in a variety of often competing regimes of power. Thus if we must avoid applying to our studies a reductive understanding of resistance, that does not mean that we should abandon the concept of reflexivity; rather, we need to refine our understanding of it, including its critical dimensions of engagement in the contexts of contemporary forms of power (Ferguson & Gupta 2002). Indeed, it could be argued that Mahmood's work highlights a particular form of reflexivity, primarily geared toward the reform of women's bodily selves.

I contend that the leaders of Malian women's secular associations and human rights activists at the centre of the present analysis are, to a different degree, critically engaged in national and transnational gender discourses. While devoted Muslims for the most part, they are increasingly more vocal in questioning public readings of Islam that reinforce male hegemony. Their questioning reflects contemporary women's search for more meaningful mediations between their identity as Muslims and their militancy in women's secular groups, reflexive engagements that are located at the interstices of often conflicting regimes of power that simultaneously limit and enhance women's forms of participation.[2]

In the first part of this chapter, I briefly describe some of Mali's recent political changes to focus on some of the major debates on gender issues that have divided Malian citizens in the democratic period. Then I analyse interventions at the women's conference and reflect on women's and men's verbal practices as well as on their reference to religious arguments in the course of presentations and ensuing debates. In my concluding remarks, I return to the issue of the public sphere, particularly its applicability and limits for the Malian context, and restate the importance of extending our research to reckon with people's reflexive views of their religiosity and their grounded engagements with a variety of public contexts.

Legislative projects and public debates on gender and the family in Mali

In 1991, mass demonstrations by students, women, and workers spurred the end of Moussa Traoré's twenty-three-year dictatorship. In the eighteen months that followed, the transitional government laid the foundations for Mali's democratic turn by reviewing and changing the constitution, reforming state institutions, and granting freedom of the press and organization. In 1992 the first free elections were held and brought to power a leading intellectual and democratic activist, Alpha Oumar Konaré, as president of the country. Konaré was re-elected in 1997 in a much-contested vote and led the country until 2002. Following this, Amadou Toumani Touré, a popular military official who arrested Traoré in 1991 and led the eighteen-month transitional government prior to Konaré's election, was elected president. Touré was re-elected in April 2007 for a second term, despite growing critiques of his leadership (e.g. Cissé 2006).

Since 1991 the 'woman's question' has been at the centre of political and legislative interventions. One of the political objectives of Konaré's presidency was to promote women's participation in various domains and uphold women's rights. Major results were the creation of a central ministry for women's and children's welfare (Ministère de la promotion de la femme, de l'enfant, et de la famille), the establishment of regional and local branches of the ministry, and an increase in the number of women elected to national, regional, and local office. For instance, 'if the first government of the third republic numbered only two women, the last is composed of more than a third women, that is, 8 out of 21' (Couloubaly 2004: 81). Another important objective was the reform of the Malian corpus of laws to eliminate discriminatory statements against women and to redress the void of legislation on important matters such as inheritance, which are typically handled according to either Islamic or customary law. I will examine some of the results (or lack thereof) of such initiatives on the part of the state and its international partners as a discursive context in which to locate the 2004 debates at the Centre Djoliba.[3]

While the creation of the ministry does not seem to have engendered much opposition, especially given its reassuring title (a ministry not just for women but also for children and the family), the prospect of legislative changes affecting women's status and the organization of the family has generated contentious debates at various levels and ultimately widespread opposition. Changes in these domains would significantly affect existing boundaries between the household and the state and bring into question the substantive power of adult males to settle household matters. This issue is especially sensitive because household heads have continued to experience the erosion of their power by young grooms who contribute a substantial part of the bridewealth to their brides' families, thus allowing them greater freedom in choosing their spouses and greater independence once married, a trend reinforced by the scale of Malian migration from rural areas to Malian cities, particularly Bamako, and abroad. In addition, women's involvement in women's organizations and Malian households' increasing reliance upon women's incomes have further shaken adult males' positions.

Debates on gender relations and women's status have been central in discursive articulations of Mali as a nation in the neoliberal era (Bhabha 1990). Such debates have led observers to question the presumed secularity of the Malian state and indeed to argue for the intertwining of secular and religious institutions and practices. In particular the lack of legal status for religious marriages has been questioned. Muntaga Tall, a descendant of the nineteenth-century Muslim ruler and *jihad* leader al-Hajj Umar Tall and the leader of one of Mali's most established parties, the Congrès national d'initiative démocratique (CNID), presented a motion in 1992 for the legal recognition of religious marriages. The marriage code establishes the primacy of civil marriages over customary and religious marriages (De Jorio 2002; Schulz 2003). Civil marriages are the only form of marriage legally recognized by the state. In practice, very few citizens marry at the city hall, a situation that often leaves women and children with no legal claim to a man's inheritance. Tall's proposal was rejected by the majority party, Alliance pour la démocratie au Mali (ADEMA), on the grounds that it would compromise the French-derived separation of church and state to which Mali formally subscribes and that it would undermine state authority.[4] The issue was reopened during regional and national discussions (several *concertations regionales* and a *forum national*) on the new family code in 2000 and 2001, with similar results. Large segments of the population would favour the legalization of religious marriages, and their position has been given voice in the media by a number of Muslim religious leaders and activists (Soares 2009). In time, several state representatives have come to modify their position and have expressed some openness towards the legal recognition of religious marriages. The women's movement itself is divided on this issue, with a number of women activists siding with the legalization of religious marriages, which would grant greater protection to women.

The government agenda for the improvement of women's legal status (in co-operation with international aid agencies) has been a battlefield for competing political interests and competing visions of the world order. In 2002, shortly prior to the end of his second term, Konaré submitted to the national assembly a draft proposal on the family code that aimed to improve women's and children's rights by eliminating discriminatory language from existing laws and by legislating in previously unaddressed areas (e.g. inheritance). It contained provisions empowering women's role within the household and granting legal rights to children born to unmarried parents. Some of the major changes included the possibility for women to become household heads in the event of divorce or their husband's death, to play a greater role in choice of family residence and the exercise of parental authority, and to have access to an equitable portion of a deceased husband's inheritance in the absence of a will. The draft proposal, which if accepted would have further reduced the authority of adult males within Malian households, was immediately met with fierce opposition by various groups within the population, particularly male *fonctionnaires* (civil servants) and Muslim religious leaders and activists. President Konaré, who had miscalculated popular reaction (Soares 2009), decided to withdraw it from the national assembly.

Given the failure of such legislative changes, state officials and representatives of international organizations have opted for a different strategy, increasing the instances of dialogue with various segments of the population, and particularly religious leaders and activists. This has translated into an effort to establish new forms of control over religious institutions, be encouraging or favouring particular readings of Islam that could eventually predispose religious actors to support the desired legal changes. In this vein, the women's ministry and some of its foreign partners (particularly the Food and Agriculture Organization) commissioned a study to increase people's knowledge of women's rights and duties according to Islam. The report was presented by L'association malienne pour l'unité et le progrès de l'Islam (AMUPI) and the Union des associations de femmes musulmanes du Mali (UNAFEM) – two of the most well-established Islamic institutions in the country (Soares 2009). The document is addressed to religious leaders and aims to 'enlighten [them] ... on issues concerning women's rights and duties according to Islam'. It also hopes to involve religious leaders in educating men 'on Islam's position in regard to reproductive rights and gender equality' (AMUPI & UNAFEM 2002: 4). This document is further testimony to women's increasing visibility within Mali's religious sphere and some of the forms of power behind such transformations. According to Malian historian Bintou Sanankoua (1991), up to the late 1980s Muslim women's organizations were struggling to find recognition by male Muslim authorities, who largely ignored them. Since then Muslim women have created a number of Islamic associations, co-ordinated by the influential UNAFEM, with the double-goal of disseminating knowledge of Islam among women and educating the society about women's rights according to Islam (FAC-MR 1999). This initiative also shows efforts by the state and foreign partners to involve religious leaders in projects of social change. The position paper includes a careful reading of the draft law and clarifies points of contact and points of divergence between Islamic law and positive law. It presents a particular reading of Islamic jurisprudence[5] exemplified, for instance, in the idea that marriage should be based on mutual consent (a provision often subverted, given that many marriages continue to be arranged to varying degrees) and that women should be free to administer their own property. On the other hand, and diverging here from positive law, Islamic law maintains that women should obey their husbands. However, women's opinions on family matters should be sought, thus encouraging co-operation between spouses. The primacy of Muslim inheritance law is reaffirmed as well as a man's right to choose the family residence. This document aims to present Islam as a religion that brings about significant advances for women *vis-à-vis* customary law and to establish some common ground with women's lay groups.

State initiatives aiming to improve women's rights, if successful, would dramatically alter local geographies of power, challenging adult males' power over household members and women in particular. The temporary failure of such initiatives reflects the fragmentation of Malian politics during Konaré's ten-year presidency as well as wide opposition to such changes by substantial and influential segments of society (e.g. civil servants and Muslim religious leaders). In addition, it can also be read as the expression of a general discontent among ordinary citizens concerning the limited gains brought about by democratization (Otayek & Soares 2007; Soares 2009). Analysis of such debates seems to suggest a greater, if ambiguous, commitment by the state and its international partners to establish some dialogue with different components of Malian society. For example, during the dictatorship of Moussa Traoré (1968-91) and in response to efforts by the Union nationale des femmes du Mali (UNFM) – the only official Malian women's organization and a powerful instrument of the dictatorship (Ba Konaré 1993) – to curb excision, a number of families stopped circumcising their daughters for fear of state retaliation but rushed to do so in the aftermath of democratic change. Diverging from previous practices, the women's ministry as well as several women's organizations and NGOs co-ordinated by the umbrella organization Coordination des associations et ONG féminines du Mali (CAFO) are attempting to broaden their support and to establish a dialogue with religious leaders and activists. As a part of this effort, they actively promote a certain version of Islam, one that foregrounds women's rights and prerogatives.

The conference on women's realities

The five-day Conference on Women's Realities was organized by the cultural association Acte Sept in conjunction with the seventh edition of the Festival du théâtre des réalités. The conference took place in the Centre Djoliba, a well-established conference centre run by a Roman Catholic order. Besides hosting a number of important national debates since Mali's democratic turn, during the dictatorship of Moussa Traoré the centre was one of the few spaces in which people could safely gather to discuss issues of public concern. Such gatherings today attract a diverse but mostly highly educated public, including a number of well-respected public intellectuals and politicians, the latter particularly assiduous around election time. The Catholic order running the centre was not officially represented; its contribution was limited to providing the conference space.

Dravé, the (male) conference moderator, remarked at the opening session that the conference was put together to recognize women's contributions to the development of the nation: 'In the house, as in the fields, in the offices, and in modern enterprises, including the highest positions of our administration, women's role in the country's development is ... unquestionable'. Yet, he noted, there were still segments of the population that failed to recognize women's contributions and that indeed undermined them. On the same occasion, Bagayogo, a man who was the Acte Sept representative in attendance, expanded that the goal of the conference was to sensitize the national and international public[6] to Malian women's 'conditions of slavery, conditions of exploitation, conditions of domination', and to find possible solutions. Despite the rhetorical flourishes and the condescending tone of the conference moderator and the Acte Sept representative, the conference was organized to create a shared discursive space in which women and men could engage in dialogue on a number of important topics, thus temporarily overcoming traditional gender barriers.

Topics debated at the conference included excision, violence against women, the history of women's organizations, and changes in women's status, among others. Each day, one main speaker (totalling four women and one man for the entire conference) was scheduled to present on a given topic. This was followed by a lively and substantive question-and-answer session (ranging between one and two hours) that offered an unprecedented opportunity to reflect on women's and men's discursive practices in a shared public space.

Bringing together women and men to discuss women's issues is, no doubt, not an easy enterprise anywhere, as men's contributions to such dialogue easily acquire condescending tones. While in many women's conferences women are the most visible participants, the gender dynamics at play during this conference in Mali were significantly different. In this context, there were certainly more men speaking up than women (although some women were equally articulate and rhetorically effective), and women's participation had to be periodically solicited by the (male) moderator, as reflected in the following comment: 'I want to ask women to speak up in great number, because the series of conferences ... is for them. ... [By not speaking] you confirm men's presuppositions. I expect that many of you will ask to talk shortly'. In part this hesitation was due to the fact that some of the women present were not comfortable speaking French, the language of the conference. Some were members of the various associations represented by the women speakers and had shown up to support their leaders. The language issue was openly addressed by some of the participants, who requested that speakers be permitted to switch to Bamana – the most widely spoken language in Mali – to allow those women to participate. The organizers, concerned about the presence of representatives from the international community, settled for some summaries in Bamana at the end of the debates. Some of the speakers (such as Traoré Oumou Touré) spoke alternately in French and Bamana, to reach both audiences. Furthermore, some women's hesitation about speaking up was a reflection of the dominant expectation that women should not speak in public settings when men are present. Traoré Oumou Touré, the president of CAFO (the umbrella organization that co-ordinates most Malian women's associations and NGOs), developed this point in her presentation on women and stereotypes.[7] One of the damaging stereotypes in Malian society, she suggested, is the expectation that 'a woman should not talk when a man is there; otherwise she is no longer a woman but a man'. This is so, she added, even when matters of concern to women are being discussed. Traoré gave a number of reasons for this situation, mentioning lack of education, traditions, and patriarchy, and provocatively invited the men in attendance to explain such stereotyping.

Contributions by several male speakers (with some notable exceptions, such as that by Victor Sy, a well-respected public intellectual and a frequent attendee of conferences at the centre) consisted of often severe if not harsh critiques of women's behaviour and activities. For instance, a certain Mr Doumbia suggested that women had not yet demonstrated the value of their social contribution, making it unlikely that their husbands would agree to any sharing of power:

> I never heard of a man waking up in the morning and volunteering to share his power with his wife. … To have your place [here he switched from the formal *vous* to the familiar *tu*] one needs to work, one needs to be useful; when you are useful you become indispensable.

This point was later fiercely rejected by the president of CAFO, who retorted that there was no need for women to show their relevance, as they were already indispensable. (This comment was greeted with cheering and nodding on the part of some of the CAFO women in attendance.) Other men criticized women for what they deemed irrational and immoral practices – including women's substantial expenditures for life-cycle ceremonies (particularly naming ceremonies and marriages) and the indecent ways in which they clothed their daughters in an effort to secure them husbands.[8] Such tirades express the popular view that women have almost exclusive responsibility for the moral conduct of their children, especially their daughters.

The most subtle and elegant effort in this direction was led by the only invited male speaker, Temo Tamboura, who presented on the issue of violence against women. In his speech, Tamboura cited the weakness of Mali's civil society as the reason for the perpetuation of violence against women. Despite the lack of precise legislation target-ing violence against women, Mali was a signatory to a number of international con-ventions that in themselves offered adequate legal protection for Malian women. However, Tamboura argued, the responsibility to make sure that the laws of the state were applied was in the hands of civil society and most of all those of women's associations and women's NGOs: 'The state cannot be omnipresent. … This means that … we need to legitimize civil society. The existing associations and NGOs must take on this role of popular control. By taking on the role of popular control, they must be able to eradicate these phenomena.'

The tendency to blame women for what are perceived as society's problems is well represented in the Malian media. One relatively recent example is the number of newspaper articles pointing to Mariam Traoré, the wife of Mali's former president, as the real architect and driving force behind the twenty-three-year dictatorship, some-thing also widely echoed in popular discourse. The women participating in the con-ference challenged some of the men's positions, as in Koumba Iaresi's ironic request to Tamboura to explain to her 'what women should do so that states respect their legis-lation in favour of women', given Tamboura's recurring critique of the ineffectiveness of women's associations in generating effective social changes. Other female partici-pants admitted to some weaknesses of the women's movement, as in the following comment by a woman named Binta, explaining violence against women: 'But we the women, we do not help one another, we are not in solidarity; this is a real problem that we experience in Mali'. Others stressed similarities between the genders, as did Traoré Oumou Traoré: 'Women and men are human beings first and foremost … [yet women] are the victims of numerous prejudices, unfounded opinions, and judgments that … marginalize them.'

Debates on gender and Islam

In this highly charged discursive context, references to Islam emerged as an authoritative idiom that some women used to question existing power relationships within Malian society and their conceptual foundations.[9] Women problematized male-centred readings of Islam and presented alternative interpretations of their faith. Interestingly, most references to Islam came in the question-and-answer periods (with the exception of the talk given by the only male presenter, Tamboura), thus showing some hesitation on the part of the women presenters, perhaps due to their public visibility as the leaders of some of the most established secular women's organizations in Mali, to explicitly incorporate religious themes or arguments in their speeches. Women's incursions into the religious realm generated heated debates among conference participants.

During the first conference day, dedicated to the analysis of women and stereotypes, a woman by the name of Sidibé commented on the main (female) speaker's presentation, which in her view should have included reference to what she called religious stereotypes. Since her comment followed on the heels of a male tirade against 'intellectual' (highly educated) women and their inability to represent the concerns of the majority of Malian women, Sidibé made sure to clarify her authorial position. 'I am not a woman from Bamako', she stated, indicating that she had not experienced the luxuries that are often attributed to city women, and also that she was in touch with the diversity of Malian women's conditions. 'I have had the opportunity to work in the most remote villages. ... Most of all I have experienced two different cultures ... Songhai and Manding'. Her rich, diverse cultural experiences had led her to reflect upon the images of women and most of all to question men's uses of Islam.

> My religion causes me some dilemmas. ... I was born a Muslim ... but was I properly educated as a Muslim? When it is said, 'God is good,' have we received such an education? If we were really properly educated to be Muslims, we [women] would not have been subjected to what we are subjected to.

Questioning the depth of her own as well as ordinary Malians' knowledge of Islam, she noted, 'I received an education in Arabic (*une formation arabe*), I recite the verses [of the Qur'an], but I do not understand their deeper meanings'. Embracing half-ironically an evolutionary paradigm (see Gosselin 2000), she suggested that Malians had too quickly moved from 'animism' to monotheism under the influence of what she referred to as 'the Arabs', without attaining an adequate degree of knowledge of religious matters. She then (provocatively) proceeded to question the identification of God with a masculine being and queried the adequacy of French translations of the Qur'an. Wishfully she added, 'One day I thought, "But we would need to create a goddess somewhere"'. Most of all she called into question Malian men's understandings of salvation and their claim that women's access to heavenly paradise depended upon their submission to their husbands' authority: 'Men tell us that in order for us to go to Paradise, the medium is them: one needs to accept what they say, one needs to be submissive so that the children one day will be worthy children, children of whom to be proud'. But, she noted, we are all human beings, all created with the primary purpose of worshipping God. 'Why does somebody [i.e. a man] cross my path in my effort to reach God?' She then went on to attack Malian 'animist' practices, such as excision, and in the process clarified that as a Songhai woman, she had not experienced this practice.

As she began to address the issue of circumcision, the moderator abruptly interrupted her because she was digressing onto the next day's topic (excision), and her speech was brought to an end.

This comment, which problematized patriarchal readings of Islam from a Muslim woman's perspective, generated strong and diverse reactions from the male audience. The first to address Sidibé's reflections on religion was Victor Sy.[10] His remarks constituted the only sympathetic and supportive reading of Sidibé's critical position by either the men or women in attendance. Sy presented himself as 'first of all a Malian, an organic intellectual, and a tireless fighter for women's rights'. In his personal and public life, he had supported the achievements of Mali's first republic and been a strong proponent of the 1962 code of marriage (which in his view had 'liberated Malian women'). In fact, Sy appears to have been one of the few Malians to have followed the provisions of the 1962 code: contrary to many men's widespread practice of opting for monogamy on the occasion of their first marriage and then later switching to polygamy without seeking their first wife's required consent (a practice he strongly attacked), he had married once according to the monogamy option, divorced, and then married again at city hall.[11] Sy justified ordinary Malian citizens' disregard for the law as the consequence of years of Western-imposed programmes of economic liberalization and the consequent loss of state power. In line with his socialist orientation, Sy identified women's limited economic and political rights as the main cause of women's subordination – a situation, he added, that was only reinforced by religious readings, which further disempowered women. In Sy's view, religion, whether Christianity or Islam, had never contributed to women's emancipation. To overcome women's state of alienation and resolve many of the country's social problems there was only one option, in his opinion: socialism. Sy's remarks were typically followed by warm rounds of applause. While the positive audience response may indicate that his political views were widely shared, they were also the reflection of more complex factors. Several in the audience had been his students (as they indicated in their comments), while others recognized in Sy a representative of a glorious period of Malian history, the struggle for independence and Mali's first socialist regime. Still others expressed appreciation for his outspoken critiques of structural adjustment programmes in the presence of representatives from international aid organizations, tourists, and anthropologists.

Later remarks by a less well-known individual, Diakité, a male member of the Association malienne des droits de l'homme, were far less sympathetic. Scolding Sidibé for her ignorance of the Qur'an, he clarified that 'in reality Islam has never put women behind', and listed three factors as supporting his argument: the importance in Islam of respecting one's mother, the moral obligation to respect the property of one's wife, and the active role played by women in disseminating the Prophet Muhammad's words, as in the case of his wife Aisha. Men's discussion of religious matters showed far greater confidence and authority compared to women's. While Sidibé emphasized ordinary Malians' and her own poor knowledge of Islam, the dangers of biased readings of Islam, and the need for greater education, Diakité dismissed her points on the grounds that they were erroneous and, indeed, a sign of the speaker's ignorance on matters of religion. He made no concession to Sidibé's insightful critiques of the uses and abuses of religion.

Significantly, Traoré Oumou Traoré, who was asked to respond to people's questions and commentaries, did not openly refer to Sidibé's critique of men's prevailing readings of Islam. In an effort to create a common platform with all Malian women, Traoré emphasized that all women experienced damaging stereotypes and social constraints: 'I and the housewife from Bouguni [a provincial town in the south of the country] have the same husband'. However, Traoré made sure not to propose an open confrontation with men (reflecting her previous emphasis on women and men's shared nature). Following a well-established motif in the rhetoric of women leaders since the first republic (1960-8), she proceeded to distance herself from Western feminism and Western women's struggle for their rights. In her view, there was no gender struggle in Mali, but rather a complementarity of roles (see also Ba Konaré 1993: 3-4; 1999). The women's ministry had been created with the objective of promoting the country's development. Malian women were first and foremost Malians, and, as such, they privileged their country's overall interests. Marching at their husbands' side, women had contributed to major historical changes such as the fall of Moussa Traoré's dictatorship and the establishment of democracy. Malian women's trajectory for the betterment of their condition was grounded in their own history, and they did not need to look elsewhere for sources of inspiration.

Malian women activists have often rhetorically asserted their distance from Western feminism (De Jorio 1997: 156-7). They have argued for the possibility of reconciling the promotion of women's greater participation in the Malian economy and politics with the reinforcement of prevailing family values. Accordingly, they have often presented their work as reinforcing the stability of the Malian household and subscribed to a view of gender relationships stressing complementarity rather than equality. Women's primary role as mothers and wives is presented as a firm basis from which to assert claims in other domains. However, the distancing from Western feminism is also to be understood as an attempt to deflect any criticism addressed by religious actors to secularly orientated leaders and activists of complicity with Western imperialism, of forgetting local 'African' values, and of introducing values that are antithetical to Malian traditional lifestyles (e.g. Abu-Lughod 1998; Soares 2009). Indeed, Malian women activists have to walk a fine line between seemingly diverging conceptions of the social order and their institutional references (Muslim religious leaders, state representatives, foreign donors, etc.).

References to Islam also surfaced during the day dedicated to the analysis of violence against women. The main speaker, Temo Tamboura, emphasized how various religions (in particular, Islam and Christianity), not only Malian 'traditional' culture, expected women to obey their husbands 'blindly and unconditionally'. What was not immediately evident was that Tamboura was in perfect agreement with such 'traditional' demands. His position became clearer in response to a provocative question a woman, Koumba Iaresi, formulated:

> I have some problems as to the message of the Qur'an, the Bible, and the Torah. You talk of the obedient woman (*soumise*). What does this term mean? Particularly, due to the fact that when one reads these sacred texts from cover to cover, these books suggest at the same time that we have to be obedient and that we have rights. How are we to understand this? You may be able to shed some light on this issue.

In responding to Iaresi's question, Tamboura suggested that she was the only one to see a contradiction. All religions (including 'animism') conceived of woman as 'a being on the side of man, thus who is submissive'. While he wholeheartedly espoused a reading of Islam as sanctioning women's subordination to men, men had specific duties towards women, in particular to protect them. In addition, he added that such a relation of subordination did not give men any right to mistreat or abuse women. To resolve the situation of violence against women a new family code was needed. (In so saying, he was somewhat modifying his previous attack on the ineffectiveness of women's associations in monitoring the application of state laws or conventions.) However, this new family code should be 'inspired by our realities, [and] ... take our culture, our history, our religions and beliefs, and our social rules into account'. Tamboura here implicitly criticized the version of the family code that President Konaré had submitted in 2002, which if passed would indeed have undermined some of the premises of men's hegemony within the household. On this day, the moderator, Dravé, invited Victor Sy to have the last word, perhaps to conclude in a more conciliatory spirit. Returning to the topic of religion, Sy noted that while religion contributes to more ethical behaviours, 'we need to make sure that fundamentalist readings of religion do not block our evolution ... that they do not end dialogue'.

On reflexivity and the public sphere

The five-day women's conference constituted one of the rare occasions in which women and men gathered together to discuss gender relationships, the Malian family, legal changes, and related topics. However, the modalities of such discursive encounters warrant further attention. In particular, what sort of publicness emerged from such debates? To what extent did those debates approximate the idea of a public sphere as a space of rational-argumentative discourse among peers on issues pertaining to the common good? Certainly it would be hard to describe the conference as a context in which actors bracketed their social identities and engaged in rational debates solely focused on matters of shared public interest (Fraser 1992; 2007). The analysis evidenced instead the relevance of people's situated positions for their discursive articulations in the context of the debates, in particular with regard to their gender identity, but also in the context of education, political affiliation, and transnational links.

Moreover, as suggested by Fraser in her critique of Habermas's unitary conception of the public sphere, when different publics come together, 'the discursive relations among differentially empowered publics are as likely to take the form of contestation as that of deliberation' (1992: 529). Contestation rather than deliberation was indeed predominant at the conference. Direct confrontation and reproach characterized many of the speeches by the adult males in attendance. Men spoke much more assertively and authoritatively than women did, and tended to assign most of the blame to women's own conduct – as in the case of women's inability to secure the application of state law, or their excessive expenditures and immoral behaviour. When making religious arguments, men presented their interpretation of Islam as the only correct one. On this basis, men (with the notable exception of Sy and a few others) tended to discount women's critical readings of religious interpretations as insufficiently informed and not credible. They either denied any validity to women's conclusions – as in the case of Diakité, who claimed that women were wrong to present Islam as a religion that did not respect women – or asserted their position of domination on religious grounds, as in this comment from Tamboura: 'Islam expects submission of women ... and men have the duty to assume women's protection'.

Women, on the other hand, were more hesitant to speak and had to be prompted to do so by the moderator or be encouraged by individuals in the audience. When they did comment, women demonstrated a critical stance toward the forms of their own political participation. They also radically questioned patriarchal traditions, including dominant readings of Islam, as, for instance, when they queried dominant views of women's unequal path to salvation and the identification of God with a masculine being. However, women's linguistic practices were significantly different from men's. As a reflection of their subaltern status, women often framed their critiques in the form of questions even when their intent was clearly polemical. Their rhetorical challenges were couched in more tentative or ironic terms, as in Sidibé's and Koumba Iaresi's public speeches. Other times, as in Traoré Oumou Traoré's speech, they tried to contain and deflect men's strings of accusatory statements by refocusing the audience's attention on men's and women's common nature as human beings, or by reminding the audience of some of women's rights according to Islam.

Women's and men's different verbal practices, and particularly men's critiques of women's form of political participation, limited any concrete building of bridges and led to little recasting of positions. Said differently, the end result of such a space of contestation appears to have been the unresolved articulation of conflicting world orders. At the conference, critical viewpoints on society and gender relationships were expressed, but they did not seem to have substantially affected the views of the dominant group, at least during the proceedings. Consequently, it is questionable whether the conference ended with any specific deliberation pertaining to the common good (and whether religious groups should indeed be the sole target of state policies as opposed to civil servants, strongly represented at the conference). I would argue that it did not. Yet this might be in part because, as several participants noted, state officials and particularly women representatives from the women's ministry were absent, which in and by itself speaks to the weakness of civil society in Mali and, particularly, the divisions within the women's movement.[12]

Despite some of the limitations noted above, the conference did mark the greater participation of women in political and religious discussions, including the potential emancipatory role of women-centred readings of Islam, thus contributing to the 'widening of spaces of discursive contestation' (Fraser 1992: 124). In such contested space, Islam emerged as one authoritative frame of reference to alternatively justify or challenge male hegemony. In particular, women privileged a reading of Islam that emphasized women's rights and challenged men's patriarchal interpretations. Conference participants' engagement with religious issues is thus a further indication of the widening and diversification, if not fragmentation, of the public sphere. Not only 'self-ascribed Muslim authorities' (Salvatore & Eickelman 2004: xii) but also ordinary Malian Muslims are taking part in religious and political debates, engaging in diverging interpretations of sacred texts, and attempting to reconcile differing dimensions of their identities (as Muslims, representatives of women's organizations, mothers, etc.). The discursive positions articulated at the conference (a seemingly secular space) thus bring further evidence to the literature on the public sphere that highlights the role of religion in 'creat[ing] a certain space for debate' (Salvatore & Eickelman 2004: 5) both within and outside the Western tradition. My chapter also suggests that religious debates do not necessarily escape some of the limitations underlined by feminist theorists in their critiques of Habermas's early conception of the public sphere. Social differences are not necessarily bracketed under the supposed search for a common good; indeed, religious discourses constitute an important medium for the articulation of differences.

My analysis of women's discourses at the conference constitutes an attempt to begin to understand some of the characteristics of the emerging Malian public sphere and the challenges that women face as they engage within wider publics. As I have shown, the conference provided women with a new participatory role in religious discussions, including a greater reliance on Islam as a self-empowering idiom, even if women still maintained a subaltern position. While the findings show the lack of a fully egalitarian public forum, they support questioning the commonly held assumption that popular forms of religious participation, in particular women's, are predominantly restricted to adherence to ritualized forms of worship and/or non-verbal, embodied expressions of religiosity. Instead, the findings indicate the importance of examining women's reflexive engagement with the religious in public debates, reflexive modalities that, as Mahmood (2005) reminds us, are grounded within specific regimes of power. Indeed, some women's critical readings of Islam emerged in their effort to mediate between conflicting world orders. Women are often caught between the patriarchal ideology of an influential sector of Malian society and the progressive view of gender equality promoted by some international funding organizations. Their participation at the conference reflects their attempts to reconcile and/or problematize some of these contradictions.

ACKNOWLEDGMENTS

I would like to thank for their critical insights and generous comments at various stages of the writing process Hans-Herber Kögler, Filippo Osella, and Benjamin F. Soares. I am also grateful to Leonardo Villalon and the participants of the Summer Institute on 'Contemporary Islam in West Africa: Senegal in Perspective' (15-29 June 2003) for the stimulating talks and conversations around related topics. This chapter builds on research I conducted from 1993 to the present on women's organizations in Mali (De Jorio 1997; 2001; 2002).

NOTES

[1] Carolyn Sargent (2006) in her study of Malian immigrants in France arrives at similar conclusions, describing how women's references to Islam motivate and strengthen their reproductive choices.

[2] While I am aware of the significant and insightful literature on Islamic feminism (for some recent developments, see Ahmad 2008; Moghadam 2002; Vatuk 2008), I hesitate to apply such a category to describe some of the positions developed by Malian women at the conference. Malian women representatives have often expressed some distance from Western feminism. Based on my conversations with women activists as well as a systematic analysis of the existing literature by Malian women's groups (see De Jorio 1997), I suggest that they do not claim gender equality as a political objective, but rather aim to improve women's rights while subscribing to a view of gender complementarity. It follows that I would qualify the women at the conference as women's rights activists rather than Islamic feminists. The topic, no doubt, warrants further investigation.

[3] Under the presidency of Amadou Toumani Touré (2002-present) no significant legal changes to bring about greater gender equality have yet been made.

[4] Brenner (1993) has insightfully questioned such a distinction by detailing instances of state incursions in the religious.

[5] Soares (2009) has underlined the impact of the Maliki school of law on Malian legislation and particularly the 1962 code of marriage: 'It is striking (but generally unremarked upon) how some of these existing Malian laws are very close – sometimes nearly identical – to some of the rules of Islamic jurisprudence, particularly those of the Maliki school long applied here'.

[6] Although the conference was primarily a site for Malian citizens to debate – and this remains the main focus of the present contribution – the presence of the international community was also significant. A number of international partners, in addition to Malian institutions, had founded the conference and a few international guests sat discretely in the audience. Their presence (as well as the mediatization of the conference) accounts for the adoption of French as the primary medium of communication at the conference. It also accounts for the critical and distancing stances towards both the feminist movement and Western-derived liberalization programmes taken by some conference participants.

[7] In his introductory speech Dravé provided some general information about Traoré Oumou Traoré. He underlined Traoré's marital status, number of children, and her public role as 'President and executive secretary of CAFO, she is a sociolinguist and consultant (*formatrice*) in participatory development as well as gender and development'. Dravé went on to underline Traoré's outstanding education in Mali and abroad as well as her fluency in several foreign languages, such as French, English, Arabic, and Russian, and a number of national languages, such as Songhay, Bamana, and Peul.

[8] The excesses of women's expenditures and the proliferation of ceremonies (as in the case of the naming ceremony for newborns, which was not an occasion for social gatherings and celebrations before the first half of the nineteenth century) is a trend that women's organizations have taken upon themselves to control since the period of one-party rule (1960-91). In 1980 the UNFM issued a circular on the curbing of expenditures and limiting of festivities on the occasion of naming ceremonies, circumcisions, marriages, and deaths.

[9] The potential contribution of women-centred readings of Islam to the improvement of women's conditions as well as some of their ambiguities have been widely discussed in the existing literature (e.g. Ahmad 2008; Moghadam 2002; Vatuk 2008). In this specific ethnographic context, Islam represented one of several intellectual frames of reference, in addition to socialism, human rights activism, the women's movement, and so on.

[10] Victor Sy is representative of the generation of women and men who brought Mali to independence in 1960. He fought the lack of civic freedom under the dictatorship of Moussa Traoré, was detained in prison for his political views, and to avoid further political repercussions left Mali from 1981 to 1991. Upon returning in 1991, Sy played a crucial role at Mali's National Conference (where he was nominated to be second vice president). He recently rejoined the ranks of his former party, the Union Soudanais/Rassemblement Démocratique Africain (US-RDA) (Diakité 2002; see also a series of four interviews with Sy by Cheickna Hamala Sylla and Issa Doumbia [2002]).

[11] References to personal details to illustrate the speaker's point were common throughout the five-day conference. Employed more frequently by women, references to personal experiences were used to pre-empt men's tendency to question women's credibility. Women activists are often accused of merely talking about certain customs (e.g. excision) and not practising what they preach. However, at the conference, several of the women speakers let the audience know they had not had their own daughters excised.

[12] The counter-public addressed here (i.e. women's secular associations) is itself characterized by limited participatory equality, given the distinctions in matters of class, status, and education between the members of women's associations (see De Jorio 1997; 2002; Gosselin 2000; Sanankoua 1991).

REFERENCES

ABU-LUGHOD, L. 1998. The marriage of feminism and Islamism in Egypt: selective repudiation as a dynamic of postcolonial cultural politics. In *Remaking women: feminism and modernity in the Middle East* (ed.) L. Abu-Lughod, 243-69. Princeton: University Press.

AHMAD, I. 2008. Cracks in the 'mightiest fortress': Jamaat-e-Islami's changing discourse on women. *Modern Asian Studies* 42, 549-75.

AMUPI & UNAFEM 2002. Guide sur femme, famille, et Islam. Bamako, Mali (available on-line: *http://www.mpfef.gov.ml/Guide_sur_Femme_Famille_Islam.pdf*, accessed 18 January 2009).

BA KONARÉ, A. 1993. *Dictionnaire des femmes célèbres du Mali.* Bamako: Éditions Jamana.

——— 1999. L'éditorial d'Adam Ba Konaré: aux sources de la vie. *Faro* 00, 3-4.

BHABHA, H. 1990. Introduction: narrating the nation. In *Nation and narration*, H. Bhabha, 1-7. London: Routledge.

BRENNER, L. 1993. Constructing Muslim identities in Mali. In *Muslim identity and social change in sub-Saharan Africa* (ed.) L. Brenner, 59-78. Bloomington: Indiana University Press.

CISSÉ, A. 2006. *Mali: une démocratie à refonder.* Paris: L'Harmattan.

COULOUBALY, P.B. 2004. *Le Mali d'Alpha Oumar Konaré.* Paris: L'Harmattan.

DE JORIO, R. 1997. Female elites, women's formal associations, and political practices in Mali (West Africa). Ph.D. dissertation, Department of Anthropology, University of Illinois, Urbana-Champaign.

——— 2001. Women's organization, the ideology of kinship, and the state in postindependence Mali. In *New directions in anthropological kinship* (ed.) L. Stone, 322-40. Lanham, Md.: Rowman & Littlefield.

——— 2002. Gendered museum, guided he(tour)topias: women and social memory in Mali. *Polar: The Political and Legal Anthropology Review* 25: 2, 50-72.

DIAKITÉ, M. 2002. Interview de Victor Sy: qui est Victor Sy? In *Bâtissons la mémoire du Mali démocratique: 26 mars 1991-26 mars 2001: Xe anniversaire*, Centre Djoliba and Mémorial Modibo Keïta, 281-3. Bamako: Centre Djoliba.

FAC-MR (Comité malien de la fondation femmes d'Afrique et culture-Memorial Rufisque) 1999. *Les associations féminines au Mali.* Bamako: Éditions Jamana.

FERGUSON, J. & A. GUPTA 2002. Spatializing states: toward an ethnography of neoliberal governmentality. *American Ethnologist* **29**, 981-1002.

FOUCAULT, M. 1982. The subject and power. In *Michel Foucault: beyond structuralism and hermeneutics* (eds) H. Dreyfus & P. Rabinow, 208-26. Chicago: University Press.

FRASER, N. 1992. Rethinking the public sphere: a contribution to the critique of actually existing democracy. In *Habermas and the public sphere* (ed.) C. Calhoun, 109-42. Cambridge, Mass.: MIT Press.

———— 2007. Transnationalizing the public sphere: on the legitimacy and efficacy of public opinion in a post-Westphalian world. *Theory, Culture & Society* **24**: 4, 7-30.

GAL, S. 1991. Between speech and silence: the problematics of research on language and gender. In *Gender at the crossroads of knowledge* (ed.) M. di Leonardo, 175-203. Berkeley: University of California Press.

GOSSELIN, C. 2000. Handing over the knife: *numu* women and the campaign against excision in Mali. In *Female 'circumcision' in Africa* (eds) B. Shell-Duncan & Y. Hernlund, 193-214. Boulder, Colo.: Lynne Rienner.

KÖGLER, H.H. 1999. *The power of dialogue.* Cambridge, Mass.: MIT Press.

———— 2005. Constructing a cosmopolitan public sphere: hermeneutic capabilities and universal values. *European Journal of Social Theory* **8**, 297-320.

LAUNAY, R. & B.F. SOARES. 1999. The formation of an 'Islamic sphere' in French colonial West Africa. *Economy and Society* **28**, 497-519.

MAHMOOD, S. 2005. *Politics of piety: the Islamic revival and the feminist subject.* Princeton: University Press.

MOGHADAM, V. 2002. Islamic feminism and its discontents: toward a resolution of the debate. *Signs* **27**, 1135-71.

OTAYEK, R. & B.F. SOARES 2007. Introduction: Islam and Muslim politics in Africa. In *Islam and Muslim politics in Africa* (eds) B.F. Soares & R. Otayek, 1-24. New York: Palgrave Macmillan.

SALVATORE, A. 2007a. *The public sphere: liberal modernity, Catholicism, Islam.* Palgrave Macmillan.

———— 2007b. Authority in question: secularity, republicanism and 'communitarianism' in the emerging Euro-Islamic public sphere. *Theory, Culture & Society* **24**: 2, 135-60.

———— 2007c. The exit from a Westphalian framing of political space and the emergence of a transnational Islamic public. *Theory, Culture & Society* **24**: 4, 45-52.

———— & D.F. EICKELMAN. 2004. *Public Islam and the common good.* Leiden: Brill.

SANANKOUA, B. 1991. Les associations féminines musulmanes à Bamako. In *L'enseignement islamique au Mali* (eds) B. Sanankoua & L. Brenner, 105-25. Bamako: Éditions Jamana.

SARGENT, C. 2006. Reproductive strategies and Islamic discourse: Malian migrants negotiate everyday life in Paris. *Medical Anthropology Quarterly* **20**, 31-49.

SCHULZ, D. 2003. Political factions, ideological fictions: the controversy over the reform of family law in democratic Mali. *Islamic Law and Society* **10**, 132-64.

———— 2006. Promises of (im)mediate salvation: Islam, broadcast media, and the remaking of religious experience in Mali. *American Ethnologist* **33**, 210-29.

SOARES, B.F. 2005. *Islam and the prayer economy: history and authority in a Malian town.* Edinburgh: University Press for the International African Institute; Ann Arbor: University of Michigan Press.

———— 2006. Islam in Mali in the neoliberal era. *African Affairs* **105**: 418, 77-95.

———— 2009. The attempt to reform family law in Mali. *Die Welt des Islams* **49**: 3/4.

SYLLA, C.H. & I. DOUMBIA 2002. Interviews de Victor Sy. In *Bâtissons la mémoire du Mali démocratique: 26 mars 1991-26 mars 2001: Xe anniversaire*, Centre Djoliba and Mémorial Modibo Keità, 281-3. Bamako: Centre Djoliba.

VATUK, S. 2008. Islamic feminism in India: Indian Muslim women activists and the reform of Muslim personal law. *Modern Asian Studies* **42**, 489-518.

7

Piety politics and the role of a transnational feminist analysis

LARA DEEB *Department of Anthropology, Scripps College*

In December 1999, towards the beginning of an extended period of field research in the pious Shi'i Muslim community in the southern suburb of Beirut, Widad,[1] the president of an Islamic women's organization where I had recently begun volunteering, asked Aziza, my closest friend in the community, about me. As a researcher from the United States, I was accustomed to understandable encounters with suspicion; however, as Aziza related their conversation to me, it became clear that this was different. Rather than trying to assess whether or not I had any ties to espionage or the US government, Widad was instead trying to assess whether I was talking to the 'right' people in her community in Lebanon. She wanted to know to which other organizations I had gone and what sort of information I had been receiving about Islam and Muslim women. Widad then concluded the conversation by emphasizing that she 'welcomed the opportunity to show Lara the way that Islam is civilized and how modern our women are'.

This sense that it was crucial to demonstrate the modernity and civilized status of Islam and especially Muslim women is one of the dominant themes that has emerged again and again in my conversations with pious Shi'i Muslims – men and women – in Lebanon over the past ten years.[2] Also ten years ago, in her introduction to the key volume *Remaking women*, Lila Abu-Lughod wrote that the volume would address

> the way that in the postcolonial world women have become potent symbols of identity and visions of society and the nation ... the way that women themselves actively participate in these debates and social struggles ... [and] the complex ways that the West and things associated with the West, embraced, repudiated, and translated, are implicated in contemporary gender politics (1998b: 3).

It is my contention that both the questions and the political implications that Abu-Lughod raised in her introduction remain relevant today. In fact, a resurgence of tropes equating certain forms of Islam with absolute 'otherness' and calling upon women's bodies and practices to mark those boundaries has amplified the echoes of the colonial and anti-colonial discourses that *Remaking women* (Abu-Lughod 1998*a*) so successfully addressed and is reflected in the concerns of my Lebanese Shi'i interlocutors. In its contemporary formations, questions of Muslim women's status have focused on two related areas: the headscarf and women's public participation. This is due in part to the long history of symbolic potency of the headscarf and assumptions about its relationship to limitations or facilitations of women's public participation (Abu-Lughod 2002; Ahmed 1992; El Guindi 1999; MacLeod 1991) and in part to particular Western feminist assumptions that public participation is an accurate indicator of women's status in society.

In anthropology, concern with these issues has emerged in recent discussions of the relationship between piety and politics in two major strands of work. Research interrogating the notion of a 'Muslim public' builds upon and critiques Habermasian notions of the public sphere in order to shed light on the ways that Muslim publics have been transformed in relation to politics, Islamisms, and new technologies (Deeb 2005; Eickelman & Anderson 1999; Göle 1997; Meyer & Moors 2006; Salvatore 2000; Salvatore & Eickelman 2004; Salvatore & LeVine 2005). Another strand of scholarship has instead focused on the formation of pious subjectivities and ethical selves through the cultivation of embodied dispositions, where moral reform is itself a political project of ethical self-fashioning (Asad 1993; Hirschkind 2006; Mahmood 2005). Both these theoretical directions begin to provide ways of thinking about the relationship between piety and politics that move away from causal reductionisms. They also allow us to begin to confront two sets of limiting ideas that plague theorizing on the relationship of piety to politics when it comes to gender in particular. On the one hand, the insights of scholarship on pious subjectivities build on the lessons of women-of-colour feminisms in the United States (e.g. Mohanty 1988), emphasizing the need to reformulate notions of feminist agency and moving away from narrow definitions of 'emancipation' in which there is no room for certain ideas about pious selves (see especially Mahmood 2005; see also Deeb 2006*a*). On the other hand, analyses of Muslim publics and public spheres have highlighted the necessity of problematizing understandings of religiosity that insist on its delineation in a separate sphere (see Asad 1986; Salvatore 2000).

These analyses contribute to the deconstruction of instrumentalist arguments that assume that piety practices are linked to identity politics or to economic, social, or political gain, arguments that are rooted in part in an unwillingness to view practices of piety as a form of agency in and of themselves. Yet in responding to such instrumentalist arguments, it is also possible to slip into another sort of reductive argument where piety becomes a singular aspect of life unto itself, fully detached from other daily practices, from politics, and from complex social environments and relationships. In this sense, the analytic danger in over-privileging individualized practices of piety and divorcing them from their social, economic, and political contexts is reminiscent of studies of Islam divorced from nation-state contexts.[3]

In what follows, I suggest that a more complete analysis of the relationship between practices of piety and politics would benefit from the incorporation of transnational feminist analyses – and especially analyses of transnational discourses on gender and Islam. Transnational discursive contexts are critical to the ways in which the stakes of piety have been raised in the contemporary world, and to the themes that have been at work in these debates for over a century, positioning women at the borders between various civilizational and moral constructs. When I refer to 'transnational analysis', I am referring not to multi-sited research, but rather to the ways in which we can attend to our interlocutors' engagements with discourses that emerge in and travel through transnational contexts of power, capitalism, and militarism,[4] most obviously nowadays with regard to US interventions in the Middle East and elsewhere.

The specific case I will consider is that of pious Shi'i Muslim gender activists in the southern suburb of Beirut – among them Widad and Aziza. After providing an overview of the necessary context for understanding their community and its concerns, I will turn to the example of a seminar on public participation sponsored by the Hizbullah Women's Committee and explore the engagements with transnationally constituted discourses about Muslim women and about Western women that were articulated by its participants. Finally, I will conclude by comparing contemporary transnational engagements with those of an earlier era, and revisiting the importance of such engagements to our analyses.

Piety/politics and civilizational status in *al-Dahiya*

The southern suburb of Beirut, referred to in Lebanon simply as *al-Dahiya* – literally, 'the suburb' – is comprised of a series of neighbourhoods whose population today is mostly but not entirely Shi'i Muslim and where Hizbullah is the most popular, though by no means the sole, political presence.[5] For heuristic purposes, I use the phrase 'pious Shi'i community' or 'pious Shi'i Muslims' as an imperfect gloss for those who identify with certain ideologies and practices of piety that are centred on a nexus represented by both the prominent religious scholar Sayyid Muhammad Husayn Fadlallah and Hizbullah.[6] Obviously, not all pious Shi'is in Lebanon fit this description, nor is sect by any means a fixed category.[7] However, it is possible to identify a (often self-identified) community of pious Shi'i Muslims defined by these shared practices and ideologies.

In addition, among pious Shi'i Muslims living in this area of the capital, recent decades have seen the convergence of particular expressions and cultivations of piety with particular definitions and expressions of modernity. By 'modern' or 'modernity', I mean to connote a value-laden and context-derived concept, which in this case distils down to notions of progress in both the spiritual and material realms.[8] But there is also another usage which holds relevance for my discussion here. Frequently, people used 'modern' almost interchangeably with 'civilized' to indicate their status along a 'civilized'-'barbaric' continuum. This emphasis on the term 'civilized', usually phrased in Arabic as 'we have civilization' (*'indna hadara*), is crucial because in addition to evoking the 'clash of civilizations' thesis and rhetoric, it evokes conflict and questions around who has the authority and the ability to define the terms of 'civilized status' along that continuum and what signifiers are utilized in doing so.

Of the many critiques of the 'clash of civilizations' thesis that underlies the binarisms set up between Islam and the West, I want to follow Amira Jarmakani's lead (2008) and highlight a feminist critique made by Minoo Moallem (2005) and Lila Abu-Lughod (1998b), among others, about the ways in which civilizational discourses are dependent on gendered assumptions.[9] Often grounded in histories of colonialism and/or nationalist movements, this critique underscores the ways in which women are frequently cast – as signifiers – in the role of 'barometer' of a society's location on a hierarchical and linear axis of 'civilizational status'. Gender is implicated here for a number of reasons, including the symbolic relationship between woman and nation, ideologies that underscore women's role in producing and reproducing communities, and a 'discourse of protection' that creates alliances between white men and women and legitimates their positions as protectors and 'free women', respectively (Moallem 2005). This is an alliance and positioning familiar to us from postcolonial studies' analyses, but it is also important to contemporary neoimperialism in the Middle East.[10]

This axis of civilizational status functions in a variety of ways. 'Women's status' may be understood to signify the level of national progress that has been achieved, as in the writings of Egyptian reformer Qasim Amin (1992 [1899]) on women's education or the historical politics of forced unveiling as part of state modernization programmes in Turkey and Iran. 'Women's status' may also signify the preservation of national culture in the face of colonialism, as in the reversal of veiling policies in Iran during and after the Islamic Revolution, or the positioning of women in the nationalist movement in Bengal (Chatterjee 1993). In the first example, the axis of civilizational status measures movement away from a state of 'backwardness' or 'barbarism'. In the second example, an age-old civilization is seen as under attack from certain aspects of modernization driven by colonialism. But in both cases, it is women's bodies that mark the location of a culture or society on this axis (cf. Jarmakani 2008). And in both cases, transnational discursive contexts are critical to these positionings of women's bodies and 'status' at the borders between various civilizational and moral constructs.

The pious Shiʻi women with whom I worked in *al-Dahiya* simultaneously articulated a sense of being responsible for representing their community's civilized status *and* reproduced the very civilizational binarisms upon which this role as signifier rested. In *al-Dahiya*, a codependence of ideas about being pious and ideas about being modern has emerged in a specifically gendered way: it is women who are primarily responsible for demonstrating and inhabiting a moral position related to *both* states (piety and modernity) in the contemporary world. In other words, women's status has come to be viewed as an indicator – perhaps the key indicator – of the community's status itself. Furthermore, to be considered fully 'civilized' or 'modern' within the community, one had to demonstrate this in both the material and spiritual registers, linking piety and political activism together in a process of subject formation that was conceptualized as 'self-improvement'.

One form in which a merged piety/politics (crucially, with neither term modifying the other) has become increasingly visible in *al-Dahiya* is in women's participation in the public arena, often, though not exclusively, through Islamic social welfare organizations. Frequently taking on a third shift, in addition to their household and employment duties, pious Shiʻi women are contributing to what they conceptualize as the continuing 'development' of their community – in both the material and the spiritual senses – through unpaid labour in these organizations. Their work ranges from the provision of basic needs (e.g. food, medicine, blankets, clothing) for poor families to leading educational seminars on topics ranging from hygiene to Qurʼanic interpretation to how best to approach the religious court system. In this sense, women's public participation is not only important to women's status in relation to its positioning as a barometer of the community's status, but it is implicated in the development and 'improvement' of that status in the first place.

Women's increased public participation in *al-Dahiya* is related to two major changes in the Lebanese Shiʻi community over the past several decades. The first is the development of an organizational network through which community welfare activity can take place. This network represents the institutionalization of a Lebanese Shiʻi Islamic mobilization that began in the 1970s, and that today is represented most prominently – though not exclusively – by the political party Hizbullah.[11] The second change is the concurrent development of a new model of ideal moral womanhood for pious

Lebanese Shiʿi women, described by one of my interlocutors as 'outspoken, Muslim, committed, and educated'.

This model emphasizes particular forms of publicly expressed and cultivated piety as a key aspect of being considered a modern person, along with active participation in the community. A woman's public participation and public piety are understood as linked, and are evaluated in terms of her contribution to the common good of the community, the cultivation of her own piety, and the demonstration of the modern status of herself and her community to the outside world. It is the latter that forms the crux of my discussion here, especially in relation to the ways that my pious Shiʿi interlocutors, like Widad in this chapter's opening, consciously and directly worked to contest transnational stereotypes about pious Muslim women as passive or oppressed. Indeed, women's public participation is being conceptualized by some pious activists in this community as 'part of religious duty', a conceptualization that emerges both from social and religious values like that of mutual social solidarity (*takaful al-ijtima'i*) and from engagements with transnational discourses about the status and image of Muslim women. As one community activist put it: 'We see these terrible images of Muslim women, images that say that we are very oppressed and backward. It is very important that we show people that this is incorrect, to show that we can be committed to our religion and be educated and cultured at the same time'.

To illustrate the ways that transnational discourses are implicated in the construction of this model of ideal womanhood, I will draw on the example of a seminar on women's public participation held by the Hizbullah Women's Committee in 2000. I want to highlight the ways in which the seminar participants themselves engaged with various transnational discourses about gender roles. These engagements are not only situational and contextually dependent, but also represent ways in which values expressed in different gender norms are productively reformulated.

Seminars held by various women's organizations in *al-Dahiya* were common venues for discussions about women's public participation and often worked to both encourage and facilitate it. This particular seminar was led by Nayla, an engineer who had recently left her job at an architectural firm in order to devote more of her time to activism within the political sphere. The twenty participants ranged from women in their forties and fifties who held only high school diplomas, to college graduates in their twenties and thirties, and a few undergraduate students. In general, they were active in their community, sometimes in opposition to their families' or husbands' wishes, and they shared the view that one of the tasks of their gender activism was to work to change that opposition. Indeed, for this group of women, as well as for many other pious Shiʿi women in *al-Dahiya* who actively participated in their community, *activism* itself necessarily included gender activism. This is the case because no matter what the proximate purposes of women's public activity – be it assisting the poor, running an educational centre, or raising funds to support martyrs' families – the mere fact of women's visibility in the public arena demanded a critical engagement with gender norms and presented a *de facto* challenge to those norms. Most women in *al-Dahiya* were aware of this, even as they tended to articulate the importance of their gender-specific struggles in terms of transnational image rather than local sexism, an emphasis related to the dynamics between these two factors in the first place.

Nayla opened the seminar by speaking about the different types of struggle – *jihad* – that women should take part in, including military, social and cultural struggles; she defined the latter as being able to learn about and discuss gender norms from 'other societies'. Throughout, she returned to textual citations from the Qur'an and *hadith*, as well as from the *ijtihad* (interpretations of religious texts) of various Shi'i scholars, especially Ayatollah Khomeini and Sayyid Muhammad Husayn Fadlallah. After about twenty minutes, she opened the seminar up for general discussion among the participants. Over the next hour and a half, the conversation tacked in myriad different ways, including among its many topics: possible strategies for facilitating women's greater political role in Lebanon and specifically how to convince Hizbullah to run a woman candidate for Parliament; a discussion of patriarchy in Lebanese society and how to teach men to take on a greater role in the domestic sphere; a pragmatic discussion of strategies to change laws in Lebanon around issues like childcare and maternity leave for working mothers; and concern with the recent interest of journalists in their work.

In addition, and most relevant to our purposes here, throughout the seminar participants drew on transnational examples and discourses to make their points. For instance, the classic example of women's participation in the Algerian anti-colonial resistance came up as an example from which a lesson was to be learned. A student at the Lebanese University who had been reading about the ways that Algerian women had been 'sent home' after the revolution brought this up as a cautionary note, asking what could be done to prevent such a reaction against women's public role in Lebanon in the event of peace with Israel.[12] Iran was also raised as another example in this vein, where the situation was described as 'better' than what happened in Algeria, but 'not good enough', in terms of women's participation in society after their work with the revolution was perceived as completed. Interestingly, however, this group of women's experience with and knowledge of Iran did not extend to the plethora of (what has been termed) 'Islamic feminist' discourse that has developed there since the 1980s.

Transnational discourses about gender norms emerged in several other ways as well, and I will focus on two of these: ideas about Western women, and ideas about the West's views of Muslim women. In this regard the seminar discussion exemplifies both the ways that binary civilizational discourses are drawn upon *and* the places where those binary distinctions collapse.

Contrasting gender discourses

Participants in this seminar, as well as many of my other interlocutors in *al-Dahiya*, often commented on the interest that journalists took in 'Hizbullah women'. Several of the seminar participants had been interviewed by reporters at various times over the years, and they observed that these reporters were – as one woman put it – 'all looking to see if Islam is modern, so what do they do? They look at the women'. Others commented that this was also because 'Westerners' all think that Muslim women are 'backward and oppressed'. They then noted that one of their tasks was to challenge such perspectives, and to 'teach the world' that their society is modern and civilized by demonstrating this through their own actions, and, most crucially, through their visibility in the public sphere and work to improve the status of other women in their community.

Outside the Hizbullah seminar too, pious Shi'i women frequently expressed an acute understanding of the importance of perceptions of women's status to perceptions of the level of modernity or civilization of a place or people. For example, in a conversation about local responses to the women-run organization where she worked, an activist told me that she hoped that the organization would provide evidence of women's public capabilities. I thought at first we were talking about providing evidence within Lebanon, but then she continued, saying: 'We have to set an example for the world ... This work is part of our religious duty, because woman is the example for everything. A culture is judged by the level of its women'.

Several years later, while another volunteer with the same organization was describing their activities to me, she emphasized the importance of the nursery they ran, saying,

> Our nursery is extremely important because it is a place for working women to leave their children when they go to work. And it is being spoken of as the best nursery in all of Beirut, not even only *al-Dahiya*. People from all over walk in to see, and they are surprised, they say, 'Wow, these are Muslims, but they understand, they are educated, they have awareness'.

Her defensive tone and recounting of the phrase 'Muslims ... but' here are indicative of the extent to which both transnational and local Lebanese discourses stereotyping Muslims – and in particular Shi'i Muslims – in negative ways have been encountered and confronted by my interlocutors.

It is also crucial to note that such transnational and Lebanese discourses are not necessarily unrelated, and in fact work in conjunction with one another in various ways. For example, I had several conversations with the co-ordinator of an explicitly feminist NGO in Lebanon. She had little patience for what she called 'local feminisms' and insisted that Islamic feminism was an 'oxymoron'. While she conceded that the 'Islamic' women who attended a training session she facilitated had been 'the most outspoken and participatory' in the group, she continued, 'It doesn't matter, because in the end, they won't take that scarf off. You can progress and progress and progress and raise the living standards and be outspoken and voice your opinions like men, but then faith will step in and stop it all'. If the listener did not know its Lebanese context, this statement might be assumed to represent that of the director of a feminist NGO based in the United States or Europe. Yet not only does it reflect stereotypes held by Lebanese about 'other' Lebanese, but it also points to assumptions, held by some in Lebanon as well as elsewhere, about the incompatibility of religiosity with modernity. More recently, the relationship between transnational and Lebanese discourses can also be seen in the ways that increased specifically anti-Shi'i sentiment within Lebanon has accompanied the alignment of the government versus opposition divide with pro- versus anti-United States political stances.

The general sense among my interlocutors is that both the public visibility of pious women in their community and the imperative to actively address transnational discourses about Muslim women have only increased since 2001.[13] Indeed, during a more recent conversation with Nayla in 2007, she related that she had ceased to grant interviews to anyone who was interested in talking about 'Hizbullah women', though she continued to communicate with a few journalists via email. She listed a number of reasons for this, including changes in her work schedule and responsibilities within the party (she is no longer running the Women's Committee but has a more direct political role), the fact that the questions had become repetitive and were often too simplistic, a desire to be viewed as a political figure regardless of her sex, and suspicions about the interviewers themselves or a sense that they were not genuinely interested in dialogue. Despite this reluctance to engage directly with journalists, Nayla confirmed that she remained interested in using the media to confront stereotypical images of Muslim women, noting that she 'always served this issue in [her] interviews. Because some people who come to interview us are open to getting to know us, they are not just stuck with what the other media tells them, no, they say, there is this thing, let me ask about it, see what it is about'.

A contrasting set of transnational discourses that emerged in the seminar were those regarding 'the liberated Western woman' – often just as monolithic a construct as 'the oppressed Muslim woman'. Yet unlike the image of the 'Westoxicated' woman that saturated the revolutionary Iranian context,[14] the Hizbullah seminar participants presented a more complex and ambivalent relationship to this notion of 'Western woman'.[15] On the one hand, for example, the figure of the Western woman emerged when one participant noted the difficulties women faced in working outside the home in Lebanon, including societal expectations that they would prioritize the domestic realm, pressure from spouses, and the gossip of neighbours and relatives. 'In the West, women don't have this problem', she concluded.

Another woman concurred, and noted that 'in the West, all parts of society are working, women and men are standing together. Here, we are a society that is missing half of our potential. They work with two teams, we have only half of that'. This assertion contains an echo of the statements of elite Egyptian reformers during British colonialism, like Qasim Amin, who used such arguments to argue for unveiling and for women's education – though *not* for women's participation in the political and economic realms (Amin 1992 [1899]).[16] It is also an assertion that contributes an added importance to pious Shi'i women's public participation – emphasizing that it is necessary for the progress of their community and underscoring comparison with ideals that are associated with the West, especially those stemming from development discourses and liberal feminist discourses.

On the other hand, several women who had lived in the United States and Canada offered the perspective that 'social relationships are coming apart in the West. There are no family ties or neighbourly relations. People are alone with no support from society'. This was also phrased as, 'In the Western civilizations, you find that a person lives for himself more than for his family, the women too'. Another problem was located in the West's notion of women's rights, as my interlocutors interpreted them. Here Nayla chimed back in, offering authoritatively the difference between the *musawa*, or equality, of the West, which she defined as 'being identical to or the same as', as opposed to the *'adala* of Islam, meaning equity or justice that allows for difference.

In the end, this part of the discussion concluded with an apparent consensus that neither the situation in Lebanon nor the situation in the West was appropriate.[17] Participants agreed that the work of women in Hizbullah's Women's Committee and in their society more generally should therefore be to forge a third way. This was envisioned as a hybrid of sorts by some participants, who described linking and fusing 'the values of the West and the values of our society'. Others disagreed, imagining instead a model that has no precedent and that may look to elements of existing models for inspiration, but without incorporating them:

> We have no examples, because the examples we have are either of oppressed women or of Western women who are equal to men in everything, even in the things that they should not be equal in. Instead, we have to set a new example for the world, an example of women who are Muslim but strong and educated.

My interest here is less in the specifics of the conclusion at which seminar participants arrived than in the process of articulation of multiple transnationally constituted discourses about gender norms that facilitated that conclusion. Participants' engage-ments with transnational discourses about gender norms and roles were not solely reactive, opposing stereotypes or constructing their own models of ideal womanhood in opposition to stereotyped 'others'. This was also a *productive* engagement, through which various elements were transformed into a new model of ideal pious womanhood that is understood – at least by some of the women present – as resembling none of the existing models discussed. In this sense, my interlocutors themselves enacted a trans-national feminist practice, moving beyond the binary divisions of civilizational discourses.

Contemporary transnational engagements

Engagements with transnational discourses about Muslim women provide a contem-porary example of the ways in which ideas about women and gender norms are understood in a Muslim community to be important to the boundaries between binary civilizational constructs – so that in the constructed opposition between 'Islam' and 'the West', women's activities, status, and visibility mark the border between 'us' and 'them' on both sides. Historically, this is a common theme, emerging again and again in literature on both colonialism and anti-colonial nationalist movements. The debate among participants in the Hizbullah seminar as to the merit of the model provided by (their notion of) the 'Western woman' is also a common one.

Consider, for example, Partha Chatterjee's analysis of anti-colonial nationalists in India (Chatterjee 1993). This analysis is one in which, against notions of a Westernized woman, Bengali women were delegated the maintenance of the spiritual domain, and material development and modernization were conceptualized as the domain of nationalist men. Women's spiritual responsibility was also linked to a gendered division of space into public and domestic spheres. This led to shifts in the nineteenth century in gender norms that facilitated elite women's emergence into public spaces – yet in this case, this shift did not alter the gendered nature of the spiritual/material (private/public) divide.

In contrast, in the Shi'i Lebanese case today, the material and spiritual domains are linked without a similarly prominent gender divide, and where such a divide can be discerned, it is in fact *women* who are allotted the greater responsibility of representing their community as developed and modern through their visible participation in the public sphere. Omnia Shakry's work on discourses about mothering in Egypt at the turn of the twentieth century highlights some of the problematics of generalizing across colonial histories, and she notes that in contrast to the Indian case,

> The 'women's question' in Egypt clearly linked both the moral and material domains and articulated in complex ways with colonial discourse. Although Egyptian nationalist discourse clearly sought to uphold women as a source of cultural integrity, it also localized them as an arena for the social, political, and cultural progress of the nation (1998: 129-30).

A key difference between the colonial case that Shakry discusses and that of my contemporary Lebanese interlocutors lies in the critical importance in colonial Egypt of notions of mothering as the sphere within which women's progress was to occur. In *al-Dahiya*, by contrast, rhetorics of progress have been taken outside the boundaries of the family so that women are charged with *community* development.

Building on this comparison, I wish to close by raising the question of what, if anything, is different about the ways in which women are positioned at the boundary between civilizations through transnational discourses about gender norms in the contemporary moment. One possibility is that the circulation of discourses itself differs. It is clear that transnational discourses about both Muslim and Western women are being engaged, circulated, interpreted, appropriated, reformulated, and contested today, but such circulations and engagements are certainly not new. As Peter van der Veer has noted, '[T]he transnational public sphere today is the successor of a public sphere that in many societies is formed in a contest of the interaction between empire and the nation-state' (2004: 29).[18]

Yet, clearly, contemporary circulations are heavily mediated, such that it is imperative that we take seriously the circuits of knowledge production that inform engagements with gender and other discourses. Electronic media and satellite television in particular contribute to the production of different sorts of public spheres and relationships to circulating information and ideas.[19] My pious Shi'i interlocutors responded in part to images of Muslim women they viewed on CNN International and the BBC, and confronted those images through their work with al-Jazeera and Hizbullah's television station, al-Manar. Over the past two decades, Hizbullah itself has built a sophisticated and media-savvy information production and distribution network that selectively targets various Lebanese and international audiences in different campaigns and that has employed numerous pious women who were unable to find employment in media in other parts of Beirut due to anti-Islam discrimination. After the summer war of 2006, for example, a recently established media office drew on its employees' advertising and design expertise to design a multilingual and internationally noted campaign declaring the party's 'Divine Victory' (a play on the meaning of Hizbullah leader Sayyid Hasan Nasrallah's name in Arabic). Other campaigns have selectively targeted an international audience, a broad Lebanese audience, or their own constituents.

The second potential difference may stem from the varying contingencies of European colonialism versus contemporary US 'neoimperialism'.[20] Since the 1970s, Islam and Muslim women have been positioned in particular ways in relation to specifically US power, often directly related to international political conflicts.[21] The figure of the 'Westoxicated' woman, whose materialism and immorality provided the point of contrast for both Islamist and leftist women during the 1978-9 Islamic revolution in Iran, is a classic example. A more recent instance is represented by the figure of the oppressed Muslim woman in need of liberation by the US military that emerged most strikingly in the case of the rhetoric around Afghanistan, where the *burka* was used to provide added moral justification for US military attack.[22]

In the United States' complicity with the summer 2006 Israeli attack on Lebanon, Muslim women were not mentioned. However, a civilizational discourse in which women play a key representative role in defining and claiming civilizational status remains a major subtext within which dynamics of US power are negotiated in Lebanon and other contemporary conflicts. This type of gender construction legitimates military adventure even when not explicit. It does so in part by bifurcating the world into those who are deemed civilized and those who are not, and by assuming that those who are have a right to 'bring' civilization to those who are not by whatever means necessary. It also does so through erasures of complexity, in favour of essentializing explanations that make claims about naturalized identities, often rooted in ideas about religious difference. Legitimations of particular military actions and policies are also bolstered through the erasure of political and economic factors and explanations of conflict and difference in favour of cultural ones (Abu-Lughod 2002), as well as through the construction of armed opposition to US military adventure as terrorists hiding behind 'helpless women and children', a construction that once again reinforces the notion that certain women require rescue from their own communities. The stakes of the politics of representation are material and military.

This is a crucial aspect of the context in which Shi'i women's public participation is viewed as central to their signifying the status of their community. Gender norms here are critical because of both local and international concern, as well as local concern about international concern. When I asked Nayla why she thought there was so much interest among journalists and others in the women of the party, she explained that this was related to a general interest in Hizbullah as well as to a sense that Hizbullah women were more active and visible than women in other Islamic movements. She continued, however, by noting that 'even the *mukhabarat* (informers/intelligence agents/spies) are working on this topic, because usually when they want to *attack any group, they study all the details about this group and especially about its women*'.

Lest her fears seem conspiratorial, or rooted in memories of colonial discourses no longer relevant to a contemporary world, consider the 1 June 2007 article from the *Jerusalem Post* that I received in my email from two other women in *al-Dahiya*, as well as two colleagues in the United States. The article was titled 'Empowered women could combat Islamic extremism' and it described a conference 'on the empowerment of Arab women at the Hebrew University's Shasha Center for Strategic and Policy Studies' (Snyder 2007). Attendees at this conference 'examined the traditions within Muslim society that prevent women from obtaining work and education outside the home and what the Israeli government and social organizations could do too in this area'. The director of the sponsoring centre, Ephraim Halevy, was 'a former head of the Mossad and the National Security Council'. Examples such as this lend credence to Nayla's fears, demonstrate the circulation of transnational gender discourses through email and other media, and point to continuities between colonial gender discourses and contemporary ones.

In this contemporary context, ideas about and acts of piety are related to a complex of practices and beliefs that cannot be divorced from the broader political and social environment, an environment in which transnational discourses about gender norms and Muslim women play a major role. A convergence has emerged among the value placed upon women's public participation, ideas about the necessity of that public participation to demonstrating the status of the Muslim community in a transnational field, and the moral imperative that constructs women's public activism as religious duty and as necessary to piety. This triangulation ensures that piety, social practices, and politics cannot be isolated from one another.

To assume that piety is a self-contained aspect of life for pious Shi'i Muslims in *al-Dahiya* would do a disservice to their own nuanced engagements with the complex social and political worlds in which they live. To focus solely on the religious milieu in this case – or to privilege an analysis of pious subjectivities and ethical selves located within a depoliticized religious milieu – would obscure both the political and economic dimensions of my interlocutors' lives (including their religious lives) and the wider frame of reference which informs their debates and practices. As I hope to have demonstrated, a transnational feminist analysis is one critical element in this broader framework.

Serious attention to transnational discourses about gender roles and norms and various articulations of and engagements with these discourses is necessary to our thinking through the complex relationships between Islamic pieties and politics, for a number of reasons. First, these circulations of and engagements with knowledge may challenge us to think through concepts of agency and its relation to religion and politics. Second, attention to these discourses is important because civilizational dichotomies are drawn through them, and those dichotomies have been called upon in support of various political-economic, social, and military interventions in the Middle East and elsewhere. The transnational discursive context also provides a lens that complicates our understandings of the ways in which various models of ideal womanhood that incorporate piety and politics as inseparable aspects of life are constructed and contested, and, lastly, it raises questions about the contrasts between the relationship of gender norms to anti-colonial nationalisms versus contemporary anti-imperialist struggles. Only by attending to these discourses and the ways in which they are appropriated, altered, and reflected can we come to a nuanced understanding of their implications and of the relationship between piety and politics on the global, national, and local levels.

ACKNOWLEDGMENTS

Thanks to Amira Jarmakani, Filippo Osella, Esra Özyürek, and Benjamin Soares for their comments. All shortcomings of course remain my own.

NOTES

[1] All names are pseudonyms.

[2] Proving that one is 'civilized' is a common rhetorical device in Lebanon. In the eighteen-month stand-off between the government and the opposition parties (of which Hizbullah is a major player) that followed the July 2006 war on Lebanon, and during the short period of violence that led to the Doha agreement ending that stand-off in May 2008, both sides frequently laid claim to being 'civilized', while implying that the other side was not. This is not happening in a vacuum or only in relation to internal Lebanese politics. The term 'civilized' is pregnant with references to value structures related to Europe, the United States, and/or other parts of the Islamic world, with different values emphasized by different speakers and in different contexts.

[3] This is one of the lacunae that *Remaking women* sought to address (see Abu-Lughod 1998b: 5-7).

[4] This notion of transnational feminist analysis builds on the work of scholars such as Inderpal Grewal, Caren Kaplan, and Minoo Moallem (Grewal & Kaplan 1994; Moallem 2005). Such a framework is also attentive to the articulations of gender, nation, race, religion, sexuality, and class within these transnational relations of power.

[5] For more on *al-Dahiya*, see Deeb (2006a: chap. 2) and Harb (1996).

[6] It is important to note that Fadlallah and Hizbullah do not represent the same views. Fadlallah is a prominent religious scholar and *marji' al-taqlid*, or 'source of emulation'. (Practising Shi'i Muslims often choose a religious scholar who has attained a certain rank to emulate on religious matters; such a scholar is known as a *marji' al-taqlid*.) Hizbullah is a political party, and while the party officially 'follows' or 'emulates' Iranian leader Sayyid Ali Khamenei, its members are free to emulate others, and many in fact emulate Fadlallah. These circles of overlap are, however, precisely that: circles of significant overlap that none the less maintain their differences from one another.

[7] For more on the fluidity and constructed nature of notions of 'sect' and sectarian identity in Lebanon, see Makdisi (2000).

[8] See Deeb (2006a) for a detailed elucidation of this argument.

[9] For a thorough discussion of the 'clash of civilizations' thesis and various critiques of it, as well as a discussion of the ways 'civilization' operates as a value-laden term in relation to notions of modernity rooted in the European Enlightenment, see Jarmakani (2008).

[10] I use the term 'neoimperialism' advisedly, taking to heart Kelly and Kaplan's cautioning that describing US power as 'imperial' or 'neoimperial' is imprecise and does not capture the complexities of US global domination, which includes an anti-European imperialism streak and affinities between neoliberal capitalist economies and identity-politics rights-based movements (2004: 144-5). See Calhoun, Cooper & Moore (2006) for discussion of differing perspectives on how to name this phenomenon, ranging from an insistence that the United States is a hegemon but not an empire, to insistence on calling a spade a spade, that is, an empire.

[11] For more on this Lebanese Shi'i Islamic mobilization, see Halawi (1992) and Norton (1987). For more on Hizbullah, see Deeb (2006b); Hamzeh (2004); Harik (2004); Norton (1999; 2007); and Saad-Ghorayeb (2002).

[12] This particular transnational parallel is a common one among women activists in the Middle East (see, e.g., Strum 1992).

[13] While I hesitate to set September 11, 2001 up as date of absolute change, it is clear that the events of that day and its aftermath, continuing today in the US occupation of Iraq and US interventions elsewhere in the Middle East and Muslim world, have had ramifications for both discourses about Muslim women and my interlocutours' own engagements with those discourses.

[14] The term 'Westoxication' (*garbzadagi*) was originally coined by Iranian philosopher Ahmed Fardid, and later made popular by leftist intellectual Jalal al-e Ahmed in his book of the same title. For discussion of 'Westoxication' specifically in relation to women during the Islamic revolution in Iran, see Moallem (2005).

[15] While it is quite possible that this complex of responses to women in 'the West' also reflects responses to those middle- and upper-class Lebanese women who my interlocutours might characterize as 'Westernized' – on the basis of both their dress and language choices – this particular discussion did not address other groups in Lebanon.

[16] Similar arguments, with similar limitations, were made by Lebanese intellectuals and reformers during the seventeenth-century *Nahda* (awakening) (see Traboulsi 2007: 63-7).

[17] Note that these constructions of both Islam and the West cast a monolithic construct of the 'East' as the source of patriarchal oppression, and also serve to mask complex histories of feminist and gender activist movements in Muslim societies that are not simply impositions or contaminations from the West, including in Lebanon.

[18] In addition to work on colonial discourses on gender and Islam, including Abu-Lughod (1998*b*) and Ahmed (1992), see also Ho's eloquent depiction of a long-globalized world and argument against the idea that transnational linkages are at all a new phenomenon (Ho 2006).

[19] See Eickelman & Anderson (1999) on the emergence of a new Muslim public sphere that has been facilitated by electronic media. See also Allen (2006) for a parallel argument in the Palestinian context and a critical analysis of the ways in which images of Palestinian suffering are deployed in transnational and local media in an effort to counteract the dehumanizing and stereotyping discourses that dominate much of the international reporting on the conflict.

[20] See note 10.

[21] I would suggest that this differs from Europe, for example, where contemporary discourses on Muslim women and the headscarf are more frequently related to questions of national identity, cultural authenticity, and internal political dynamics.

[22] For an eloquent critique of this discourse, see Abu-Lughod (2002).

REFERENCES

Abu-Lughod, L. (ed.) 1998a. *Remaking women: feminism and modernity in the Middle East.* Princeton: University Press.

———— 1998b. Introduction: feminist longings and postcolonial conditions. In *Remaking women: feminism and modernity in the Middle East* (ed.) L. Abu-Lughod, 3-31. Princeton: University Press.

———— 2002. Do Muslim women really need saving? Anthropological reflections on cultural relativism and its others. *American Anthropologist* **104**, 783-90.

Ahmed, L. 1992. *Women and gender in Islam: historical roots of a modern debate.* New Haven: Yale University Press.

Allen, L. 2006. Witnessing the *shahid*: aesthetic politics in the Palestinian media. Presented at 'Dying to Kill, Dying to Win: Contexts and Conditions of Suicide Terrorism', a symposium and workshop of the Institute for Comparative and International Studies, Emory University, Atlanta, Ga., March.

Amin, Q. 1992 [1899]. *The liberation of women* (trans. S. Peterson). Cairo: American University in Cairo Press.

Asad, T. 1986. *The idea of an anthropology of Islam.* Washington, D.C.: Georgetown University Center for Contemporary Arab Studies.

———— 1993. *Genealogies of religion: disciplines and reasons of power in Christianity and Islam.* Baltimore: Johns Hopkins University Press.

Calhoun, C., F. Cooper & K.W. Moore (eds) 2006. *Lessons of empire: imperial histories and American power.* New York: New Press; London: Social Science Research Council.

Chatterjee, P. 1993. *The nation and its fragments: colonial and postcolonial histories.* Princeton: University Press.

Deeb, L. 2005. 'Doing good, like Sayyida Zaynab': Lebanese Shi'i women's participation in the public sphere. In *Religion, social practice, and contested hegemonies: reconstructing the public sphere in Muslim majority societies* (eds) A. Salvatore & M. LeVine, 85-108. New York: Palgrave.

———— 2006*a*. *An enchanted modern: gender and public piety in Shi'i Lebanon.* Princeton: University Press.

———— 2006*b*. Hizbullah: a primer. *Middle East Report Online,* 31 July (available on-line: *http://www.merip.org/mero/mero073106.html*, accessed 19 January 2009).

EICKELMAN, D.F. & J.W. ANDERSON (eds) 1999. *New media in the Muslim world: the emerging public sphere.* Bloomington: Indiana University Press.

GÖLE, N. 1997. *The forbidden modern: civilization and veiling.* Ann Arbor: University of Michigan Press.

GREWAL, I. & C. KAPLAN (eds) 1994. *Scattered hegemonies: postmodernity and transnational feminist practices.* Minneapolis: University of Minnesota Press.

EL GUINDI, F. 1999. *Veil: modesty, privacy and resistance.* Oxford: Berg.

HALAWI, M. 1992. *A Lebanon defied: Musa al-Sadr and the Shi'a community.* Boulder, Colo.: Westview.

HAMZEH, N. 2004. *In the path of Hizbullah.* New York: Syracuse University Press.

HARB, M. 1996. *Politiques urbaines dans la banlieue-sud de Beyrouth.* (Les Cahiers du CERMOC). Beirut: Centre d'Études et de Recherches sur le Moyen-Orient Contemporain.

HARIK, J. 2004. *Hezbollah: the changing face of terrorism.* London: I.B. Tauris.

HIRSCHKIND, C. 2006. *The ethical soundscape: cassette sermons and Islamic counterpublics.* New York: Columbia University Press.

HO, E. 2006. *The graves of Tarim: genealogy and mobility across the Indian Ocean.* Berkeley: University of California Press.

JARMAKANI, A. 2008. *Imagining Arab womanhood: the cultural mythology of veils, harems, and belly dancers in the US.* New York: Palgrave.

KELLY, J.D. & M. KAPLAN 2004. 'My ambition is much higher than independence': US power, the UN world, the nation-state, and their critics. In *Decolonization: perspectives from now and then* (ed.) P. Duara, 131-51. London: Routledge.

MACLEOD, A. 1991. *Accommodating protest: working women, the new veiling, and change in Cairo.* New York: Columbia University Press.

MAHMOOD, S. 2005. *Politics of piety: the Islamic revival and the feminist subject.* Princeton: University Press.

MAKDISI, U. 2000. *The culture of sectarianism: community, history and violence in nineteenth-century Ottoman Lebanon.* Berkeley: University of California Press.

MEYER, B. & A. MOORS (eds) 2006. *Religion, media and the public sphere.* Bloomington: Indiana University Press.

MOALLEM, M. 2005. *Between warrior brother and veiled sister: Islamic fundamentalism and the politics of patriarchy in Iran.* Berkeley: University of California Press.

MOHANTY, C. 1988. Under Western eyes: feminist scholarship and colonial discourses. *Feminist Review* **30**, 61-88.

NORTON, A.R. 1987. *Amal and the Shi'a: struggle for the soul of Lebanon.* Austin: University of Texas Press.

———— 1999. *Hizballah of Lebanon: extremist ideals vs mundane politics.* New York: Council on Foreign Relations.

———— 2007. *Hezbollah: a short history.* Princeton: University Press.

SAAD-GHORAYEB, A. 2002. *Hizb'ullah: politics and religion.* London: Pluto.

SALVATORE, A. 2000. The Islamic reform project in the emerging public sphere: the (meta-)normative redefinition of *shari'a.* In *Between Europe and Islam: shaping modernity in a transcultural space* (eds) A. Hofert & A. Salvatore, 89-108. Brussels: PIE-Peter Lang.

———— & D.F. EICKELMAN (eds) 2004. *Public Islam and the common good.* Leiden: Brill.

———— & M. LEVINE (eds) 2005. *Religion, social practice, and contested hegemonies: reconstructing the public sphere in Muslim majority societies.* New York: Palgrave.

SHAKRY, O. 1998. Schooled mothers and structured play: child rearing in turn-of-the-century Egypt. In *Remaking women: feminism and modernity in the Middle East* (ed.) L. Abu-Lughod, 126-70. Princeton: University Press.

SNYDER, E. 2007. Empowered women could combat Islamic extremism. *The Jerusalem Post,* 1 June (available on-line: *http://www.yunusnews.com/node/105*, accessed 19 January 2009).

STRUM, P. 1992. Introduction: the women of Palestine will not be like the women of Algeria. In *The women are marching: the second sex and the Palestinian revolution,* P. Strum, 1-23. New York: Lawrence Hill.

TRABOULSI, F. 2007. *A history of modern Lebanon.* London: Pluto.

VAN DER VEER, P. 2004. Secrecy and publicity in the South Asian public arena. In *Public Islam and the common good* (eds) A. Salvatore & D.F. Eickelman, 29-52. Leiden: Brill.

8

Mukadas's struggle: veils and modernity in Kyrgyzstan

Julie McBrien *University of Amsterdam*

In the autumn of 2003, after protracted consideration, Mukadas Kadirova,[1] aged 25, altered her mode of public dress. She changed the way she fastened her headscarf, pinning it securely under her chin so that it completely covered her hair and neck. She no longer bared her arms and she started wearing skirts which revealed only her feet. Mukadas deliberated for so long neither because she felt uncertain about a Muslim woman's obligations, nor because she lacked the desire to adhere to them. Her hesitation resulted from the possible consequences of her actions. Would she be perceived as a religious extremist? Would she be permitted to teach? How would her family react? And, perhaps most importantly, would she still be a modern woman?

Mukadas's worries are not particularly remarkable; they resonate with the contemporary experience of many Muslim women. The history of the veil as an anti-modern symbol has been well documented (e.g. Ahmed 1992). Through critical ethnographies, anthropologists have challenged one-dimensional, Orientalist readings of the headscarf, demonstrating its subaltern uses as a sign of protest (McLeod 1991), a means of creating an alternative modernity (Brenner 1996), or part of pious self-fashioning (Mahmood 2005). Others have examined the veil in its role as Islamic fashion (Moors & Tarlo 2007) or political chic (White 1999). Nevertheless, the headscarf's ubiquitous anti-modern image remains.[2] Mukadas's dilemma is tied to this globalized interpretation.

To analyse Mukadas's struggle as a challenge to narratives of modernity, gender, and Islam is, quite frankly, theoretically redundant. Yet the redundancy itself is intriguing for Mukadas is not from one of the regions – Europe or 'the Muslim majority world' – that have figured prominently in such analyses. She is a citizen of Kyrgyzstan, a former Soviet Central Asian Republic that underwent seventy years of anti-religious and other modernizing campaigns. I present Mukadas's struggle not to critique once more familiar 'modernist' narratives. Rather, Mukadas's dilemma is intriguing because it shows that she and her community read her decision to veil through these same discourses.

The similarity reveals not only the effects of contemporary 'globalization', but a longer history of global interconnectedness as it unfolded in Central Asia over the twentieth century.

Before the seventy years of Soviet modernization, Central Asia was a region of diverse populations with shifting social, economic, political, and cultural forms which had been under Tsarist domination for at least fifty years. There was no single, primordial 'Central Asia' which the Soviet regime sullied. However, the consequences of Soviet policies and practices did profoundly alter the material and ideological landscapes of the region. Soviet modernization efforts (unintentionally) objectified and systematized notions of tradition and modernity, and transformed conceptions of Muslimness, joining them with a newly developed sense of ethno-national identity. While atheist campaigns failed to eradicate religion, they aided the creation of a secular sphere and altered practices and notions of religion, resulting in a conceptual and institutional environment congruous with those of other modern nation states. Importantly, the modernization campaigns succeeded not only in turning Central Asians into Soviet citizens, but also in creating people who believed they were modern.

Understanding the Soviet Union as modern – in terms of its construction of the category of religion and its production of discourses on Islam, women, and modernity – helps explain parallels between Mukadas and Muslim women from other areas of the world. However, it is equally significant that Mukadas's problematic is not identical to theirs. The dilemmas faced by Mukadas reveal the erosion of the Soviet normative order, the rising influence of alternative orders in local and national communities, as well as the continued saliency of some Soviet-era notions – most notably, negative discourses about the veil. When Mukadas contemplated veiling, she perceived herself as fully modern, even as she watched the modernity of her society crumble. The economic and social decay of the post-Soviet period precluded the institutional enactment of either Soviet norms or the new capitalist, consumption-orientated vision of modernity. Mukadas's decision to veil thus involved a re-evaluation of her vision of modernity as well as a creative attempt to overcome the material and social constraints impeding her decision.

The distinctiveness of Mukadas's struggle suggests that even as modernity is multiple in its political and cultural forms (Eisenstadt 2000), individuals can experience these multiple modalities simultaneously. This chapter thus seeks to answer the following question: If visions and dreams of modernity are shaped by modernizing regimes, how is Mukadas's struggle related to the distinctive versions of Soviet and post-Soviet modernity? Answering this question poses a second. How do people experience modernity, especially regarding its temporal trajectory? For while modernity has often been understood as something experienced either as a present state or a desired future, Mukadas's dilemma demonstrates that the experience can likewise include a longing for a modern past. This has important consequences for how we theorize these experiences. Simply put, what do we do when actors see themselves concomitantly as being, becoming, and *having been* modern?

Soviet Muslims

Mukadas is the second eldest child of Zeba Osmonalieva and Ulugbek Kadirov. Zeba, born in 1950 in the city of Osh,[3] was the daughter of an illiterate mother and a father who was a history professor. Zeba was partly raised by her grandmother, who regularly took her as a young child to pray at the nearby pilgrimage site of Suleiman's Mountain, the bans on religious expression notwithstanding. Nevertheless, Zeba's teenage and adult years were devoid of religious experience and she gave little thought to such matters, she said. She was, however, very occupied with studying and 'advancing' herself.

Ulugbek was an artist of mixed Uzbek-Tatar origins from Bazaar-Korgon. He met Zeba at a summer camp in his home region where they both worked as youth leaders. After the summer, Zeba continued her university studies while Ulugbek travelled extensively throughout the USSR and painted. Following his return to Bazaar-Korgon, he and Zeba married. She moved to Bazaar-Korgon and began teaching. Between 1974 and 1985 their five daughters – Muyassar, Mukadas, Delnura, Delfuza, and Shasta – were born. At that time Bazaar-Korgon was a small agro-town of around 15,000 inhabitants (now 30,000) with some industry. Zeba and Ulugbek were part of the town's intelligentsia, and they taught their daughters to appreciate the arts and education.

While the Kadirova girls were growing up, the town of Bazaar-Korgon underwent a transformation. In the late 1970s it became the capital of a newly created administrative region: Bazaar-Korgon *raion*. As such, following the logic of Soviet planners, the town had to be 'modernized'. Government offices, a hospital, a new school, and a House of Culture (*dom kultura*) were constructed. A second statue of Lenin was erected in the new town centre. Water mains were run throughout the town bringing potable water nearer to every home. Residents of Bazaar-Korgon had already seen the transformation of nearby cities. Recalling this period, they remember how pleased they were that their town, too, was finally modernizing.

Clearly, the Soviet Union was a powerful modernizing regime. It forcibly sedentarized nomadic populations and introduced new forms of agricultural production. The reorientation of Central Asian agricultural production to cash crops meant a transformation of the ecological environment through massive irrigation schemes which eventually almost completely emptied the Aral Sea. Local development meant the provision of infrastructure for everyday conveniences like running water, telephones, and electricity. New political structures extensively politicized and bureaucratized everyday life. While a communist utopia was never realized, the decades of socialist campaigns wrought changes producing what has been called one of the 'original alternative modernities' (Eisenstadt 2000: 11).[4] And while Bazaar-Korgonians indexed material alterations as the 'arrival of modernity', it was the cultural changes engendered by Soviet projects which gave rise to Mukadas's struggle and which locate her dilemma as part of the larger story of modernity.

A strong component of all modern nation states has been what Talal Asad has called the political project of secularism, in which states have attempted to 'construct categories of the secular and the religious in terms of which modern living is required to take place' (2003: 14). The atheist campaigns of the USSR were among the most extreme cases of this kind of categorical transformation. For those engaged in the early anti-religious campaigns in Central Asia, religion had already been objectified and redefined in ways consistent with modern, secularized notions. With this notion of religion, and the Orthodox Church as a model of how religious life was structured, early Soviet atheizers – many of whom were Russian – looked for 'religion' in Central Asia and targeted what they understood to be the bedrock of Islam, namely the institutional and publicly visible aspects of Muslim life (Keller 1992).

These early anti-religious campaigns in Central Asia were fairly unsuccessful. The Soviets authorities therefore changed tactics many times and tried various means to discredit Islam throughout Central Asia. In the Ferghana Valley, where Bazaar-Korgon is located, Tashkent party leaders eventually decided to focus on women's emancipation as a new means of attack on Islam because, as they argued, it would upset 'the basis of social order' and destabilize the authority of religious leaders (Northrop 2004: 76). The transformation of gender relations fitted the multiple goals and ideologies of the Bolshevik agenda, but importantly party leaders hoped that it would also 'make millions of Muslim women into passionately loyal Soviet boosters', and 'jump-start the faltering anti-religious campaign' (Northrop 2004: 76-7).

By 1926 local party officials saw unveiling women as tantamount to their liberation (Massell 1974; Northrop 2004). They therefore aimed their efforts at veiled woman, arguing that her imprisonment in the *paranji*[5] represented the evils of fanatical Islam. The assault (*hujum*) on veiled women began in 1927. While early attacks on Islam – including the *hujum* – were ineffective, long-term efforts succeeded in nearly completely eliminating some of the most central Muslim institutions and practices, such as *waqf* property, religious education, highly modest forms of dress and veiling, fasting at Ramadan, collective prayer, the networks of religious scholars and leaders, and knowledge of the most basic tenets and practices of textual Islam. But the anti-religious assaults did more than eradicate institutions and practices; they also transformed the way these were understood.

When atheist agitators attacked 'religion', they targeted a set of institutions and practices which they believed to constitute that category. However, 'religion' had not yet been objectified for Central Asian Muslims, and therefore there was no 'religion' as such to attack. Thus, while the anti-religious campaigns targeted and eventually eliminated public aspects of Muslim life, other notions and practices which were equally important to Central Asian ways of being Muslim – especially the marking of life-cycle events and rituals related to the home – were left untouched (Shahrani 1984). The former set of public acts, discourses, and institutions became known as 'religion', hence labelled as harmful, extreme, subversive, and anti-modern, and made illegal. The latter became known as Muslimness (*musulmanchilik*).

The anti-religious campaigns of the 1920s and 1930s were concurrent with the Soviet nationalities policies. The concomitant programmes had important (if unintended) effects on the way religion, culture, and ultimately politics would be understood, enacted, and valued from the mid- to late Soviet period. Soviet nationalities policies, begun in the 1920s, created the boundaries of nations within the Union, the ethno-national consciousness that became tied to the newly delineated territories and the 'cultural stuff' which became associated with each nationality (Grant 1995; Hirsch 2005; Pelkmans 2006; Slezkine 1994). The point is not that such cultural forms were invented – they were largely based on existing material – but that the materials were systematized, standardized, displayed, and taught to the 'titular groups' involved as well as to other nationalities. The material need to create the contents for the national repertoire of traditions – national dishes, language, clothing, instruments, heroes, and religion – for each ethno-national group was largely 'gathered' by Soviet ethnographers, who looked to women and home life, among other places, for sources of inspiration. Importantly the elements being identified were congruous with those aspects of Muslimness untouched by Soviet anti-religious campaigns. Thus, Muslim identity became intrinsically tied up with national identity and became romantically celebrated as 'culture'. To be Kyrgyz, or Uzbek or Kazak was to be Muslim. But again, it was a sense of Muslimness which excluded formerly central Islamic observances as essential practices and which labelled them as fanatical and unmodern.

Notwithstanding this creation of particular identities and their centrality in every-day life, as well as the anti-religious campaigns and other brutalities of the early Soviet period, by the mid- to late Soviet period Central Asians none the less conceived of themselves as Soviets; they largely supported the Union, its visions, and programmes. Bruce Grant has argued similarly for one of the Soviet Union's small ethnic groups, the Nivkh. Despite all the contradictions of the Soviet experience and the reified dualisms of public political discourse – traditional/modern, local/federal, Nivkh/Soviet – these oppositions were less distinct at the local level. As he claims, '[M]ost Nivkhi thought of themselves as Soviets first and Nivkhi second; a good number of others, especially younger people, thought of themselves as Soviets only' (1995: 159). This feeling of being Soviet may be one of the most important differences between residents of the USSR and inhabitants of many places colonized by Western powers. A colonizer/colonized dichotomy did not exist in Central Asia. By the mid- to late Soviet period, the USSR was not perceived by Central Asians themselves as a colonial endeavour. They were Soviets and they were modern people, even if these identities were built upon seeming con-tradictions – like an 'atheist' Muslim.

This was at least partly due to measurable and observable changes that Central Asians witnessed in their lives and the discursive politics promoting them. While women unveiled, they were offered new possibilities for work, recreation, and home life. Notions of gender equality were advanced and discursively tied to Soviet modern-ization projects. Rational, scientific investigation was touted as the means to personal and societal advancement, and certain real technological accomplishments – small ones at the local level like electricity, plumbing, and telephones as well as large prestige projects such as steel plants and a space programme – helped shore up faith in these ideals. Not all Soviet rhetoric was reality. However, as Deniz Kandiyoti has argued, if we compare the Middle East and Central Asia through the rubric of postcolonialism, one of the most striking differences is 'the diffusion of the fruits of Soviet development to the lower strata of society [that] separates Central Asian societies from those of the Middle East' (2002: 295).

While parallels can be drawn with Ataturk's modernizing campaigns and the cre-ation of Turkish citizens or to a lesser degree with long-term reforms in Egypt, the exceptionality of the Soviet campaigns – their militant intensity and long duration along with the closed nature of the USSR – suggests limits to this comparison. If in the 1950s in Turkey Islamic groups were already vying for power during a brief period of political pluralism (Göle 1996: 20) and the 1970s witnessed a worldwide Islamic resur-gence, it was not until the 1990s that a similar space for political opposition was even imaginable in the former Soviet Republics of Central Asia.

In fact, even when the Union collapsed, the leaders of the five Central Asian repub-lics were among the last to accept its demise and it was not until the turn of the millennium that a Central Asian 'Islamic revival' became palpable in public spaces. Even then in Kyrgyzstan Islamist groups have been absent from the political scene. The unfolding of the 2005 'Tulip revolution' is instructive in this regard. Reports about the demonstrations and marches that culminated in the toppling of the Akaev regime did not make a single reference to religious symbolism or motivations. Certainly some of the post-Soviet changes were welcomed. The material wealth of capitalism enticed many and religious freedom was widely celebrated. But as post-Soviet realities set in, former Soviet Muslims' relationship to both their Soviet past and capitalist present became much more complex.

Post-Soviet changes

Mukadas was 13 when the Soviet Union collapsed. When asked about the changes in the early years, the first thing she recalled was how expensive everything had become. Others in her community around her age remembered waiting in line for hours to acquire scarce resources. While they had similarly queued for items during the Soviet era, the difference was the dearth of even the most basic items such as bread. Mukadas remembers things were particularly difficult for her father. As an artist, he had received regular payment for his work. Such payments ended with the demise of the Soviet Union, and the ensuing economic crisis meant that there was no private demand for his paintings. Mukadas's father did not live through the collapse of the Union. He died in 1994 under mysterious circumstances. Despite the double-shock and hardship of personal loss and societal collapse, Mukadas's mother worked out a modicum of economic success trading gold jewellery. The girls thrived in the seemingly inhospitable environment and grew up to be well-liked and respected young women.

Mukadas talked of her father often. Though in the years just preceding his death there had been friction between them – mostly as a result of Mukadas's burgeoning independence – she remembered her father tenderly. Mukadas recounted how he taught her about the nature of life and how she should live it. She talked very pointedly about wanting to be a cultured person, to better herself, and to be intelligent and well read. She was pleased with the freedoms of the post-Soviet period, especially freedom of conscience. She said that only since the end of the USSR were people learning to think for themselves, rather than listening to the dictates of others.

Mukadas's positive evaluation of the post-Soviet period expressed her satisfaction more with the change – with the loosening of certain unsavoury elements of the USSR – than with an endorsement of the new forms of political, economic, societal, and moral organization that had replaced that of the Soviet era. Her actual encounter with the realities of post-socialist life provoked more disillusionment and disappointment than celebration. Dreams and values nurtured in the Soviet period were accompanied by institutional arrangements that provided for their possible fruition. Socialist ideals of modernity had been possible to enact, even if they were never fully attainable. As Frances Pine argues, criticism during the socialist period focused not on socialist ideals but on the incompleteness of specific projects (1996: 133-4). There was a sense that some dreams could be reached – for example, the education and employment of women, along with their full participation in society – and that the system could be changed to make the implementation of these ideals more complete. However, when these same dreams and values were set in the radically new context that we may loosely term 'capitalist', the possibility of their fulfilment was largely curtailed. A deficit of jobs, absence of child care, lack of money, and limited access to 'quality goods' meant Mukadas was constantly frustrated by the mismatch of her dreams and realities.

She was equally disappointed by the hollowness of 'Western' modernity. Actually lived socialist modernity was characterized by infrastructural improvement, scientific advancement, a certain ethos of community and communal effort to create a new, superior society, and, importantly, a set of values – gender equality, mass literacy, economic equality, and meaningful work for all – that were, if only partly, attainable. Post-socialist modernity, by contrast, was not about lived experiences and values – it was almost exclusively about dreams. These were dreams of Western consumption and material standards of living that did not fit the logics of Soviet life and were rather unattainable in the economic realities of post-socialist life. Thus, while hopes for a prosperous 'modern' future abounded, they were coeval with nostalgia for an equally modern, if different, past (Pine & Bridger 1998).

The material prosperity that Western forms of modernity promised – though often failed to deliver – was not the only source of unease in the post-Soviet period. In the early 1990s Kyrgyzstan elected for 'shock therapy', enacting not only radical economic transformations to hasten its 'transition' to capitalism, but also political ones – including freedom of conscience – to accelerate its passage to democracy. This resulted in the growth of multiple religious communities. While Christian and Muslim missionaries from outside the country certainly took advantage of Kyrgyzstan's liberal policies, in places like Bazaar-Korgon the local religious scholars and leaders facilitated the expansion of Islam more directly.

By the early 2000s, the number of Bazaar-Korgonians who had turned to scripture-based interpretations of Islam was sizeable enough – and their public acts of piety became visible enough – that the town had become known throughout the region as a 'religious' place. I have designated this category of people 'the newly pious', borrowing Robert Hefner's terminology from his discussion of the resurgence of public religion in the Muslim world (2005: 21). He notes that

> [m]ost of the newly pious were primarily interested in just what they claimed to be: religious study, heightened public devotion, expressing a Muslim identity, and insuring that public arenas were subject to ethical regulation. The key symbols of the resurgence were similarly pietistic: reciting the Qur'an, keeping the fast, wearing the veil, avoiding alcohol, giving alms (2005: 21).

Importantly, he notes, the newly pious were not 'especially *political* in any formal sense of the word' (2005: 21, emphasis original). In Bazaar-Korgon, the main actors involved in the return of religion to public life can be similarly described. Locally they would be labelled 'religious' – literally 'those who have gone over to religion' (*dinge burulup getkin adamdar*) and 'close to religion' (*dinge jakin*).

Unlike descriptions of the so-called 'Islamic resurgence' elsewhere, the newly pious of Kyrgyzstan are demographically distinct. While 'new veiling' has often begun in capital cities and universities (Brenner 1996; Göle 1996; White 2002), newly veiled women in Kyrgyzstan are largely absent in Bishkek's universities and public spaces. Instead they are found in southern cities and small towns predominately populated by Uzbeks. They rarely have more than high school degrees and tend to be lower-middle class or lower class, in contrast to middle-class ranks of piety movements elsewhere.[6]

In most of the Muslim world, recent instances of widespread veiling have been preceded or accompanied by Islamist projects ensuring that women's veiling is embedded within larger political struggles (Göle 1996; Mahmood 2005; Saktanber 2002; White 2002). But in the case of Bazaar-Korgon, and Kyrgyzstan more generally, women's veiling became politically charged despite women's lack of (formal) political involvement and the non-existence of Islamist movements. The political consequences of their actions can only be understood then in reference to alternative narratives of Muslim-ness and modernity (cf. Mahmood 2005). As the number of newly pious in the com-munity increased, their alternative visions, articulations, and representations of Muslimness sparked public debates not only over religious observance and doctrine, but also over wider notions of religion and politics. Changing modes of veiling and the increased public visibility of these new forms played a prominent role in these discus-sions. By wearing headscarves and dresses that more fully covered their bodies, women like Mukadas presented a challenge to community members who read their actions as reversals of one of the biggest triumphs of Soviet modernizing campaigns – women's emancipation.

Though most married women in Bazaar-Korgon wear a headscarf – usually tied at the nape of the neck with a swathe of hair revealed at the top – the covering is considered part of age, familial, and social roles, not of religious commitments. Many professional women even choose to forgo head covering. The mode of veiling known outside the region as *hijab* – in which all the hair and neck is covered but the entire face is revealed – is the most common and most rapidly spreading form among the newly pious. The word *hijab*, however, is not locally used for such headscarves, not even by the women who wear them. Instead, people generally talk about women who have 'closed their headscarves' (*joluk japdi*) or who 'wear their headscarves like *this*' (*joluk mundai slanip jueruet*), simultaneously tracing an oval with two fingers around their faces, beginning at the forehead, following the curve of their face, and meeting just below the chin. Normally the *hijab* is combined with a long-sleeved, loose fitting dress found or made either in Bazaar-Korgon or in one of the nearby cities. Although the new style is usually locally produced, the manner in which it is worn, the kinds of colours, fabrics, and clothing combinations that are chosen, and the fact that it is all worn by young women (under age 40) raises eyebrows in the community. Women who cover their bodies as fully as those wearing *hijab* but who do so in 'local' styles generally do so out of religious conviction as well. Yet they draw little attention in public and are not stigmatized in discussions critical of emerging public expression of religiosity. When people in town talk about women who have 'gone over to religion' (*dinge burulup getkin*) or who have come 'closer to religion' (*dinge jakin*), they never indicate women wearing veils in non-*hijab* styles.

When a young woman wears a *hijab*, she is automatically assumed to take part in a locally new cluster of religious practices – attending religious study groups, learning to recite the Qur'an, and praying regularly. For example, not long after she began wearing the *hijab*, Mukadas met a small group of girl neighbours who asked her if she could recite the Qur'an. When she replied that she could not, the girls responded with shock, 'But you wear your headscarf like that!' For many community members the *hijab* is a conspicuous form of head-covering because of its style as well as the religious com-mitments assumed to have inspired its wearer. While a certain degree of religious commitment is acceptable, wearing the *hijab*, perceived as part of being 'close to religion', is also closely associated with excessive religious fervour. The association has multiple roots. First, the *hijab* is locally understood to be an 'Arab' form of dress (cf. Brenner 1996: 674) and often associated with 'Wahhabis'. In Central Asia, the word 'Wahhabi' became synonymous with 'extremist' in the late 1970s and early 1980s (Babadjanov & Kamilov 2001; Shahrani 2005). More recent global deployments of the term have given it new salience, especially considering the influence of foreign powers in the region. Russia, the United States, and China – all with vested stakes in authorizing discourses on Muslim extremists – have used their economic and political weight to push Kyrgyzstan into a 'tougher stance' in its anti-terrorism measures. On the local level, residents of Bazaar-Korgon have become convinced that there must be 'extremists' in their midst. As they gossiped about this supposed threat, they often speculated on who might be a 'terrorist', the *hijab* often taken as a sign of someone's radicalization (McBrien 2006).

Contemporary stereotypes surrounding the veil carry weight precisely because they are consonant with Soviet-era notions in which the veil had come to symbolize the apparent oppressive, backward, and fanatical nature of Islam. The veil was doubly problematic for residents – it indicated excessive religious commitment and a departure from the norms and practices of gender equality established during the Soviet era. It thus signalled a retreat from Soviet modernity. Female interlocutors, especially those in their forties and fifties, often told me that women who 'wear their headscarves like *that*' were backward and unmodern. They suggested that these women had been coerced into the practice. Men likewise questioned the women's motives for veiling, wondering why they would have given up their independence (see McBrien & Pelkmans 2008).

Community perception was not the only thing that delayed women from veiling. Women were usually confronted with difficult material circumstances that made them postpone their decision. The vast majority of women choosing to wear the *hijab* were relatively young. They wanted to set themselves apart from older women who veiled more fully. They were also keenly interested in fashion and beauty, especially given all the newly available consumer products and images in the post-Soviet period. Yet, for those wishing to wear the *hijab*, there were not many clothes available. Some young women had clothes made by local seamstresses. Even then, the selection of fabric in town was limited. Others travelled to nearby cities to search for garments that would meet their desires. But the garments they found were often deemed unattractive. Finding something that covered them, and was beautiful, was a great challenge. One unique solution was to 'import' veils. Women who went on the hajj occasionally brought back scarves and other clothing for their family, friends, and acquaintances. But the number of women doing this was small. No traders in the bazaar catered to these women's needs, and foreign traders had yet to capitalize on such a niche market.

While the newly pious may not have been able to overcome all the stereotypes surrounding the *hijab*, their attempts at beautiful, fashionable veiling at least challenged some. Beautiful veiling for young women went against the grain concerning local aesthetics of the veil and its role in women's life-cycle. These young women attempted to reconfigure the veil not as 'tradition' from the pre-Soviet past, but as contemporary and in line with new visions of modernity. In their search for beauty and fashion, they often employed images of Western modernity that they were seeking to blend with their religious devotion. Perhaps an even greater challenge to young women's veiling was economics: most women simply did not have the resources they needed to wear the kind of clothing they desired. This dilemma was particularly intense for women who chose to wear the *hijab* after marriage, because their wish to dress 'religiously' meant that they had to give up their trousseau (*sep*) as the garments that came as a part of the *sep* were not designed for *hijab*-wearing women.

Economic constraints were the downside of the new capitalist modernity. Post-Soviet life, in a sense, forced Kyrgyzstani citizens to face the dark sides of Western modernity while simultaneously being flooded with its promises and desires. This disjuncture in many ways stimulated longing for the Soviet era – for its perceived security, morality, and stability (cf. Özyürek 2006 on Turkey). Post-Soviet citizens were nostalgic, but not blindly so. They had not forgotten the negative aspects of the Soviet system. But for many, the balance between good and bad seemed a bit better then than now.

Kyrgyzstani citizens' relationship to both Soviet and post-Soviet modernity was mixed; neither modality was fully embraced or rejected. It is perhaps better to speak of a realignment of cultural and material frameworks, a process which became all the more complex for those Muslims who, in the post-Soviet period, decided to 'draw close to religion' (*dinge jakin*). Recent ethnographies of the 'Islamic resurgence' have portrayed these movements as articulating strong criticism of Western, secular-liberal projects, and thereby launching various alternative discourses and projects of modernity in many cases through and by veiling women (e.g. Brenner 1996; Göle 1996; Mahmood 2005). These accounts depict a bifurcated discourse where veiled women see Western projects and norms as inimical to Islamic principles. What is perhaps most striking about the post-Soviet Central Asia case is the more ambivalent relationship with the West. The concern of Muslims in the region has been focused on what Westernization would do to Soviet structures and values, rather than Islamic ones. Westernization and its form of secularism was in fact viewed by those concerned with religion of any sort as an improvement, even if morally, economically, and socially Westernization soon exhibited its downsides. Yet these were still measured against an imagined Soviet past rather than an Islamic one. Western secularism sustained and supported Soviet-era narratives about women's agency and modernity but in an institutional environment which allowed relatively more freedom for religious expression. Soviet-era accomplishments, institutions, and values often became the basis of comparison and debate, with Western secularism playing a more ambiguous role in these discussions.

Throwing stones at fruitful trees: Mukadas Kadirova's story

There was a black-and-white photograph at the Kadirova home that showed a young woman standing on Red Square, the onion domes of Saint Basil's Cathedral behind her. Her hair was braided, and she had on a small square hat (*dopi*). She wore a smart dress of Uzbek atlas that fell just above her knees. She smiled. The Kadirova sisters loved to look at that photograph of their mother. Through it they could imagine their mother as a young girl – someone like themselves. But they also commented on how differently their mother's youth had been – more opportunities to travel, an easier life with more hope for the future. Their lives were different. Especially the older ones among them had been steeped in the discourse of becoming intelligent, modern people who were part of the great Soviet project. But these were dreams that they, unlike their mother, were unable to realize. Taught by their parents that education was the key to a fruitful, modern life, the sisters witnessed the depreciation of these values in the post-Soviet era.

Even though the rhetoric of communist modernity was never an accurate reflection of the realities of Soviet life, Soviet citizens were active participants in creating and sustaining the rhetoric and largely felt part of its overarching goals. The dreams and values of the Kadirova sisters started in the Soviet era. Even after the collapse, their ideas, visions, and hopes were nurtured by family, teachers, and community members who grew up during socialist times (see Lampland 2002). And yet, though links to the past are durable, the way people evaluate bygone eras changes in shifting environments and new situations. Pine argues that many of the positive achievements of the socialist states, especially with regard to gender equality, were not recognized until after the collapse, when the experience with 'actually existing capitalism' cast new light on former socialist realities (1996: 133). Thus in some cases, re-evaluation shores up and even strengthens notions created and sustained in a social and political environment that no longer exists (cf. Pelkmans 2006). Furthermore, such notions can even be reinvigorated in the new environment when old and new rhetorics align. For example, the role of education in individual and societal advancement is central to both Soviet and Western discourses. Western campaigns on educational reform and massive foreign funding for study abroad programmes consolidated the Soviet/post-Soviet value of education. Unfortunately, the promises of education, partly fulfilled in the Soviet years, are unattainable in contemporary Kyrgyzstan.

Three out of five of the Kadirova sisters attended university. Despite their training – Mukadas in education, Delnura in border control, and Delfuza in art – only one found employment in her chosen field. Delfuza's study of art seemed rather hopeless from the outset. Mukadas worked as a teacher for one year, before leaving to have her first child. She never returned to work, partly because child care systems had broken down. Delnura's failure to secure work as a border guard shows another odd twist of the post-Soviet period. Ironically, while Mukadas herself lauded the independence period for allowing people to think critically and independently, the education system became even more riddled with corruption than during Soviet times. Everything could be bought for a price in post-Soviet universities – admission, grades, exam results, even diplomas. This continued into the job market such that, while Delnura was still able to earn her degree the old-fashioned way – by studying – she could not pay the bribes necessary to secure work as a border guard or customs officer. Delnura pursued an alternative dream. In partnership with another young woman, she opened a small clothing stall in the bazaar. Delfuza and Shasta helped out as well. In the first few months of business they never made a profit.

In addition to fulfilling, well-paid work the sisters longed for love, good husbands, kind mother-in-laws, and nice homes. They all wanted children. Mukadas had some of these desired things. Unlike most of her age cohorts, she had married for love – with the full consent of her mother. However, her marital life had not been easy. Her husband and in-laws were considerably less well educated than her own family. They were also quite poor. The differences between her natal and marital families, combined with a mother-in-law whom Mukadas described as unkind and critical, and who looked unsympathetically on her less-than-robust constitution, made for a difficult home life for her.

The difficulties Mukadas faced at home were, in the end, a major impetus in her religious awakening. In 2002 she dreamed about troubles she was having with her mother-in-law and husband. In the dream, she explained, the trials in her home life manifested themselves in the form of a snake which, coiled around her body, was constricting and killing her. She called on God to rescue her from the snake, and He instructed her that she must pray and come 'close to religion' (*dinge jakin*) to find relief. She took the dream literally and began praying five times daily. Around the same time, her husband also had a self-described religious awakening. He had also begun to pray and attend a Qur'anic study group where he learned to recite the Qur'an and received religious instruction. Mukadas likewise had begun to learn more about Islam by visiting a female religious specialist (*atincha*).[7]

One afternoon in the early autumn of 2003, Mukadas and I sat in her mother's small orchard and talked. She told me she was considering wearing the *hijab*. Her husband had brought up the subject some months before. Mukadas told him she was not ready at that moment. However, she agreed to think about it. She had been considering it for some time and decided that she was nearly ready to do it. She felt sure that it was her duty before God and her responsibility as a Muslim woman. At the same time she was unsure of herself because, as she explained, she wanted to be a modern woman. She considered herself different from many other young women who attended Islamic study groups. 'They finished 9th form and after that they stayed at home. They go to the *atincha* and return home. That's it. They don't think, they don't question. But I am modern, I am educated'.

Mukadas decided to wear the *hijab*, though she postponed her veiling until late autumn. It would be easier, she explained, because in autumn and winter one wore long sleeves and thus she would not have to buy new clothes. She would only have to change the way she pinned her scarf. Mukadas's husband was pleased with her decision, as were her mother-in-law, her mother, and two of her sisters. All three girls had become 'interested in religion' (*dinge kiziktuu bolop kaluu*). The three sisters had prayed the five times daily *namaz* when they were younger. Mukadas had returned to it in 2002, Delfuza in 2003. Shasta was learning how to pray *namaz* from Delfuza. Mukadas's husband often brought home locally produced audio recordings of religious teachings from the bazaar which the sisters listened to and discussed. When Mukadas decided to wear the *hijab*, Delfuza and Shasta went shopping with her, offering advice on which scarf to buy and how best to style it. Delnura, however, was upset with her decision. Delnura told her sister, 'What matters is what you believe on the inside, and how you treat others. That is more important then what you wear on the outside. Veiling is for old women. We are modern', she said.

As the winter wore on, Mukadas doubted the attractiveness of the new scarf and took to wearing an older, pink one that she thought suited her better. Her sisters and mother chided her that it was out of fashion. Mukadas, hurt by their comments, said she was angered at their focus on 'things'. She argued that clothes and other material objects were not important. She said that God teaches people to look at others and be thankful for what they have.

> When we think about religious knowledge, we should look ahead to those who have more than us so that we may strive forward to have what they do. When we think about the things of this world, we should look behind to those who have less so that we are thankful for what we have and so that we may share with them, through *zakot* (alms).

Though Mukadas had thought through many of the potential consequences of her changed mode of dress, and was certain of the correctness of her decision, she none the less felt the tensions of competing visions and desires. She wanted to veil, but to do so fashionably and with good-quality clothes. She was motivated by her appreciation of beauty and a desire to participate in the lures of the new consumerist environment. Her wish to overcome Soviet-era notions that marked more fully covered forms of veiling as for the old informed her wish to veil fashionably as well. However, her poverty, the dearth of locally available goods, and her own interpretation of the overly consumption-orientated attitudes of her family as incongruent with proper Muslim behaviour counteracted her own desires for beauty.

As the weather became warmer, Mukadas faced a new dilemma – her spring and summer clothes did not fit with her new notions of appropriately modest dressing. After an exhaustive search of a regional bazaar, she bought a new outfit. Despite her sisters' validation concerning the beauty of her new clothes, Mukadas waited almost two weeks before wearing the brightly coloured outfit in public. It was quite different from anything she had worn before, she said. She explained that the new form of dress made her decision to wear the *hijab* more tangible and final. It set her apart more demonstrably from other women in town. She was nervous. The dress and *hijab* did indeed draw more attention to her and she began to hear people whispering about her as she walked about town. She went to an *atincha* with her difficulties and was advised to count them as tests from God.

One afternoon she had a particularly unsettling experience. As she was walking through the bazaar, a woman approached her, stared her in the face, and said, 'I hate women who cover themselves'. Mukadas walked away. She ignored the woman and went to see her husband, who worked in the bazaar.

> When I told him what had happened, I felt very happy. I knew it was a test from God. The woman only said what she did for one of two reasons. One, she wanted to cover herself and knew she could not. Two, she really liked my clothes, thought I looked beautiful, and thus tried to push me down to make herself feel better.

Mukadas's confidence grew. She recalled a proverb '*No one throws stones at a tree that does not bear fruit*'. She reasoned that the difficulties were a sign of her obedience; she must be bearing the fruit of her devotion.

Despite her desires for beauty, Mukadas chose to veil first and foremost in obedience to God and in an effort to ease familial tensions. Yet, she feared not being allowed back to work, she faced public admonishment, and she felt the weight of unheard community gossip. She also feared a change in her status as a modern woman. Not only had she confronted the stereotypes of her community which equated wearing the *hijab* with extremism and the overturning of Soviet-era notions of gender equality, but she dealt with an internal struggle of redefinition. In some ways, Mukadas, too, saw the *hijab* as anti-modern – as a symbol of backwardness, of the uneducated, of a tradition given up long before the period of modernity in which she lived.

But her story also illustrates how modernity had become more complex since the fall of the USSR. Thus, while Mukadas dealt with certain tensions inherent in veiling and being modern – tensions provoked by a century and a half of Western and Soviet/Russian interpretations of the veil – she simultaneously drew on new interpretations of the *hijab* and modernity in her community. Post-Soviet emphasis on consumption and the importance of exteriority, fashion, and youth had informed her desires to veil beautifully, but the emptiness of Western consumption and the perceived immorality of the post-Soviet period had forced her to reconcile these desires with the principles for ethical conduct she found in Islam. While Mukadas had not completely merged consumption with certain values in Islam, her attempts to veil fashionably none the less counteracted community notions that the headscarf was ugly or only for the old, redefining the veil in relation to at least one stereotype of modernity.

When Mukadas and other women like her seek to come 'close to religion' (*dinge jakin*) – whether through veiling or other techniques – and attempt to reconcile this with redefined notions of modernity, they confront, at least implicitly, one of the greatest tensions between Soviet and Western modernity. The Soviet version of modernity in Central Asia encompassed, however incompletely, individual as well as societal desires. It succeeded in providing institutional means to obtain these goals and provided a framework of morality to encompass the goals and the institutions. Despite imperfections, it was more inclusive and coherent than the fragmented, dis-embodied, desire-focused yet unattainable visions of Western modernity circulating in Kyrgyzstan since the fall of the USSR. Mukadas's attempt to reinterpret modernity, to create herself as obedient, modest, modern, educated, and 'close to religion' – in short her creation of an Islamic modern – may be an antidote to these Western projects. Fashionable veiling intertwines with Western consumption while correcting its perceived immorality. If, as Mahmood rightly urges, the veil is about more than 'women's (un)freedom' (2005: 195), it can equally be about more than just creating piety (see also Marsden 2005: 251-2). Mukadas certainly understood her veiling as a pious act and one that transformed her inner dispositions, but her conception of what 'the veil was performing', to borrow Mahmood's terms, was not limited to this. The veil was also a means of realigning cultural landscapes and of creating herself as a modern individual through, within, and in reaction to 'Western', 'Soviet', and 'Islamic' normative frameworks.

Conclusion: modernity in the past

Contemporary Kyrgyzstan is not simply a place *still* in transition to modernity or in retreat from it. It is a place, like many the world over, where multiple modernities compete. But these various *contemporary* visions also compete with dreams from the *past* held by people who were already modern, who remained modern but who had to cope with the decay of their society into a state of 'post-modernity'. The tension that Mukadas felt arose not only from the variance between Western and Soviet notions of the modern, but also from the disjuncture in how the two were enacted. Mukadas understood Soviet dreams to have been at least partially attainable. Western images, on the other hand, incongruously mapped onto the realities she experienced in post-Soviet life, realities which in fact were the dark side of the West's development programmes. The tensions provoked a sense of nostalgia for Soviet life as well as a criticism of the present. They also fuelled an alternative imagination of the future (cf. Rofel 1999: 128-31). In Mukadas's case, her religious turn sparked the form that this reimagination took. But that religious turn – which was at odds with both Soviet and contemporary Western notions of gender equality and proper, moderate, religious behaviour – neces-sitated yet another rethinking of the contentious notion 'modernity'. Mukadas's was a complicated, multi-level dilemma; it was an attempt to realign and reinterpret the competing frameworks and material circumstances so that she could be a modern, veiling Muslim woman.

What light does Mukadas's struggle cast on anthropological understandings of how modernity is experienced? In an introduction to anthropological approaches on modernity, Bruce Knauft asserts the need to address 'the issues that surround the process of *being* or *becoming* differently modern in different world areas' (2002: 4, emphasis mine). He offers a minimal definition of modernity as 'the images and insti-tutions associated with Western-style progress and development in a contemporary world' (2002: 18). However, in light of Mukadas's struggle, and the role of the socialist world as modern, we need to rethink this articulation. My questions are twofold. First, how do we deal with a situation in which central images of progress and development come not from the contemporary West but from a socialist past? And, second, what happens when we seek to interpret people who see themselves as *having been*, as *being*, and as in need of *becoming* modern?

Knauft fleshes out his discussion by providing a diagram which locates modernity as an articulatory space between traditional/subaltern culture on one side and the modern/dominant on the other. He argues that the alternative modern is 'the articulatory space through which notions of modernity and tradition are co-constructed' (2002: 26). However, how would his diagram adequately map out Mukadas's experience? While she certainly has a notion of tradition, it is one of a past long removed, one which occurred before the Soviet era. Similarly she must position herself with reference to the dominant capitalist political economy and its incumbent culture. But where would the Soviet era – Mukadas's most immediate referent and source of contrast with the dominant vision of modernity – fit on such a schema?

In her study of Kemalist nostalgia in Turkey, Esra Özyürek has uncovered a similar disjuncture in temporal experiences of modernity. She contends that Turkish citizens' 'nostalgic take on modernity' is a sentimental position and political ideology which attempts to make sense and use of a *history* marked by multiple modernizing regimes and their variegated visions of modernity (2006: 18-19). Turkish citizens deal with contemporary neoliberal politics through the lens of past state-led modernization projects, she argues, leading her to conclude that anthropological literature needs to consider not only the spatial variation of modernity but its temporal one as well (2006: 18).

Similarly, I suggest that despite our attempts to overcome our own 'modernity' in anthropological writings, we still too strongly reflect a forward-looking thinking in our analysis. We end up with tradition behind us, modernity ahead, and the modern as the present. But is this the complete story? When James Ferguson charted the social experience of decline in the Zambian Copperbelt, he not only described the decline, but offered means of interpreting the non-linear, non-teleological trajectories he studied. In this way he critiqued the notion of progress and development found not only in modernization theory, but also in much ethnography of developing countries. My argument parallels his attempt to 'follow a range of reactions and strategies that shift over time in ways that do not sustain a simple linear narration' (Ferguson 1999: 20). However, I argue that in Kyrgyzstan it is not just a matter of a modernity that was almost achieved, but rather one that was realized. Diverging from Ferguson, I see the contemporary situation in Kyrgyzstan not merely as one of decline. While there is this sense especially regarding reduced living standards and the loss of societal modernity, the fact that Mukadas none the less sees herself as still modern despite the changed circumstances and attempts to create a new type of modernity – which incorporates Soviet, Western, and Islamic elements – signals that the experience of modernity is not just a matter of moving towards or away from something. The experience can be simultaneously one of loss, one of fulfilment, and one of desire – modernity as past, present, and future.

ACKNOWLEDGMENTS

The research and write-up of this chapter were supported by the Max Planck Institute for Social Anthropology, Halle, Germany, the Eurasia Program of the Social Science Research Council (Title VIII), New York,

USA, and the International Institute for the Study of Islam in the Modern World, Leiden, the Netherlands. Particular gratitude goes to Filippo Osella, Mathijs Pelkmans, Richard Rottenberg, Benjamin Soares, and Olaf Zenker for their comments.

NOTES

[1] All names are pseudonyms.

[2] See Abu-Lughod (2002) and Moors (2007) for examples.

[3] Osh, Kyrgyzstan's second largest city, is 80 kilometres from Bazaar-Korgon.

[4] Eisenstadt deals only with the communist and socialist revolutions. For a fuller discussion of the Soviet Union as modern, see Arnason (1993; 2000).

[5] The *paranji* was a large, shirt-like covering that was combined with a *chachvan*, a rough horse-hair veil worn by some female inhabitants of the Ferghana Valley.

[6] Locally this demographic pattern is attributed to something 'essential' in Uzbek ethnicity – that is, Uzbeks are more religious than Kyrgyz and Uzbeks live in the south. I have argued elsewhere that at least in the case of Bazaar-Korgon this seeming ethnic pattern has more to do with socio-economic class of the Soviet era (McBrien 2008). In essence, those less tied into and monitored by the state and its incumbent secularism, and those located in former centres of Islamic textual learning – that is, the late-Soviet era Uzbek peasants of Kyrgyzstan's Ferghana Valley – were more likely to become interested in interpretations which appeal to scripture as a basis of authority after the Union's demise.

[7] An *atincha* is a female religious specialist who, among other things, teaches women to recite the Qur'an, instructs them about their Islamic duties, and offers advice.

REFERENCES

ABU-LUGHOD, L. 2002. Do Muslim women really need saving? Anthropological reflections on cultural relativism and its others. *American Anthropologist* **104**, 783-90.

AHMED, L. 1992. *Women and gender in Islam: historical roots of a modern debate.* New Haven: Yale University Press.

ARNASON, J. 1993. *The future that failed: the collapse of communism in Eastern Europe.* London: Routledge.

——— 2000. Communism and modernity. *Daedalus* **129**, 61-90.

ASAD, T. 2003. *Formations of the secular: Christianity, Islam, modernity.* Stanford: University Press.

BABADJANOV, B. & M. KAMILOV 2001. Muhammadjan Hindustani (1892-1989) and the beginning of the 'Great Schism' among the Muslims of Uzbekistan. In *Islam in politics in Russia and Central Asia (early eighteenth to late twentieth centuries)* (eds) S.A. Dudoignon & K. Hisao, 195-219. London: Kegan Paul.

BRENNER, S. 1996. Reconstructing self and society: Javanese Muslim women and 'the veil'. *American Ethnologist* **23**, 673-97.

EISENSTADT, S.N. 2000. Multiple modernities'. *Daedalus* **129**, 1-29.

FERGUSON, J. 1999. *Expectations of modernity: myths and meanings of urban life on the Zambian Copperbelt.* Berkeley: University of California Press.

GÖLE, N. 1996. *The forbidden modern: civilization and veiling.* Ann Arbor: University of Michigan Press.

GRANT, B. 1995. *In the Soviet house of culture: a century of perestroikas.* Princeton: University Press.

HEFNER, R. 2005. Introduction: modernity and the remaking of Muslim politics. In *Remaking Muslim politics* (ed.) R. Hefner, 1-36. Princeton: University Press.

HIRSCH, F. 2005. *Empire of nations: ethnographic knowledge and the making of the Soviet Union.* Ithaca, N.Y.: Cornell University Press.

KANDIYOTI, D. 2002. Post-colonialism compared: potentials and limitations in the Middle East and Central Asia. *International Journal of Middle East Studies* **34**, 279-97.

KELLER, S. 1992. Islam in Soviet Central Asia, 1917-1930: Soviet policy and the struggle for control. *Central Asian Survey* **11**, 25-50.

KNAUFT, B. 2002. Critically modern: an introduction. In *Critically modern: alternatives, alterities, and anthropologies* (ed.) B. Knauft, 1-56. Bloomington: Indiana University Press.

LAMPLAND, M. 2002. The advantages of being collectivized: cooperative farm managers in the postsocialist economy. In *Postsocialism: ideals, ideologies and practices in Eurasia* (ed.) C. Hann, 31-56. London: Routledge.

McBRIEN, J. 2006. Extreme conversations: secularism, religious pluralism, and the rhetoric of Muslim extremism in Southern Kyrgyzstan. In *The postsocialist religious question* (eds) C. Hann *et al.*, 47-73. Munich: Lit Verlag.

———— 2008. Fruit of devotion: Islam and modernity in Kyrgyzstan. Ph.D. dissertation, Max Planck Institute for Social Anthropology.

———— & M. PELKMANS 2008. Turning Marx on his head: missionaries, 'extremists', and archaic secularists in post-Soviet Kyrgyzstan. *Critique of Anthropology* **28**, 87-103.

McLEOD, A. 1991. *Accommodating protest*. New York: Columbia University Press.

MAHMOOD, S. 2005. *Politics of piety: the Islamic revival and the feminist subject*. Princeton: University Press.

MARSDEN, M. 2005. *Living Islam: Muslim religious experience in Pakistan's North-West Frontier*. Cambridge: University Press.

MASSELL, G. 1974. *The surrogate proletariat : Moslem women and revolutionary strategies in Soviet Central Asia, 1919-1929*. Princeton: University Press.

MOORS, A. 2007. '*Burka*' in parliament and on the catwalk. *ISIM Review* **19**, 5.

———— & E. TARLO 2007. Introduction. *Fashion Theory: The Journal of Dress, Body and Culture* **11: 2-3**, Special Issue (eds) A. Moors & E. Tarlo, 133-42.

NORTHROP, D. 2004. *Veiled empire: gender and power in Stalinist Central Asia*. Ithaca, N.Y.: Cornell University Press.

ÖZYÜREK, E. 2006. *Nostalgia for the modern: state secularism and everyday politics in Turkey*. Durham, N.C.: Duke University Press.

PELKMANS, M. 2006. *Defending the border: identity, religion, and modernity in the Republic of Georgia*. Ithaca, N.Y.: Cornell University Press.

PINE, F. 1996. Redefining women's work in rural Poland. In *After socialism: land reform and social change in Eastern Europe* (ed.) R. Abrahams, 133-56. Providence, R.I.: Berghahn.

———— & S. BRIDGER 1998. Introduction: transition to post-socialism and cultures of survival. In *Surviving post-socialism: local strategies and regional responses in Eastern Europe and the former Soviet Union* (eds) F. Pine & S. Bridger, 1-15. London: Routledge.

ROFEL, L. 1999. *Other modernities: gendered yearnings in China after socialism*. Berkeley: University of California Press.

SAKTANBER, A. 2002. *Living Islam: women, religion, and the politicization of culture in Turkey*. London: I.B. Tauris.

SHAHRANI, N. 1984. From tribe to *umma*: comments on the dynamics of identity in Muslim Soviet Central Asia. *Central Asian Survey* **3: 3**, 27-38.

———— 2005. Reclaiming Islam in Uzbekistan. Paper presented at the conference 'Post-Soviet Islam', Max Planck Institute for Social Anthropology, Halle, Germany, June.

SLEZKINE, Y. 1994. The USSR as a communal apartment, or how a socialist state promoted ethnic particularism. In *Stalinism: new directions* (ed.) S. Fitzpatrick, 313-47. London: Routledge.

WHITE, J. 1999. Islamic chic. In *Istanbul: between the global and the local* (ed.) Ç. Keyder, 77-91. Oxford: Rowman & Littlefield.

———— 2002. *Islamist mobilization in Turkey: a study in vernacular politics*. Seattle: University of Washington Press.

9

Genealogy of the Islamic state: reflections on Maududi's political thought and Islamism

IRFAN AHMAD *Monash University*

Across the disciplinary divides, it is a truism to assert that Islam, in contrast to other religions, does not make a distinction between religion and the state, or *sacerdotium* and *regnum*. The idea of an Islamic state, as the argument goes, flows from the theological character of Islam itself. The vast literature on Islamic fundamentalism testifies to such an assumption. Ismael and Ismael thus argue that 'the classical paradigm of politics was founded on an image of the state that presupposed religion as the source of power and *Khalafah* [caliphate] as the framework of government' (1991 [1985]: 25). In the words of prominent Orientalist Bernard Lewis, 'In Islam ... there is from the beginning an interpenetration, almost an identification, of ... religion and the state' (1996: 61). Lewis further argues that the state in Islam is at the mercy of divinity, for 'the state does not create the law, but is itself created and maintained by the law, which comes from God' (2002 [1988]: 31). Lambton elaborates on this argument as follows: 'From the very beginning religion and state were one and this remained a characteristic of Islam down to the modern times ... *The sharia, the divinely revealed law of God, has absolute authority. It precedes the state and was its law*' (1988: 3, emphasis added). While most versions of this argument posit that Islam fuses religion and the state, many, including Lambton, believe that Islam indeed did not require such a fusion since it was a state from its inception. In Gellner's parsimoniously forceful rendition, 'It [Islam] *was* the state from the very start' (1992: 9, italics in original). It is this theological character of Islam, Gellner continues, which renders it a 'dramatic, conspicuous exception' to the otherwise universal process of secularization (1992: 5). Advancing the same argument, Dumont avers that whereas in its long course of history Hinduism was secularized (cf. Geertz 1980: 125-9; Madan 1997), Islam was not (1970: 68, 91-2).[1] Huntington's (1996) is probably the most well-known articulation of this premise in recent times.

I will call the above line of argument the 'fusion framework'. Against this hegemonic framework – also shared by influential Islamist ideologues such as Abul Ala Maududi and Egypt's Sayyid Qutb – a few scholars argue to the contrary. According to this second argument, Islam indeed makes a separation between religion and the state. And theologically, it does not entail an Islamic state. In the nineteenth century, Sayyid Ahmad Khan of India (d. 1898) was probably one of the first scholars to argue that Islam asked its believers to be loyal to whatever state they were part of, no matter whether it was Muslim or non-Muslim (1982). His associate, Shibli Nomani (d. 1914), further pursued this line of thought (1999). In the so-called 'heartland' of Islam, the Middle East, it was the Egyptian Ali Abd Ar-Raziq who presented this argument in its full-blown form. Published in the wake of the abolition of the Caliphate, Ar-Raziq's (1982) treatise generated much debate. In recent times, Maulana Wahiduddin Khan (1963) of India and Egypt's Al-Ashmawy have questioned the fusion framework. According to Al-Ashmawy, a former judge, the Qur'an does not guide Muslims to a distinct form of government. If the state were part of Islam, he argues, 'it would have been ... sketched out in general outlines in the Qur'an' (1998: 78).

Let us call Al-Ashmawy's line of argument the 'anti-fusion framework'. Evidently, the conclusions of both fusion and anti-fusion frameworks are radically different, even antagonistic. However, there is an arresting unity in the methods they employ to arrive at their respective conclusions. Their approach is theological. That is, they employ a method which accords centrality to canonical religious texts, particularly the Qur'an and *hadith* (the Prophet Muhammad's statements and actions), to derive a given conclusion. Central to this approach is a philological way of deciphering meanings of key words in the texts. Among the proponents of the fusion framework, Lewis's *The political language of Islam* (2002 [1988]) is a classic example of this approach. He traces the roots and meanings of such words as *dawla* (state), *khalifa* (caliph), *hukuma* (government), *amir* (leader), *sirat al-Mustaqim* (straight path), and so on, not only in the Islamic traditions but also in the Hebrew and Latin traditions. The advocates of the anti-fusion framework adopt the same textualist approach. Wahiddudin Khan's *Folly of interpretation* (1963), almost every page of which is laced with citations from the Qur'an and *hadith*, is a representative example, as is Al-Ashmawy's *Against Islamic extremism* (1998).

The argument

Until recently, anthropology has been rather disinterested in the salience of the modern state. Anthropology's indifference, if not hostility, to the state is probably best expressed by Radcliffe-Brown. In his preface to *African political systems*, he dismissed the state as a 'fiction of the philosophers' (1940: xxiii). Though as a sub-discipline, political anthropology gave attention to politics and the government (hence its abiding interest in factions, networks, action-sets, and so on), and also studied, as Fuller and Harriss (2001) note, the 'traditional' princely states (e.g. Dirks 1987; Geertz 1980), it remained until recently largely uninterested in the study of the valences and practices of the modern state (Gledhill 2000; Spencer 1997; 2001; Swartz, Turner & Tuden 1966; Vincent 1990; 1996). In recent times, several anthropologists have begun to pay attention to the dynamics of the state. In the South Asian context, Gupta's (1995) article bears special mention. The volumes edited by Fuller and Bénéï (2001) and by Sharma and Gupta (2006) offer valuable contributions to the anthropological debates on the state. The two outstanding volumes edited by Hansen and Stepputat (2001; 2005) are presently perhaps the most comprehensive anthropological explorations of the state in the non-Western world.

My main objective is to question the validity of the theological approach to understand the dynamics of Islamism. As an alternative, I call for a historically embedded anthropological approach to the idea of the Islamic state – a subject that anthropology has been even more disinterested in than in the notions and practices of the state in general. Historically, the debate on the Islamic state has been conducted mostly in the field of Islamic studies or area studies (exceptions include, *inter alia*, Gellner). Not surprisingly, theological factors have weighed heavily in these debates. While sensitive to theology, my approach gives primacy to the political factors and historical context in which philological interpretation is made and unmade. My call, then, is not to abandon theology, but rather to subject it critically to the historical-political matrixes that shape the enterprise and, more importantly, the product of interpretation. Analytically speaking, an exclusively theological approach to the canonical texts, for example the Qur'an, has serious limits. It is not a pristine text that yields meanings on its own and by itself; it is rather the distinct social condition and the biography of the person reading the text which produces its meanings. My point would become clearer with the following quotation. As the contemporary Egyptian scholar Nasr Abu Zayd observes, '[T]he Quran is at the mercy of the ideology of its interpreter. For a communist, the Quran would thus reveal communism, for a fundamentalist it would be a highly fundamentalist text, for a feminist it would be a feminist text, and so on' (in Ahmad 2008: 551). While I agree that study of theology and texts is important, far more significant are the political dynamics and historical context in which a given theology ascends, wins, or loses salience.

Based on this methodological approach, I propose a set of two interlocking arguments. Contra Gellner, for whom Islam 'was the state from the very start', I argue that the idea of an Islamic state is a distinctly modern development. The proposition by Lewis and Lambton that in Islam from the beginning religion and the state were one and that the latter was an unsullied embodiment of sharia, '*the divinely revealed law of God*' (Lambton), is an ideologically de-historicized abstraction. It helps us understand neither the modern nature of the state nor the complexity of sharia, including how the meaning of sharia itself changed over time and the ways in which it was humanly recast.

Clearly, the concept of 'the state' is quite modern. The term entered the lexicon of the social sciences in the nineteenth century to understand the dramatic changes in early modern Europe from the seventeenth century onwards (Kaviraj 1999). To impose the modern concept of the state on seventh-century Arab society is misleading (Asad 1997). This is not to suggest that seventh-century Arabia was bereft of any political formation. My point is that the nature of the political configuration of the seventh century was radically different from the state as it evolved in modern Europe. The medieval European state, it is well known, governed mostly by not governing. It barely intervened in most affairs of its subjects. It stood above the societal structure without intending to change it. Even if the state desired to alter the social arrangements, it would not have been possible due to its infrastructural weakness. As such its executive scope was far too limited. It was a 'puny leviathan' (Hall & Ikenberry 1997 [1989]: 23; also see Held 1996; Poggi 1978; Tilly 1975) interested in simply extracting taxes. In contrast, the modern state developed a more penetrative reach. With the rise of print media, transportation links, and a series of other innovations, the state assumed what Giddens calls 'heightened administrative power' (1985: 256) and went beyond mere extracting taxes to impact on daily life. In Europe around the sixteenth century, notes Foucault, there was a 'veritable explosion of the art of governing' (1996: 383 see also 1982), with the result that the state acquired the pastoral power to legislate everyday life, including the intimate arenas of sexuality and care.

This admittedly synoptic account of the modern state enables us to question the premise that Islam possessed a state from the very beginning. It also allows us to debunk the assumption – basic to the fusion framework – that Islam had a fully fledged theory of the state. Indeed it would be erroneous to say that Islam had a neatly crafted political theory. 'There is no political theory as such in Islamic political thought', writes Al-Azmeh (1990: 9). As I will show, it is during the early twentieth century that a fully developed political theory of the Islamic state emerged in the discourse of Islamism. Equally flawed is the assumption that sharia is the revealed law of God and hence immutable. It is divine for Muslims to the extent that its frame of reference is the Qur'an and *hadith*. But it is fallible humans who have made and interpreted over time the body of conflicting juridical rules, instructions, and ethics called sharia. Sharia is thus humanly shaped and contested (Eickelman & Piscatori 1996; Eickelman & Salvatore 2002; Masud 2001; Messick 1993). In a recent study, Muzaffar Alam, a medieval historian, notes that the meaning of sharia itself varied from one context to another.[2] As generally understood, sharia was not simply a body of religious edicts pronounced by theologians. In medieval India, for example, it also included writings of *akhlaq* (ethics) texts[3] by Muslim philosophers. Among several texts of this genre, Alam (2004) discusses Khawaja Nasiruddin Tusi's (d. 1274) *Akhlaq-e-Nasiri*, in particular. In his writings on politics, Tusi departed from the conventional sharia positions. He drew on 'Hellenic philosophical writings and blended them with his own "Islamic" view of man and society' (2004: 47). In the Nasirean tradition (that which follows Khawaja Nasiruddin's approach) an ideal ruler was one who 'ensured the well being of the people of diverse religious groups, and not Muslims alone' (2004: 49; also see Alam 2000).

Seen from this perspective, the two Muslim dynasties – the Sultanate (1206-1526), which indeed comprised several different dynasties, and the Mughal (1526-1750), which ruled India – were not mere executers of the divine, as Lewis and Lambton suggest. Independent of sharia, Muslim rulers invented *zawabit*, state laws (Alam 2004; Rashid 1979). This is not to say that sharia was irrelevant. But it coexisted with *zawabit*. Thus, along with the laws of *hadd*, sharia-derived punishment for severe crimes, there also existed *tazir* (state-mediated punishments for crimes which the Qur'an or *hadith* does not specify), in the exercise of which state policy was crucial (Kugle 2001). In many ways *zawabit*, not sharia, were central to the Mughal polity (Alam 2004; Rashid 1979; Rizvi 1975). The abolition of *jizya*, a tax levied on non-Muslim subjects, by the emperor Jalaluddin Akbar (r. 1556-1605) was the most authoritative example of *zawabit*. Such legislation as Akbar's calls into question the premise that religion and the state were fused. If it were so, how could Razia Sultana (d. 1240), a woman of the Sultanate dynasty, have become the ruler of Delhi? In fact, Muslim rulers in India mostly followed secular policies in that they did not fuse Islam and politics (Ashraf 1970; Eaton 2001; B. Metcalf & T. Metcalf 2002; Rashid 1979; Rizvi 1970; Tirpathi 1998; Uberoi 1994; cf. Krishna 1972; Madan 1997; Majumdar 1960; Qureshi 1962). When asked about his policy and the place of religion therein, Alauddin Khilji (r. 1296-1316) remarked, 'I do not know whether these orders are in conformity with sharia or contrary to it. Whatever I consider to be for the good of the administration, and expedient, that I decree' (in Rizvi 1975: 20). In a curious phrase, Rashid described the Mughal state as a 'religion-oriented secular state' (1979: 146). It was 'secular' in that it upheld an ecumenical policy towards non-Islamic religions at the core of which lay respect for and inclusion of non-Muslims in the state bureaucracy. Unlike in the Ottoman Empire, where non-Muslims were required to convert to Islam to join the military, the Mughals recruited Hindus *qua*

Hindus in the military (Eaton 2001: 30).[4] Between 1594 and 1595, Akbar appointed twelve finance ministers; eight of them were Hindu. His wife, moreover, followed Hindu rituals within the royal palace (Smith 1963).[5] As I illustrate below, it was precisely against this separation between religion and politics by Indian sultans that Maududi later called for a fusing of Islam and the state.

My second argument, which follows from the first, is that the reason why the state became central to Islamism was not because Islam theologically entailed it. Rather it did so because of the configuration of the early twentieth-century socio-political formations under which the state as an institution had acquired an unprecedented role in expanding its realm of action and the scope of its penetration. Since Islamism was a response to the modern colonial state formation with its far-reaching consequences, it was only logical that the state became the centre of its discourse. My argument is thus substantially different from some recent works questioning the thesis that Islam fuses religion and politics (see, e.g., Ayubi 1991; Eickelman & Piscatori 1996; Roy 1994). The focus of my chapter is not the broader field of politics but the specific idea of an Islamic state which Maududi conceptualized as being indispensable to Islam.

To substantiate my argument, I will discuss the writings and political role of Abul Ala Maududi (1903-79), arguably the foremost ideologue of Islamism. Founder of the Jamaat-e-Islami in India, Maududi has influenced Islamist movements beyond South Asia, most notably Egypt's Muslim Brotherhood and one of its ideologues, Sayyid Qutb (Shepard 2003). In the first part of the chapter, I outline the contours of the pre-modern Mughal state to show its marginal role in terms of its impact on social life. Next, I describe the ways in which the colonial British state that replaced the Mughal state assumed an unprecedented interventionist role to impact on social lives. While the colonial state influenced all segments of Indian society, its impact was particularly unsettling for the Muslim elite to which Maududi belonged and with whom he identified. Drawing on Maududi's life, in the second part, I show how at a time when the slogan of the anti-colonial movement was 'self-rule', or the Indian/communist/Hindu/Muslim state, he advanced the idea of an Islamic state. Here I demonstrate how Maududi's theoretical elaboration about Islam being identical with the state was an upshot of the electoral politics of colonial India.

The modern leviathan and its power

Much like the puny leviathan of medieval Europe, the scope and the capacity of the pre-modern Indian state was severely limited. The demands of a predominantly agrarian socio-political formation did not entail an interventionist role by the state. It lacked the basic infrastructure that the modern state came to acquire later. It did not have the centralizing aims. Nor did it possess the apparatus to impose a uniform, standardized structure. Though the Mughal dynasty served as the centre of power, in practice the authority rested with the regional rulers and autonomous chieftains. The Mughal state did not interfere with the regional chieftains as long as the latter obeyed the sovereignty of the former. Based on his work on south India, Stein (1980) describes the pre-modern state as a 'segmentary state'. Summing up the debates on the pre-modern state, Hansen concludes that 'pre-colonial India had indeed a long-standing tradition of segmented, overlapping and stratified forms of sovereignty' (2005: 115).[6]

Anthropologically, the pre-modern Indian state was high in titles and spectacles but fairly low in its ambition and capacity to regulate the everyday lives of its subjects. Villages where most people lived most of their lives enjoyed considerable autonomy from the state. In fact, the patterns of community lives in villages survived the over-throw or installation of royal power. The key mode of relation between villages and empire, mediated through local landlords and regional kingdoms, was that of rent-giving. Beyond extracting taxes from the villages, the state did not aspire to disturb, much less refashion, the social order. According to Kaviraj, '[T]he state was of curious marginality to the fundamental processes of everyday life of society'[7] (1999: 42; also see Bayly 1983). Interestingly, this marginality of the state (cf. Blake 1979, 1991; Moosvi 2005) went hand in hand with its majesty.

In marked contrast to the pre-modern state, the modern state instituted by British colonialism assumed an unprecedented role. It would be an exaggeration to say that it possessed pastoral power similar to that of the modern European state. But the legis-lative scope of the colonial state was surely more far-reaching than that of the Mughal state. The colonial state thus marked 'a radical departure ... from its pre-colonial predecessor states [the Mughal]' (Pantham 2003: 1428). This argument obviously goes against the thesis of continuity. The historian Percival Spear claimed that the colonial state was a faithful continuation of the Mughal state. Early British India, he contended, 'was really the Mughal India writ large', and the colonial state 'never intended to ... disrupt society' (1979: 171, 169; cf. Bayly 1988). Spear based his argument on the policy of the colonial state from the early eighteenth century to 1835. This is the period when the British East India Company (hereafter the Company) had not yet fully conquered India. Its rule was limited to Bengal. It is true that the impact of the colonial state during this phase was less pervasive. It intensified following the Revolt of 1857, after which the British Crown directly took control of India. However, the argument of continuity, which plays down the intensely interventionist role of the colonial state, avers a historian of the Aligarh school (see note 6), is also made to redeem colonialism (Moosvi 2005). Contrary to Spear, below I show that both during its early and latter phases the colonial state inaugurated a series of initiatives which altered the existing socio-economic and cultural configurations. In many ways, these initiatives indeed led to the breakdown of traditional social arrangements. In discussing these state-induced changes, my focus is on the Muslim community.

Historians take 1757 as the formal start of colonial rule, when the Company con-quered Bengal after the battle of Plassey. With the conquest the Company set in motion many extraordinary changes. To begin with, it secured the *diwani* whereby the Company assumed the right to collect revenue from three provinces of Bengal, Bihar, and Orissa. More importantly, it passed the Permanent Settlement Act in 1793. The Act introduced the notion of private ownership of land (Desai 1946) and created a new class of landlords loyal to the Raj. This was done by replacing the old class of *zamindars*, mostly Muslims, with a new one, mainly comprising Hindus. The Company did not spare the lower-class Muslims either. Owing to the commercialization of agriculture by the Company and its interests in crops like opium, indigo, and jute as well as the competition with the manufacturers in England, the condition of weavers, craftsmen, and cultivators – a large number of them being Muslim – worsened. This shift in the mode of economy, however, benefited bankers and moneylenders, who were mostly Hindus (Hardy 1972; Malik 1963; Rizvi 1970). The next major step was the Resumption Regulation of 1820, whereby the Company assumed *lakhiraj*, the revenue-free land granted to Muslims. Even the Muslim *waqfs* (endowments) were not spared. This gave a further blow to Muslim elites as it led to the virtual collapse of their traditional educational system, which was based primarily on *waqfs* (Kabir 1969).

Another crucial result of the Company's rule was the overnight change of court language. The circular of Lord Macaulay replaced Persian with English in 1833. For Muslims it meant the further closing of doors to administrative posts. The middle layers of Muslims received yet another blow when the Company introduced the modern criminal law replacing the traditional legal system, which provided jobs to Muslims in the judiciary. As a result of the transformation of the legal system, in 1869, there was not a single Muslim among the attorneys, proctors, and solicitors of Bengal's High Court. Summarizing the impact of the first seventy-five years of colonial rule, Malik writes that 'the Moslem upper and middle classes either disappeared or were submerged beneath the new Hindu upper classes which developed as a result of the English policy' (1963: 146).

The series of extraordinary interventions by the Company, especially those pertaining to land relations, led to numerous protest movements by Muslim peasants in Bengal. Dubbed as 'Wahabi' by the British, these movements employed the vocabulary of Islam. The Faraizi movement, initiated by Haji Shariatullah (d. 1840), was one such protest movement. It was called *faraizi* because of the emphasis the movement put on the adherence to religious obligation, *fard*. The movement activists declared that India under the British rule was *darul harb* (the abode of war) and hence Muslims could no longer perform either the Friday prayers or prayers for Eid. They opposed the levying of taxes by landlords and indigo planters. Such episodes of protests made Muslims suspect in the eyes of the British. In his book *The Indian Musalmans: are they bound in conscience to rebel against the Queen?* (1871), W.W. Hunter, a British official, described Muslims engaged in such protests as 'fanatic swarms' and their activities as 'enterprise of treason' (1871: 9). The Revolt of 1857 against colonial rule only intensified the British suspicion of Muslims. Though Hindus also participated in the Revolt, the British believed that it was the handiwork of Muslims. After the Revolt, Muslims became the chief target of the British (Nehru 1946). In Delhi alone several hundreds of Muslims, including the members of the Mughal family, were indiscriminately killed, hanged, or imprisoned.

After the suppression of the Revolt, India came directly under the purview of the Crown. Thereafter the colonial state became even more interventionist. Based on the idea of an essential difference between India and Britain and buoyed by the 'White Man's Burden' to rule, manage, and alter India in the image of Britain (T. Metcalf 1995), the colonial state undertook a range of measures. Codification or what Hansen (1999: 33) calls 'scripturalization ... of customary laws', including those of sharia (Kugle 2001), enumerations of caste and religious categories through census (Appadurai 1996; Dirks 2001; also see Chatterjee 1993; van der Veer 1996), and formation and conquest of knowledge systems (Cohn 1996) were some of the crucial measures. The state also introduced many fundamental changes in the political arena. In 1861, it passed the Indian Council Act, which formed the basis of subsequent reforms towards the forming of a representative government. The Morely-Minto Reforms of 1909 were crucial in that they introduced separate electorates for Muslims and Hindus. Pertinent to my argument is also the Government of India Act of 1935, under which for the first time elections were held, in 1937, to form provincial governments (Brass 1994). It was in the wake of the 1937 elections that Maududi advanced his political theology of an Islamic state. He did so because the state had emerged as the new master vocabulary of the time.

The invention of the Islamic state: Maududi's political theology
From the foregoing historical account, it should be clear how the modern colonial state deeply impacted on Indian society, particularly Muslims. In contradistinction to the

Mughal state, its reach was far more penetrating and ubiquitous. Given the centrality of the state, all social movements in colonial India related to the role of the state, even if their target was non-state actors (see I. Ahmad 2009). The anti-colonial movement, spearheaded by the Indian National Congress (formed in 1885; hereafter the Congress) under M.K. Gandhi's leadership, was the largest. From the early twentieth century, its goal became *swaraj*, self-rule. Clearly, self-rule was all about the state. It was in such a context that Maududi, still a teenager, appeared as an Urdu journalist on the scene. Never schooled in a madrasa, an Islamic seminary, and largely self-educated (on Maududi's life, see Nasr 1996), initially he was a devoted Congressman. He wrote admiring biographies of Gandhi and Madanmohan Malaviya, a Congress revivalist and a key leader of the Hindu Mahasabha whom he called 'sailor of India's boat' (Maududi 1992 [1919]: 28-9). In 1920, Maududi became an editor of *The Muslim*, an Urdu newspaper published by the Jamiatul Ulema-e-Hind, a party of *'ulama* (those educated in an Islamic seminary; theologians) allied to the Congress. However, Maududi grew disenchanted with the Congress, which he believed favoured Hindus against Muslims. Under the cloak of secularism, he maintained, the Congress pursued the ideology of the Hindu Mahasabha, a party with avowedly Hindu goals (1938: 151).

In 1928, Maududi left Delhi for Hyderabad, capital of the Muslim princely state of the Nizams. As military generals, his mother's ancestors had served the Nizams. On his father's side too, he had a royal connection. An educated notable of Delhi, Maududi's grandfather had relations to the court of Bahadurshah Zafar, the last Mughal king (Nasr 1996; Sampradaikta Virodhi Committee n.d.). While devoting himself to the study of Islam at Hyderabad, he realized that, like the Mughals, the Nizams would also disintegrate. He began to investigate the causes of Muslims' decline. He discovered that the decline set in because Muslim rulers had abandoned 'pure Islam', *asali Islam* (1937: 71). He bemoaned the fact that most rulers were more busy conquering lands than following sharia. Maududi did not consider the Mughal rule Islamic because it did not fuse Islam and politics. In particular, he attacked King Akbar for his ecumenical, secular policies (1937: 9-13; 1938: 170; 1940: 310-14). Chiding Muslims who cited the Taj Mahal as a shining achievement of the Mughals, he argued that it was un-Islamic to bury the dead in acres of land occupied at a cost of millions of rupees to erect a monument thereon. 'From a purely Islamic framework of history', he averred, 'a major part of the achievements of these people [the Saljuq, and the Mughals] have to be written ... in ... the catalogue of crimes' (2001 [1939]: 138). Worried about the decline of Muslims, he offered a blueprint to the Nizams to revitalize it. It called for overhauling the educational system and propagating a 'pure' Islam. To his dismay, the Nizams showed no interest in it. In 1932, Maududui launched an Urdu journal, *Tarjumanul Qur'an* (herafter *Tarjuman*) as a part of his own plan.

In 1937, while busy with the publication of *Tarjuman*, Maududi got swept up in the elections, which had been authorized by the Government of India Act two years earlier. Consequently, he moved from composite nationalism to communalism and finally to Islamism. The electoral contest was between the Congress and the Muslim League (hereafter the League), a party founded in 1906. In principle, the Congress upheld secularism and believed in the united nationalism of Hindus and Muslims. Its aim was to unite Indians of all faiths to fight against the colonial order. The objective of the League, by contrast, was Muslims' interests and loyalty to the Raj. The League rejected the Congress's claim to represent Muslims. Yet, it lost the elections. The Congress clinched victory to form provincial ministries. It was then that Maududi turned

Tarjuman into a weapon against the Congress. He equated the policy of the ministries (1937-9) with heralding a 'Hindu Raj' (1938: 161). Before proceeding further, let us note that these were the first ever ministries that Indians, still under British suzerainty, had formed by themselves. Maududi critiqued the Congress ministries on a variety of issues. For brevity, I will focus on his critique of the educational policies of the state.

Provision of primary education was central to the ministries' agenda. To this end, they prepared the syllabus, set up committees to select textbooks, and ran schools. Maududi believed that as a minority Muslims were being subjected to the whims of the Hindu majority and made to lose their Islamic identity.[8] He accused the ministries of erasing the identity of Muslim students in schools. He discussed at length the educational plan, the Wardha Scheme, based on Gandhi's philosophy and designed by Zakir Husain, a 'nationalist Muslim'. He criticized it for presupposing that India comprised only one nation and thereby denying the existence of a Muslim nation. To Maududi, the Wardha Scheme was devised to forge 'Indian nationalism by eliminating Islamic nationalism' (1938: 168). The Wardha syllabus, he held, trivialized Islam by presenting its prophets in the list of figures like Lincoln, Tolstoy, Marx, and the musician Tan Sen. Gandhi's ideas, however, dominated the syllabus. He sarcastically called Gandhi 'the prophet of modern India' and likened Zakir Husain to Macaulay, the British official who scorned non-Western knowledge and wanted to manufacture an anglicized class of Indians (1938: 171, 172).

Maududi continued his critique of the Congress ministry by citing its practices in the Central Provinces (CP). The CP's policy was named Vidya Mandir, 'educational temple', derived from the Hindu education system, *gurukul*. Maududi objected as much to the naming of the school (which was the same as the policy) as to the exclusion of Muslims in the syllabus and textbook committees. Furthermore, Maududi argued that Muslim students were coerced to sing the anti-Islamic Sanskrit anthem *vande matram*[9] with their hands folded and head bowed. The President of the Sagar municipality threatened that those refusing to sing the anthem would be expelled from school. Muslim students were forced to worship Saraswati, the Hindu goddess. Instead of using Islamic greetings, they were made to greet a visitor with *jai Ram ji ki* (victory to [the god] Ram). Likewise, they were forced to wear Hindu dress, *dhoti* (a lower garment worn by Hindu men[10]) and treated like untouchables. Maududi supported his allegations with reports and eyewitness accounts from the English and Urdu press (1938: 116-17, 177-9).

Language was another ground of Maududi's critique of the Congress. He saw the 'Hindu Raj' coming in the imposition of Sanskritized Hindi and the elimination of Urdu. In the elimination of Urdu, he saw the elimination of Muslim culture, *tahzeeb*. He noted how even those Urdu words intelligible to all Indians were being expelled from the documents and speeches of the Congress ministries. He gave a list of such words and their Sanskritized substitutes (1938: 180-90). In his view, Vidya Mandir smelled of Hindu religion, as did the Sanskritized renaming of places like Central Provinces as Mahakaushal. He concluded that these policies aimed at marginalizing Muslims and 'bringing the age of Ramayana back to India' (1938: 117). Clearly, Maududi's allegations pertained to the role of the modern colonial state – a role the pre-colonial state scarcely had. Having critiqued the practices of the Congress ministries, Maududi came to the following conclusion:

> From these details, it can easily be inferred how the policy adopted [by the Congress] to gain political power in the name of 'independence struggle' under the shadow of British rule is being used to

extinguish the power of Muslims and their identity (*qaumiat*); and how our neighbourly friend [the Congress or Hindus] is appropriating all those devices of national imperialism which they have learned from their English masters (1938: 180).[11]

After the elections of 1937, both Maududi and the League thus opposed the Congress. This did not make them allies, however. Actually, as the possibility of Pakistan's creation intensified, so did Maududi's critique of the League. In the late 1930s, the national politics revolved around the question of the state: the League demanded a separate Muslim state; the Congress attempted to avert it by having a secular state of united India; and the communists wanted to secure a socialist state. In a context where the 'state' was the reigning idiom of politics, Maududi advanced his own, a sharia state. From this standpoint, he found the League un-Islamic. He saw no difference between the Congress and the League; both desired a secular state. He called the League a 'party of the pagans' (1942: 69). Since the League had no agenda for a sharia state, Maududi declared that future Pakistan would be 'napakistan', a profane land (1942: 78). He even called it an 'infidel state of Muslims' (1942: 109). It was for this reason that in 1941, he formed Jamaat-e-Islami and set its goal as *hukumat-e-ilahiya*, 'Allah's Government' or 'Islamic State' (*Tarjuman*, May 1941: 11).

To Maududi's amazement, there were only a few enthusiasts for *hukumat-e-ilahiya*. As a party of *'ulama*, the Jamiatul Ulema-e-Hind believed in a secular, composite India and did not regard the state as essential to Islam. Maududi realized that Muslims would rally around him if he proved, through the Qur'an, why the state was central to Islam. He wrote, 'Without a proof from the Qur'anic verses ... people consider my every interpretation as personal, and my view at least cannot be acceptable to my opponents' (*Tarjuman*, May 1941: 216). A radically new theology of the state was on the anvil.

Maududi was clearly cognizant of the power of the modern state. It was in the context of the Congress ministries' policies *vis-à-vis* Muslims that the state became central to his thought. His exposition on the state was first elaborated in the March 1938 issue of *Tarjuman*, where he critiqued Sampurnanand, the Congress education minister of the United Province known for his enthusiasm for Hindu nationalism. Maududi wrote:

> The conceptualization of the state by the nineteenth-century scholars of politics is now utterly outdated. ... Gone are the days when if the state presented its economic, educational, industrial, or social scheme people made fun of it by calling it grandmotherly legislation.[12] The situation has completely changed. Now the state's arena has almost become as all-encompassing as that of religion. Now it also decides what you are to wear or what not to wear; whom you are to marry and at what age; what you are to teach your kids and what mode of life you are to choose; ... what language and script you are to adopt. So, the state has not left even the most peripheral issues of life independent of its ultimate right to intervene (*Tarjuman*, March 1938: 5).

As this quote demonstrates, not only did Maududi comprehend the nature of the modern state, but also his views reflect a critique of the policies of the Congress ministries on issues of dress, language, curriculum, and religious identity. Deploying a religious metaphor, he remarked, 'The first and the last loyalty of an individual is to the state, and any breach in this respect is no less than disbelief, *kufr*' (*Tarjuman*, March 1938: 6). Given the radically interventionist role of the modern state and the manner in which it shaped the daily lives of Muslims, he equated Islam with the state. That was why, in 1941, he founded the Jamaat to attain an Islamic state. As I noted earlier, most 'ulama had rejected Maududi's views, largely because he had no degree from a madrasa. Maududi thus felt compelled to legitimize the goal of the Jamaat through the Qur'an.

The key text of Maududi's political theology is *Four fundamental concepts of the Qur'an* (1979 [1941]).[13] Later published as a booklet, he first wrote it as a long essay the first instalment of which appeared in the same May 1941 issue of *Tarjuman* that carried the Constitution of the Jamaat. In his essay, Maududi argued that to know the 'authentic objective' of the Qur'an it was crucial to grasp the 'real and total' (7) meanings of the four Qur'anic words: *ilah* (Allah), *rabb* (Lord), *ibadat* (worship), and *deen* (religion). Did not 'ulama know their "real and total" meanings? Maududi claimed that they did not, for soon after Qur'an's revelation, their real meanings were lost (see below).

Of the four Qur'anic words, Maududi considered 'Allah' the most important one because one becomes Muslim by reciting the *kalimah*, there is no God except Allah and Muhammad is His messenger. The crucial word in the *kalimah* is Allah; unless one understands its real meaning the very declaration of one's faith would be in doubt. Maududi's exposition on Allah is premised on a distinction between the 'metaphysical' and 'worldly political' life which together constitute an indivisible organic whole. To be a Muslim is to worship *Allah alone* not just in the metaphysical realm but also in political realm because He is the master of both. Accordingly, Maududi contended that Allah must also be the 'Ruler, Dictator (*aamir*), and Legislator' of the political domain (28). Consequently, if someone claimed to be the ruler of a country, his claim would be equivalent to a claim to be God in the metaphysical realm. Thus, to share political power with someone who disregards the laws of Allah, he declared, would be polytheism in the same sense as someone who worships an idol (29). Elaborating on the meaning of *rabb*, a cognate term for Allah, he wrote that it was 'synonymous with sovereignty, *sultani*' (79). Since he viewed sovereignty in political terms, he argued that Allah is also a 'political *rabb*' (73). Thus *taghoot*, another Qur'anic word, does not just mean Satan or idol. It means a political order not based on Allah's sovereignty. Maududi chided the 'ulama for reducing the meaning of *taghoot* to a literal idol. For him, the Qur'anic injunction to worship Allah and shun *taghoot* meant securing a sharia state and rejecting any non-Islamic polity.

Like Allah, worship also meant obeying the political authority. Maududi lamented that Muslims had squeezed its meaning to worshipping Allah in metaphysical life and banished Him from their political life (81-98). Elsewhere, he equated rituals like prayer to military training and considered them as bare means to achieve the goal of an Islamic state. He wrote, 'The prayer, fasting ... is indeed a ... training precisely for that purpose [installation of an Islamic state]' (1968 [1940]: 315). Maududi interpreted *deen*, religion, similarly. 'The word of the contemporary age, the state, has ... approximated it [the meaning of *deen*]' (108). In a different text, he wrote, 'In reality, the word *deen* has approximately the same meaning which the word "state" has in the current age. To accept and obey a superior authority by a people is the state. This is precisely also the meaning of religion' (*Tarjuman*, February-March 1941: 13). Because of the centrality of the state in his thought, Maududi reasoned that 'the ultimate objective of the missions of all prophets has been to establish the Kingdom of God' (1940: 281). He likened the mission of the prophet Yusuf (Joseph) with the 'dictatorship' of Mussolini[14] (1999 [1939]: 122). Against the position that the assumption of the ministry of finance by Yusuf under the sovereignty of the non-Muslim king of Egypt meant that Muslims could participate in a non-Muslim polity, he argued that Yusuf did not just want to hold the finance ministry. Rather he wanted dictatorship.

Many of Maududi's other theorizations also echo the spirit of modern politics: for instance, the conceptualization of Islam as a movement and Muslims as a party (see I. Ahmad 2003). He introduced such innovations in the name of reclaiming 'pure' Islam. Clearly, his call for pure Islam (*asali Islam*) was an invention of tradition (Eickelman & Piscatori 1996; Hobsbawm 1983). Maududi's novel reading of these Qur'anic words stunned *'ulama* across the board, including his former comrade and Deoband theologian, Manzoor Nomani. Nomani accused him of 'politically interpreting' the Qur'an, and added that it also raised doubts if other words of the Qur'an were correctly understood. In his view, *Four fundamental concepts of the Qur'an* opened the 'door for sedition (*fitna*)', offered 'legitimacy for the atheists', and shook 'the very foundation of Islam'. It is instructive to note Maududi's response. When Nomani asked him if none before him understood their real meanings, Maududi said that Ibn Taimiyah (d. 1328) nearly did, but even he could not get them right (M. Nomani 1998: 94, 84, 88, 90).

Conclusion

Given the neglect of the state by anthropology, in an important article van der Veer called for according adequate attention to the state in anthropological explorations. 'The history of the colonial state', he observed, 'is crucial for the anthropological understanding of postcolonial religious formations in South Asia' (2002: 173). Following his lead, in this chapter I have tried to show how the logic and all-encompassing power of the colonial Indian state shaped the political theology of Maududi, arguably the most influential ideologue of Islamism in the twentieth century. The call for an Islamic state by Maududi, I have demonstrated, was distinctly modern as it arose in the milieu of colonial, electoral politics. In arguing for an Islamic state, Maududi did not replay the idea of an Islamic state allegedly intrinsic to Islam since inception because of its unique theological character. He indeed invented the notion of an Islamic state. The reason why he did so was because of the extraordinary capacity and reach of the modern state to impact on collective lives, including everyday practices. In the wake of the 1937 elections held to form ministries in various provinces, the state had become the master vocabulary of Indian politics. It was as much central to the Congress as to the League and various streams of the left. At a critical moment in South Asian history when the state was a key slogan, Maududi advanced his own notion of an Islamic state. Obviously, communal politics played a key role in shaping his ideas.

The argument of Gellner that Islam was the state from the very start is thus deeply flawed and ahistorical. In the sense that the state was used in the lexicon of the nineteenth-century social sciences, there was no state in the Arabian Peninsula in the seventh century or subsequently (Asad 1997). To argue that Islam was the state from the very start is, then, to impose a distinctly modern term on a pre-modern social formation. Equally misleading is the dominant assumption – widespread across the academic disciplines – that the so-called 'theological' character of Islam forces it to fuse religion and politics. The history and practices of the Indian Muslim rulers show that most of them did not follow sharia. Rather, independent of sharia, they framed secular laws, *zawabit*. Moreover, the meaning of sharia itself varied. It was far from stable. It was not only a body of juridical rules propounded by theologians. It also included *akhlaq* texts by Muslim philosophers like Nasiruddin Tusi. In many important ways, these ethical-philosophical texts transcended the conventional positions of sharia to address the concerns of the larger humanity (Alam 2004). The Mughal state was, to invoke a curious phrase of the historian Rashid, a 'religion-oriented secular state' (1979: 146). It was in the context of this separation between religion and the state that Maududi argued for a fusion of the state and Islam. He made this argument because the colonial state had emerged as an omnipotent institution influencing every domain of life.

It is not uncommon to read philosophy such as Tusi's as Islam's 'pragmatic' gesture in a non-Muslim Indian environment, as Gilmartin and Lawrence (2000: 14-15) seem to suggest. Even Alam appears to read such philosophical-ethical treatises as Islam's 'accommodation' in a non-Arab milieu (2000: 239). Clearly, the word 'pragmatic' presupposes a given entity out there: 'original', 'real', 'ideological', and 'pure'. It has been my contention that Islam is not a preset entity with an original, pure, real core against which Muslims – whether in the periphery or in the 'heartland' – fashion pragmatic adjustments. Islam is a process. What often passes under the flag of 'pragmatic' carries, if only unwittingly, a strong slant of deviation from an assumed original. In my view, that which is usually construed as 'pragmatic' is not deviation from the 'original', 'real', or 'pure'; both are simply work in progress.

My main objective in this chapter has been to rethink critically the received wisdom on the dynamics of the state and Islamism. Methodologically, I have also attempted to offer an immanent critique of a purely textualist approach to the study of Islam and politics. In my view, philological approaches to religious texts – the Qur'an and Prophet's sayings – have many limitations. My suggestion, however, is not to discard such approaches altogether, but rather to use them as an ancillary to a more historically grounded anthropological approach. Central to Maududi's political theology – as outlined in his monumental tract *Four fundamental concepts of the Qur'an* – was not just religious text but, more importantly, the wider matrix of the modern colonial state formation and its extraordinary impact on socio-political lives. To understand Maududi's Islamism and his invention of the notion of an Islamic state is to unlock the complex matrix of the modern state formation. My argument is thus also a critique of Mahmood (2005), who depicts pious activism in Egypt taking place in some kind of an Islamic island disengaged from the larger socio-political field which crucially bears on the performance of piety. We need to pause and ask why in the 1970s, for example, there were not many devotees in the mosques of Aligarh Muslim University (India) and why their number dramatically increased in the 1990s? Is this rise in piety disconnected from the rise of virulent Hindu nationalism and the threats it posed to the already precarious position of Indian Muslims (also see Osella & Osella 2008 and Lara Deeb this volume)?

An anthropological genealogy of the notion of an Islamic state as articulated in the South Asian context in the political activism and writing of Maududi opens up further frontiers of research. Did Dutch, French, or British colonialism in other parts of the world also lead to the development of Islamist thought similar to Maududi's? A historical-anthropological line of future research may help us understand not only the genealogies of the Islamic state in the twentieth century or before in the region beyond South Asia but also forms and shades of contemporary Islamism in its diverse settings.

ACKNOWLEDGMENTS

Earlier drafts of this chapter have been presented at the seminar 'Cool Passion: The Political Theology of Conviction', the Department of Anthropology, University of Amsterdam (May 2007) and at the European Conference on Modern South Asian Studies, Manchester (July 2008). I am thankful to Thomas Blom Hansen for the invitation to Amsterdam. I particularly wish to thank Faisal Devji and Gyanendra Pandey for their comments. At the Manchester conference I received valuable feedback from Barbara Metcalf and Margrit Pernau. I am indebted to both, especially to Barbara Metcalf for emailing her thoughtful suggestions to me. Thanks are also due to the anonymous reviewers of the *JRAI* for their highly encouraging comments. I am deeply grateful to Benjamin Soares and Filippo Osella for their many critically engaged remarks and nuanced suggestions, which shaped the final form of this chapter.

NOTES

[1] In different ways, this position informs most writings on Islam, especially Islamic fundamentalism. Representative examples include Bruce (2000); Krishna (1972); Lawrence (1995); Madan (1997); Vatikiotis (1987); von Grunebaum (1953); Watt (1988); Weiner (1987).

[2] Here I am inspired by Koselleck's (2004 [1979]) revealing reading of changing meanings of terms – like *legitimitat*, *bund*, and *stand* – in the German traditions (see also Evans-Pritchard 1965: 7-8). Alam's engagement with Koselleck would have added comparative weight to his elegant argument. I am indebted to Sheldon Pollock for bringing Koselleck's work to my notice. I benefited from my participation in the Master Class with Sheldon Pollock, Michael Cook, Peter Burke, and Benjamin Elman on 'Comparative Intellectual Histories of Early Modern Asia', Leiden (30 May-2 June 2006).

[3] Alam does not clarify what he means by '*akhlaq*'. He uses it to refer to a tradition of dissidence that redefined sharia in a 'philosophical, non-sectarian and humane' way. Its concern was not just ethically good actions but also the issues of 'statecraft, political culture, and philosophy' (2004: 12).

[4] Many European travellers (e.g. France's François Bernier and Portugal's Fari Souza) to Mughal India were somewhat shocked to note such practices of non-discrimination against Hindus in the bureaucracy and deference to their religious lives (see Alam 2000: 237; R. Prasad 1947 [1945]: 39-40).

[5] In Indian historiography, Akbar (r. 1556-1605) is regarded as the epitome of tolerance and secularism and Aurangzeb (r. 1658-1707) as the archetype of Muslim bigotry. (For an unconventional reading of Aurangzeb, see Ali 1997; Brown 2007; O.P. Prasad 1998.)

[6] For a brief analysis of the Mughal state, see Subrahmanyam (1992). The volume edited by Alam and Subrahmanyam (1998) offers a comprehensive treatment of the Mughal state. The main poles in this debate are the 'Aligarh school', with its left-nationalist leanings, and the 'Cambridge school' (see Moosvi 2005; Subrahmanyam 1992).

[7] It is perhaps due to its peripheral role that Kaviraj puts the pre-modern 'states' in quotation marks (1999: 39). While my argument about the nature of the pre-modern state does not take into account the full complexity and evolving character of the Mughal state across time and the culturally heterogeneous regions, such generalizations can be justified. My objective is not so much to go into the elaborate details of the Mughal state but to outline its key features, which differentiated it from the modern colonial state. My description of the colonial state is based on the same objective.

[8] In Urdu, Maududi uses phrases such as *qaumi tashakhkhus*, community/national identity, *milli imtiaz*, community distinctiveness, *Islami zindegi*, Islamic life, and *Islami tahzeeb*, Islamic culture (1937: 20, 1938: 176, 181). *Islami/Muslim qaumiat* is the most recurring phrase in his prose. To Maududi, India comprised many nations, *qaum* (adj, *qaumi*; noun, *qaumiat*; pl. *qaumon* or *qaumen*), Hindus and Muslims being two important nations. Contra the Congress and the Jamiatul Ulema-e-Hind, he believed that neither territory, nor language nor culture defined a nation. In his view, only religion did. Furthermore, he believed that the Congress's claim that India was one nation basically aimed at erasing the distinct identity of Muslims, *Islami qaumiat*. For him, there was no difference between the Indian nationalism of the Congress and the overt Hindu nationalism of parties like the Hindu Mahasabha (Maududi 1962).

[9] A Sanskrit song written by Bankim Chatterjee. While Hindus consider it as an archetype of nationalism, even now Muslims consider it un-Islamic (see I. Ahmad 1999).

[10] Though considered typical Hindu dress, many Muslims wore it in the past. My late maternal grandfather as well as paternal uncles wore the *dhoti* on special occasions.

[11] This as well as the previous and subsequent translation from Urdu into English is mine. I use Maududi's works in original Urdu. Many of his works have been translated into several languages. The volume edited by Khursid Ahmad and Zafar Ishaq Ansari (1979) lists his works in English. Maududi's works in English are also available for purchase at *http://www.mmipublishers.net/english1.html*.

[12] The phrase 'grandmotherly legislation' is Maududi's inserted in English.

[13] Henceforth the page number in the text without a reference is from Maududi's *Four fundamental concepts of the Qur'an* (1979 [1941]).

[14] Maududi used dictatorship in transliterated Urdu.

REFERENCES

AHMAD, I. 1999. Contextualizing *vande matram. Manushi* **111**, 29-30.

———— 2003. Ninety-nine percent individuals of this *qaum* are ignorant of Islam, ninety-five percent are deviant ...': discourse of purity and purity of discourse. Paper presented at the Dutch Anthropological Association Conference, Leiden, November.

———— 2008. Cracks in the 'mightiest fortress': Jamaat-e-Islami's changing discourse on women. *Modern Asian Studies* **42**, 549-75.

———— 2009. *Islamism and democracy in India: the transformation of Jamaat-e-Islami*. Princeton: University Press.

AHMAD, K. & Z.I. ANSARI (eds) 1979. *Islamic perspectives: studies in honor of Sayyid Abul Ala Mawdudui*. Leicester: Islamic Foundation.

ALAM, M. 2000. Sharia and governance in the Indo-Islamic context. In *Beyond Turk and Hindu: rethinking religious identities in Islamicate South Asia* (eds) D. Gilmartin & B. Lawrence, 216-45. Gainesville: University Press of Florida.

———— 2004. *The languages of political Islam in India, c. 1200-1800*. Delhi: Permanent Black.

———— & S. SUBRAHMANYAM (eds) 1998. *The Mughal state, 1526-1750*. Delhi: Oxford University Press.

AL-ASHMAWY, M.S. 1998. *Against Islamic extremism: the writings of Muhammad Said Al-Ashmawy* (ed. C. Fluehr-Lobban). Gainesville: University Press of Florida.

AL-AZMEH, A. 1990. Utopia and Islamic political thought. *History of Political Thought* **11**, 9-19.

ALI, A.M. 1997. *The Mughal nobility under Aurangzeb*. (Revised edition). Delhi: Oxford University Press.

APPADURAI, A. 1996. *Modernity at large: cultural dimension of globalization*. Minneapolis: University of Minnesota Press.

AR-RAZIQ, A.A. 1982. The Caliphate and the bases of power. In *Islam in transition: Muslim perspectives* (eds) J. Donohue & J. Esposito, 29-37. Oxford: University Press.

ASAD, T. 1997. Europe against Islam: Islam in Europe. *The Muslim World* **LXXXVII**, 183-95.

ASHRAF, K.M. 1970. *Life and conditions of the people of Hindustan*. (Second endition). Delhi: Munshiram Manoharlal.

AYUBI, N. 1991. *Political Islam: religion and politics in the Arab world*. London: Routledge.

BAYLY, C.A. 1983. *Rulers, townsmen and bazaars: North Indian society in the age of British expansion, 1770-1870*. Cambridge: University Press.

———— 1988. *Indian society and the making of the British Empire*. Cambridge: University Press.

BLAKE, S. 1979. The patrimonial-bureaucratic empire of the Mughals. *Journal of Asian Studies* **39**, 77-94.

———— 1991. *Shahjahanabad: the sovereign city in Mughal India, 1639-1739*. Cambridge: University Press.

BRASS, P. 1994. *The politics of India since Independence*. (Second edition). Cambridge: University Press.

BROWN, K.B. 2007. Did Aurangzeb ban music? Questions for the historiography of his reign. *Modern Asian Studies* **41**, 77-120.

BRUCE, S. 2000. *Fundamentalism*. Cambridge: Polity.

CHATTERJEE, P. 1993. *Nation and its fragments: colonial and postcolonial histories*. Princeton: University Press.

COHN, B.S. 1996. *Colonialism and its forms of knowledge*. Princeton: University Press.

DESAI, A.R. 1946. *Social background of Indian nationalism*. Bombay: Popular Prakashan.

DIRKS, N. 1987. *The hollow crown: ethnohistory of an Indian kingdom*. Cambridge: University Press.

———— 2001. *Castes of mind: colonialism and the making of modern India*. Princeton: University Press.

DUMONT, L. 1970. *Religion, politics and history in India*. Paris: Mouton.

EATON, R. 2001. Who are the Bengal Muslims? Conversion and Islamization in Bengal. In *Understanding the Bengal Muslims: interpretative essays* (ed.) R. Ahmad, 26-51. Delhi: Oxford University Press.

EICKELMAN, D. & J. PISCATORI 1996. *Muslim politics*. Princeton: University Press.

———— & A. SALVATORE 2002. The public sphere and Muslim identities. *European Journal of Sociology* **43**, 92-115.

EVANS-PRITCHARD, E.E. 1965. *Theories of primitive religion*. Oxford: Clarendon Press.

FOUCAULT, M. 1982. Afterword: the subject and power. In *Michel Foucault: beyond structuralism and hermeneutics* (eds) H. Dreyfus & P. Rabinow, 208-28. Chicago: University Press.

———— 1996. What is critique? In *What is enlightenment?* (ed.) J. Schmidt, 382-98. Berkeley: University of California Press.

FULLER, C. & V. BÉNÉÏ (eds) 2001. *The everyday state and society in modern India*. London: Hurst.

FULLER, C. & J. HARRISS 2001. For an anthropology of the modern Indian state. In *The everyday state and society in modern India* (eds) C.J. Fuller & V. Benei, 1-30. London: Hurst.

GEERTZ, C. 1980. *Negara: the theatre state in nineteenth-century Bali*. Princeton: University Press.

GELLNER, E. 1992. *Postmodernism, reason and religion*. London: Routledge.

GIDDENS, A. 1985. *The nation-state and violence*. Cambridge: Polity.

GILMARTIN, D. & B. LAWRENCE 2000. Introduction. In *Beyond Turk and Hindu: rethinking religious identities in Islamicate South Asia* (eds) D. Gilmartin & B. Lawrence, 1-20. Gainesville: University Press of Florida.

GLEDHILL, J. 2000. *Power and its disguises: anthropological perspectives on politics*. (Second edition). London: Pluto.

GUPTA, A. 1995. Blurred boundaries: the discourse of corruption, the culture of politics and the imagined state. *American Ethnologist* **22**, 375-402.

HALL, J.A. & G.J. IKENBERRY 1997 [1989]. *The state*. Delhi: Worldview.

HANSEN, T.B. 1999. *The saffron wave: democracy and Hindu nationalism in modern India*. Princeton: University Press.

——— 2005. Sovereigns beyond the state: on legality and public authority in India. In *Religion, violence and political mobilization in South Asia* (ed.) R. Kaur, 109-44. Delhi: Sage.

——— & F. STEPPUTAT (eds) 2001. *States of imagination: ethnographic explorations of the postcolonial state*. Durham, N.C.: Duke University Press.

——— & ——— (eds) 2005. *Sovereign bodies: citizens, migrants and states in the postcolonial world*. Princeton: University Press.

HARDY, P. 1972. *The Muslims of British India*. Cambridge: University Press.

HELD, D. 1996. The development of the modern state. In *Modernity: an introduction to modern societies* (eds) S. Hall, D. Held, D. Hubert & K. Thompson, 55-89. Oxford: Blackwell.

HOBSBAWM, E. 1983. Introduction: inventing traditions. In *The invention of tradition* (eds) E. Hobsbawm & T. Ranger, 1-14. Cambridge: University Press.

HUNTER, W.W. 1871. *The Indian Musalmans: are they bound in conscience to rebel against the Queen?* London: Trubner and Company.

HUNTINGTON, S. 1996. *The clash of civilizations and the remaking of world order*. New York: Simon & Schuster.

ISMAEL, T.T. & J.S. ISMAEL 1991 [1985]. *Government and politics in Islam*. Delhi: CBS Publications.

KABIR, H. 1969. *Muslim politics and other essays, 1906-47*. Calcutta: Firma K.L. Mukhopadhya.

KAVIRAJ, S. 1999. The modern state in India. In *Politics and the state in India* (ed.) Z. Hasan, 37-63. Delhi: Oxford University Press.

KHAN, Sir S.A. 1982. Indian and English government. In *Islam in transition: Muslim perspectives* (eds) J. Donohue & J. Esposito, 38-40. Oxford: Oxford University Press.

KHAN, W. 1963. *Tabir ki ghalti* (Folly of interpretation). Delhi: Ar-risala Books. Reprinted in 1995. In Urdu.

KOSELLECK, R. 2004 [1979]. *Futures past: on the semantics of historical time* (trans. K. Tribe). New York: Columbia University Press.

KRISHNA, G. 1972. Piety and politics in Indian Islam. *Contributions to Indian Sociology* (N.S.) **6**, 143-71.

KUGLE, S.A. 2001. Framed, blamed and renamed: the recasting of Islamic jurisprudence in colonial South Asia. *Modern Asian Studies* **35**, 257-313.

LAMBTON, A.K. 1988. Introduction. In *Islam: state and society* (eds) K. Ferdinand & M. Mozaffari, 1-10. London: Curzon.

LAWRENCE, B.B. 1995. *Defenders of god: the fundamentalist revolt against the modern age* (with a new preface by the author). Columbia: University of South Carolina Press.

LEWIS, B. 1996. A historical view: Islam and liberal democracy. *Journal of Democracy* **7**, 52-63.

——— 2002 [1988]. *The political language of Islam*. Karachi: Oxford University Press.

MADAN, T.N. 1997. *Modern myths, locked minds*. Delhi: Oxford University Press.

MAHMOOD, S. 2005. *Politics of piety: the Islamic revival and the feminist subject*. Princeton: University Press.

MAJUMDAR, R.C. 1960. Hindu-Muslim relations. In *The Delhi Sultanate: Bharatiya vidya bhavan's history and culture of the Indian people*, vol. VI (ed.) R.C. Majumdar, 615-636. Bombay: Bharatiya Vidya Bhavan.

MALIK, H. 1963. *Moslem nationalism in India and Pakistan*. Washington, D.C.: Public Affairs Press.

MASUD, M.K. 2001. Social construction of Sharia in Pakistan. Paper presented at Von Humboldt Foundation's workshop on Public Spheres and Muslim Identities, Berlin, July.

MAUDUDI, S.A.A. 1937. *Musalman aur maujudah seyasi kasmakash* (Muslims and the present political predicament), vol. 1. Pathankot: Maktaba Jamaat-e-Islami. All the following references to Maududi are in Urdu unless indicated otherwise.

——— 1938. *Musalman aur maujudah seyasi kasmakash* (Muslims and the present political predicament), vol. 2. Pathankot: Maktaba Jamaat-e-Islami.

———— 1940. Tajdeed-e-ahya-wo deen (Renewal and revival of religion). *Tarjumanul Qur'an* **17**, 265-346.

———— 1942. *Musalman aur maujudah seyasi kasmakash* (Muslims and the present political predicament), vol. 3. Pathankot: Daftar Resala Tarjumanul Quran.

———— 1962. *Masla-e-qamiat* (The issue of nationalism). Delhi: Markazi Maktaba Islami.

———— 1968 [1940]. *Khutbaat* (Sermons). Delhi: Mrkazi Maktaba Islami Publishers. Reprinted 2003.

———— 1979 [1941]. *Qur'an ki chaar bunyadi istelahen* (Four fundamental concepts of the Qur'an). Delhi: Mrkazi Maktaba Islami.

———— 1992 [1919]. *Pundit Madanmohan Malaviya*. Patna: Khuda Bakhsh Oriental Library. In Hindi.

———— 1999 [1939]. *Tafheemaat* (Explanations), vol. 2. Delhi: Mrkazi Maktaba Islami.

———— 2001 [1939]. *Tafheemaat* (Explanations), vol. 1. Delhi: Mrkazi Maktaba Islami.

Messick, B. 1993. *The calligraphic state: textual domination and history in a Muslim society*. Berkeley: University of California Press.

Metcalf, B. & T. Metcalf 2002. *A concise history of India*. Cambridge: University Press.

Metcalf, T. 1995. *Ideologies of the Raj*. Cambridge: University Press.

Moosvi, S. 2005. The pre-colonial state. *Social Scientist* **33**, 40-53.

Nasr, V.R. 1996. *Maududi and the making of Islamic revivalism*. New York: Oxford University Press.

Nehru, J. 1946. *The discovery of India*. New York: John Day.

Nomani, M. 1998. *Maualana Maududi ke saath meri refaqat ki sarguzashta aur ab mera mauqaf* (The story of my friendship with Maulana Maududi and my current stand). Lucknow: Al-furqan Book Depot. In Urdu.

Nomani, S. 1999. *Maqalaat-e-Shibli, mazhabi* (Essays of Shibli, religious), vol. 1. Azamgarh: Darul Mosannefeen. In Urdu.

Osella, F. & C. Osella 2008. Islamism and social reform in Kerala, South India. *Modern Asian Studies* **42**, 317-46.

Pantham, T. 2003. The Indian nation-state: from pre-colonial beginnings to post-colonial reconstructions. In *The Oxford Indian companion to sociology and social anthropology*, vol. 2 (ed.) V. Das, 1413-46. Delhi: Oxford University Press.

Poggi, G. 1978. *The development of the modern state*. Stanford: University Press.

Prasad, O.P. 1998. *Aurangzeb – ek naya zawiaya-e-nazaria* (Aurangzeb – a new perspective). Patna: Khuda Bakhsh Oriental Public Library. In Urdu.

Prasad, R. 1947 [1945]. *Indian divided*. (Third edition). Bombay: Hind Kitabs.

Qureshi, I.H. 1962. *The Muslim community of the Indo-Pakistan subcontinent (610-1947)*. The Hague: Mouton.

Radcliffe-Brown, A.R. 1940. Preface. In *African political systems* (eds) M. Fortes & E.E. Evans-Pritchard, xi-xxii. London: Oxford University Press.

Rashid, Shaikh A. 1979. The Mughal state. In *Tradition and politics in South Asia* (ed.) R.J. Moor, 128-50. New Delhi: Vikas.

Rizvi, S.A.A. 1970. The breakdown of traditional society. In *The Cambridge history of Islam*, vol. 2 a (eds) P. Holt, A.K. Lambton & B. Lewis, 67-96. Cambridge: University Press.

———— 1975. *Religious and intellectual history of the Muslims in Akbar's reign with special reference to Abul Fazal (1556-1605)*. Delhi: Munshiram Manoharlal.

Roy, O. 1994. *The failure of political Islam* (trans. C. Volk). London: I.B. Tauris.

Sampradaikta Virodhi Committee n.d. *Jamat-e-Islami ka haqiqi kirdar* [The real character of Jamaat-e-Islami]. Delhi. In Urdu.

Sharma, A. & A. Gupta (eds) 2006. *An anthropology of the state: a reader*. Malden, Mass.: Blackwell.

Shepard, W.E. 2003. Sayyid Qutb's doctrine of Jahiliat. *International Journal of Middle East Studies* **35**, 521-45.

Smith, D.E. 1963. *India as a secular state*. Princeton: University Press.

Spear, P. 1979. The British and the Indian state to 1830. In *Tradition and politics in South Asia* (ed.) R.J. Moor, 151-71. Delhi: Vikas.

Spencer, J. 1997. Post-colonialism and the political imagination. *Journal of the Royal Anthropological Institute* (N.S.) **3**, 1-19.

———— 2001. Political anthropology. In *International encyclopaedia of the social & behavioral sciences* (ed.) N.J. Smelser, 11628-31. Oxford: Elsevier.

Stein, B. 1980. *Peasant state and society in medieval south India*. Delhi: Oxford University Press.

Subrahmanyam, S. 1992. The Mughal state – structure or process? Reflections on recent Western historiography. *Indian Economic and Social History Review* **29**, 291-321.

Swartz, M., V. Turner & A. Tuden (eds) 1966. *Political anthropology*. Chicago: Aldine.

TILLY, C. (ed.) 1975. *The formation of national states in Western Europe*. Princeton: University Press.

TIRPATHI, R.P. 1998. The Turko-Mongol theory of kingship. In *The Mughal state, 1526-1750* (eds) M. Alam & S. Subrahmanyam, 115-25. Delhi: Oxford University Press.

UBEROI, J.P.S. 1994. The elementary structure of medievalism: religion, civil society and the state. *Contributions to Indian Sociology* (N.S.) **28**, 1-34.

VAN DER VEER, P. 1996. The ruined centre: religion and mass politics in India. *Journal of International Affairs* **50**, 254-77.

———— 2002. Religion in South Asia. *Annual Review of Anthropology* **31**, 173-87.

VATIKIOTIS, V.J. 1987. *Islam and the state*. London and New York: Routledge.

VINCENT, J. 1990. *Anthropology and politics: visions, traditions and trends*. Tucson: University of Arizona Press.

———— 1996. Political anthropology. In *Encyclopaedia of social and cultural anthropology* (eds) A. Barnard & J. Spencer, 428-34. London: Routledge.

VON GRUNEBAUM, G.E. 1953. *Medieval Islam: a study in cultural orientation*. (Second edition). Chicago: University Press.

WATT, M.W. 1988. *Islamic fundamentalism and modernity*. London: Routledge.

WEINER, M. 1987. Political change: Asia, Africa and the Middle East. In *Understanding political development* (eds) M. Weiner & S. Huntington, 33-64. Boston: Little Brown.

10

Talking *jihad* and piety: reformist exertions among Islamist women in Bangladesh

MAIMUNA HUQ *University of South Carolina*

Two themes have been prominent in the proliferating scholarship on contemporary Islamic revival or resurgence since the late 1970s. One is *jihad* (literally 'struggle', 'exertion', or 'striving'), usually discussed in its aspect of violent engagement to establish the hegemony of Islam at the state level (e.g. Kepel 1985; 2002; Roy 1994). The other is a tidy distinction between the political and the religious whereby Islamic efforts to secure political power are characterized as merely 'political'[1] and therefore divorced from the truly 'religious'. On this view, traditions within Islam that do not seek political ascendancy, such as Sufism, liberal Islamic modernism, or orthodox pietism, are more genuinely religious or desirable than Islamic movements with explicit political goals.

Recently, these dominant themes have been complicated in several ways. The emergent scholarship introducing these complications focuses, however, less on localized Islamic movements than on globalized forms of Islamist aggression. For example, Faisal Devji (2005) argues that the attention-grabbing violence of terrorist groups such as Al-Qaeda is grounded in ethical sensibilities similar to those of other global movements such as the environmentalist and peace movements. Yet Devji also continues to subscribe to the conventional view that localized Islamic movements seeking to establish Islamic states belong largely to the realm of 'traditional politics' and so are divorced from religious-ethical concerns.

David Cook (2005) broaches the topic of *jihad* from a religious-studies perspective grounded in meticulous historical research using original Arabic sources. He shows, among other things, that Sufis have participated in armed *jihad* at different periods of Islamic history, both to expand the territory of Islam and to defend its borders from real and perceived threats. While unsettling certain conventionalities, however, he tends to reproduce others. For example, he argues that *jihad* in both historical and contemporary Muslim societies has been mostly violent rather than devotional-spiritual. Dismissing as apologists those scholars and activists who have sought to privilege *jihad*'s spiritual aspect over its militant one, he predicts that as non-Arabic-speaking Muslims gain greater access to original Arabic (and hence, in his view, more authentically

Islamic) textual sources, *jihad* in its violent form is likely to spread from the 'heartland' of Islam – the Arab world – to 'peripheral' Muslim communities. Devji argues nearly the opposite, namely that in the landscape of contemporary global *jihad*, violence is being exported from the 'peripheral' Muslim societies to the Middle East. Both scholars rely primarily on texts and discourses produced by the 'big men' of Islamic radicalism and revivalism: leading members of Al-Qaeda in Devji's case; male Muslim writers and swashbuckling religio-political activists from classical Islam to the present in Cook's.

Islamic activism in South Asia
Here I examine the activism of a non-stereotypical group of 'warriors of Allah', the Bangladesh Islami Chatri Sangstha (BICSa; Women Students' Islamic Association of Bangladesh). BICSa is the female student wing in Bangladesh of the Islamic political party Jamaat-e-Islami, a leading Islamic socio-political movement in South Asia and the dominant Islamic political party in Bangladesh. (BICSa's association with Jamaat-e-Islami is unofficial but integral.) Although BICSa's activities are rarely reported in the mainstream Islamic media in Bangladesh, much less the locally dominant liberal-secular-nationalist media or the international media, they are important for at least three reasons.

First, examining these activities allows us to shift our focus on *jihad* slightly from the global to the local, the operational site of most contemporary Islamic movements, extremist and otherwise. Drawing on ethnographic field research conducted in Bangladesh between 1999 and 2003, I here seek to contribute to the de-essentialization of *jihad* and Islamic activism and to destabilize essentializing tendencies in the scholarship on Islam and Muslims in general.

Second, there is a dearth of scholarship on Islamic groups in contemporary South Asia, especially as regards various understandings and practices of *jihad*.[2] Although most Muslims live in South and Southeast Asia, these regions are still understood as 'peripheral' to the Muslim world by many otherwise well-informed scholars (e.g. Cook 2005).

Third, the gap in scholarship on women in Islamic movements in South Asia in general and on women's regional views and practices of *jihad* in particular is even more striking.[3]

Women in Islamic activism
A growing body of work on women in Islamic movements provides an increasingly rich picture of the public-sphere activities of Islamic activist women (e.g. Arat 2005; Deeb 2006; Hale 1996; White 2002). Emphasis on women's public projects, however, has encouraged a prevalent idea of women's Islamic activism as an expression of identity politics. Women and men in Islamic movements are understood as *performing* religious forms and symbols as instrumental means to essentially material, secular, and political ends.

An alternative, emerging trend in scholarship on women in Islamic movements – e.g. Barbara Metcalf on the history of South Asia (1998), Saba Mahmood on the anthropology of Egypt (2005), and Lara Deeb on the anthropology of Lebanon (2006) – has focused on women's efforts to *embody* Islam through the cultivation of pious selves. Some of these scholars (notably Metcalf and Mahmood) touch upon the texts widely read in the Islamic movements they describe. This attention to textual encounter has been notably absent in most scholarship on women in Islamic movements. Yet little has yet been said, even by Metcalf and Mahmood, about the *micro-mechanics* of the processes whereby these devoutly committed women, who mostly hail from non-religious educational backgrounds, come to acquire textual-scriptural knowledge and are persuaded by the texts they read. Among other questions, we wish to know what textual and theological questions, if any, participants and recruits in these movements pose.

Moreover, devotion, self-reform, and piety, perceived by many religio-political women activists as their central concerns, are largely either ignored by scholars (including Metcalf and Mahmood) or defined as essentially an Islamic disguise for secular concerns. These explicitly religious preoccupations are treated as religiously inauthentic, smacking of self-alienation at best and political expediency at worst. In effect, conventional scholarly discourse implies that the analyst alone can accurately locate the activist's genuine motivations.

Women and *jihad*

Much emerging scholarship on women who explicitly consider themselves as enacting *jihad* has centred on the Middle East, where some women have been and in certain contexts still are engaged in militant resistance to colonizing or occupying non-Muslim forces. For example, many women participated actively in the Algerian war of liberation from the French, some fighting as armed combatants (Bouatta 1994; Cherifate-Merabtine 1994). Women affiliated with the Muslim Brotherhood of Egypt, notably Zainab al-Ghazali, viewed themselves as conducting *jihad* against the regime of Gamal Nasser, which Islamists considered oppressive (Hoffman 1985). Some Palestinian women's participation in suicide bombing has been understood as *jihad* both by the bombers themselves and by other Islamists. The Palestinian context is one of the few to date where women's *jihad* has received major attention, whether from scholars (e.g. Mishal & Sela 2006 [2000]) or from journalists. According to Palestinian Islamic Resistance (a chapter of Hamas), every man and woman is obliged to conduct *jihad*, and the requirement for spousal consent is suspended wherever Muslim territory has been invaded. Hamas expands *jihad* to include all activities that aid the Islamist cause, including publication (Allen 2005).[4]

In the Lebanese context, women engage in *jihad* in four distinct ways: (1) in association with the anti-Israeli Islamic resistance led by the Lebanese Shi'i political party Hizbullah; (2) by disciplining the 'baser desires of the self' (a standard phrase in this context); (3) by participation in community service targeting socio-economic ills such as poverty; and (4) through 'gender *jihad*', efforts directed at establishing equity between men and women (Deeb 2006). Deeb's work on the Shi'i community in Lebanon is unique in its substantive exploration of women's discourses and practices of *jihad* in the modern and post-colonial era. This kind of scholarship has yet to be undertaken in the context of Sunni Muslims, the dominant sect in Islam, or in other Middle Eastern settings and beyond. Yet even in Deeb's work[5] we do not hear of the minutiae of those processes whereby women come to acquire their understanding of *jihad*. Such minutiae are not incidental to understanding the large, complex phenomena often lumped as 'Islamization' and 'political Islam', but are the essential mechanism by which Islamist ideology is transmitted to particular people – albeit not always smoothly.

This chapter seeks to fill this gap concerning the acquirement of *jihad*-related knowledge among its practitioners and in the scholarship on women's *jihad* in South

Asia. More generally, it seeks to begin to understand Islamization in its complexity, particularity, and dynamism and to draw attention to the views and practices of important Islamist groups engaged primarily in non-violent *jihad*. This departs from the prevalent focus on violent *jihad* in the contexts of Palestinian resistance to Israeli occupation, Iraqi and Afghani resistance to US occupation, and global extremist projects like Al-Qaeda.

Ideas and practices of *jihad* – mostly non-violent – centrally define highly organized religio-socio-political movements such as the Jamaat-e-Islami (Jamaat) in South Asia[6] for their participants. Yet little information is available about the Jamaat's engagement with *jihad*. Moreover, among the few works that have treated the Jamaat exhaustively (e.g. Nasr 1994; 1996), none describes the texts read and study circles so assiduously conducted in this movement, its women participants,[7] or the discourses and practices of *jihad* among these women.

Working primarily with young, urbanized, well-educated women in high school and university, BICSa produces the core cadre of activist Jamaat women. Reading sessions (study circles) are central to BICSa socialization and training. By focusing on these sessions, we can discern how ideas of *jihad* and piety, as articulated from particular Qur'anic verses and propounded in the writings of the 'big men' of contemporary Islamic resurgence (especially Abul Ala Maududi, who founded Jamaat-e-Islami in colonial India), are discussed and practised on the ground among young, educated women adherents of Jamaat.

Islamic reading sessions

Religious reading circles are proliferating throughout Muslim-majority societies and in Muslim communities elsewhere. These circles conduct informal religious study of the Qur'an, *hadith* (see note 5), and literature by medieval Islamic theologians (e.g. Abu Hamid al-Ghazali, 1058-1111) and iconic figures in the contemporary Islamic revival (e.g. Hasan al-Banna, 1906-49; Sayyid Qutb, 1903-66; Abul Ala Maududi, 1903-79; Muhammad Zakariyya Kandhalawi, 1898-1982). With a few exceptions (see, e.g., Limbert 2005; Mahmood 2005), this practice has drawn only passing attention from scholars of Islamic phenomena.[8]

Many contemporary Islamic movements claim to return to the primary sources of Islam, namely the Qur'an and the life of the Prophet Muhammad. Thus, in Jamaat, certain verses of the Qur'an are assigned by organizational syllabi for study by both male and female activists. These verses are also intensively discussed and explained among BICSa activists in study circles. Examining these practices reveals in outline the culturally specific contours of the life-world of Islamic study circles in contemporary Bangladesh. Transposing Charles Hirschkind's cogent argument for the simultaneously disciplinary and deliberative nature of the orthodox Islamic counter-public sphere in contemporary Egypt (2001) to the realm of the Islamic revivalist movement in Bangladesh, I identify the Islamist reading circle as a primary site for the production of a specific kind of Islamic subjectivity, one inclined to submit to prescriptions understood as religiously binding even while questioning some precepts central to movement ideology.

BICSa, violence, and *jihad*

Women's Islamic activism in Bangladesh can be understood partly as a response to the perception that local and global life-worlds are increasingly wracked by violence, injustice, and oppression. Bangladeshi Islamists believe that the liberal state's failure to deliver on its promises of socio-economic security for all is evidenced by increasing violence, corruption, and class disparities. The Islamist movement therefore deploys a scripturally referenced emphasis on 'social justice' in calling for the establishment of a 'pristine' Islamic polity through *jihad* (primarily non-violent). BICSa, for example, offers a systematic path to 'peace and success both in this world and in the hereafter' (a phrase often repeated in its official discourse), a path offered as a refreshing contrast to the overwhelming threats that inundate Bangladeshi women today through print media, street violence, and satellite TV images. A small but growing number of educated women are persuaded by this Islamist vision of a salvific, pristine polity to be achieved through the cultivation of pious, pristine selves. BICSa harnesses their anxieties by interweaving religious texts with narratives pertaining to local and global current events and issues in its study programmes. It uses global and local forms of violence to constitute a landscape of suffering, insecurity, and disorder in the nation and the world at large, with orthodox Islam explicitly construed as the only hope for cure.

This combined appeal to visceral insecurity and pious desire to ground oneself in orthodox Islam is manifest in key BICSa discourses and practices. Veiling and other forms of pious modesty, for example, are construed as not only religiously correct but also personally protective in a context where Bangladeshi women from the middle and especially the lower-middle classes (including most BICSa activists) are more vulnerable to violence than are elite women. Secular women's groups and the daily newspapers increasingly provide a platform for addressing the more overt forms of physical violence against women (Hashmi 2000; Monsoor 1999), but various 'covert' forms of sexual harassment and 'the violences of everyday life' (Kleinman 2000; Scheper-Hughes 1992) to which average Bangladeshi women are subjected are virtually ignored in such venues. BICSa steps into this gap, hitching practical concerns about everyday violence and its attendant anxieties to religious concerns about bodily modesty and mental peace. It proposes a prevention-orientated approach to safety that is based on self-protection (secluding oneself through veiling from the predictably objectifying, potentially harmful male gaze), moral reform of society (including men), and reaffirmation of women's contributions as sisters, wives, mothers, and homemakers to nation-building and the construction of the global Muslim *umma* (community of Muslims). BICSa's project of social-ethical change is best summarized in its trope 'security of life, property, and dignity'. It is this particular project of reforming the quality of daily life in present-day Bangladesh within an Islamic framework and living with the sacrifices that undertaking such a reformist project might entail that undergirds BICSa's notion and practice of *jihad* as essentially opposed to all forms of violence, including violence in the very structures of one's articulations, thoughts, emotions, desires, and imaginings. It is this BICSa paradigm for *jihad* that will be explored in the remainder of this chapter.

A BICSa study circle in Dhaka, March 2003
Explicit discussion of jihad
At this particular reading session, attended by eight members including the chairwoman (a higher-level BICSa member), a participant named Tanya[9] was asked by the chairwoman and moderator, Nabila, to launch the discussion by commenting on the pre-assigned Qu'ranic verses (sura as-Saff), which deal with the issue of *jihad*.

Following traditional Islamic scholars, Tanya suggested that there are two kinds of *jihad*, namely *jihad akbar* (the greater struggle) and *jihad asghar* (the lesser struggle). The greater *jihad* is that against one's *nafs* (baser self, animalistic instinct), which, being subject to the *waswasa* (whisperings) or influence of Satan, constantly tries to divert one from righteousness. Tanya tied this distinction to another which she made, between mere 'believers' and 'true believers'. *Nafs*, she suggests, thwarts a believer's efforts to become a *true* believer. A believer's constant struggle to overcome her *nafs* is therefore her most important battle, and socio-political struggle is *internal* to this larger struggle against desires of the self: that is, a pure self is more easily achieved in a pure society. Socio-political struggle is therefore lesser struggle, *jihad asghar*. In particular, Tanya defined lesser *jihad* as struggle waged in the cause of Allah through the commitment of one's life and property, and argued that time, career, intellect, and creative talent are at least as important for the success of the contemporary Islamic movement as the sacrifice of wealth, even life itself.

Living or dying for jihad?

In reflecting on Tanya's comments, one of her fellow participants, Bilkis, questioned the comparability of the sacrifice of life with that of time, energy, or wealth. A fellow participant, Nur Jahan, responded as follows:

> One can die in combat at a whim, or for glory, or personal vengeance. Anti-Islamic forces such as the boys of Chatra Dal kill and die for their cause as well.[10] In Islam, however, to be rewarded by Allah as a martyr, one's intention must be pure and exclusively to defend Islam for the pleasure of Allah alone. We know the *hadith* that in the course of a battle, Ali [the Prophet's son in-law and the fourth caliph] was about to kill an enemy solider. At that moment, the soldier spat on Ali, who then released his adversary. At the soldier's puzzlement, Ali explained that if he were to kill his foe at that moment, he could not be certain that part of [his] motivation was not personal anger, since the soldier had spat on him. Thus Ali could not bring himself to kill an enemy because he could not be certain that his only intention at the moment of killing was to defend Faith. It is virtually impossible to muster this kind of purity of intention today. Also, it is a sin to realize an Islamic practice such as martyrdom but for the most just of causes. Therefore, it seems to me that conducting *jihad* in other ways that entail living rather than dying is much more fruitful today.

Another participant, Najma, commented:

> I think there is another reason why living rather than dying entails greater commitment to Allah's cause today. When one dies, everything ends. One must no longer deal with the troubles of life. One may *think* that sacrificing one's life for the sake of Allah is the most difficult thing to do, since life seems to be the most precious thing we have. But I feel that spending one's wealth for Islam, for example, requires greater love for Allah since one must *live* with the consequences of that, one may have to face a lifetime of economic hardship ... Thus these kinds of sacrifice involve greater hardship for the cause of Islam. Dying takes but a moment. There are no consequences to suffer.

Rikta added that given the dearth of Islamic workers (in Bangladesh) today, the Islamic movement needs live workers much more than dead ones. In her view (and in that of many other activists I spoke with), it is not on the conventional battlefield that Muslims face today the most serious of attacks, but in the spheres of culture, the arts, and media indoctrination and in the temptations of upward socio-economic mobility. 'The Prophet Muhammad said that the pen is mightier than the sword, and this is more true than ever before today', she reminded her audience. Nowadays, she said, activists can serve Islam best through study of a wide range of books, writing articles and books, and through preaching among family, friends, fellow students, and neighbours.

Discourse on violent jihad

BICSa's policy of nonviolent *jihad* does not go unquestioned among junior activists, however. One participant asked: 'If Islam can be served best through writing and speaking, then why did the Prophet Muhammad engage in so many battles? Why did even some among female companions (*mahila sahabi*) accompany him to the battle-field? Why did they not simply continue to preach?'

Nabila, the chairwoman, responded that to her knowledge the Prophet fought only where the Muslim community was under physical attack and, later, whenever ruling elites would not allow the Prophet to preach the message of Islam peacefully. This, she explained, was not the situation facing BICSa – yet. 'Violence is a last resort, when one's very survival is in question, and that moment has not arrived', said Nabila. Despite being banned from certain key campuses such as Dhaka University,[11] she argued, there was still much scope for BICSa activists to propagate the Islamic message peacefully. The media offer the most effective means today for propagating the call for an Islamic revolution. These means for getting past oppressive rulers and gaining access to publics were not available in the time of the Prophet. 'But do we not emulate the Prophet?' asked a participant. Nabila responded that to propagate the divine message of libera-tion, practical strategies for propagation must change with context.

Rikta responded that it is humiliating to have to flee from the dormitory when faced with the possibility of violence from rival activists (e.g. in the aftermath of violent conflicts between BICSa's male counterpart group Chatra Shibir and the student wings of the ethno-secularist Awami League and the conservative-liberalist Bangladesh Nationalist Party).[12] Sometimes it is important to stand and fight so that one's oppo-nents do not consider one weak and try to terrorize one into silence. 'They consider us timid, in our veils', she fumed. Not only does this dishearten activists, she argued, but unopposed secularist shows of strength discourage women who might otherwise join BICSa.

Despite Rikta's dissent, many BICSa activists are content with BICSa's normative avoidance of violence. Furthermore, neither BICSa authorities nor the parent organi-zation Jamaat have thus far relaxed the policy of strictly non-violent *jihad* for women, which bans even verbal violence. Why?

Importantly, BICSa's non-violence helps it attract members. In Bangladesh, politics is often violent, and many families oppose participation in politics by young sons and daughters (especially the latter). BICSa's meticulous avoidance of violent encounters with secular and liberal-nationalist groups helps activists garner and retain familial support.

But how does BICSa distance itself ideologically from violence, given its own emphasis on *jihaad fii sabiilillah* (struggle in the way of God) and, for that matter, the Prophet Muhammad's own willingness to wage literal war in the latter part of his life, following his migration to the town of Madina from his hometown Makka?

As partly seen in Nabila's responses to questions, BICSa does this in a number of ways. First, it effectively recasts South Asian Islamist Abul Ala Maududi's vision of socio-political *jihad*, which emphasizes Islamization of Muslim polities equally for hegemonic and self-defence purposes, as a vision justified primarily by self-defence against and socio-political resistance to 'un-Islamic socio-cultural influences and anti-Islamic political and economic domination'.[13] In this context, self-defence means cultural, political, and economic self-defence.

Second, it shifts the popular understanding of *jihad* as violent resistance to liberal-secularist, Indian (Hindu), and Western domination to an understanding of *jihad* as the investment of one's time, effort, money, influence, credentials, skills, and creative and performative abilities, a form of *jihad* that I call civic persuasion. The object of civic persuasion is the Islamization of the polity simultaneously from above (through moral-ethical reform among the social and political leadership and Islamization of the state) and from below (through the Islamic socialization and politicization of ordinary citizens).

Third, having constituted themselves in opposition to the multiple forms of violence that afflict Bangladeshi women, BICSa activists are reluctant to reproduce other forms of violence. They therefore tend to privilege notions of peace, patience, and reasoning in both ideology and praxis.

Finally, the painstaking cultivation of feminine Islamic virtues by BICSa, including 'shyness' (*lajja*) and 'modesty' (*shalinata*), 'humility' (*binay*), and the related, urban attributes of 'politeness' (*bhadrata*), 'decency' (*shalinata*), and 'civility' (*shabyata*) in deportment and interpersonal relations disinclines BICSa women to any kind of violence. This holds for public situations where 'talking back' to verbally aggressive rivals and sometimes even physically repulsing aggressors instead of seeking refuge in BICSa offices might boost group morale. Withdrawal and non-confrontation accord better with *lajja* and *bhadrata* than does brawling in the street or on campus.

On the other hand, BICSa staunchly defends and glorifies the violent engagement of its male organizational counterpart, Chatra Shibir, on the ground that its members have no choice: they operate openly as a political party, and political culture in Bang-ladesh is such that one is disempowered, even annihilated, if one refuses to fight back. Violence, BICSa argues, cannot be altogether renounced in an essentially violent world, but must be used judiciously and authorized by 'authentic Muslim leaders'. Indeed, the violent encounters of Shibir men empower BICSa members with a rousing repertoire of tales of sacrifice and martyrdom, which provides them with a moral vocabulary of justification for mobilizing against and dislodging from power those perceived as oppressors. In these circulating tales of Islamist men's sacrifice of life or limb, anti-Islamists are always understood to instigate the violence.

Some scholars have characterized the violence practised by Islamist men in South Asia as essential to political Islam (Ahmed 1993). In showing that Islamist women affiliated with these same male Islamist groups and studying virtually the same texts on *jihad* as their male counterparts studiously avoid violent behaviour, my fieldwork points to the need for cultural contextualization of violence in the name of religious ideology. BICSa women are just as Islamist as Chatra Shibir men. Nor is it clear that Qur'anic verses mobilizing violence are addressed specifically to men. Nevertheless, BICSa women are strictly non-violent in practice.[14] There is, in effect, a culturally specific, gendered division of pious labour, with women specializing in virtues such as 'shyness' and men taking on what is seen as the heroic, necessary work of defensive violence.

In BICSa, the possibility of violence is both articulated and contained within its piously gendered bounds by encouraging patience with, compassion towards, and prayers for the divine guidance of misguided adversaries. Such encouragement is integral to these sites of communication, even though seemingly contradictory sensibilities of violence (e.g. anecdotes of martyrdom of Shibir men in street fighting) simultaneously infuse Qur'anic lessons and book discussions. BICSa urges activists to exercise patience and 'sincerity' (*antarikata*) in their relationships with all persons, including or especially adversaries, since the organization's primary strategy is to persuade others to see the 'irresistible beauty of Islam' through the religion's embodiment in the character of individual activists.

Many BICSa activists therefore form friendships with women who are supportive of secularist-nationalist or liberalist-nationalist political groups, however tenuous some of these friendships prove to be in the long run and however un-strategically and spontaneously they may unfold. A side-benefit of these friendships is the possibility of protection from violence from the more aggressive men or women in these dominant groups. Such friendships are not simply manipulative or instrumental: some friendships persist not because there is much possibility for recruitment but because of mutual respect and fondness, which may persist despite tension over ideological differences. Often a BICSa activist not only influences her liberal-secular friend's view of Islamism but is also shaped by the latter's views. Indeed, BICSa leaders sometimes express concern about this tendency.

BICSa discussions of patience, civility, and friendship or at least 'cordial relationship' with potential foes therefore become 'a labour of peace' in the sense elaborated by Laura Ring (2006) in her work on women and sectarian violence in Karachi. Ring suggests that women's routine neighbourly exchange practices of borrowing and visiting are a form of peacemaking that is grounded in an 'ethic of suspense', whereby socio-cultural tension is painstakingly suspended or *sustained* rather than *resolved*. Rather than seeing daily co-existence 'as the static context or backdrop against which "things" (like riots, violence, or "breakdown") happen' (2006: 4), she conceives it as a positive, indeed remarkable, achievement.

While *jihad* is one of the most widely discussed topics in BICSa's training programmes – an emphasis that helps distinguish Islamist groups such as Jamaat-e-Islami from piety movements such as the transnational Tablighi Jama'at – it is also an area in the BICSa discursive regime that is characterized by internecine tensions and ambivalences. We have glimpsed these in play already, in the fragment of study-circle discourse described above; other aspects are discussed below.

The 'balanced life' of the 'middle road'

BICSa's call to commit time, physical-mental labour, and skills to its Islamic movement and thus to the *jihad* of persuading others to the Islamist cause encounters reluctance and doubt from many activists, especially recent recruits and younger members. For example, the study-circle participant Bilkis asked in the course of discussion of sura as-Saff from the Qur'an:

> We know that *jihad* must be conducted in an organized manner to be effective. But in many cases, committing time and energy to organizational work results in poor grades. This makes many parents even more hostile to BICSa, and this then impairs our ability to garner support from our family members for the Islamic movement, thus hindering *jihad*. Also, when we oppose our parents, this becomes sinful since Islam tells us to obey our parents. Furthermore, as poor students, it is difficult for us to attract other students to our cause, let alone our teachers. I think we end up spending too much time on bureaucratic work necessary to sustain this type of an organization. Organizing events, attending meetings, and filling out forms, for example, are time-consuming. I think groups like

Tablighi Jama'at, which are not as organized as we are, are therefore more able to spend more time than we are on worship and thus on conducting the *jihad* of self-purification. Thus they become more God-fearing Muslims. This quality, in turn, shines through to others when these Tablighi women talk to others about Islam, and they are then able to attract more followers than we.

In Bangladesh, as a result of the opportunities opened up by the spread of mass higher education, the efforts of feminist or woman-centric groups, state discourses of modern nation-building, and growing difficulties in attaining a middle-class lifestyle, educated women have begun to enter the white-collar job market in increasing numbers, especially in the education, health, and NGO sectors. Thus, despite Islamist ideology's formal insistence that the home is the most 'natural' place for a woman, most Islamist women are aiming for a college education and more are entering such fields as teaching and medicine every day. In general, top BICSa leaders have both Bachelor's and Master's degrees. Thus, while Islamists have conventionally had to persuade women to rescue time for organizational work from household responsibilities, BICSa now must increasingly compete with women's desires for good grades and good jobs as well. This competition is reflected in BICSa's growing emphasis on the need for using one's talents and for sacrificing time from schoolwork and jobs ('worldly preoccupa- tions') – even sacrificing a career altogether – as being at least as central to *jihad* as martyrdom itself. Nabila, the chairwoman of the particular group described here, suggested several things in response to Bilkis's criticism of the highly organized *jihad* that BICSa considers essential for bringing about a successful 'Islamic revolution'. First, she disagreed with the conventionally assumed separation between the two types of *jihad*, one against the self and one against 'un-Islamic' and 'anti-Islamic' socio-political norms. The Islamic work of the pietist organization Tablighi Jama'at – focused, in Bangladesh at least, on self-purification through ritual worship and on preaching among others to do the same – she characterized as as an 'incomplete' form of Islam. In the view of groups such as Jamaat-e-Islami, Tablighi's reluctance to challenge those in positions of social and political power and willingness to court these elites result in the downright neglect of *jihad*. Furthermore, senior BICSa activists, following Jamaat, contend that Tablighi's inclination to separate religion from politics, and its emphasis on individual moral reform alone impede the efforts of groups such as Jamaat that practise *jihad* in struggling for comprehensive reforms.

According to Nabila (and BICSa officialdom), self-purification cannot ultimately be realized exclusively in private. Both private and public *jihad* must be conducted simul- taneously and are mutually constitutive: pure selves thrive in pure societies. Nabila suggested that the perceived conflict between the two types of *jihad* can be resolved by living a life of 'balance' where one is so disciplined in one's use of time that neither schoolwork nor organizational work nor household work suffers. In order to partici- pate successfully in the Islamic movement, an activist must garner the support of family members, fellow students, teachers, and neighbours. One must be an 'all-rounder', for Islam represents 'the middle path'. According to Nabila, 'There is no scope for excessiveness (*barabari*) in Islam'. She cited the Prophet Muhammad as stating that 'extremism destroys religion' and followed this up with another tradition:

Once a companion of the Prophet declared that he would fast every day in his devotion to Allah. The Prophet said that not even he fasts every day or prays all the time, but that he does other things as well, that one should have a family, earn a livelihood, care for their parents in old age, serve their community, etc.

In her conclusion, Nabila sought to motivate other activists by referring to liberal-secular Muslims:

> If a non-religious Muslim can attend school and learn to sing, dance, and act all at once for success in this temporary life, then as true Muslims committed to securing happiness in the permanent life of the Hereafter, we should be able to work much harder and work simultaneously on many fronts.

Virtues integral to the success of jihad

On BICSa's view, for *jihad* to be waged successfully and in an authentic Islamic manner it must be conducted in a highly specific spirit. This essential spirit was described in the discussion by one of the participants, Rikta, of the fourth verse of sura as-Saff, which proclaims 'divine love for those who fight in His path in rows as though they were a wall forged out of steel'. Following a style of presentation and analysis not only common in Qur'anic lessons and study circles but also typical of argumentation, lecturing, and note-taking in Bangladeshi classrooms, Rikta followed a strictly point-by-point exposition. She interpreted the verse on three interrelated levels, closely following the contours of Maududi's exegetical style in his exegetical work *Tafheem-ul Qur'an*: zero in on certain segments and words of the verse, then unfold and amplify these materials.

Firstly, she clarified what it means to 'fight in Allah's path' – more precisely, what kind of commitment to God's cause is endearing to Him. Rikta stated 'that only those believers able to assume any kind of risk and to make any kind of sacrifice necessary, be it in terms of wealth, life, time and/or skill, in struggling for Allah are able to earn His satisfaction'.

At the second level of interpretation, she focused on the latter half of the verse: 'fight in ... rows, as though they were a wall forged out of steel'. Rikta enumerated the three virtues that BICSa, Jamaat, and Chatra Shibir consider essential for a warrior of Allah to possess based on the teachings of Maududi: (1) they must fight in Allah's path with a 'profound awareness' (*gabhir chetana*) or thoughtfully and not 'whimsically' (*hujuger boshe*) or in a sudden fit of emotion; (2) they must not indulge in 'organizational disobedience' (*sangatanik birudhdhata*) but should struggle in a 'well-organized' (*sus-angbadhdha*) and 'disciplined manner' (*niyomanugatyata sahakare*); and (3) they must be unyielding and unwavering, 'like a wall forged out of steel'.

Rikta began her third level of interpretation through an elaboration of what 'fighting in His path in rows as though they were a wall forged out of steel' specifically entails. 'Advanced moral character' and a 'sincere commitment to goals' are among the several virtues that one must possess to be able to stand in such a manner. Commitment, she observed, inspires every warrior in any army to sacrifice his or her life. In other words, every soldier is rendered capable of standing before the enemy like an impenetrable wall, regardless of the enemy's superiority in numbers or weapons. She illustrated this final virtue and concluded her discussion by harkening back to the time of Prophet Muhammad, perceived as exemplary, then shifting forward in time to critique the current Islamist movement in Bangladesh and to issue a call to action. The Prophet's army was made up of Muslims who possessed all the virtues discussed:

> Consequently, we know from various *hadith* that no sooner did the Prophet utter a command than his companions carried it out without any hesitation. The Qur'an says that a true believer says: 'We hear and obey'. Then why are we unable to rise above our petty differences (*sankirnata*) today? The reason is we are weak in faith. The level of our moral character (*naitiak charitrer man*) is far lower than required. We must therefore strive for greater vigilance against these shortcomings by focusing on cultivating an intimate relationship with Allah.

The virtue of patience

One of the most important ways in which an Islamic worker can cultivate her relationship with Allah and thereby engage in *jihad akbar* or self-purification, suggested the group moderator Nabila, is through practising the virtue of '*sabar*' (Arabic *sabr*) or patience, a disposition greatly valued in the orthodox Islamic tradition. This emphasis illustrates the primacy for BICSa of building of 'advanced moral character', which undercuts the charge – made by secularist groups, the orthodox '*ulama* (traditional religious experts), and Tablighi – that Islamist groups 'use religion for political purposes'.

For BICSa members, BICSa's authority and legitimacy as an Islamic organization does not derive primarily from its political sophistication: Islamism as a political ideology has been historically suspect and controversial in Bangladesh, and some activists continue to raise questions about Islamist opposition to the independence war of 1971, in which secular nationalists enabled 'East Pakistan' to become the independent nation of Bangladesh. In BICSa's understanding, this organization's authority is grounded in its emphasis on the Islamic ethical virtues (*Islamic noitik gunaboli*) and its success hinges on organizational leadership by especially pious BICSa activists. As study-circle chairwomen and moderators often emphasize, particularly in the view of BICSa's strict policy of non-violent *jihad* for women, 'We must be so exemplary as persons that even our adversaries will be forced to wonder that while there are good people around us, why are these women so exceptionally good?'[15] Therefore, in BICSa ideology, the most effective means of waging *jihad akbar* is through upholding oneself in daily life as an exemplary Muslim to all. In BICSa's moral landscape, *jihad akbar* ultimately involves rendering Islam victorious over other ideologies through simultaneous engagement on myriad interconnected levels – personal, social, and political.

To this end, BICSa study circles pay particular attention to the virtue of patience, as, for example, by Nabila on this occasion. Patience enables *taqwa* (an inclination to fear God), strengthens relationships between activists, and enhances a member's capacity to recruit others.

In following up on Rikta's comments on *jihad*, group moderator Nabila referred to the booklet by Maududi on the criteria for Islamist success that Rikta had mentioned. She described the five qualities mentioned in this book, namely the cultivation of a sincere relationship with God, anxiety concerning the Day of Judgment, sweetness of character, patience, and wisdom. Through traditional Islamic virtues such as patience, on which Nabila dwelt the most, a link is constantly sustained between the lesser *jihad* of public activism and the most fundamental criterion for Muslimhood – belief or faith (*iman*), to which the greater *jihad* of self-purification is integral. As Nabila explained,

Some people use coercion to persuade others, but the effects of fear are short-lived. Islam commends patience as crucial for *dawati kaj* (preaching, inviting others to the path of Islam), for convincing people, our key means for *jihad*, for establishing Islam. Hence patience is even more crucial for an Islamic worker than for an ordinary believer. Thus an Islamic worker feels more compelled to acquire Islamic virtues than an ordinary Muslim and thereby to strengthen her faith. The Islamic movement propels her into public view as a role model, and public scrutiny motivates her to perfect herself as a representative of authentic Muslimhood. In order to preach, she must strive to realize every virtue of a true believer. Our acutely flawed realization of even the most fundamental virtues such as patience is reflected in our inability to attract members. No matter how poorly others treat us for our belief, we must persevere in showing them kindness and winning them over to Islam through our personal attributes and logical argumentation.

Nabila's comment drew from earlier words by Rikta, who had expressed anger at the alleged repeated vandalism perpetrated by fellow secularist students against the posters she put up on campus announcing Islamic events: 'How can patience in the face of this kind of persistent behaviour solve anything?'

In support of the importance of the virtue of patience for conducting *jihad*, Rikta cited a *hadith* that reads,

> In the course of preaching, the Prophet Muhammad was being persecuted by the people of a region named Taif near Makka. Suddenly the angel Gibreel appeared and asked the prophet whether he would crush the populace of Taif between its two mountains given the way they were assaulting him. The Prophet replied that were Gibreel to kill these people, to whom would he convey his message?

Jaheliyat: *a society of ignorance*

Najma pointed out that while the Prophet Muhammad clearly waged the lesser *jihad*, some argue that this type of *jihad* is no longer important, since Bangladesh is already a society where the majority of the people are Muslims. The current need for *jihad akbar* should therefore be clarified, she said, in order both to persuade potential recruits and to make things clearer in her own mind.

Najma was calling attention to an aspect of the BICSa ideology that requires regular maintenance. Many Islamic scholars agree that the lesser *jihad* is obligatory for every Muslim in a setting dominated by non-Muslims and where Muslims are not allowed to practise the essentials of their faith. However, *jihad* is often considered obligatory for only some Muslims in an Islamic society, since sustenance of an Islamic environment does not require as much striving as the supplanting of an un-Islamic way of life with an Islamic one. In such a case, the requirements of *jihad akbar* are fulfilled by the state and groups of Muslims assigned with the task of sustaining and nurturing Islam in the public sphere.

BICSa's call for *jihad* in contemporary Bangladesh must therefore be rooted in an understanding of contemporary Bangladeshi society as essentially un-Islamic, Muslim 'only in name', not in practice. Its configuration of contemporary Bangladeshi society as equivalent to the pre-Islamic era of *ayyame jaheliyat* (the Days of Ignorance or Dark Ages), therefore equally in need of prophetic *jihad*, is crucial for legitimizing the kind of holistic Islamic reform that BICSa envisages.

This theme's appearance in the study-circle discussion described here and in many other training programmes that I attended is an example of how central BICSa para-digms are repeatedly worked into the fabric of meetings through graphic narratives, references to daily events (e.g. crime, poverty, corruption, and violence), and the articulation and confirmation of views that study-circle participants, often being of the advanced cadre level, tend to be familiar with already. Against the prevalent liberal-secular view of faith as a private matter and opposition to religious activism in the political/public sphere, BICSa asserts that the private and public are intricately linked, especially where the cultivation of faith is concerned.

Individual piety and socio-political activism

That core Islamic virtues such as patience are far less difficult to cultivate adequately and sustain in a 'comprehensively Islamic' environment than in an 'un-Islamic' society is a theme at numerous BICSa study circles. Both liberal Muslims in Bangladesh and the pietist-traditionalist Tablighi, which focuses almost exclusively on the cultivation of personal religiosity rather than social reform, argue that religion should be kept separate from politics, and that as long as individuals are free to practise religion in the private sphere there should be no conflict between religion and the state. Islamist groups such as BICSa, however, reject such a view of the state. They argue that given the intimate relations between state and society and the power the state wields over society in the present-day world, the Islamization of the public sphere is essential to the successful cultivation of individual faith at home. For example, an Islamic state could ban access to un-Islamic forms of cultural knowledge such as those conveyed from Bollywood and the USA via satellite television and could encourage religious sentiment by Islamizing the national educational curriculum.

In response to a comment from a study-circle participant who said she sometimes felt she might be better able to cultivate an Islamic self if she could spend more time on quiet worship at home than on performing organizational tasks, the chairwoman Nabila repeated that it is important to continue to struggle to transform the existing society into an Islamic one. In Nabila's view, an Islamic, reformed society significantly aids the individual Muslim in his or her efforts to cultivate Islamic virtues such as patience and thus a closer relationship with God:

> Today our patience is constantly on trial. Many of our sisters are from un-Islamic families. At home, however troubled she might feel at heart, such a sister must put up with her brothers' habit of watching nudity on satellite television or her sisters' lack of modesty in dressing or her father's involvement in corruption. As for those of us who are fortunate enough to be from Islamic families, we cannot escape the condition of the larger society. As soon as we step outside the home, many un-Islamic things assail us. Large billboards with scantily clad women advertising products are everywhere. Indecent Hindi, English, and Bangla music assail our hearing. Our fellow students are far more interested in watching titillating Hindi films on satellite television in the student lounges than in offering the daily prayers. Sights and sounds have a powerful impact on our senses. Things would be different in an Islamic environment. There would be fewer occasions for frustration for authentic Muslims struggling to practise Islamic virtues such as patience to not yield to temptation. Also, impious Muslims would more likely be drawn to the beauty of Islam that they would then have an opportunity to witness and experience every day.

Thus, a circular logic is linking individual piety, the larger environment, and social action. The Islamic virtue of patience is easier to realize in an overall Islamic atmosphere. In turn, a more Islamic environment, in better embodying the conditions necessary for the cultivation of Islamic virtues, significantly eases the hardship that the practice of patience specifically and piety generally entails. This relationship is used to exhort and mobilize activists to participate in the *jihad akbar* of public religious activism that seeks to transform both society and state. It is also offered, in an implicit manner, as a critique of the liberal-secular view – shared somewhat by some madrasa-trained religious scholars as well as by Islamic pietist groups such as Tablighi – that the practice of religion ought to be a personal matter to be confined to homes and designated religious spaces such as mosques, with as few linkages as possible to the public sphere, specifically the political sphere.

A relationship between individual belief and *jihad* is established not only through the belief-environment linkage and through the linkage of certain traditional Islamic virtues to the success of *jihad*, but also through connecting *jihad* to the 'five pillars of Islam', those obligatory acts of worship that most Muslims, whether Islamists, pietists, or secularists, agree are central to the faith. BICSa establishes this connection through Maududi's notion that Islamic forms of worship are intended to produce a particular kind of subjectivity.

Such acts should therefore be performed not merely as isolated acts of worship and not only for their intrinsic value but also for the sake of their profound, long-term, interlinked effects on a person's disposition. While this may sound similar to secular-liberal percep- tions of the significance of Islamic rituals within some Muslim communities, BICSa's views differ both from such perceptions and from the orthodox understanding charac- teristic of the pietistic mosque movement in Egypt (Mahmood 2005).

Secular nationalists regard Islamic rituals such as prayer as helping to produce the kind of disciplined, diligent, and honest individual so urgently needed and valued by a post-colonial, liberalizing nation such as modern Egypt (Starrett 1998). Pietist move- ments such as Tablighi or the mosque movement in Egypt regard Islamic rituals as instilling a virtuous disposition that is constantly and comprehensively orientated towards God in every aspect of life. BICSa, however, considers the essential divine intent in making these acts of worship obligatory as that of producing a form of individual piety that can thrive adequately and be sustained in the long run only in an Islamic environment. According to Maududi, the architect of the particular form of Islamist ideology to which BICSa adheres, the underlying purpose of obligatory acts of worship such as prayer and fasting is to produce the impetus within a person for keeping his or her consciousness *constantly* orientated towards God, so that even when that person is not praying or fasting, that established impulse keeps him or her focused on pleasing God. This impulse, however – a crucial difference from the Egyptian mosque movement's view of piety – can be sustained in the long run only when it is supported by an orientation of the polity towards pleasing God (see Maududi 2002 [1989]).

In BICSa's ideology, therefore, Muslims are perceived as responsible not only for cultivating their own piety, but also for Islamicizing their life-world (or sustaining and nurturing Islam's primacy in an already Islamized locale) through organized activism. It is only in the establishment of Islam as the dominant working ideology that the ultimate potential of one's personal beliefs is realized. Those who neglect or even refuse to promulgate and uphold Islam at the social, national, and political levels are sus- pected of hypocrisy, of a weakness in faith that prevents them from taking risks and making sacrifices for Islam. Socio-political, activism-centred 'lesser' *jihad* is thus con- ceptualized as an essential aspect of personal belief, just as integral to the 'five pillars of Islam' as the obligatory prayers or fasting. The triad of belief-hypocrisy-*jihad* around which so many BICSa discussions unfold, and which I explore elsewhere at length (Huq 2008), embodies this paradigm.

Conclusion

The specific discursive practices of BICSa complicate the conventional scholarly dichotomy of piety or the moral-ethical versus the political or instrumental. While BICSa unquestionably has political goals, its members perceive their pious and reli- gious practices as primary, not instrumental to those goals. There is little ethnographic ground for dismissing these perceptions as simply inauthentic, rhetorical, or cosmeti- cally performative: on the ground, an ongoing, dynamic, and fluid interpenetration of political concepts and goals and practical strategies with devotional religious sensibili- ties is found. In BICSa, this interpenetration of the religious and the political takes a highly gendered form, with women being socialized into a form of *jihad* that strongly discourages even verbal violence. In this view, militant *jihad* is a defensive project undertaken primarily by men against other combatants with the understanding that it is not compulsion by force but intellectual persuasion that has the most enduring impact on a person, community, and socio-political relations. BICSa emphasizes a kind of *jihad* or sacred struggle that privileges endurance, disciplined yet creative living, and constructive spiritual and socio-political engagement despite formidable odds over overtly emotional zeal, whim- and passion-driven dying, and impulsive acts of rage and destruction. BICSa's discursive practices thus also complicate the conventional view of *jihad* as violent in essence.

The process of Islamic activist socialization through study circles is, at least in BICSa's case – which is probably not unique – not only disciplinary (i.e. top-down, organizationally prescribed, hierarchically structured) but also deliberative and dialogic. However much BICSa leaders might prefer to manufacture perfectly indoctrinated activists, this does not occur. Rather, organizational efforts to convince recruits of the correctness of BICSa's Islamist doctrines through discussion, argumentation, and activists' openness to questions both inculcate and allow for varying degrees and styles of questioning – within bounds – of those tenets. Activists who challenge organizational prescriptions and recommendations do so on the basis of their practical experiences of these doctrines and their efforts to realize these teachings in the course of their daily lives as aspirants to Muslim devotion in an age perceived as increasingly secular, worldly, and materialistic. Such challenges that participants offer up in the course of BICSa study circles are only partly deflected or absorbed by the openness that permits them. The result is strikingly non-monolithic.

ACKNOWLEDGMENTS

I am thankful for the comments of the anonymous *JRAI* reviewers of this chapter. I am grateful to Filippo Osella and Benjamin Soares for their rigorous comments and patience. Research was supported by a dissertation fellowship from the Bangladesh Studies Program of the Social Science Research Council and a Social Science Research Council International Dissertation Fellowship. I was able to write this chapter by virtue of a postdoctoral fellowship at the International Institute for Advanced Studies at New York University, where I presented key portions under the auspices of the larger research project 'The Authority of Knowledge in a Global Age' directed by Tim Mitchell. Stimulating conversations with fellow IIAS seminarians at NYU and support from colleagues in the Department of Anthropology and in the Islamic Cultural Studies Program at the University of South Carolina has enabled the final draft of this chapter. I thank Lila Abu-Lughod, Lori Allen, Elaine Combs-Schilling, Dale F. Eickelman, Engseng Ho, Naveeda Khan, Barbara Metcalf, and Amira Mittermaier for their comments on earlier versions. I have benefited singularly from my dearest friend Larry Clifford Gilman's editorial insights and detailed comments on the various reincarnations of the chapter. All errors and inconsistencies remain my responsibility alone.

NOTES

[1] This is most evident in the scholarship on groups such as the Muslim Brotherhood in Egypt and Jordan (see Kepel 1985; Wickham 2002; Wiktorowicz 2001). On the Islamist group Hamas in Palestine, see Mishal & Sela (2006 [2000]) and Robinson (2004). On the Jamaat-e-Islami in Bangladesh, see Ahmed (1993), and on JI in Pakistan, see Nasr (1994; 1996).

[2] A pioneering contribution is a paper by Barbara Metcalf (2003) where she draws on primary sources to analyse specific religious discursive practices including that of *jihad* as it informs the perceptions and activities of members of Tablighi Jamaat, a Muslim missionary movement that originated in colonial India to develop into a global movement with a particularly significant and growing presence in South Asia.

[3] This is evident, for example, in the entry on women's *jihad* in South Asia by Michel Boivin, *Encyclopedia of women and Islamic cultures* (2005). More generally, however, pioneering inquiries into the various aspects of women's diverse practices of Islamic activism in South Asia have begun to address this gap, although none offers a substantive treatment of the particular issue of *jihad* in connection with broader Islamic activist practices (see Haniffa 2008; Hegland 1998; 2003; Huq 2008; Metcalf 1998; Shehabuddin 1999; 2008).

[4] This essay by Allen is an excellent overview – the best, to my knowledge, to date – of women's *jihad*, particularly in the Arab context.

⁵ Scholarship exploring women's *jihad* in some detail is emergent in religious studies (e.g. Cook 2005).

⁶ The Islamist or Muslim religio-political party Jamaat-e-Islami was founded in colonial India in August 1914 with an agenda for religio-moral, social, and political transformation. Today, it operates independently in India, Pakistan, and Bangladesh and seeks to establish an Islamic state in Bangladesh and Pakistan specifically. The founder, Abul Ala Maududi (1903-79), received his early education at home from his father, who received both religious and modern English education and had practised law in the British courts for a time. Maududi also had home tutors in Urdu, Persian, Arabic, the Qur'an, and *hadith* (authoritative records describing actions and speech of the Prophet Muhammad but not authored by him). It would seem Maududi also read widely on his own in Arabic, Persian, and English. He launched a public career as a journalist in 1920, at the age of 17. He was an effective orator with notable organizational skills and wrote abundantly, including an Urdu commentary on the Qur'an titled *Tafheem-ul-Qur'an*. This work of exegesis, written in a very readable style, has been translated, along with many of his other works, into a variety of languages and is read widely today in Islamist circles in South Asia and beyond, including those in South Asian diasporic communities around the world. (See also Ahmad this volume.)

⁷ An exception is the pioneering work of Elora Shehabuddin (1999; 2008), who focuses on the activities of adult women leaders of this movement, particularly their practices of targeting rural and often uneducated women in lobbying for votes for Jamaat.

⁸ In his work on the Islamic *Nur* movement in Turkey, for instance, Hakan Yavuz (2003) briefly mentions the 'conversational readings' (*sohbet*) that apparently constitute an important part of the Nur movement he discusses. Indeed, it is through movement-sponsored *sohbet* that members engage the teachings of movement founder Bediuzzaman Said Nursi, which members use to reconstruct themselves as moral agents. We get a fairly good notion of what Nursi actually taught, just as we know from a variety of scholarly works what the key architects of the contemporary Islamic revival, Hasanal-Banna, Abul Ala Maududi, and Sayyid Qutb, wrote. However, we know very little of the specifics of audience engagements with these texts.

⁹ Pseudonyms are used for all of my interlocutors.

¹⁰ Chatra Dal is the student wing of the Awami League, one of the two national political parties that have dominated the political landscape of Bangladesh since its inception as an independent country in 1971. The other dominant national political party, the Bangladesh Nationalist Party or BNP, upholds a relatively conservative Muslim nationalist ideology rooted in the cultural and political experiences of Bangladesh as a nation-state where Bangali Muslims comprise the distinct majority of the population. In contrast, the Awami League adheres to a secular ideology grounded in ethnic (i.e., Bangali) nationalism. A majority of Bangali Hindus reside just across the border in India, which is also home to a large and ethnically diverse Muslim minority, including a Bangali Muslim minority.

¹¹ In the course of informal conversations with several non-partisan faculty and staff members at Dhaka University and other institutions of higher education in Dhaka between 1999 and 2003, I learned that the authorities instituted this ban to maintain peace in view of the remarkably concerted and sometimes violent opposition from the student wings of the two dominant political parties, the AL and BNP, that Islamist activism had often sparked on the campus throughout the 1980s. Reportedly, opposition to an Islamist ideology and activism constituted one of the few grounds that the rival and sometimes violently clashing political parties, the AL and BNP, had shared since the early years after Bangladesh's secession from Pakistan in 1971. According to these interlocutors, Chatra Union, the student wing of the Bangladesh Socialist Party with a notable presence at Dhaka University at the time, had also joined Chatra League, the student wing of the AL, and Chatra Dal, the student wing of the BNP, on many occasions in calling for the 'extermination' of 'fundamentalism' from the Dhaka University campus and beyond. In the view of such concerted political activist opposition to Islamism on campus, the then Dhaka University authorities decided that allowing Chatra Shibir, the student wing of Jamaat-e-Islami, to operate on the campus alongside other student political groups would only exacerbate already politically volatile campus conditions. According to these interlocutors, while Chatra Shibir activists and their supporters were just as militant and dedicated as their rivals, the former were far fewer in number than the latter and less likely to enjoy state patronage and thus genuine protection from the police, who had to enter the campus to contain and sometimes pre-empt political violence. The decision to impose the ban was thus represented to me as a 'practical' one taken for the 'common good'.

¹² Some BICSa activists, in the course of informal conversations with the author, recalled events where their dormitory rooms were vandalized by women activists of Chatra League, Chatra Dal, and Chatra Union. Some recalled days when BICSa posters were torn down from campus walls 'in an effort to silence'. Others narrated events where BICSa activists were trapped in dormitory rooms with rival activists attempting to break down the doors. Yet others complained that in the aftermath of conflicts between Shibir and

anti-Islamist students, university authorities would order BICSa activists to leave the campus premises as their presence might 'excite' opponents. Within my small group of liberal-secularist women student interlocutors, many denied these charges and some refused to comment on these allegations in most instances. However, none accused BICSa activists of violence. Some remarked that BICSa women collaborate in the violent perpetrations of Shibir in that these women help propagate the fundamentalism of Shibir and Jamaat.

[13] Formal interview of a leading BICSa activist, 11 December 1999.

[14] In contrast to this, scholars such as Miriam Cooke have shown that female companions of the Prophet Muhammad not only accompanied the Prophet in battle but they also fought with him. Thus a woman named Nusayba bint Ka'b is reported to have physically defended the Prophet at the battle of Uhud in 625 CE (Cooke 2002). Indeed, leading BICSa activists increasingly cite these female companions' participation in battle in persuading recruits, many among whom lose determination along the way, that the sacrifices BICSa asks of them are smaller than those made by the women from the time of the Prophet for the causes of Islam.

[15] Informal conversation with a leading BICSa activist and a veteran conductor of study circles, April 2003.

REFERENCES

AHMED, R. 1993. Redefining Muslim identity in South Asia: the transformation of the Jama'at-i Islami. In *Fundamentalisms and society: reclaiming the sciences, the family, and education* (eds) M.E. Marty & R.S. Appleby, 669-705. Chicago: University Press.

ALLEN, L. 2005. Jihad, Arab states. In *Encyclopedia of women and Islamic cultures 2*, 319-21. Leiden: Brill.

ARAT, Y. 2005. *Rethinking Islam and liberal democracy: Islamist women in Turkish politics.* Albany: State University of New York Press.

BOIVIN, M. 2005. Jihad, South Asia. In *Encyclopedia of women and Islamic cultures 2*, 326-7. Leiden: Brill.

BOUATTA, C. 1994. Feminine militancy: *moudjahidates* during and after the Algerian War. In *Gender and national identity: women and politics in Muslim societies* (ed.) V. Moghadam, 18-35. London: Zed.

CHERIFATE-MERABTINE, D. 1994. Algeria at a crossroads: national liberation, Islamization and women. In *Gender and national identity: women and politics in Muslim societies* (ed.) V. Moghadam, 40-51. London: Zed.

COOK, D. 2005. *Understanding jihad.* Berkeley: University of California Press.

COOKE, M. 2002. Islamic feminism before and after September 11th. *Duke Journal of Gender and Law Policy* **9**, 227-36.

DEEB, L. 2006. *An enchanted modern: gender and public piety in Shi'i Lebanon.* Princeton: University Press.

DEVJI, F. 2005. *Landscapes of the jihad: militancy, morality, modernity.* Ithaca, N.Y.: Cornell University Press.

HALE, S. 1996. *Islamism, socialism, and the state.* Boulder, Colo.: Westview.

HANIFFA, F. 2008. Piety as politics amongst Muslim women in contemporary Sri Lanka. *Modern Asian Studies* **42**, 347-75.

HASHMI, T. 2000. *Women and Islam in Bangladesh: beyond subjection and tyranny.* Basingstoke: Macmillan; New York: St Martin's Press.

HEGLAND, M.E. 1998. Flagellation and fundamentalism: (trans)forming meaning, identity, and gender through Pakistani women's rituals of mourning. *American Ethnologist* **25**, 240-66.

———— 2003. Shia women's rituals in northwest Pakistan: the shortcomings and significance of resistance. *Anthropological Quarterly* **76**, 411-42.

HIRSCHKIND, C. 2001. Civic virtue and religious reason: an Islamic counterpublic. *Cultural Anthropology* **16**, 3-34.

HOFFMAN, V. 1985. An Islamic activist: Zainab Al-Ghazali. In *Women and the family in the Middle East: new voices of change* (ed.) E.W. Fernea, 233-54. Austin: University of Texas Press.

HUQ, M. 2008. Reading the Qur'an in Bangladesh: the politics of belief among Islamist women. *Modern Asian Studies* **42**, 457-88.

KEPEL, G. 1985. *Muslim extremism in Egypt: the Prophet and the Pharaoh.* Berkeley: University of California Press.

———— 2002. *Jihad: the trail of political Islam.* Cambridge, Mass.: The Belknap Press of Harvard University Press.

KLEINMAN, A. 2000. The violences of everyday life: the multiple forms and dynamics of social violence. In *Violence and subjectivity* (eds) V. Das, A. Kleinman, M. Ramphele & P. Reynolds, 226-41. Berkeley: University of California Press.

LIMBERT, M. 2005. Gender, religious knowledge and education in Oman. In *Monarchies and nations: globalisation and identity in the Arab states of the Gulf* (eds) P. Dresch & J. Piscatori, 182-202. London: I.B. Tauris.

MAHMOOD, S. 2005. *Politics of piety: the Islamic revival and the feminist subject.* Princeton: University Press.

MAUDUDI, A.A. 2002 [1989]. *Islami ibadater marmakatha* (The crux of Islamic worship). (Fourth edition). Dhaka: Shatabdi Prakashani.

METCALF, B.D. 1998. Women and men in a contemporary pietist movement. In *Appropriating gender: women's activism and politicized religion in South Asia* (eds) P. Jeffery & A. Basu, 107-22. London: Routledge.

———— 2003. Travelers' tales in the Tablighi Jamaat. *Annals of the American Academy of Political Science* **588**, 136-48.

MISHAL, S. & A. SELA 2006 [2000]. *The Palestinian Hamas: vision, violence, and coexistence.* New York: Columbia University Press.

MONSOOR, T. 1999. *From patriarchy to gender equity: family law and its impact on women in Bangladesh.* Dhaka: University Press Ltd.

NASR, S.V.R. 1994. *The vanguard of the Islamic revolution: the Jama'at-i Islami of Pakistan.* Berkeley: University of California Press.

———— 1996. *Mawdudi and the making of Islamic revivalism.* Oxford: University Press.

RING, L.A. 2006. *Zenana: everyday peace in a Karachi apartment building.* Bloomington: Indiana University Press.

ROBINSON, G.E. 2004. Hamas as social movement. In *Islamic activism: a social movement theory approach* (ed.) Q. Wiktorowicz, 112-39. Bloomington: Indiana University Press.

ROY, O. 1994. *The failure of political Islam* (trans. C. Volk). Cambridge, Mass.: Harvard University Press.

SCHEPER-HUGHES, N. 1992. *Death without weeping: the violence of everyday life in Brazil.* Berkeley: University of California Press.

SHEHABUDDIN, E. 1999. Beware the bed of fire: gender, democracy, and the Jama'at-i Islami in Bangladesh. *Journal of Women's History* **10**: 4, 148-71.

———— 2008. Jamaat-i-Islami in Bangladesh: women, democracy and the transformation of Islamist politics. *Modern Asian Studies* **42**, 577-603.

STARRETT, G. 1998. *Putting Islam to work: education, politics, and religious transformation in Egypt.* Berkeley: University of California Press.

WHITE, J. 2002. *Islamist mobilization in Turkey: a study in vernacular politics.* Seattle: University of Washington Press.

WICKHAM, C.R. 2002. *Mobilizing Islam: religion, activism, and political change in Egypt.* New York: Columbia University Press.

WIKTOROWICZ, Q. 2001. *The management of Islamic activism: Salafis, the Muslim Brotherhood, and state power in Jordan.* Albany: State University of New York Press.

YAVUZ, H. 2003. *Nur* study circles (*Dershanes*) and the formation of new religious consciousness in Turkey. In *Islam at the crossroads: on the life and thought of Bediuzzaman Said Nursi* (ed.) H. Yavuz, 297-316. Albany: State University of New York Press.

11

Market Islam in Indonesia

DAROMIR RUDNYCKYJ *University of Victoria*

At about ten minutes before noon one Friday in May 2004, employees from Krakatau Steel's slab steel plant ambled toward the Baiturrahman mosque adjacent to the mammoth mill. Small clumps of dingy bamboo with greyish-yellow leaves were planted around the building's perimeter just beyond a small gutter aligned with the roof edge above. The acrid odour of smelting steel pervaded the dusty, heavy air as the sun beat down on a mercilessly hot midday. The mosque's high, Javanese-style roof provided some relief from the otherwise sweltering heat. A smattering of workers had already assembled to perform optional *sunnah* prayers prior to the main collective prayers, while others hurriedly finished their obligatory ablutions at a row of metal spigots adjacent to the mosque. Shortly, against a background of heavy machinery and massive equipment that roared in semi-muted cacophony, Asmianto,[1] the plant employee who would serve as the *khatib*, the prayer leader who delivers a religious lecture, launched into an ominous sermon.

His oration concerned Indonesia's ongoing economic problems, the country's upcoming presidential elections, and the political and ethical responsibilities of plant employees. Asmianto began by explaining to the assembled, 'We are here to enact our duty (*melaksanakan kewajiban*) of Friday prayers'. He then linked Indonesia's political and economic problems to what he termed a 'moral crisis', intoning,

> Events in our country cause us to take notice. Since 1997 there has been an economic crisis that has been getting worse (*makin parah*). There is also a political and social crisis, but what is most threatening is the prospect of a moral crisis that is now gripping the country ... Given these conditions we face the future pessimistically.

He then launched into a long Qur'anic recitation in Arabic and suggested the crisis was a challenge presented by Allah that employees of the company could address through pious action guided by Islamic principles. Referring to Indonesia's upcoming election for president of the republic, he said that pious acts included electing 'a better leader, one who is comfortable with the people (*senang kepada rakyat*), and with whom the people are content ... If we return to the true road the people will receive the grace (*nikmat*) of Allah ... Thus, we must implement the orders of Allah (*perintah Allah*)'. He urged workers to fulfil religious duties as a means of resolving the crises that plagued the country. He said that they should develop proper moral behaviour in their everyday activities. Finally, he enjoined the workers to 'remember that work is worship (*kerja adalah ibadah*) ... our work is part of our service to Allah!'

Later that afternoon I sat with Tata, a foreman in the slab steel plant who had attended the prayers, drinking small cups of the instant coffee that was popular among plant workers. I asked him about the sermon and the relationship between the crisis, the future of the company, and matters of work and religious worship. He explained that recently he had noticed an increasing focus on relating Islamic practice to daily work at official company functions. Referring to Asmianto's discussion of time during the oration, Tata said that after each *rakaat* (the basic unit of Muslim prayer, consisting of a set of bows and prostrations) the *khatib* had quoted two Qur'anic passages. After the first *rakaat* he quoted from the Sura at-Takathur.[2] This was intended to remind Muslims 'that people may not be greedy (*rakus*) ... they shouldn't be orientated towards worldly (*duniawi*) things like money, objects, or women'. Tata interpreted this as an injunction against corruption, like taking tools from the factory or deliberately misreporting one's hours on a time card.

Tata then explained that the Qur'anic citation after the second *rakaat* specifically addressed questions of time management at work. This one was from Sura al-Asr[3] and 'reminded us not to waste time ... that we cannot be relaxed at work (*membuang-buang waktu diingatkan ... santai tidak boleh*)'. Tata explained:

> We made a promise with a representative of God (*janji di wakil Tuhan*) – the company – not to waste time. This is not a regulation made by humans, but by Allah (*bukan aturan manusia, tapi Allah*). We made a promise (*janji*) with the company; if we violate it, it is a betrayal (*khianat*) ... The company may not know, but God knows. God notes all the violations (*Tuhan mencatat pelanggaran*). Not God specifically, but one of his angels. Later there will be a verdict after death (*nanti hukum sesudah mati*).

With this portentous injunction, Tata finished his cup of coffee and returned to work. His comments and the day's earlier sermon reflected an emerging emphasis on cultivating religious practice to instil labour discipline and enhance corporate competitiveness. It was a message I would hear repeatedly during the period between 2003 and 2005 when I carried out ethnographic research in Indonesia.

The notion that intensified attention to Islamic practice would redress Indonesia's political and economic crises resonated widely at Krakatau Steel and beyond. Not only was it a common topic of sermons at factory mosques as demonstrated by workers like Tata and Asmianto, but managers also sought to make it part of the company's regular human resources training sessions. They had contracted a Jakarta-based company, the ESQ Leadership Center, to hold intermittent 'spiritual training' programmes for employees. These sessions, called Emotional and Spiritual Quotient (ESQ) training, fused business management, life-coaching, and self-help principles with Islamic history and examples from the life of the Prophet Muhammad, creating what I term 'market Islam'. Market Islam, a combination of religious practice and business management knowledge, was seen as conducive to success in an increasingly competitive global economy.

Conceived by the charismatic businessman-turned-spiritual reformer Ary Ginanjar, ESQ was embraced by managers at Krakatau Steel and scores of other state-owned enterprises, private companies, and government offices in Indonesia. During the period of my field research, Ary Ginanjar and his brother, Rinaldi Agusyana, delivered monthly (or sometimes bi-monthly) training sessions at Krakatau Steel in a distinctive style that blended zealous religious oratory and fervent motivational speaking. These sessions consisted of emotionally evocative programmes that were designed to configure a new type of Muslim practice intended to reconcile the ethical, economic, and moral predicaments of middle- and upper-middle-class Indonesians.

I argue that this articulation represents the emergence of market Islam. Market Islam refers to how Islamic practices are mobilized to facilitate the transition from an authoritarian regime of state-fostered development to organizing labour and commercial activity according to market principles. Although there are points of overlap with what has been called 'civil Islam', I argue that market Islam seeks less to create commensurability between Islam and democracy and is instead designed to merge Muslim religious practice and capitalist ethics.

Islam and modernity

Partially in response to the widely circulating arguments of Samuel Huntington and others, Robert Hefner identifies civil Islam in contemporary Indonesia as the reconciliation between Islamic religious authority and democratic political institutions. Civil Islam does not stand in conflict with the West, but rather sees precedents for ideas central to democratic polities in Islamic history and certain Qur'anic injunctions. It accepts both democratic norms such as free speech, participation, and toleration and a division between state and society in which society is the proper domain of religious practice. Furthermore, in contrast to Huntington's emphasis on uniformity and homogeneity across 'civilizations', Hefner instead argues that Indonesia, in part due to deep pluralist traditions that predate colonial intervention and in part due to the role of civic associations in its recent democratic transformation, is a paradigmatic example of an 'emergent tradition' of civil Islam. According to Hefner, civil Islam is characterized by 'denying the wisdom of a monolithic "Islamic" state and instead affirming democracy, voluntarism, and a balance of countervailing powers in a state and society ... this democratic Islam insists that formal democracy cannot prevail unless government power is checked by strong civic associations' (Hefner 2000: 12-13).

The vigorous debates in the Muslim world and the pluralism of political forms within a discursive tradition of Islam (Asad 1986) identified by Hefner are confirmed by others as well. Anthropologists have chronicled how, far from being characterized by tyrannical forms of authoritative knowledge, the Muslim world is rife with debates over religious practice and proper ethical choices, although these debates do not always conform to the norms of a public sphere rooted in a European historical tradition (Hirschkind 2001; Ong 1990; Othman 2003; Peletz 2002).

Hefner's attention to the commensurability of contemporary Islam and civil democratic traditions begs a related question: how do Muslims perceive the relationship between Islamic practice and the norms of contemporary capitalism? While there has been considerable work on political Islam, the articulation between Islam and economic globalization has received much less attention.[4] This chapter sheds light on this articulation by analysing the mobilization of Islamic ethics to meet the challenges of globalization. I argue that market Islam has come into being alongside, but distinctly from, civil Islam in contemporary Indonesia.

My attention to market Islam also builds on earlier approaches to Islam and capitalist transformation in Southeast Asia. Scholars of the region have long focused on 'modernist' Muslim movements that have sought to reconcile Islamic practice with modernization (Geertz 1960; Noer 1973; Peacock 1978). However, my analysis differs on important methodological grounds from these earlier accounts. In the ethnographic material presented below, it is not the analyst who posits the relationship between Islam and capitalism, but the participants in my research project themselves who sought to forge this assemblage (Ong & Collier 2005).

Rather than imposing a certain theoretical model on empirical reality, I focus on the way in which contemporary Indonesians posed questions about their contemporary lives that might enable anthropologists to see the theory that we use in a different light (Boyer 2001).[5] The concept of market Islam emerges, then, out of my efforts to break down the boundary between anthropological theory and the theories used by those studied anthropologically (Ferguson 1999; Maurer 2002; Miyazaki 2004; Riles 2000). In short, I dissolve the distinction between anthropological theory and empirical reality by uncovering the models that are practised by those who are the focus of ethnographic investigation and suggesting how they might further anthropological knowledge. Market Islam refers to efforts of self-styled spiritual reformers and corporate managers to enhance Islamic practice to better compete in an increasingly transnational economy. Although Indonesians themselves did not refer to 'market Islam', I use it to refer to the practical models they deployed to address the challenges presented by 'the free market' and the way in which Islamic practice was mobilized to address those changes.

This approach differs from previous analyses of Islam and capitalism in Southeast Asia (Alatas 1963; Geertz 1963; Peacock 1978) insofar as the Indonesian Muslims involved in the project of spiritual reform explicitly connect Islamic practice to economic development. That is to say, they are developing a model of how to live *in practice* as Muslims in an economy no longer defined in national terms. This project consists of a set of discursive practices intended to make Indonesian Muslims amenable to what they term the 'free market'. Underlying this approach is the presumption that proper Islamic practice necessarily entails greater productivity, less corruption, and more diligent work habits. Furthermore, this is an avowedly self-reflexive process. Participants in spiritual reform directly connected their own previous moral failings to the political and economic problems in Indonesia at large. Perhaps due to past acts of corruption or, at lower levels of the company hierarchy, labour shirking, they see the problem of resolving this moral crisis as an impetus to work on themselves in order to improve both themselves and the larger community.

Market Islam differs from other new forms of popular religious practice and new religious movements in Southeast Asia. Peter Jackson and Katharine Wiegele have recently discussed the widespread popularity of prosperity religions in Thailand and the Philippines. While Jackson focuses on the Buddhist veneration of amulets and the worship of saints and monks and Wiegele on the enormously popular El Shaddai Catholic movement, both scholars define these recent phenomena as 'prosperity religions' (Jackson 1999; Wiegele 2005). Followers of prosperity movements believe that enhanced religious devotion will net them economic success through divine intervention (Coleman 2000). Herein lies the main difference between prosperity movements and market Islam. Adherents of a prosperity movement are encouraged, following Wiegele, to 'invest in miracles' by making donations to religious groups as a means of 'eliciting miracles from God' (Wiegele 2005: 21). Market Islam, in contrast, is designed to inculcate the kind of ethical dispositions deemed conducive to greater competitiveness in a global economy. Rather than expecting miracles as the result of previous economic exchanges, market Islam emphasizes an ethics of hard work, responsibility, and accountability as the means to economic well-being. Thus, spiritual reformers in Indonesia see initiatives like ESQ training as a means of both enhancing Islamic piety and developing Indonesia's human resources to further the project of national development.

Market Islam offers a different analytical stance from that entailed in what political scientist Patrick Haenni (2005) has recently called 'Islam de marché'.[6] Whereas 'Islam de marché' is represented as 'conservative' and 'fundamentalist', market Islam is neither. This is due to the fact that a scale like liberal-conservative appears very different from the perspective of people in Indonesia than it does from Europe or North America. Indonesians did not see Ary Ginanjar as conservative because he was not trying to conserve a tradition perceived to be under threat. Rather, they saw ESQ as progressive (or even radical) because it represented a completely new way of practising Islam to make it commensurate with modern life and labour.

'Breaking the boundary': spectres of the free market

Employees of Krakatau Steel would often invoke the 'free market' (*pasar bebas*) as the greatest threat to the future of the company. The free market served as an all-purpose phrase that referred to a number of distinct, yet interrelated phenomena. These included the end of Krakatau Steel's monopoly on marketing steel, global integration of the steel market, the elimination of both tariffs on imported steel and state subsidies to support modernization of ageing plant facilities, and the end of an exclusive national zone of economic activity.

Krakatau Steel had long enjoyed a monopoly position on the sale of steel in Indonesia. However, in 2004, the central government under pressure from downstream consumers fully eliminated tariffs on imported steel. Employees of the company felt further threatened by plans to form the 'AFTA plus three' free trade area, which would include Southeast Asian countries and China, Japan, and South Korea. These plans, announced at an October 2003 ASEAN (Association of Southeast Asian Nations) summit in Indonesia and widely reported in the Indonesian press, were a recurring topic of my conversations with Krakatau Steel workers. The inclusion of China, Japan, and South Korea in a free trade zone with Indonesia was particularly alarming, as employees were well aware that these countries had achieved economies of scale in steel production that far exceeded Indonesia's meagre output.[7] The prospect of a free market in which Indonesia would have to compete with these three steel titans did not portend well for the company's long-term viability.

The free market had far-reaching ramifications for employees of Krakatau Steel. Long-standing practices deemed inefficient and not conducive to global competitiveness were under re-evaluation. Thus, the company sought to introduce various reforms, including basing promotions on merit rather than personal ties; eliminating corruption; restructuring the employee salary scale; and eliminating guaranteed lifetime employment. According to managers, these changes meant that employees had to become more industrious, honest, independent, and responsible. This involved a wide-ranging overhaul of existing norms. Thus, the abstract notion of the free market presented a very practical problem: how to elicit labour practices that would ensure the company's long-term viability given increasing transnational competition? Krakatau Steel would no longer occupy the dominant position in the domestic steel market, but would become one company competing among others in a global economy. It chose to address these challenges through particularly high-profile means, by enhancing the Islamic practice of company employees.

Krakatau Steel employees repeatedly invoked the free market as the foremost threat to the company's future. Suryawardi, an employee in production planning and control, showed how this problem was articulated. In a conversation he explained that

> globalization is the world market. If the world market becomes free (*pasar dunia sudah bebas*), it is a foregone conclusion. If we don't do things correctly, then we'll lose to the others. Other companies will come to Indonesia and send their products to Indonesia. We won't be anything because they are brave enough to sell [their products] inexpensively.

He then invoked the spectre of the growth of the Chinese steel industry, which had the potential to flood the Indonesian market with cheaper steel, rendering Krakatau Steel non-competitive and moribund.

The spectre of a free market and increasing transnational competition marked a drastic change in the way business had been conducted during Krakatau Steel's short history. Most notably, while there were other steel companies in the country, the company had long held a monopoly on marketing steel domestically within Indonesia. Fajri, a fourteen-year veteran of the company who worked in human resources planning, said that the government had sought to promote the development of Krakatau Steel by giving it a domestic monopoly on steel sales. Thus, while other companies could produce steel, they were obliged to use Krakatau Steel's marketing department to access the domestic market. Fajri explained that although Krakatau Steel became 'the sultan of steel' (*raja baja*), this had precipitated poor customer service. He continued, 'since there was no competition, there was no pressure to provide good service to Krakatau Steel customers; it was a culture of being served, not serving others', explaining that if customers required a special order, needed expedited delivery, or had some other extraordinary request, then they often had to pay a bribe to the employee in the marketing department who handled the account. The monopoly position also had led to instances in which company employees used their quasi-official positions for personal benefit.[8] This poor record continued even after Krakatau Steel's marketing monopoly was ended in the mid-1990s. Fajri said that this problem had become increasingly acute with the prospect of a free market: 'Now with globalization (*globalisasi*), now with the free market (*pasar bebas*), we must be competitive, the steel business must be competitive. We must serve the customer. If not we will be destroyed!'

Fajri's concern over Krakatau Steel's lack of competitiveness and poor customer service was reiterated by Effendi. He had long worked in the cold rolling mill, which produced the thin sheets of steel that were among the company's most marketable commodities due to their numerous industrial applications. He said the company was facing considerable competition from new smaller mills in Indonesia. Echoing Fajri's point that the company's past monopoly had led to lax customer service in the marketing department, he bluntly stated: 'It isn't clear how to make an order from Krakatau Steel. The marketing department don't understand their jobs'. Effendi explained that he had a friend who owned a small business in Bandung that made exhaust pipes for motorcycles. The man had sought to place a standing order of 20 tons of cold rolled steel per month from Krakatau Steel, but the marketing department showed little interest in fulfilling the order. Ultimately, he found another supplier more accommodating to his needs.

Anxieties over the free market were not only expressed in private conversations and interviews. In June 2004 I attended a large meeting in honour of the five-year anniversary of the founding of Krakatau Steel's newly formed labour union, in which senior company managers met with 100 union representatives. Fazwar Bujang, the vice-president of corporate finance, presented the union with the five major challenges that he claimed threatened the company's viability. The first, he argued, was the fluctuation of the price of raw materials and steel. He explained that due to the increasing global integration of the steel market, Krakatau Steel had much less power to set prices domestically. The second challenge was the elimination of tariffs on imported steel. These reductions could allow foreign companies to flood the Indonesian market with 'below-standard' steel. After listing other challenges, including the ageing of both machinery and employees, Bujang admonished the workers in decidedly neoliberal terms of personal responsibility, claiming that 'the responsibility for the future is not just the onus of the company, but of the employees themselves' (see Rose 1999). He explained that the workers must be disciplined and productive to ensure the long-term survival of the company. Shortly thereafter I met with another senior manager, Fauzi, who, even more bluntly, argued that the greatest problem facing Krakatau Steel was 'breaking the boundary between the inside and the outside … we must be ready to compete in the global era'. Thus, employees at all levels of the company hierarchy identified the free market as the biggest challenge facing the company.

Marketing Islam or Islamizing the market?

The course of action that Krakatau Steel undertook in order to address the problems presented by the free market was unprecedented in company history. Managers contracted a Jakarta-based company, the ESQ Leadership Center, to implement a programme of moderate Islamic spiritual and leadership training for employees and thus to make the company more competitive in a globalizing steel market. The creator of ESQ, Ary Ginanjar, developed an elaborate model, the 'ESQ model', which is based on the claim that the five pillars of Islam and the six pillars of the faith (*iman*) contain ethics conducive to business success. Through the spiritual training sessions that his company offers, Ginanjar stresses that Islamic piety should not be simply restricted to religious worship, such as during one's daily prayers. Rather, drawing on the principle of *tauhid*, or the unity *of* and faith *in* God, Islam should animate all of one's worldly activity, from interactions with one's family to everyday work in the world.

During these sessions, Ginanjar argues that principles conducive to modern business and management can be found in Islamic practice and Qur'anic doctrine. For example, participants in these training programmes are instructed that the third pillar of Islam, the duty to give alms (*zakat*), is divine sanction for 'synergy', 'strategic collaboration', and exercising a 'win-win' approach in both business transactions and relations with co-workers. Further, Ginanjar asserts that the fourth pillar of Islam, the duty to fast during Ramadan, is a model for self-control and self-management. ESQ draws on this principle to inculcate the obligation to constrain this-worldly desires in order to ensure other-worldly salvation. Corruption, which is represented as a result of the longing for material possessions, is depicted as contrary to this divine injunction of individual accountability.

At Krakatau Steel, ESQ training sessions were held once or twice per month except during Ramadan and the hajj pilgrimage season.[9] ESQ sessions were most often held in the large multi-purpose room of the factory's education and training centre, which could accommodate over 300 participants. The sessions ran for three consecutive days, usually from Friday through Sunday, but occasionally also mid-week. The first two days started at 7:00 a.m. and lasted until just before the *maghrib*[10] prayers, which usually begin around 6:00 p.m. The third day of the training involved a dramatic self-confession session in which participants simulated the experience of being interrogated by the angels of death, Mungkar and Nakir, to judge their fitness for salvation. The final event was the programme's dénouement, which consisted of a simulation of three of the events that take place during the hajj pilgrimage to Mecca: *tawaf*, the circumambulation of the *kaaba* (the shrine at the centre of the Al-Haram mosque); the *sa'i*, the ritual of running seven times back and forth between the hills of Safa and Marwah in Mecca;[11] and the stoning of *jamrat al-aqabah*, in which pilgrims hurl rocks at three representations of the devil.[12] This final day ran from 7:00 a.m. until almost midnight.

Like many other forms of management knowledge, the training was structured through what is becoming a ubiquitous global form for conveying information, a Microsoft PowerPoint presentation. This consisted of the usual slides with graphs, charts, tables, and a litany of bullet points, but also with spliced film clips, colourful photographs, and popular music. The training was delivered primarily as an interactive lecture in which the main trainer would alternate between engaging with the audience in the familiar style of a television talk show host and delivering fiery and deeply emotive lectures asking for collective atonement from Allah for past indiscretions.

In addition to lectures, assistant trainers would often perform skits to illustrate the main points of the training. Interactive games, participatory role-playing activities, and callisthenics were deployed to break up the monotony of sitting and listening. In order to elicit certain affective states, the physical environment during the training was carefully calibrated. The sound in the hall was sometimes elevated to ear-splitting volume and the lights in the room were manipulated to maximize the dramatic effects of the points made. Further, the air conditioning was turned to its lowest setting, creating a disconcerting chill in an otherwise steamy tropical climate. The careful manipulation of the environment and the sheer mental and physical exhaustion of so many hours of training no doubt contributed to the profound outpouring of affect exhibited by participants in the programme.

Ary Ginanjar's idiosyncratic combination of discourses and practices drew on North American and Japanese management theories and practices,[13] Islamic history and Qur'anic recitation, popular science, Javanese culture, popular psychology, Hollywood blockbusters, and more. This assemblage was neither wholly Indonesian nor American, but global in the sense that it found inspiration in a wide multiplicity of sources. Nevertheless, Ginanjar's originality lies in the combination of elements that constituted ESQ, not in the specific elements themselves. ESQ is evocative of what Tom Boellstorff (2003), in another Indonesian context, has referred to as 'dubbing culture', insofar as it involves a subtle negotiation of what is Indonesian and what is foreign.

While most multi-national firms in Indonesia were oblivious to the programme, ESQ was well received by educated Muslims. In 2001, after Ginanjar finished the ESQ book that serves as the basis for the training, he began visiting various Qur'anic study groups (*pengajian*) affiliated with middle- and upper-middle-class mosques in Jakarta. After his ideas were well received, he offered the first ESQ leadership training sessions in 2002. At the end of the year he counted forty-three 'alumni', but the programme quickly grew so that by the end of 2007 over 465,000 people had completed his spiritual training. This included senior managers in state-owned enterprises, officials in national, regional, and local government, and small and medium-sized business owners. In 2005 weekly ESQ pages began to appear in *Republika*, the most prominent national Islamic daily paper. Ginanjar was also named to the board of experts of ICMI (Ikatan Cendekiawan Muslim Indonesia – the Association of Indonesian Muslim Intellectuals), a New Order body founded by Suharto as a means of cultivating support among the growing legions of educated, middle-class Indonesian Muslims. The organization has maintained an important role in Islamic affairs in the post-Suharto period. Marwah Daud Ibrahim, the head of ICMI and a candidate for vice-president of Indonesia in the 2004 elections, cited Ginanjar's efforts to 'develop human resources' as the reason for his selection (Hamid 2006) and expressed the hope that his methods for strengthening human resources through the intensification of Islamic practice would benefit national development.

Although Krakatau Steel was one of the first companies to embrace ESQ, the programme subsequently spread widely across Indonesia. In 2002, as he was in the early stages of developing ESQ, Ary Ginanjar identified a niche market in state-owned enterprises and government departments. In addition to Krakatau Steel, training programmes were initiated at the Directorate General of Taxation, Pertamina (the national oil company), Telkom (the country's largest telecommunications company), and Garuda (the nation's flag air carrier). A number of (current and former) Indonesian armed forces generals were also avid supporters of and participants in ESQ. Several training sessions specifically for military leaders were offered at the Army's officer candidate training school in Bandung.

State ministers, both past and present, were enthusiastic proponents of ESQ. In late 2004, Sugiharto, then the newly appointed Minister for State-Owned Enterprises, issued a letter 'recommending' that employees of all state-owned enterprises in Indonesia complete the ESQ training programme. This is a vast pool of over 100 companies, all of which have established budgets for employee training. During a news conference when journalists asked the Minister how he intended to combat rampant corruption, he invoked ESQ as the primary means his new administration planned to use towards this end.

In just five years the growth of ESQ was nothing short of spectacular. The company also does a brisk business in so-called 'public' trainings, where people pay up to US$350 out of their own pockets to participate. Ary Ginanjar said that these events, which attract as many as 1,000 people at a time, are his biggest growth market. Recently ESQ has met its goal of becoming a national movement by establishing branch offices in thirty out of thirty-three Indonesian provinces.[14] In late 2005 the ESQ Leadership Center initiated construction of a new headquarters – a twenty-five-storey office tower and convention centre in south Jakarta – which was partly funded through investment shares sold to past participants. By May 2008 the convention centre had been completed and work continued on the office tower. The company planned to lease much of the office space to multinational corporations with offices in Jakarta.

Ary Ginanjar's ESQ training programme and associated books, DVDs, tours, and other branded commodities are a manifestation of a wider trend in Indonesia in which Islamic values are mobilized to meet the challenges of globalization. Another exemplary figure in this regard, as described by Watson (2005) and Hoesterey (2008), is the charismatic engineer-turned-television preacher Abdullah Gymnastiar, who, until his controversial decision in 2006 to take a second wife dimmed his star, was one of the most visible celebrities in Indonesia. Gymnastiar, better known under the abbreviated moniker Aa Gym, is the founder of the Islamic media and direct marketing conglomerate called the Manajemen Qolbu Corporation. He used first an English-derived term (*manajemen*) and then an Arabic word (*qolbu*) to yield a corporation and form of spiritual practice that Indonesians understand as 'Management of the Heart'. In addition to his successful televangelism, Gymnastiar also designed human resources training sessions that combined the principles of business organization and the teachings of Islam, which he called 'Management by Conscience' (*Manajemen Suara Hati*). Over forty state-owned and some private companies have sent staff to his Bandung headquarters for training. Market Islam refers to these efforts to design a form of Islamic practice conducive to the free market by transforming the way in which corporate employees viewed their own labour.

In addition to ESQ and Management by Conscience training there are a growing number of similar initiatives that combine Islamic practice and management and life-coaching techniques in Indonesia, including Syariah Management and Celestial Management. These groups are moderate insofar as they do not advocate the seizure of state power as a means of enforcing Islamic strictures. Rather, proponents of and participants in these movements consider Indonesia's political and economic 'crisis' a result of the separation of religious ethics from economic practice. They argue that this disjunction has resulted in rampant corruption, inefficiency, and a lack of discipline in the workplace. This phenomenon is not limited only to Indonesia, but is increasingly found elsewhere in the Islamic world as well (Haenni 2005; Osella & Osella this volume; Wise 2003).

At Krakatau Steel, Ary Ginanjar and his brother Rinaldi Agusyana delivered the standard ESQ training session that had been replicated at hundreds of sites across Indonesia. However, they tailored portions of the programme specifically to address issues troubling the company's workforce. For example, in one session in May 2004, Ginanjar presented economic globalization and the free market as divine challenges that demanded enhanced attention to Islamic practice by company employees. Effectively merging globalization and monotheism, he declared that a recent decision by Indonesia's central government to eliminate import tariffs on steel was in fact a divine blessing. He said,

> Ladies and gentlemen ... our faith in Allah is the key to all the problems that we face in this global era! This era has brought the elimination of import tariffs on steel. For humans it is darkness, but for Allah it is light. Because the elimination of tariffs is a blessing from Allah! The reduction of import tariffs to zero per cent is a blessing from Allah!

He continued with this line of reasoning, proclaiming that global competition was the effect of godly intervention that sought greater corporate efficiency and productivity:

> Achieving our potential is not only dependent on the government. In fact, we are ready to compete with the outside world! The way things are going in Indonesia and with international competition –

this is what Allah has confronted us with ... Allah wants to prove to every level of the company that we have entered the global era (*kita masuk era global*) and that we are able to compete.

The free market was represented not as a matter of global economic restructuring, but rather as a divine challenge, whereby problems were posed in explicitly religious terms and enhanced Islamic practice was invoked as the means to their resolution.

This message resonated profoundly with Krakatau Steel employees. Hadi, an operator in the hot strip mill, supported ESQ because it offered tools to address the challenge presented by the free market. He said, 'ESQ can raise the human resources. It shows how bad waste and cheating are. The employees will become aware (*jadi sadar*) that Allah doesn't like waste and loss. We must work honestly (*tulus*). With ESQ the employees will become aware (*sadar*) and work motivation will be increased'.

Furthermore, Ary Ginanjar's message that individual fate was part of a divine plan led some employees to see ESQ as a means to resolve obstacles to the privatization of Krakatau Steel. Eliani, who worked in the human resources department and was one of the company's small number of female employees, conveyed this point. She was an active participant in ESQ training programmes. In one session that I observed, she conducted what the trainers referred to as 'sharing'. This was a kind of personal audit in which a participant tearfully repented for past misdeeds or impious actions in order to elicit similar existential introspection from other employees. In her words, it was a chance to 'describe one's religious experience in a collective setting ... It is a form of self-evaluation and introspection'. She said that many employees were scared of privatization because they thought it would mean massive job losses, but ESQ offered a means to confront these fears. Plans were afoot to divest state ownership of the company, either through a strategic sale to a foreign investor or via a public offering through the stock market. Eliani said that, in light of this impending privatization,

the mentality must be different. People must be prepared to be fired! This means changing the mindset ... In state-owned companies, employees think that they can depend on the company for a long time. It is safe, people can wait around for their pension ... ESQ prepares people to face changes, so they will not be afraid (*tidak takut*).

Thus, employees in the human resources department hoped that Islamic spiritual reform would encourage employees to accept the transition from the stability of state guarantees to the uncertainty of the market.

Proponents of spiritual reform saw spirituality as something located within participants. The market, on the other hand, was conceived of as something external to both participants and the boundaries of the nation. Market Islam breaks these boundaries by representing individual religious practice as directly tied to corporate success in the free market. This point was made by Aris, who worked in the hot strip mill. He stressed that ESQ was successful because it encouraged people to improve themselves, rather than forcing them to act in certain ways. He told me that the training was intended to 'make people better from the inside ... to give us a sense of where we are from and where we are going'. He then stressed that ESQ was not about setting up a set of rules to obey, but rather created a system that elicited certain forms of behaviour from participants, a point that was also reiterated by Rinaldi Agusyana (see below). Aris said 'there is no regulation and no force' involved in the training, thus emphasizing the way in which employees see the training, largely because it is represented as religious, as something that they are doing for themselves, rather than something that others are doing to them. After all, commitment to Islam is taken as a personal decision requiring individual piety. The relationship is between God and an individual, with no intermediaries. Participants in spiritual reform found this compelling because they saw it as a manifestation of the outside world conforming to Islam rather than the religion succumbing to outside forces.

Fauzi, the senior manager quoted earlier, spoke enthusiastically about the benefits of ESQ. Unprompted, he told me that 'ESQ is one of the best methods that Krakatau Steel had for improving the quality of its human resources' because it enhanced 'loyalty, honesty, discipline, and productivity' and reduced corruption. He said that it was effective because it reminds employees that 'they will die and they need to prepare for the afterlife'. I asked him why ESQ was necessary to ensure honesty and prevent corruption, given that Krakatau Steel had an internal audit department responsible for ensuring that company business was conducted transparently. He said that ESQ was superior to company audits as a means of reducing corruption because it trained employees to monitor themselves, rather than relying on company employees to scrutinize the actions of other employees. Thus, spiritual reformers and managers had recast the problem of development as a matter of cultivating the individual ethics inherent in a familiar tradition. It was no longer solely a question of acquiring external knowledge and technology.

From civil to market Islam

Market Islam emerges in response to a specific set of moral, political, and economic challenges. In contrast to the active role in democratic reform that has been played by Islamic groups like those described by Hefner, proponents of ESQ present themselves as explicitly non-political. Ary Ginanjar and his brother Rinaldi eschewed any connection to party politics and Islamic social organizations like Nahdlatul Ulama (NU) and Muhammadiyah that increasingly served as the bases for political campaigns in the post-New Order period. Unlike the leaders of NU and Muhammidiyah, who used their vast networks as springboards to enter party politics, Ary Ginanjar viewed participation in political activity as a possible threat to his religious credentials and thought that it would only make ESQ look opportunistic. He and Rinaldi adamantly insisted that ESQ was 'non-political', perhaps also fearing that engaging in party politics would present a threat to their lucrative franchise.

Their hesitation at being involved in political activity reflected the widely held sentiment in Indonesia that religion and politics should be kept separate. This orientation was often expressed by employees of Krakatau Steel, who were deeply suspicious of religious scholars (*kiyai*[15]) who got involved in politics. One operator in the direct reduction plant said that he supported 'religion in politics, but not politics in religion'. Thus, although he approved of *syariah* law (i.e. that based on Islamic principles), he did not believe that religious figures should enter politics. He explained that the activities of a politician were incongruous with those of a religious figure who, he thought should 'calm the *umma* (global community of Muslims), motivate worship, and promote a peaceful environment' (*menentramkan umat, motivasi ibadah, dan menyampaikan lingkungan damai*). Political leaders, in contrast, might inflame the passions of the 'masses' (*massa*) with incendiary pronouncements and fiery rhetoric.

ESQ and other movements for spiritual reform in contemporary Indonesia have emerged alongside of, but separately from, those groups that Hefner views as characteristic of civil Islam. Hefner described this form of Islam as 'a public culture' that

> depends on mediating institutions in which citizens develop habits of free speech, participation, and toleration. In all this, they say, there is nothing undemocratic about Muslim voluntary associations (as well as those of other religions) playing a role in the *public* life of civil society as well as in personal ethics (2000: 13, original emphasis).

While the groups described by Hefner fall into this category, movements for spiritual reform active in state-owned enterprises, private corporations, and government bureaucracies in contemporary Indonesia represent a different phenomenon. Democratization has enabled freer rein for groups like ESQ, but these groups are not necessarily interested in achieving broad social transformation through party politics or direct advocacy. They are not concerned with questions of human rights, social justice, or political liberalism: those who represent Islam as holding the key to economic success are, in general, not outspoken advocates for democracy.[16] Thus, their representations of reform do not necessarily align with those groups involved in developing civil society. Rather, their primary objective is to enhance Islamic practice as a means of improving Indonesia's economic performance and competitiveness. The medium through which they do so is the market, by offering Islam-inflected training programmes and selling a wide-range of books, videos, and manuals that offer advice on how to live as a Muslim in an increasingly global, free market.

However, market Islam does not only refer to the fact that the market enables new forms of Islamic practice. It also refers to the ways in which enhanced Islamic practice is designed to address the challenges presented by the free market. Market Islam instils religious practices seen as conducive to market-orientated reforms. The elimination of generous state subsidies and a domestic steel market protected by tariffs led Krakatau Steel to implement Islamic spiritual reform as a means of producing steel producers fit for international competition. Further, market Islam involves designing a form of Muslim practice commensurate with the goals of eliminating corruption, promoting privatization, and enhancing productivity in an increasingly global market. In looking for analogues between Islamic spiritual reform movements and the classic texts of Western social science, the point of reference is not so much Tocqueville's *Democracy in America* (Tocqueville 1990 [1835]) (as it is for civil Islam), but rather Weber's *Protestant ethic* (Weber 1990 [1905]). ESQ reconfigured work as a divine calling rather than forming a civic association that could further democratic reform. At other ESQ trainings that I observed away from Krakatau Steel, many participants sought to develop their own business networks and investment opportunities, in addition to enhancing their faith. Spiritual reform is surely producing new collectivities. However, these are not the kind of collectivities that necessarily constitute a democratic public culture.

Even in domains where market and civil Islam appear to converge, there are important differences. Proponents of civil Islam reject Islamic law based on maintaining a division between state and society in which religion is restricted from the former and consigned to the latter. Like politically liberal Muslims, those enmeshed in market Islam steadfastly reject efforts to implement uniform Islamic *syariah* law in Indonesia. However, the terms which those who are creating market Islam criticize *syariah* are different from the terms that Hefner's civil Muslims use. They do so on ethical rather than political grounds. Market Islam does not reject *syariah* law out of a fear of protecting religion from the state, but rather on the grounds that religious practice is a matter of individual initiative. Thus, adherents of ESQ resolutely affirmed the notion that individuals must choose Islam, not have it imposed on them.

To advocates of market Islam, Indonesia's recent history reveals the inevitable failure of the use of force to implement Islamic principles. The authoritarian, hierarchical Suharto regime governed through violence (or the threat of violence) and its collapse was invoked as evidence of the failure of such approaches. In contrast to other groups in contemporary Indonesia like Hizbut Tahrir that advocate state enforcement of *syariah* law, the proponents of spiritual reform saw such efforts as doomed to failure.

Rinaldi specifically contrasted the ESQ spiritual training programme with initiatives dedicated towards the implementation of *syariah* law. He told me that participants in ESQ were not being indoctrinated in a system of 'more rules'. He said 'we already have enough rules ... but if you touch them here, in the heart, they don't need rules. They won't accept commission even without more rules'. Thus, forming a subject conducive to the norms of the free market was not something that Rinaldi thought could be approached through external regulation. Rinaldi here evokes similar principles to those to which I referred earlier, such as Aris's idea that ESQ makes people 'better from the inside'. Spiritual reform seeks to elicit a new ethical subject who governs him- or herself in accordance with religious norms that are conceived of as internal to the subject, not because of external compulsion.

The failure of external compulsion to elicit desired ethical dispositions was reiterated during ESQ, which advocated self-surveillance. On the morning of the first day of training Rinaldi asked the audience rhetorically, 'Is there a method to make someone honest?' He answered the question himself, suggesting that 'rules, regulations, standard operating procedures, and more supervisors (*pengawas*)' would not ensure integrity. Rinaldi spoke about the futility of merely multiplying forms of surveillance. He said:

> Supervision keeps a close eye. For every unit, surely there is a supervisory committee, but how about the supervisor? They too must be supervised, of course! So a supervisory board for the supervisory board – even administrators must be supervised, of course! So you have a supervisory committee for the supervisory committee of the supervisory committee, and it goes on. Until when?

Thus, the problem of non-sovereign forms of power in which there is no position external to the operations of power is the central problem of ESQ training. Corruption, inefficiency, and indolence are the objects of intervention, but spiritual reformers recognize the inability of regulations and coercion to eliminate such behaviour.

Market Islam has emerged alongside civil Islam in contemporary Indonesia. The project of producing workers for the free market presents a different solution to the perceived oppositions between Islam and modernity. Proponents of spiritual reform accept a distinction between religious and political spheres. At the same time, however, they argue that a historical separation between religious and economic spheres is directly responsible for Indonesia's crisis. Whereas civil Islam demonstrates affinities between Islam and democracy, market Islam illuminates efforts to resolve the tension between Islam and capitalism. Market Islam captures efforts to design a self-regulating subject who 'worships through work'. The extent to which this is commensurable with the subject of civil Islam is an open question, but the possibility of their overlap suggests the ongoing problem of the entanglement of democracy and capitalism in the contemporary world.

Conclusion

Islam has long been linked to the expansion of trade in Southeast Asia; however, market Islam captures a different manifestation of this articulation. According to prevailing historical interpretations, traders from the Indian subcontinent and the Arabian peninsula spread Islam through the region as early as the thirteenth century (Azra 2004; Reid 1993). In these accounts the extension of Islamic ethics was facilitated through market relations. In contrast, market Islam captures the dissemination of a market ethic through Islam. Market Islam refers to the way in which spiritual reformers work to mobilize Muslim ethics to meet the challenges of the free market, yielding Islamic practices conducive to economic liberalization. In this articulation, the free market was represented as a divine test. Enhanced Islamic practice was the means to address it. Further, the prospect of the elimination of guaranteed employment was given religious justification. By introducing a programme of spiritual training grounded in moderate Islam, managers and self-styled spiritual reformers sought to create a set of practices that resembled those that Nikolas Rose and others have identified as characteristic of neoliberalism (Barry, Osborne & Rose 1996; Rose 1999). They sought to create a responsible, accountable, self-managing subject who acted according to the norms of the free market.

During my fieldwork there was a pervasive sense that the political and economic crisis afflicting Indonesia was the result of a deeper moral crisis. However, representations of these problems in the media – the decline of the country's currency, political instability, corruption, and a volatile economy – were abstract insofar as there was not much that individuals could do to resolve them. They appeared distant from the everyday lives of many Indonesians. Connecting these abstract problems to individual practices made them more comprehensible to contemporary Indonesians. An intensification of individual religious practice was a way through which individuals could address problems that otherwise appeared removed.

Those who presented political and economic problems as a moral and religious crisis argued that the challenges that the country faced were not the result of abstract forces affecting Indonesia from the outside, but rather effects of the individual ethical practices of the nation's citizens. Thus, Indonesian Muslims, by enhancing their religious practice, could solve these problems. These efforts, referred to as spiritual reform, sought to produce a workforce capable of competing globally by investing everyday practices with what were represented as Islamic ethics. Proponents of spiritual reform specifically emphasized honesty, self-discipline, accountability, and considering work a form of worship. Market Islam simultaneously draws on immersion in an Islamic discursive tradition, calculating economic rationality, and instilling principles and practices of self-management. While market Islam is commensurable with both capitalism and Islam, it is reducible to neither.

The methodological approach used in this chapter builds on recent approaches to dissolve the boundary between anthropological theory and the empirical material that anthropologists encounter during fieldwork. This choice of approach enabled me to avoid making an artificial split between anthropological theory and method (and observation and participation). Thus, this chapter works reflexively between anthropological knowledge and the perspectives of the Indonesian participants that I endeavour to accurately reproduce. My questions are not so much dedicated to uncovering what kind of definitive statements social science can make about their social world. Rather, I show what the implications of the models encountered in the field are for anthropological thought regarding religion and political economy today. I use the models and theories developed by spiritual reformers to reflect back on concepts like civil Islam and 'Islam de marché'. Thus, I focus on the practical models that prominent Indonesians have developed to address what they perceive as some of the greatest challenges that they face. Market Islam dissolves the distinction between theory and the empirical world by showing how spiritual reformers in contemporary Indonesia are developing sophisticated models and theories to address the challenges presented by the free market.

Just as I have sought to dissolve the boundaries of anthropological theory and the empirical material I encountered during fieldwork, the project of producing workers for the free market creates an assemblage that breaks the boundaries that were constitutive of Indonesian modernity. The corporate managers and spiritual reformers who sought to mobilize Islam to enhance the ability of Indonesian firms to compete in an increasingly global economy want to 'break the boundary between the inside and the outside'. ESQ introduced examples from the life of the Prophet Muhammad and represented forms of Islamic practice to show how Islam was compatible with modern life and labour in a vast corporation. Breaking the boundary does not involve seeking to conserve tradition in the face of modernity, but reinvents it in order to meet new challenges. The boundaries ruptured in this reinvention are numerous. One is the boundary between religion and economic development, once seen as a cornerstone of secular modernization. Another is the boundary between Indonesia and the outside world, which was assumed under the programme of nationalist development. A third is the boundary between the individual and the corporation, as spiritual reformers assert that individual interest in personal salvation is merged with corporate success. By breaking these boundaries, spiritual reformers seek to form a new subject capable of the kind of self-government conducive to development in new conditions of economic crisis and transformation.

ACKNOWLEDGMENTS

I would like to recognize the generosity of Krakatau Steel employees who tolerated my queries between 2003 and 2005. I regret that in order to ensure their anonymity I am not able to thank them individually by name. I also thank Ary Ginanjar, Rinaldi Agusyana, and the rest of their staff from the ESQ Leadership Center for patiently addressing my entreaties. Filippo Osella, Benjamin Soares, and two anonymous reviewers provided insightful comments and careful readings of this chapter, greatly improving the final draft. A faculty fellowship at the Centre for Studies in Religion and Society at the University of Victoria enabled me to revise the chapter. I am also grateful for the engaged responses I received from members of the Center regarding my main arguments. Of course, any errors of representation or interpretation are my own. Research for the chapter was enabled with material support from the International Dissertation Research Fellowship Program of the Social Science Research Council, the Wenner-Gren Foundation for Anthropological Research, the University of California's Pacific Rim Research Program, and Fulbright-Hays.

NOTES

[1] With the exception of public figures, I have followed anthropological practice and used pseudonyms to conceal the identities of all individuals referred to directly in this chapter.

[2] This is chapter 102 of the Qur'an.

[3] This is chapter 103 of the Qur'an.

[4] Recently, however, anthropologists have begun to address this articulation (Maurer 2005; 2006; Otayek & Soares 2007; Sloane 1999).

[5] I have used this approach to explain other phenomena in contemporary Indonesia (Rudnyckyj 2004).

[6] I began to formulate the notion of market Islam while writing my dissertation (Rudnyckyj 2006) and only became aware of Haenni's work in Egypt while composing this chapter. While 'Islam de marché' could be translated into English as market Islam, the respective analytical stances towards similar research objects differs significantly. Commensurate with the methodological stance put forward in this chapter, I contend that the language in which one articulates a concept affects its meaning.

[7] In 2004 China, Japan, and Korea were ranked first, second, and fifth in steel production with a combined output of almost 450 million tons per year. Krakatau Steel produced about 2.5 million tons per year.

[8] These practices resembled the earlier pattern of *hulu-hilir* trade in Southeast Asia in which sultans profited from trade by virtue of their position, not by producing or adding value to commodities (Bronson 1977). This provided the economic underpinnings for early Southeast Asian states. Prior to and after European contact, sultans in Sumatra and on the Malay peninsula controlled the points where river systems met the sea and taxed both upstream and downstream trade. Joseph Conrad supplements Bronson's functionalist account with a vivid account of the conflicts precipitated by this system of political organization in *Lord Jim* (Conrad 1900).

[9] For more details on these training sessions, see Rudnyckyj (2008; 2009).

[10] *Maghrib* is the first evening prayer for Muslims and occurs at sundown. It is a particularly important prayer for employees of Krakatau Steel because it represents the end of the workday for non-shift employees. Departing work for home before *maghrib* sometimes served as a justification for leaving work early 'in time for prayers'.

[11] This is a re-enactment of Hagar's search for water, before Allah revealed the well of Zamzam to her.

[12] The stoning of *jamrat al-aqabah* takes place in Mina just outside of Mecca and physically enacts rebuking the devil. The ritual involves hurling the pebbles at three pillars, which represent the devil. The pillars are three different representations of the devil: the first and largest is where he tempted Abraham against sacrificing Ishmael; the second is where he tempted Abraham's wife Hagar to induce her to stop him; and the third is where he tempted Ishmael to avoid being sacrificed. He was rebuked each time, and the throwing of the stones symbolizes those rejections.

[13] Among other sources, he borrowed ideas and practices from business management and life-coaching sessions such as *The seven habits of highly effective people*, which have greatly expanded in North America, Europe, and Asia in recent decades (Thrift 1998; 1999).

[14] As of early 2009 the three Indonesian provinces with no ESQ presence were Gorontalo, Maluku Utara, and Nusa Tenggara Timur. These are among the poorest and least developed provinces in Indonesia.

[15] A *kiyai* is a learned scholar of Islam who is the leader of an Islamic boarding school (*pesantren*).

[16] This is not to say that they are critical of Indonesia's fledgeling democratization. Rather, it shows that there are multiple ways in which Islam intersects with the institutions characteristic of modernity in Indonesia.

REFERENCES

ALATAS, S.H. 1963. The Weber thesis and South East Asia. *Archives de Sociologie des Religions* **15**, 21-34.

ASAD, T. 1986. *The idea of an anthropology of Islam*. Washington, D.C.: Center for Contemporary Arab Studies.

AZRA, A. 2004. *The origins of Islamic reformism in Southeast Asia: networks of Malay-Indonesian and Middle Eastern 'Ulama' in the seventeenth and eighteenth centuries*. Honolulu: University of Hawai'i Press.

BARRY, A., T. OSBORNE & N.S. ROSE 1996. *Foucault and political reason: liberalism, neo-liberalism and rationalities of government*. Chicago: University Press.

BOELLSTORFF, T. 2003. Dubbing culture: Indonesian *gay* and *lesbi* subjectivities and ethnography in an already globalized world. *American Ethnologist* **30**, 225-42.

BOYER, D. 2001. Foucault in the bush: the social life of post-structuralist theory in East Berlin's Prenzlauer Berg. *Ethnos* **66**, 207-36.

BRONSON, B. 1977. Exchange at the upstream and downstream ends: notes toward a functional model of the coastal state in Southeast Asia. In *Economic exchange and social interaction in Southeast Asia* (ed.) K. Hutterer, 39-52. Ann Arbor, MI: SEAS Program.

COLEMAN, S. 2000. *The globalisation of charismatic Christianity: spreading the gospel of prosperity*. Cambridge: University Press.

CONRAD, J. 1900. *Lord Jim*. Edinburgh: William Blackwood and Sons.

FERGUSON, J. 1999. *Expectations of modernity: myths and meanings of urban life on the Zambian Copperbelt*. Berkeley: University of California Press.

GEERTZ, C. 1960. *The religion of Java*. Glencoe, Ill.: Free Press.

——— 1963. *Peddlers and princes: social change and economic modernization in two Indonesian towns.* Chicago: University Press.

HAENNI, P. 2005. *L'islam de marché: l'autre révolution conservatrice.* Paris: Seuil.

HAMID, A. 2006. Ary Ginanjar terpilih sebagai salah satu dewan pakar ICMI (Ary Ginanjar selected to the ICMI board of experts), 14 February (available on-line: *http://www.icmi.or.id/ind/content/view/366/64/*, accessed 22 January 2009).

HEFNER, R.W. 2000. *Civil Islam: Muslims and democratization in Indonesia.* Princeton: University Press.

HIRSCHKIND, C. 2001. Civic virtue and religious reason: an Islamic counterpublic. *Cultural Anthropology* **16**, 3-34.

HOESTEREY, J. 2008. Marketing morality: the rise, fall and rebranding of Aa Gym. In *Expressing Islam: religious life and politics in Indonesia* (eds) G. Fealy & S. White, 95-112. Singapore: Institute of Southeast Asian Studies.

JACKSON, P. 1999. Royal spirits, Chinese gods and magic monks: Thailand's boom-time religions of prosperity. *Southeast Asia Research* **7**, 245-320.

MAURER, B. 2002. Anthropological and accounting knowledge in Islamic banking and finance: rethinking critical accounts. *Journal of the Royal Anthropological Institute* (N.S.) **8**, 645-67.

——— 2005. *Mutual life, limited: Islamic banking, alternative currencies, lateral reason.* Princeton: University Press.

——— 2006. *Pious property: Islamic mortgages in the United States.* New York: Russell Sage Foundation.

MIYAZAKI, H. 2004. *The method of hope: anthropology, philosophy, and Fijian knowledge.* Stanford: University Press.

NOER, D. 1973. *The modernist Muslim movement in Indonesia, 1900-1942.* Singapore: Oxford University Press.

ONG, A. 1990. State versus Islam: Malay families, women's bodies, and the body politic in Malaysia. *American Ethnologist* **17**, 258-76.

——— & S.J. COLLIER. 2005. *Global assemblages: technology, politics, and ethics as anthropological problems.* Malden, Mass.: Blackwell.

OTAYEK, R. & B.F. SOARES 2007. Introduction: Islam and Muslim politics in Africa. In *Islam and Muslim politics in Africa* (eds) B.F. Soares & R. Otayek, 1-23. New York: Palgrave Macmillan.

OTHMAN, N. 2003. Islamization and democratization in Malaysia in regional and global contexts. In *Challenging authoritarianism in Southeast Asia: comparing Indonesia and Malaysia* (eds) A. Heryanto & S. Mandal, 117-44. London: Routledge Curzon.

PEACOCK, J.L. 1978. *Muslim puritans: reformist psychology in Southeast Asian Islam.* Berkeley: University of California Press.

PELETZ, M.G. 2002. *Islamic modern: religious courts and cultural politics in Malaysia.* Princeton: University Press.

REID, A. 1993. Islamization and Christianization in Southeast Asia: the critical phase, 1550-1650. In *Southeast Asia in the early modern era: trade, power, and belief* (ed.) A. Reid, 151-79. Ithaca, N.Y.: Cornell University Press.

RILES, A. 2000. *The network inside out.* Ann Arbor: University of Michigan Press.

ROSE, N.S. 1999. *Powers of freedom: reframing political thought.* Cambridge: University Press.

RUDNYCKYJ, D. 2004. Technologies of servitude: governmentality and Indonesian transnational labor migration. *Anthropological Quarterly* **77**, 407-34.

——— 2006. Islamic ethics and spiritual economy in contemporary Indonesia. Ph.D. dissertation, University of California, Berkeley.

——— 2008. Worshipping work: producing commodity producers in contemporary Indonesia. In *Taking Southeast Asia to market: commodities, nature, and people in the neoliberal age* (eds) N.L. Peluso & J. Nevins, 73-89. Ithaca, N.Y.: Cornell University Press.

——— 2009. Spiritual economies: Islam and neoliberalism in contemporary Indonesia. *Cultural Anthropology* **24**, 104-41.

SLOANE, P. 1999. *Islam, modernity, and entrepreneurship among the Malays.* New York: St Martin's Press.

THRIFT, N. 1998. The rise of soft capitalism. In *An unruly world? Globalisation, governance and geography* (eds) A. Herod, G.Ó Tuathail & S. Roberts, 25-71. London: Routledge.

——— 1999. The globalisation of the system of business knowledge. In *Globalisation and the Asia Pacific: contested territories* (eds) K. Olds, P. Dicken, P.F. Kelly, L. Kong & H.W.-C. Yeung, 57-71. London: Routledge.

TOCQUEVILLE, A. DE 1990 [1835]. *Democracy in America* (trans. H. Reeve). New York: Vintage.

WATSON, C.W. 2005. A popular Indonesian preacher: the significance of Aa Gymnastiar. *Journal of the Royal Anthropological Institute* (N.S.) **11**, 773-92.

Weber, M. 1990 [1905]. *The Protestant ethic and the spirit of capitalism* (trans. T. Parsons). London: Unwin Hyman.

Wiegele, K.L. 2005. *Investing in miracles: El Shaddai and the transformation of popular Catholicism in the Philippines*. Honolulu: University of Hawai'i Press.

Wise, L. 2003. 'Words from the heart': New forms of Islamic preaching in Egypt. Master's thesis, Oxford University.

12

Muslim entrepreneurs in public life between India and the Gulf: making good and doing good

FILIPPO OSELLA *University of Sussex*
CAROLINE OSELLA *School of Oriental and African Studies*

While historians have written extensively about the participation of elites in processes of social and religious reform in late colonial India (see, e.g., Gupta 2002; Joshi 2001; Robinson 1993 [1974]; Walsh 2004; cf. Sharma 2001), the role of contemporary elites has been largely neglected (Fuller & Narasimhan 2007; 2008; Harriss 2003 are exceptions).[1] Meanwhile, analyses of contemporary Muslim politics focus on phenomena such as 'political Islam' (e.g. Eickelman & Piscatori 1996; Roy 1996), private/public piety (e.g. Deeb 2006; Hirschkind 2006; Mahmood 2005), or Muslim 'public spheres' (e.g. Salvatore & Eickelman 2003; Salvatore & LeVine 2005), with little attention paid to articulations between politico-religious orientations and economic practice in the production of contemporary Muslim subjectivities (exceptions are Hefner 1998; Rudnyckyj 2009; this volume; Sloane 1999; Soares 2005).

We are engaged in exploring relationships between Islamic reformism and contemporary forms of capital accumulation in Kerala, at India's southwestern coast. We discuss ways in which reformist Islam is invoked to encourage participation in practices named in current literature as 'neoliberal', global capitalism. At the same time, we suggest that the economic environment constitutes the ground against which contemporary reformist religious discourse seeking to transform Muslim selves is articulated, discussed, taken up, or contested.

A small group of very wealthy male entrepreneurs' lives are intertwined through friendships, business interests, marriage links, and high-profile public involvement with Muslim community life. They stand at the forefront of India's post-liberalization economy – sharp innovators who have adopted the business and labour practices of global capitalism in both Kerala and the Gulf.[2] Embodying the dream of success, these entrepreneurs are recognized as 'community leaders'. Self-avowedly concerned with the *'upliftment'* of Kerala's Muslim community, they are involved in community associations, orphanages, schools, trade organizations, and everyday politics. Their orientation towards 'reform' is intimately enmeshed, on the one hand, with an effort to produce a

'Muslim modernity' (where the main referents are the Gulf and, more recently, Malaysia and Indonesia), and, on the other, with business interests. In Kerala, education remains the yardstick by which *progress* is measured and imagined.[3] Jeffrey, Jeffery, and Jeffery (2008) remind us that 'education' in India is an over-determined marker of 'development'. It is by cultivating themselves as enlightened educationalists and by promoting 'modern education' that contemporary entrepreneurs inscribe their specific business interests and practices into rhetorics of the 'common good', eventually legitimizing wider claims to leadership.

The role of Kerala's elites in reform is neither unusual nor recent (F. Osella & C. Osella 2000). Among Muslims (as in other communities), early twentieth-century orientations towards socio-religious reform, modernization, and 'progress' found support especially amongst the educated property-owning classes, who become drawn towards a growing reformist *'ulama* (religious scholars) (Abdul Haque 1982; Miller 1992 [1976]; F. Osella & C. Osella 2008; Samad 1998; Sikand 2005). Similarly to Lebanese Shi'is (Deeb 2006), Kerala's turn-of-the century middle-class Muslims made themselves 'modern' through a generalized distancing from 'tradition', be that social, economic or religious. Reformists' success undoubtedly comes down to their ability to join forces with the wider modernizing middle class on a platform of socio-religious reforms, producing a confluence of orientations towards 'community progress' which coalesce around a perceived fundamental need for 'modern education' – with considerable slippage between ideas of 'education' as reformism, modernized morality, technocratic qualifications, and civilizing process. Kerala reformism produces itself on the ground both through practice and through dialogue with significant others, Muslim and non-Muslim alike, giving it a particularly 'progressive' flavour (see F. Osella & C. Osella 2008; Sikand 2005). While reformists[4] have only 10 per cent of Kerala's Muslim population formally affiliated as followers, they – especially Kerala's Naduvathul Mujahideen (KNM) – have set the wider agenda. Nowadays all Kerala Muslims support moderate reform – from education, business, and employment, to family life and everyday sociality: for the sake of community 'progress'; to compete with Kerala Hindus and Christians; to be self-reliant in the face of a state dominated by or host to unsympathetic Hindu revivalist parties (F. Osella & C. Osella 2008).

Coming to prominence in the wake of post-1970s Gulf migration and post-1991 economic liberalization, the entrepreneurs we discuss are committed to a 'moderate' modernizing Islam which is neither over-critical of 'traditionalism' nor openly supportive of (organized) Islamic reformism. Their keen promotion of community development projects and their very public participation in charitable activities brings to mind the early twentieth-century shift from religious gift-giving to modern forms of charity which underscored North Indian entrepreneurs' successful participation in the colonial economy (Bayly 1983; Haynes 1987; Palsetia 2005). In South India, religious endowments and gift-giving are a time-honoured means for the production and reproduction of status and political leadership (see, e.g., De Neve 2000; Mines 1994; Mosse 2003; F. Osella & C. Osella 2000: 200ff.; Price 1996; Rudner 1987). While in the name of 'Muslim unity' they show allegiance to the Muslim League[5] – with which they maintain relationships of reciprocal patronage – they are seldom interested in political office. This caution could be read as the pragmatism of traders and entrepreneurs who hedge their bets in order to forward business regardless of political circumstances. One might also argue that public-sphere activity is anyway essential for entrepreneurs, who need to garner goodwill among both the wider community and politicians.

Indeed, accusations of self-interested instrumentalism – of using charity as a means of enhancing prestige, extending patronage, and eventually forwarding economic interests – are routinely made by detractors in response to these men's public interventions. Emerging from the aesthetics of cynicism popularly deployed in Kerala to scrutinize the morality of participants in public life (see C. Osella & F. Osella 2000: 154ff.; cf. Waggoner 2005), such accusations cannot be simply dismissed as malicious gossip. But it is also apparent that these men are not merely hard-nosed profiteers callously exploiting popular religiosity for their own ends. Many Kerala observers consider entrepreneurs' involvement in community development as expressions of genuine piety arising from dual concerns over the fate of fellow Muslims and their own afterlife. Entrepreneurs themselves talk about their 'social mindedness' as a combination of piety and economic calculation, in their minds the two clearly not excluding, but actually reinforcing, each other. After all, they often reminded us, how could one help the poor and needy – or the community as a whole – without money?

These entrepreneurs strive to live moral lives, beyond simple observance of religious obligations: as wealthy Muslims, they do feel responsible to the community as a whole and they are committed to its progress. Their preoccupations with making and using money in a 'correctly Islamic way', and their interest in how to shift their entire community away from practices or lifestyles considered 'backward' and towards modern (conscious) Islam, bring these Muslim businessmen close to the Malay entrepreneurs discussed by Sloane (1999).[6] Writing about Malaysia, Sloane (1999) notes that when it comes to questions of business ethics and spending, Malaysian entrepreneurs frame their activities within an Islamic framework concerned with morality, with making money ethically, and with helping everyone to benefit. Sloane argues that networks of information and mutual help, the continual search for synergy and 'win-win' situations, and the wise use of profit in socially responsible ways, all mark out Malay business style. At the same time, Rudnyckyj (2009; this volume) discusses, via a notion of 'spiritual economies', ways in which Islamic ethics have become part of management practices in an Indonesian steel plant. These ethnographies are deeply resonant here: entrepreneurship – combining material success with moral connectedness – is coming to be seen as the exemplary contemporary way of being a modern, moral, Muslim.

One might cynically argue that, since Muslims are bounden to give *zakat*, the donations of the rich to worthy causes are no cause for comment, being simply within the bounds of mere obligation (Kuran 2006: 19ff., 41ff.; Tripp 2006: 24ff; cf. Kozlowski 1985; A. Singer 2005). But instrumentalist arguments cannot adequately explain the amount of time and money which Muslim entrepreneurs put into innumerable 'social' projects, nor would they account for why actual and considerably energetic public activity rather than mere donation is adopted (for a critique of instrumentalist analysis, see Deeb this volume; Metcalf 1976; Robinson 1993 [1974]). But we are also dissatisfied with recent studies which, we feel, suggest a uniqueness to Muslim religious-moral experience, thereby at once exceptionalizing Islam among religions, and also setting organized pietism as a uniquely 'Muslim' way – perhaps the only Muslim way – to be modern (e.g. Deeb 2006; Hirschkind 2006; Mahmood 2005). We prefer to explore the lived complexity and multi-layered forms of political engagement within contemporary Muslim communities, a framework which better allows for appreciation of contradictions and plurality of interests, glossed over or dismissed as insignificant in many accounts of contemporary pietism, where coherence of subject and action are privileged (see Bayat 2007; Marsden 2005; this volume; Schielke this volume).

As in Sloane's and Rudnyckyj's cases, Kerala Muslim entrepreneurs seek ways of framing their business practices within frameworks of ethics and moral responsibilities deemed to be Islamic, and they are also committed towards re-orientating local Muslim subjectivities and practices towards the requirements of contemporary capitalism. Promotion of wholesale self-transformation through education, rationalization of practices, and goal-orientated planning in daily life (expressed locally in notions of 'systematic life') – all of which is acquiring wider currency with reformism – is mobilized to sustain novel forms of capital(ist) accumulation. This apparent appropriation of religious values for economic ends is possible, we argue, because the 'morality of political economy' and the 'political economy of morality' – to use Marx's words (Marx 1964: 173) – here neither denote competing socio-cultural orientations towards economic practice (see, e.g., Scott 1976; Gudeman & Rivera 1990), nor do they stand for different forms of reproduction pitting individual and societal interests against each other (e.g. Bloch & Parry 1989). On the contrary, attempts to harness the possibilities offered by the colonial and post-colonial economy and to master the dispositions underpinning a successful engagement with capitalism have been constitutive of projects of self-fashioning cultivated by Kerala Islamic reformism since the early twentieth century (F. Osella & C. Osella 2008; cf. Rudnyckyj 2009; this volume; Tripp 2006). Economic success via business, entrepreneurship, or professions – made possible by the adoption of a 'systematic' orientation – underpins community-wide projects of self-transformation and takes on the connotation of a virtuous act which produces and expresses a sense of the self as a *'proper' Muslim* – in Islamic reformists' terms (cf. Bornstein 2005; Coleman 2000; Gifford 2004 on relations between economic practice and evangelical Christianity; see also Laidlaw 1995). We argue, then, for a convergence between differently grounded processes of subjectification, produced within neoliberal capitalism and Kerala Islamic reformism, respectively, thence underscored and articulated by a shared preoccupation with 'education' as the privileged site for the production of modern *and* Islamic subjects. And it is because of this convergence that the businessmen we discuss – perceived as embodiments of Muslims' dual goal of economic success and piety – are then expected to provide leadership to the community and can then legitimately attempt to translate their economic clout into claims to political authority.

Muslim entrepreneurs

We meet PV in Nilambur, a small hill town in north Kerala famous for colonial teak plantations. He left here as a young man in the 1970s to seek his fortune in the Gulf and from modest beginnings built up a thriving business empire in the United Arab Emirates, including a major company providing maintenance and supply of tools for the oil industry, warehousing and shipping, franchises of Euro-American industrial vehicles, and so on. Unlike many Malayali Gulf entrepreneurs, PV has never been shy of investing in Kerala, famous – or notorious – for buying loss-making companies and restructuring them into competitive businesses. His money and clout were also crucial for the construction of Kozhikode's airport.

PV enjoys a reputation as a 'people's man': he has brought hundreds of people to the Gulf and is always ready 'to help out'. When we arrive for our meeting, we find a crowd of people, and as we walk together, PV stops to listen to the pleas of two elderly women – one Hindu and one Muslim – to whom he readily gives Rs 500 (around £8.50) each, two crisp notes taken from a fat wallet. When one woman keeps following him, PV soon gets annoyed. 'You had 500 rupees', he hisses to her. 'What else do you want?'

Sitting behind the director's desk of the private residential school – which he has built along the lines of the famous British-style private schools of colonial 'hill stations' – PV is not shy to talk about his 'humble origins'. His is an exceptional 'rags-to-riches' tale, known to all Malabar Muslims and part of Kerala's Gulf migration mythology. His story exemplifies the resilience and entrepreneurship of Malabar's Muslims, who, in the span of thirty years, have reversed their economic fortunes through Gulf migration. It also evokes rhetorics of brotherhood and mutual help deemed to be central to Islam and characteristic of Muslims: PV benefited from the trust and goodwill of Arab Gulf Muslims; in turn he actively helps his Muslim brethren in Kerala. Admirers say that PV's philanthropic orientation springs from his modest origins, which enable him to empathize with 'the problems of ordinary people'.

Fidgeting with his not-so-ordinary platinum diamond-encrusted wristwatch, PV recounts, 'I grew up [financially] with the growth of Dubai, and Dubai also grew up with me. I was only a shop assistant in a clothes shop here in Nilambur; my family had only eight *cents* of land and a small house'. For six months in Dubai in 1974, he tells us, he stayed in one of his uncle's houses, with no job. PV had eight people to support back home and his uncle lent money to send as a remittance. When his uncle started his own company, dealing in spares and tools, PV joined him. In 1981, his uncle retired, leaving PV all the assets on condition that PV 'would not ruin the reputation the company had built, nor ruin his [uncle's] reputation' and that uncle would not be liable for any debt made by PV. PV agreed. 'And, by the grace of God, things went very, very well'. He now employs around 5,000 people.

Like many others, PV argues that Kerala Muslims 'have remained backward' because of their lack of education. 'Muslims suffered because of the British',[7] he tells us.

> So they began to hate the British and everything that the British brought, including education, English language, etc. So they opted out from the mainstream and did not benefit from British education. But nowadays, Muslims know that opting out is not possible and therefore they will not boycott Bush and American products. In the last fifty years, there has been a real Muslim renaissance under a very good leadership and Muslims are almost equal to other communities, especially with regard to education. For example, this year [2003], out of fifteen Malayalis who passed the civil service examination, five were Muslims. This is the first time that this has happened, and it shows that Muslims have understood that they must take on prominent position in politics, government, administration, and professions.

The fact that PV chooses to be interviewed from the grounds of his school is highly significant. He established this private residential school to cater for the children of middle-class Muslim Malayali Gulf migrants. PV's involvement in education does not stop in Kerala: his group of companies also runs two 'international schools' for Indian migrants in Saudi Arabia (Jeddah and Riyadh). PV stresses the role of education in the *upliftment* (English term used) of the community and argues for a long-term relationship between Muslims and education – in its widest sense – via historical trade links: 'Muslims brought prosperity, technology, education and culture to Kerala. When Arabs first came to Kerala, Malayalis did not even know how to wear clothes'. Yet he is also keen to stress that education itself might not be enough to bring economic development, for education might be a double-edged sword.

> The problem [for the development of Kerala] is the attitude of Malayalis. Because they are educated, they think that they know best, that any one of them should be prime minister. This is good, in that Malayalis think with their own heads and cannot be easily manipulated, but it is bad for business: you can't make them work! Then, those who have no job are not destitute because they can always rely on income from relatives in the Gulf. This means that Malayalis are never desperate enough to take any job at any salary.

PV highlights the entrepreneurial spirit of Muslims against this generalized malaise of Malayali society: 'Prosperity came to Kerala via trade and business, which Muslims dominated', PV argued:

> Muslims do not put money away nor enjoy interest – it is *haram* (forbidden) ... If things go well today, you cannot be sure about tomorrow. You live and enjoy day by day at God's will ... So, we have a culture of investment and risk-taking. Malayali Muslims are, for example, the main smugglers in Kerala: this is an example of people prepared to take very, very high risks. Because of this risk-taking culture, they are number one in business.

But Muslims' entrepreneurial ethic is tempered by a strong 'community orientation'. PV reminds us, 'A Muslim cannot enjoy his wealth and life if people around him are suffering. A Muslim should help needy neighbours, that is why we give *zakat* (mandatory alms) and *sadaqah* (voluntary alms)'. As seen, PV is famed for being always ready 'to help out' and is involved in countless charities and social projects directed towards the 'Wellbeing of all Muslims'. Alongside the private school he opened in 1992 – with hefty annual fees of Rs 60,000 – he has also started an English medium *day school* (English term used) recruiting only local students, paying just Rs 375 per year. PV notes, 'Many come for free – this school is for the benefit of the whole community'.

To his many detractors, especially the established trading middle class, which chides him for having 'more money than sense', PV's success is attributed solely to political connections – in Kerala and the Gulf alike – and shrewd practices rather than genuine business expertise. PV's philanthropic activities are criticized as the self-advertising stunts of a parvenu. Critics mention that when a committee for the construction of Kozhikode airport was formed, businessmen were asked to donate up to Rs 50,000 for the campaign, but PV gave one million without batting an eyelid, simply because he wanted an airport near his house to impress Arab business partners. It is PV who is said to have started the fashion of giving large donations to mosques and Muslim organizations, a practice which has increased his popularity within the community and most lately gained him a nomination to the Rajah Sabha as a Muslim League MP.

Our next entrepreneur, MK, is managing director of an Abu Dhabi-based group most famous for its department stores and hypermarkets across the Gulf. Employing more than 10,000 people worldwide, this company has set up production and export units in East Africa, China, and Southeast Asia to supply the retail business, which is predominantly directed towards the Gulf's lower middle classes (especially Indian migrants). Unlike PV, MK has little direct business investment in Kerala, but does maintain an extremely public presence, giving speeches to public meetings (invited by reformist and non-reformist organizations alike) and contributing to Muslim educational institutions and to infrastructure (such as Cochin airport). MK appears on the management committees/board of directors of many business and educational institutions in both Kerala and the Gulf, and he is a member of the Indian government's Central Waqf Council.

MK left Kerala as a young man to join his uncle's small food-exporting business in Gujarat. He soon followed his uncle to Abu Dhabi to work in the latter's small supermarket, started in 1966. The big break came in the early 1990s, during the first Gulf war. MK, by now managing director, launched a chain of supermarkets. 'Everyone was hesitant to invest in those days', he remembered (in an interview published by NRIinternet.com[8]),

> and it was a big risk to build on a new concept ... You have to take risks at some point of your life. Without risks there is no success. It is like driving a car. If you think of all those big trailers, the speeding vehicles, and that old man trying to cross the street, you will never be able to drive.

No one doubts MK's business acumen, but he is also praised as shrewd for surrounding himself with able staff and for developing strong connections with Arabs. 'He speaks very good Arabic and understands very well Arab people's ways and minds', one of his business acquaintances tells us: 'He has a very sharp business mind'. On the walls of MK's headquarters in Abu Dhabi and in his sprawling Kerala house hang framed photos of his meetings with various members of United Arab Emirates ruling families and ministers, who, he tells us, 'have always been very supportive of [my] business'.

We meet MK in his Kerala house, a peripatetic conversation taking us around the house and its sprawling grounds, where replies to questions are interspersed by MK pointing out the property's many features: central a/c system, private Ayurvedic massage centre, swimming pool, collection of American vintage cars, and so on. MK arrives exactly on the agreed time, telling us that we were 'lucky to get an appointment at all. I've been here for six days, attended eight weddings and some inaugurations, and a meeting to congratulate me on my election to the Waqf Board. And every time I come back, I also have to look after more than 400 people here!' It is no surprise when MK says: 'My main concern is education, especially that of Muslim girls. I'm chairman of the new MES [Muslim Education Society] medical college dedicated to the development of Muslim education. It will become a "deemed" university, starting courses such as nursing for Muslim girls'. Here, he quickly corrects himself: 'It is for the whole society. I respect people of all religions, but not atheists!'

MK continues, 'After the *Khilafat* movement,[9] Muslim clergy refused English and modern education, but now they should change and recognize education's importance. What development can there be if the wife of a businessman cannot even answer the phone because she does not speak English?' Later on, introducing his wife, he comments, 'She, for example, does not speak a word of English!' But then he calls upon one of his daughters, a young woman who studies at the American University in Abu Dhabi: 'You can ask her anything – she's very clever'. If education is directed towards community economic development, for MK it also plays a wider role in transformation of Muslim social practices. 'The big problems for Muslims are divorces and dowries, both arising from Gulf migration. It is very bad and the clergy should educate people that for Islam it's *haram*. Educated people', he concludes, 'Do not behave improperly'.

We hear MK a few months later addressing a 'Sunni' (see note 4) public meeting. His speech – delivered to sympathizers of an organization that until very recently advocated boycott of any form of Western education – focuses on the need for Muslims to study English, to learn modern sciences, and to become professionals and 'Ph.D. holders' – essential skills which the Gulf experience proves, according to him, vital if Kerala is to 'be part of globalization'. But the first part of his speech is about 'the value of Muslim brotherhood' and the need for Muslims to be united 'to achieve progress'.

PMA is our third exemplar of this emerging breed of Malayali Muslim businessmen. PMA's company, with more than 14,000 employees, is one of the largest construction companies in the Gulf, recently diversifying into mechanical, electro-mechanical, and heavy civil engineering sectors. The company has also landed in India, entering the hotel and construction business in Kerala and Karnataka. PMA attributes his success to a mix of calculated risk-taking and technical/ business skills. 'I do take risks', he declared (in an interview in *Oman Economic Review*),[10] 'but I do not jump into the fray without doing my homework'. He continues,

> Whenever and wherever my people need me I will be, physically, there for them, no matter what. We have to make people believe in themselves and in their capabilities in order to motivate them. You need your people to trust you; when they believe in you and in themselves, the company moves forward.

This image of a modern and enlightened business manager is what PMA presented to us when we met him in his Muscat office, keen to stress all the benefits – free food and accommodation to labouring staff, company cars and free petrol to technical/ managerial staff – which his company provides to employees on top of their salaries. He tells us that in recruiting, his first concerns are qualifications and work experience, although, he admits, he does give preference to Indians – especially those who have some family members or friends already in the company.

PMA has also branched out into the education sector, building private schools and colleges (a medical school and an engineering college in collaboration with a UK University) in Oman. He justifies these investments, saying that,

> I'm not a saint, but raking in money does not goad me anymore. I won't deny it was enjoyable when I could afford to meet my first few needs ... However rich the country may be in terms of its GDP and economic indicators, if its citizens are not educated and competent to handle its wealth and resources, what is the use of money? Education is the key to developing people and the community (interview in *Oman Economic Review*).[11]

PMA is determined, he tells us, to bring 'this vision' to Kerala via the construction of a new university.

From business interests to community 'upliftment' and back

PV, MK, and PMA rhetoricize their lives as 'rags-to-riches' tales, speaking of success as built from hard work, dedication, and business skills, where 'traditional' Muslim skills honed in the bazaar – such as risk-taking, hard work, familiarity with *wasta* (Arabic: favours, contacts) – are refined via adoption of modern business techniques – learned on the job in the Gulf as much as by studying in management institutes. Gulf-based Malayali businessmen have been successful not just because they were at the right time in the right place, but also because they combine inclinations for risk-taking in business and an affinity to the politics of Arab *wasta* with modern forms of management learned during early days in the Gulf. They now insist that entering and succeeding in the global labour market requires both 'traditional' business acumen and familiarity with new skills and technologies.

They thrive in the Gulf and have an affinity to Arabs – both as Muslims and as Malayali Muslims, with long-term Arab world connections (see F. Osella & C. Osella 2007) – but they also benefit from close links with Indian politicians, who support their investments in Kerala (cf. Sloane 1999). Like the contemporary Malaysian entrepreneurs discussed by Sloane, who sharply criticize 'old-style' fatalism and limited horizons, framed as un-Islamic because wasteful of the opportunities given by God, these men wish to see others follow their lead and adopt their dynamic approach.

These men's tales set them as iconic figures for all Muslims, an image they are keen to cultivate. They appear regularly on television, in newspapers, and so on. But they are not distant heroes: any Muslim will know someone – a friend or relative – who works for them and has a story to tell. And here a degree of accountability comes in: these men are also subject to wider public criticisms. As we might expect, the established middle classes commonly claim that these men are to be discounted, simply *nouveaux riche* and with 'no family history'. They are also sometimes portrayed as men who have simply extended the slippery rules of business beyond the usual rule-bending/bribery, and so on, which is taken for granted as necessary common practice to *all* businesspeople. And those who work for them might have different experiences of their apparent enlightened benevolence. One accountant told us, 'We have to work ridiculously long hours, just so that if MK decides to pass by our office, one of us will be there to explain to him what is happening and show him the books. We never know when he is coming, we always have to be ready'. And everyone well knows that Gulf-based businessmen make money by ruthlessly exploiting (predominantly) Malayali labour: in a deregulated labour market, workers work long hours, often live in spartan conditions, and are paid barely above Kerala rates.

All the entrepreneurs described here link the need for education to reform and future progress of Kerala Muslims, and this is not mere talk: they promote and build schools, colleges, and universities in both Kerala and the Gulf. This relationship between private interests and the common good, the advancement of business while working for the 'upliftment' of the whole community, unfolds in the Social Advancement Foundation of India (SAFI). The brainchild of PMA, the SAFI trust is constructing a new university on the outskirts of Kozhikode, inaugurated in 2006.

SAFI's glossy publicity, directed towards attracting donors from both Kerala and Gulf, connects the university-to-be to the re-awakening of the great scientific traditions of Islamic civilization. 'The inheritors of those treasures of knowledge', one of the brochures reads, 'are today the poorest and backward people'. 'It is time we move on from self-pity to self improvement', we read in the same text,

> from servility to leadership, from ignorance to the frontlines of scientific and social advance ... A few philanthropists, educationalists, jurists and other leaders met and resolved to take practical measures to realize [this] dream. It is a colossal plan to liberate the intellectually colonized sections of India, and to enable them to excel in all areas of knowledge, particularly science and technology ... SAFI will strive for the transformation of the backward sections into a society competent in every respect in the contemporary world, upholding ethical and religious values and achieving excellence in social, educational, and economic spheres.

Donors are asked to support construction of a university consisting of 'a network of centres of advanced study' in IT, medical sciences and biotechnologies, and social sciences. While the science centres are described through a list of sub-disciplines which are to be taught, the social sciences are presented through the role they will play in the wider ideological struggle of Muslims and Islam to counteract 'the entry of several pseudoscientific theories and social concepts ... [which] are targeted to rupture of the very fabric of religious faith ... our duty is to restore the healthy relation between rational knowledge and ethical values'. PMA tells us that SAFI aims to set itself as an alternative for those (Indian and non-Indian) Muslims no longer willing to send their children to study in non-Islamic environments. SAFI will provide 'cutting-edge teaching and research in an Islamic environment'. Although this move attracted substantial cash donations, it somewhat backfired. Arab donors insisted that Islamic studies should be a major component of the university curriculum and, bending to their wishes, one of the first two programmes inaugurated in 2006 was that of Islamic studies.

In SAFI, Kerala Muslims are offered not only the chance of doing good for the community, but also a very good investment opportunity. SAFI bought – at low cost – around 600 acres of agricultural land in an excellent location – 10 kilometres from Kozhikode, 15 kilometres from the airport, and 5 kilometres from the national highway – but only half of this property will be used for construction of the university campus. The rest will become a residential (25 per cent) and commercial (25 per cent) area, promising top-class infrastructure and amenities. People 'donating' Rs 200 000 (£2,500) are given full title over ready-to-build plots of 20 *cents* each, a real bargain given Kozhikode's current land prices. The children of 'donors' are also guaranteed entry to the university and all the nurseries, schools, and colleges which will be built in the new township.

'Donations' came in ready and fast, collected through public meetings organized by SAFI in collaboration with community and trade organizations. Filippo attended a Kozhikode meeting in early 2004 – an all-male Muslim audience of businessmen, bazaar traders, and entrepreneurs. After a slick PowerPoint presentation where, through maps, flow charts, and statistical tables, construction plans and predicted land price growth were illustrated, the stage was taken by Dr HR,[12] chair and medical director of Mangalore's 'Unity Health Complex' (hospital and medical school) and vice-chair of SAFI. Dr HR shifted the focus of the meeting from business to education. 'SAFI will focus on cutting-edge subjects. An important American economist has written that the sectors of biggest future growth will be biotechnologies, IT, and moral-religious values. SAFI will follow this path'. Education is to be framed in the context of Muslim development and renaissance. 'Muslims have to develop and re-invent themselves. They should not be scared of the future! Muslims must go forward with times and become again leaders in India and the world'. A well-known local businessman takes the stage, telling the audience that it was dynamic entrepreneurs like himself who had convinced SAFI that 'Kozhikode Muslims should be given an opportunity to participate in the project. 10 *crores* [100 millions] of rupees have already been raised. We are also eager to contribute. Don't let me down!' In less than fifteen minutes, thirty-seven plots were sold - to the total value of Rs 7 million - to a number of professionals, businessmen, and returned migrants.

Projects like SAFI are not at all unique in Kerala. Migration and Gulf business-led investment have brought the development (as among Kerala's other communities) of private services (hospitals, schools). Muslim-owned and Muslim-run, these then tend to become perceived as specifically Muslim and to attract a Muslim clientele. An often-expressed argument within the community runs that communalized investment is necessary for Muslims' 'development'. The need for this turn is reinforced by political events: locally, the emergence of strong and successful Hindu and Christian communal/caste organizations which dominate the public sphere and have built a whole string of 'community-owned' services; nationally, generalized Muslim marginality and the state of living 'post-Ayodhya' and under the rise of Hindutva; internationally, the Afghanistan and Iraq invasions and global post-9/11 Islamophobia. All produce a sense of being a 'community under siege' which must stick together and develop self-reliance. Muslims, it is argued, should follow other Kerala groups in building their own networks of professionals, skilled workers and businessmen to strengthen the community and provide 'economic and political leadership'. At the same time, an educated, self-reliant, and economically secure community would not, according to community leaders, 'fall into the hands of extremists and terrorists'.

But SAFI has much wider objectives: participation in a 'worldwide renaissance of Islamic "moral values" and culture'. It is argued – predominantly, but not exclusively, by Islamic reformist organizations – that an Islamic renaissance would not just rid Kerala of the social problems brought to bear on Muslim lives by 'globalization' – the negative side of Gulf migration – but also set the basis for counteracting 'Western imperialism', understood to be a problem faced by Muslims worldwide. While such pan-Islamic orientations are not new – consider, for example, not just pre-colonial networks across the Indian Ocean, but also the circulation of religious scholars and reformist ideas between the mid-eighteenth and early twentieth century (F. Osella & C. Osella 2007) – they have been significantly strengthened over the last thirty years. SAFI seeks to foster this renewed sense of participation in a wider *dar-al-Islam* (land where Islam prevails) – which is, of course, open to very different interpretations and experiences on the opposite shores of the Indian Ocean – while also tapping into the business opportunities it opens up.

Amongst Kerala Muslims, the Gulf stands for the successful blending of Islam with cutting-edge technologies and modern business practices (F. Osella & C. Osella 2007; cf. Tripp 2006 on 'Islamic capitalism'; Springborg 1989). Regardless of the unevenness and ambivalence of migrants' experiences, Dubai's skyscrapers, Kuwait's sprawling oil refineries, or Riyadh's opulent neighbourhoods stand for a world where Muslims are both wealthy and self-confident, a stark contrast – as we were reminded many times – to the circumstances of India's many Muslims (C. Osella & F. Osella 2008; F. Osella & C. Osella 2008; cf. Hansen 2007; Jeffrey et al. 2008).

PMA reminded us that, although he is committed to the 'upliftment of Muslims', he is 'no saint'. As we have seen, the SAFI project is sold to potential donors as a good investment opportunity. But the business orientation of the project does not end there. As in all Kerala's self-financing colleges, only 50 per cent of SAFI students will be recruited on merit. The remainder, in Kerala's usual way, will enter through a 'management quota', which normally demands higher fees and payment of hefty 'donations'. And while SAFI insists that it will provide scholarships to 'meritorious needy students', it is clear that actually only solidly middle-class Muslim students will either achieve the grades for merit admission, or have the resources ('donation' and/or connections) to enter through 'management quota'.

Muslim parents spend much time worrying about their children's education. In Kozhikode, some lobby for admission to the two old-established Muslim schools whose syllabi include Qur'anic classes and good standards of Arabic teaching alongside both

English and Malayalam medium streams of the Kerala syllabus. Others worry that something more dynamic and *modern* is required for upcoming generations, but few have any idea where to find it or even how to recognize it. Among the established middle classes, the relative merits of the Kerala syllabus versus the national (CBSE, central board) syllabus are debated and mothers compare notes on which English-medium schools have teachers who are truly competent in the English language. But many Muslim families have been cut off from Kerala's educational mainstream for so long that, with the best will and all the Gulf remittances in the world, parents still do not have the competence to track down and secure admission to a good school.

In an interview with the principal of the up-and-coming new cosmopolitan school[13] which our own children attended for two years, the difficulties of bringing Muslim mothers into the school's 'systematic' and Gulf-style 'modern' educational culture was a major theme. The principal despaired of the degree of absenteeism, late morning arrivals, children falling asleep mid-morning, children with poor concentration – having missed breakfast – children who had no exposure to English language at home, and so on. She expelled many pupils and we saw her many times haranguing mothers (in English): 'This child must sleep early, rise early, take proper breakfast and learn to understand some simple English. Otherwise he is out!' Bewildered mothers, who often clearly did not themselves understand (either linguistically or substantially) much of what was being said to them, promised to get more 'systematic', desperate as they were to push their children into mainstream middle-class culture and higher education. When MK highlights the anomaly of having a wife who cannot even answer the telephone in English, he is probably also thinking about the difficulties of having a wife who cannot properly help 'bring on' the next generation. PV's boarding school in Nilambur has, of course, neatly addressed exactly this issue by figuring mothers out of the picture. Here we are reminded of earlier and contemporary reformist efforts at civilizing womenfolk (Jeffery, Jeffery & Jeffrey 2004; Metcalf 1990; cf. Abu-Lughod 1998) and colonial projects of educating Indians for success by placing them away from their 'backward' mothers and into residential schools (see, e.g., Haynes 1991; Whitehead 2003); but how much higher are the stakes and how much more exacting the demands in contemporary Kerala, where global standards are setting the pace.

Conclusions

Debates amongst Kerala Muslims regarding community long-term 'progress' are neither simply informed by local concerns nor self-contained; they articulate with – and respond to – discussions taking place both within a transnational Muslim public sphere and within Kerala's wider public sphere (cf. Deeb this volume). Our entrepreneurs do not focus only on the situation of Kerala's Muslims or respond to issues arising within the community, but are continuously reflecting on and responding to their wider Gulf experience as well as the practices of Kerala's other communities.

When successful Muslims propose solutions for the common good, education becomes the core focus of charitable and activist energies. But there is considerable ambivalence about what sort of education is required and to what purpose it should be aimed. Debates have raged in the past – even to violence – between 'traditionalists' and 'reformists' or between different reformist groups over issues such as Arabic versus Malayalam versus English as teaching medium; or the relationship and relative proportioning of religious and secular education (F. Osella & C. Osella 2008).

The position of women is, as ever in Kerala, interesting. When reformist groups insist upon education for girls, this seems to be simply a question of some sort of human rights in line with contemporary (global) interpretations of Islam as granting equality to women in many arenas, including education (cf. Huq 2008; Mahmood 2005). While a photograph of girls learning to use computers while wearing *pardah* (here, a coat and headscarf, see C. Osella & F. Osella, 2007) invariably appears in reformist publications, at the same time reformists stress that women's employment should not be encouraged. 'Educated women' – by which reformists invariably intend women with good religious education and basic Secondary School Leaving Certificate qualifications – are envisaged as the prop for the family as a whole, fostering religious morality and supporting their children's education (cf. Jeffery *et al.* 2004; Metcalf 1990). In line with Kerala's general social and gender conservatism, there is here absolutely no suggestion of women becoming entrepreneurs, unlike Malaysia, where modern Muslim morality via business activity is incumbent on both sexes (Sloane 1999; see Deeb and De Jorio in this volume).

As in Sloane's Malaysian case, businessmen believe in the possibility of a win-win situation: the uplift of the entire Muslim community and access to a flexible and qualified workforce shaped into global standards. Illiterate labourers are brought in by Kozhikode entrepreneurs from Bihar or Uttar Pradesh; meanwhile one's own community can be educated, moulded, and targeted to provide the accountants, middle-managers, software specialists, and so on, which contemporary business needs. India splits into the 'backward' other regions and the 'modern', to which Kerala stakes a strong claim (C. Osella & F. Osella 2006). But within Kerala, the Muslim community is outstripped every time by Kerala's Christians and Hindus. As we found in our earlier work on Hindu reformism, the Christian community and its institutions – such as Malabar Christian College in Kozhikode – are felt to offer not simply top-class education, but also necessary training in rational and 'systematic' lifestyles, offering 'exposure' and inculcating discipline (see Froerer 2007). But use of or even emulation of such institutions is, for Muslim community leaders, no longer an appropriate goal. While the 1930s Kozhikode Muslim elite were, like the Hindu elites of the time, happy to adopt practices they drew both from the colonial modern and from the local Christian modern, in contemporary Kerala the situation is more complex. Long-standing participation in and familiarity with trans-oceanic Islam has fostered affinities to Islamic reformism and has revived romanticized notions of *dar al-Islam*. This heightened sense of the self *as a Muslim*, in turn, underpins community-wide projects of self-transformation. The Arab Gulf provides a direct example of the existence of another modern, an Islamic modern stripped of what are perceived as the excesses (atheism, sexual freedom, individualism) of 'Western' modernity (C. Osella & F. Osella 2008).

Ultimately, entrepreneurs' public-sphere activity focused on education has a dual effect. It satisfies the moral and communitarian aspirations of Muslim elites; but we perceive as an equally motivating factor the production of the sort of workforce that entrepreneurs feel they need: young men (*sic*) who are flexible, educated, and equally competent in English- and Arabic-speaking environments. An emerging public discourse attributes the relative 'underdevelopment' of Kerala Muslims, and of Muslims worldwide, not only to their alleged aversion to 'modern' education, but more generally to their lack of ambition, inability to defer gratification, or outright laziness, all marked out as deleterious to individual and community. Entrepreneurs hope to reproduce amongst youngsters their own dynamism, which ties in well with local Islamic reformism: attitudes of individual responsibility, energetic activity, and self-advancement are all part of the self cultivated by reformists. As in Sloane's Malaysian example, entrepreneurship is called upon to stand at the core of contemporary reformulations of Muslim morality. Here it allows – actually encourages – ideas of a synergistic interplay between business and morality, where material progress and religious reform become intertwined indexes of modernity (see Deeb 2006).

As in the early twentieth century, we are again seeing – in the Muslim businesses which have emerged over the last twenty years – convergence between middle-class practices and Islamic reformist discourse, by now thoroughly imbricated with gener-alized ideas about 'progress' and resonating with middle-class aspirations. Ordinary Muslims are encouraged – often in public speeches made by 'community leaders' such as our entrepreneurs – to embrace 'modern Western education', to re-craft themselves as disciplined and 'systematic', to learn English, and to perfect their Arabic in order to compete in the West-Asian-South Asian nexus of the global labour market; but they are also being asked to accept a high degree of competition and uncertainty – for example, flexible labour practices, the key to future employment. Entrepreneurs' enthusiasm for the sharp practices of global capitalism reveal the unfolding of a class-specific road map towards community development.

As one might expect, a discourse linking religious virtuosity to economic perfor-mance cannot but entail and generate unevenness, slippages, and tensions. While not everyone has benefited from the opportunities offered within India's post-liberalization economy, access to higher education remains more than ever determined by class, and all that many young Malayali Muslims can aim for is a low-paid Gulf job. Predictably, those who fail either to 'modernize' or to make the most of life's chances – e.g. old-style bazaar traders and the working classes – are increasingly marked out as morally lacking and thereby become the object of middle-class reformist intervention, often via Muslim NGO activity (cf. Elyachar 2005).

The notion of elective affinity (Weber 1985 [1905]) might seem an all-too-obvious framework to make sense of the processes at hand. But articulations between economic and religious practices remain contingent and contextual and any possible outcomes (including 'rationalization') are unpredictable. We wish at this point to make clear that we are adopting none of the clearly discernible and common positions found in analyses of Muslims' relationships to the economy. The Weberian thesis, attributing fatalism and an undeveloped rationalism, is obviously rejected by us, as are post-Weberian analyses which would trace out developmentalist teleologies of the growth of 'rationality', especially associated with Islamic reformism (e.g. Geertz 1963). More recently, two different arguments have emerged: Roy and Kuran explore moves towards production of 'Muslim economies', but conclude that these are doomed to fail, being ultimately at odds with the goals and the institutional architecture of capitalism (Kuran 2006; Roy 1996, cited in Feillard 2004). Feillard discusses the production in Malaysia of an 'ethique islamique du travail' (2004: 95) and attempts to argue – against Roy and Kuran – that the Islamist stress on personal transformation, individual responsibility, and accountability to God (e.g. in matters of *riba* or *zakat*), and in particular the production of new subjectivities, is both sufficient to transform economic activity and neither incoherent with nor antagonistic towards existing structures of capitalism. This is similar to the position taken by Rudnyckyj (this volume), and we find ourselves in agreement with both authors, and with Sloane, on this particular point; vigorous engagement in entrepreneurship, Muslim public spheres, and Islamic reformism have clearly been running together comfortably in recent years. We absolutely reject, then, the wholesale assumptions of negativity and predictions of failure to be found in the writings of Weber, Roy, and Kuran, and share with Feillard and Rudnyckyj an interest in how Islamic work ethics and new entrepreneurial subjectivities may be compatible with contemporary forms of capitalism.

But here we do also wish to mark some divergence. We take a very cautious line and absolutely avoid projections or discussions of the 'success' or probable outcome of such projects. We also want very strongly to distance ourselves from any suggestions of sheer instrumentality on the part of entrepreneurs. We insist upon maintaining an equivocal stance on the issue of whether contemporary Islam is perfectly compatible with forms of contemporary capitalism, and we are also strongly arguing for an appreciation of the complexity within any individual subject's relations to economic activity – a complexity which allows for both pragmatic instrumentalism and pious sincerity coexisting within the same persons (cf. Marsden 2005). We refuse to answer what is for us a non-question, but is, sadly, often posed: that of whether these entrepreneurs are 'really' sincere Muslims or are 'really' canny capitalists (cf. Coleman 2000).

The experience of our entrepreneurs suggests that success in the neoliberal economy depends just as much on 'new' technocratic management and rational calculation as it does on 'old' connections and luck (cf. Geertz 1963; for a critique see Fanselow 1990 and Ray 1995); and even amongst the most reformist-orientated, 'traditional' charitable practices continue to be mobilized alongside more engaged forms. At the same time, Kerala Islamic reformism, increasingly preoccupied with the possible excesses of 'Western capitalism' – individualism, hyper-consumerism, and corruption – seeks ways to set ethical boundaries for engagement with the neoliberal global economy (see Hefner 1998: 232ff.; Maurer 2005; Tripp 2006: 150ff.). This is neither a condemnation of wealth accumulation and consumerism *per se*, nor a rethinking of the need to cultivate 'systematic' dispositions, but is, rather, a continual critical reflection of the perceived effects of contemporary economic practice on everyday lives.

Elite projects of hegemony might indeed prove elusive. Reformist organizations have lately become vociferous in their critique of 'globalization': globalization is deemed to be synonymous with American imperialism, the cause of many problems faced by contemporary Muslims and hence demanding resistance. At the same time, unlike Malaysia (Sloane 1999), Turkey (Buğra 2002; Erensü n.d.) and Indonesia (Rudnyckyj 2009; this volume; cf. Hefner 1998), Kerala's Islamic reformism has become deeply concerned with the consequences of adoption of 'Western' models of economic development. Corruption in business and politics, hyper-consumerism, individualism, and increased socio-economic inequalities are discussed as negative outcomes of rapid economic change. What is desired is a properly Islamic globalized modernity which provides a moral and restraining framework for workers and entrepreneurs alike and also sets clear limits to capitalist activity. Reformists' far-reaching moral critiques are experienced by emerging entrepreneurial and professional elite fractions as an obstacle to their desire for full participation in national and global middle-class lifestyles. At the same time, a good dose of pragmatism often informs engagement with the ethical demands of Islamic reformism. Entrepreneurs needing to rely on modern banking argue, for example, that the sin of usury (*riba*) applies to lenders and not to borrowers, leaving them free to rely on bank or government loans to expand their businesses.

Reformist critique led organizations such as Jama'at-e Islami to declare full support for the (Communist Party-led) Left Democratic Front during 2006 assembly elections, while the KNM advised supporters to vote on the basis of individual candidate's 'moral standing'. This unexpected turn – given Muslims' historical hostility to the atheist left – contributed to the defeat of many Muslim League candidates in what normally had been safe seats. Significantly, amongst the defeated we find many former ministers closely associated with entrepreneurs discussed here. It remains to be seen whether, over time, this apparently opening chasm between the demands of contemporary business and labour markets and orientations towards community development and reform can continue to be mediated by entrepreneurs' service and donations to community and charitable organizations working for the 'upliftment' of all Muslims. As Elyachar (2005) has noted, there may be ways in which, in recent years, capitalism has been able to 'occupy' the ground where people place the very fundamental values of their social life; and as Maurer (2005) has explored, attempts to wrest out a 'pure' sphere of Islamic finance (or other moral economies) may be over-determined by existing market conditions and rhetorics; but at the same time, we can also think about the ways in which Islam may come to permeate capitalism. Finally, we note that such processes are not linear progressions nor do they have stable outcomes. 'Assemblages' – whether constituted before or within capitalism's neoliberal moment – can unravel with the same ease with which they come together.

ACKNOWLEDGMENTS

Research for this chapter was undertaken at various sites in Kozhikode (erstwhile Calicut, a bazaar town, pop. c.500,000) and Gulf Cooperation Council states and was funded by the Economic and Social Research Council, the Nuffield Foundation, the Arts and Humanities Research Council, and the School of Oriental and African Studies. Thanks for comments on earlier drafts to: Simon Coleman, Geert De Neve, Jon Mitchell, Daromir Rudnyckyj, Atreyee Sen, Benjamin Soares, Jock Stirrat, and Leila Zaki.

NOTES

[1] Recent debates have moved instead to consider the emergence of the so-called 'new middle classes', their engagement with novel consumption practices apparently underscoring a shift away from the redistributive logics of Nehruvian developmentalism (Corbridge & Harriss 2000; Fernandes 2000; Khilnani 1997; Mankekar 1999; Srivastava 2006).

[2] Gulf Indian workers often come from Kerala (Prakash 2000: 4534; see also Nair 1989: 343). Throughout the 1990s, Gulf remittances amounted to up to 50 per cent of GDP (Kurien 1994: 765), more than doubling Central Government budgetary support (Zachariah, Mathew & Irudaya Rajan 1999: 18ff). Despite recent shifts, Zachariah, Prakash & Irudaya Rajan (2002) estimate that 58 per cent of all United Arab Emirates remittances received within India still come via Kerala migrants.

[3] Although Kerala Muslims nowadays participate enthusiastically in mainstream education, they continue to lag behind other communities (see F. Osella & C. Osella 2007; 2008). Until the beginning of Gulf migration in the 1970s, rural Muslims, especially in Muslim majority Malappurram district, suffered from long-term economic marginalization (Miller 1992 [1976]; Panikkar 1989).

[4] All Kerala Muslims are Shafi Sunnis, but 'Sunni' is nowadays used to mean 'orthodox' or 'traditionalist' Muslims. Kerala has a few adherents of Tablighi Jama'at and Jama'at-e Islami, but by far the two biggest groupings and most culturally salient distinction is that between 'Sunni' traditionalists and 'Mujahids' (supporters of the KNM, Kerala Naduvathul Mujahideen; Abdul Haque 1982; Miller 1992 [1976]: 275ff.; Samad 1998; Sikand 2005: 130ff.; see also F. Osella & C. Osella 2008).

[5] Formed in 1948 from the ashes of Jinnah's Muslim League, the Indian Union Muslim League has since established itself as the bearer of Kerala Muslims' political interests.

[6] More than to their Hindu Tamil neighbours – industrialists made famous by Milton Singer (1972) and re-studied by John Harriss (2003).

[7] On the Mappila *lahala* (uprisings), see Dale (1980); Miller (1992 [1976]); Panikkar (1989); Randathani (2008).

[8] http://www.nriinternet.com/NRIentrepreneurs/Middle_East/A_Z/A/Yousuf_Ali/Pravasi_2004.htm, accessed 22 January 2009.

[9] The *Khilafat* Movement (1919-24) sought to preserve the Turkish Sultan as Kahlifah of Islam (Minault 1982).

[10] *http://www.oeronline.com/php/2002_march/main2.php*, accessed 22 January 2009.

[11] As previous note.

[12] Renowned for his piety, every year he publishes the 'Unity Islamic Diary', a 'practical guide to success with a brief outline on '11 Principles for Successful Islamic Living' (cf. Harriss on the Gita as a technique for dynamic living – 2003: 352, 357; 'Jesus CEO', cited in Feillard 2004).

[13] Muslim-owned/managed; Muslim business class parents; Christian head-teacher recruited from a Dubai UK school to bring aspects of UK-style school culture to Kozhikode; National (CBSE) rather than regional syllabus; majority of teachers North Indian non-Malayalam-speakers.

REFERENCES

ABDUL HAQUE, P.P. 1982. Islahi Movement in Kerala. *Almuneer* February: 61-7.

ABU-LUGHOD, L. 1998. *Remaking women: feminism and modernity in the Middle East.* Princeton: University Press.

BAYAT, A. 2007. Radical religion and the habitus of the dispossessed: does Islamic militancy have an urban ecology? *International Journal of Urban and Regional Research* **31**, 579-90.

BAYLY, C.A. 1983. *Rulers, townsmen, and bazaars: North Indian society in the age of British expansion.* Cambridge: University Press.

BLOCH, M. & J. PARRY 1989. Introduction: money and the morality of exchange. In *Money and the morality of exchange* (eds) M. Bloch & J. Parry, 1-32. Cambridge: University Press.

BORNSTEIN, E. 2005. *The spirit of development: Protestant NGOs, morality, and economics in Zimbabwe.* Stanford: University Press.

BUĞRA, A. 2002. Labour, capital, and religion: harmony and conflict among the constituency of political Islam in Turkey. *Middle Eastern Studies* **38**, 187-204.

COLEMAN, S. 2000. *The globalisation of charismatic Christianity: spreading the gospel of prosperity.* Cambridge: University Press.

CORBRIDGE, S. & J. HARRISS 2000. *Reinventing India: liberalization, Hindu nationalism and popular democracy.* Cambridge: Polity.

DALE, S.F. 1980. *Islamic society on the South Asian frontier: the Mappilas of Malabar, 1498-1922.* Oxford: University Press.

DE NEVE, G. 2000. Patronage and 'community': the role of a Tamil 'village' festival in the integration of a town. *Journal of the Royal Anthropological Institute* (N.S.) **6**, 501-19.

DEEB, L. 2006. *An enchanted modern: gender and public piety in Shi'i Lebanon.* Princeton: University Press.

EICKELMAN, D.F. & J. PISCATORI 1996. *Muslim politics.* Princeton: University Press.

ELYACHAR, J. 2005. *Markets of dispossession: NGOs, economic development and the state in Cairo.* Durham, N.C.: Duke University Press.

ERENSÜ, S. n.d. Neo-liberal elements in the transformation of Islamism in Turkey: changing conceptions of social justice. Unpublished conference paper.

FANSELOW, F. 1990. The bazaar economy or how bizarre is the bazaar really? *Man* (N.S.) **25**, 250-65.

FEILLARD, G. 2004. Insuffler l'esprit du capitalisme à l'Umma: la formation d'une 'éthique islamique du travail en Indonesie'. *Critique internationale* **25**, 93-116.

FERNANDES, L. 2000. Restructuring the new middle class in liberalizing India. *Comparative Studies of South Asia, Africa and the Middle East* **20**, 88-111.

FROERER, P. 2007. Disciplining the saffron way: moral education and the Hindu *rashtra. Modern Asian Studies* **41**, 1033-71.

FULLER, C.J. & H. NARASIMHAN 2007. Information technology professionals and the new-rich middle class in Chennai (Madras). *Modern Asian Studies* **41**, 121-50.

——— & ——— 2008. From landlords to software engineers: migration and urbanization among Tamil brahmans. *Comparative Studies in Society and History* **50**, 170-96.

GEERTZ, C. 1963. *Peddlers and princes.* Chicago: University Press.

GIFFORD, P. 2004. *Ghana's new Christianity: Pentecostalism in a globalising African Economy.* London: Hurst.

GUDEMAN, S. & A. RIVERA 1990. *Conversations in Colombia: the domestic economy in life and context.* New York: Cambridge University Press.

GUPTA, C. 2002. *Sexuality, obscenity, community: women, Muslims, and the Hindu public in colonial India.* Delhi: Permanent Black.

HANSEN, T.B. 2007. The India that does not shine. *ISIM Review* **19**, 50-1.

HARRISS, J. 2003. The great tradition globalizes: reflections on two studies of 'the industrial leaders' of Madras. *Modern Asian Studies* **37**, 327-62.

HAYNES, D. 1987. From tribute to philanthropy: the politics of gift giving in a western Indian city. *Journal of Asian Studies* **46**, 339-60.

————— 1991. *Rhetoric and ritual in colonial India: the shaping of a public culture in Surat City, 1852-1928.* Berkeley: University of California Press.

HEFNER, R.W. 1998. *Market cultures: society and morality in the new Asian capitalisms.* Boulder, Colo.: Westview.

HIRSCHKIND, C. 2006. *The ethical soundscape: cassette Sermons and Islamic counterpublics.* New York: Columbia University Press.

HUQ, M. 2008. Reading the Qur'an in Bangladesh: the politics of 'belief' among Islamist women. *Modern Asian Studies* **42**, 457-89.

JEFFERY, P., R. JEFFERY & C. JEFFREY 2004. Islamisation, gentrification and domestication: an 'Islamic course for girls' and rural Muslims in Bijnor, Uttar Pradesh. *Modern Asian Studies* **38**, 1-54.

JEFFREY C., P. JEFFERY & R. JEFFERY 2008. *Degrees without freedom? Education, masculinities, and unemployment in North India.* Stanford: University Press.

JOSHI, S. 2001. *Fractured modernity: making of a middle class in colonial North India.* Delhi: Oxford University Press.

KHILNANI, S. 1997. *The idea of India.* London: Penguin.

KOZLOWSKI, G.C. 1985. *Muslim endowments and society in British India.* Cambridge: University Press.

KURAN, T. 2006. *Islam and Mammon: the economic predicaments of Islamism.* New Delhi: Tluka Books.

KURIEN, P.A. 1994. Non-economic bases of economic behaviour: the consumption, investment and exchange patterns of three emigrant communities in Kerala, India. *Development and Change* **25**, 757-83.

LAIDLAW, J. 1995. *Riches and renunciation: religion, economy, and society among the Jains.* Oxford: Clarendon Press.

MAHMOOD, S. 2005. *Politics of piety: the Islamic revival and the feminist subject.* Princeton: University Press.

MANKEKAR, P. 1999. *Screening culture, viewing politics: an ethnography of television, womanhood, and nation in postcolonial India.* Durham, N.C.: Duke University Press.

MARSDEN, M. 2005. *Living Islam: Muslim religious experience in Pakistan's North-West Frontier.* Cambridge: University Press.

MARX, K. 1964. *Karl Marx: early writings* (ed. & trans. T. Bottomore). New York: McGraw-Hill.

MAURER, B. 2005. *Mutual life, limited: Islamic banking, alternative currencies, lateral reason.* Princeton: University Press.

METCALF, B. 1976. Review of *Separatism among Indian Muslims. Journal of Asian Studies* **35**, 339-41.

————— 1990. *Perfecting women: Maulana Ashraf Ali Thanawi's Bihishti Zewar.* Berkeley: University of California Press.

MILLER, R.E. 1992 [1976]. *Mappila Muslims of Kerala: a study in Islamic trends.* Madras: Orient Longman.

MINAULT, G. 1982. *The Khilafat Movement.* New York: Columbia University Press.

MINES, M. 1994. *Public faces, private voices.* Berkeley: University of California Press.

MOSSE, D. 2003. *The rule of water: statecraft, ecology, and collective action in South India.* New Delhi: Oxford University Press.

NAIR, P.R.G. 1989. Incidence, impact and implications of migration to the Middle East from Kerala (India). In *To the Gulf and back* (ed.) R. Amjad, 343-64. New Delhi: International Labour Organization.

OSELLA, C. & F. OSELLA 2000. The return of king Mahabali: the politics of morality in South India. In *The everyday state and society in India* (eds) C.J. Fuller & E.V. Benei, 137-62. Delhi: Social Science Press.

————— & ————— 2006. Once upon a time in the West? Stories of migration and modernity from Kerala, South India. *Journal of the Royal Anthropological Institute* (N.S.) **12**, 569-88.

————— & ————— 2007. Muslim style in South India. *Fashion Theory: The Journal of Dress, Body & Culture* **11**, 233-52.

————— & ————— 2008. Nuancing the migrant experience: perspectives from Kerala, South India. In *Transnational South Asians: the making of a neo-diaspora* (eds) S. Koshy & R. Radhakrishnan, 146-78. Delhi: Oxford University Press.

OSELLA, F. & C. OSELLA 2000. *Social mobility in Kerala: modernity and identity in conflict.* London: Pluto.

————— & ————— 2007. 'I am Gulf': the production of cosmopolitanism in Kozhikode, Kerala, India. In *Cosmopolitanism contested: the confluence of history and anthropology in the Indian Ocean* (eds) E. Simpson & K. Kress, 323-55. London: Hurst.

———— & ———— 2008. Islamism and social reform in Kerala, South India. *Modern Asian Studies* **42**, 317-46.

PALSETIA, J. 2005. Merchant charity and public identity formation in colonial India: the case of Jamsetjee Jejeebhoy. *Journal of Asian and African Studies* **40**, 197-217.

PANIKKAR, K.N. 1989. *Against lord and state: religion and peasant uprisings in Malabar 1836-1921.* Delhi: Oxford University Press.

PRAKASH, B.A. 2000. Exodus of Gulf emigrants: return emigrants of Varkala town in Kerala. *Economic and Political Weekly* **35**, 4534-40.

PRICE, P. 1996. *Kingship and political practice in colonial India.* Cambridge: University Press.

RANDATHANI, H. 2008. *Mapilla Muslims: a study on society and anti-colonial struggles.* Calicut, Kerala: Other Books.

RAY, R.K. 1995. Asian capital in the age of European domination: the rise of the bazaar, 1800-1914. *Modern Asian Studies* **29**, 449-554.

ROBINSON, F. 1993 [1974]. *Separatism among Indian Muslims: the politics of the United Provinces Muslims 1860-1923.* Delhi: Oxford University Press.

ROY, O. 1996. *The failure of political Islam* (trans. C. Volk). Cambridge. Mass.: Harvard University Press.

RUDNER, D. 1987. Religious gifting and inland commerce in seventeenth-century South India. *Journal of Asian Studies* **46**, 361-79.

RUDNYCKYJ, D. 2009. Spiritual economies: Islam and neoliberalism in contemporary Indonesia. *Cultural Anthropology* **24**, 104-41.

SALVATORE, A. & D.F. EICKELMAN (eds) 2003. *Public Islam and the common good.* Leiden: Brill.

———— & LEVINE, M. (eds) 2005. *Religion, social practice, and contested hegemonies: reconstructing the public sphere in Muslim majority societies.* New York: Palgrave Macmillan.

SAMAD, M.A. 1998. *Islam in Kerala: groups and movements in the 20th century.* Kollam: Laurel Publications.

SCOTT, J. 1976. *The moral economy of the peasant: rebellion and subsistence in Southeast Asia.* New Haven: Yale University Press.

SHARMA, S. 2001. *Famine, philanthropy and the colonial state.* Delhi: Oxford University Press.

SIKAND, Y. 2005. *Bastions of the believers: madrasas and Islamic education in India.* Delhi: Penguin.

SINGER, A. 2005. Serving up charity: the Ottoman public kitchen. *Journal of Interdisciplinary History* **35**, 481-500.

SINGER, M. 1972. *When a great tradition modernizes: anthropological approach to Indian civilization.* Chicago: University Press.

SLOANE P. 1999. *Islam, modernity and entrepreneurship among the Malays.* New York: St Martin's Press.

SOARES, B. 2005. *Islam and the prayer economy: history and authority in a Malian town.* Edinburgh: University Press.

SPRINGBORG, R. 1989. *Mubarak's Egypt: fragmentation in the political order.* Boulder, Colo.: Westview.

SRIVASTAVA, S. 2006. *Passionate modernity: sexuality, class, and consumption in India.* New Delhi: Routledge.

TRIPP, C. 2006. *Islam and the moral economy: the challenge of capitalism.* Cambridge: University Press.

WAGGONER, M. 2005. Irony, embodiment, and the 'critical attitude': engaging Saba Mahmood's critique of secular morality. *Culture and Religion* **6**, 237-61.

WALSH, J.E. 2004. *Domesticity in colonial India: what women learned when men gave them advice.* Delhi: Oxford University Press.

WEBER, M. 1985 [1905]. *The Protestant ethic and the spirit of capitalism* (trans. T. Parsons). London: Unwin.

WHITEHEAD, C. 2003. *Colonial educators: the British Indian and colonial educational service, 1858-1983.* London: I.B. Tauris.

ZACHARIAH, K.C., E.T. MATHEW & S. IRUDAYA RAJAN 1999. Impact of migration on Kerala's economy and society. *CDS Working Paper* **297**.

————, B.A. PRAKASH & S. IRUDAYA RAJAN 2002. Employment, wages and working conditions of Kerala emigrants in the United Arab Emirates. *CDS Working Paper* **326**.

13

Islam and the politics of enchantment

GREGORY STARRETT *University of North Carolina at Charlotte*

The first trick-or-treater arrived at my front door promptly at 6 p.m. A boy about 7 or 8 years old, he was wearing a white turban, white slacks, a long white jacket [and] a rubber-like mask of Osama bin Laden. In one hand he carried his treat bag, in the other a toy replica of an M-16 ... I'm still outraged that any company in this country would sell a Bin Laden mask and that any parent, perhaps one of my neighbors, would purchase it for a child's costume.
Gene Hetzel, Matthews, N.C., in a 2 November 2006 letter to the *Charlotte Observer*

[T]he point is that between ... the 'thin description' of what the rehearser (parodist, winker, twitcher ...) is doing ('rapidly contracting his right eyelids') and the 'thick description' of what he is doing ('practicing a burlesque of a friend faking a wink to deceive an innocent into thinking a conspiracy is in motion') lies the object of ethnography: a stratified hierarchy of meaningful structures in terms of which twitches, winks, fake-winks, parodies, rehearsals of parodies are produced, perceived and interpreted, and without which they would not ... in fact exist, no matter what anyone did or didn't do with his eyelids.
Geertz 1973: 7

Islam is a problem. It is held responsible for terrorism, the oppression of women, economic underdevelopment, repressive political systems, and a host of other difficulties around the world. Islam and modernity, Islam and progress, Islam and liberalism appear, in the minds of many, to be perennially at odds, perhaps irreconcilable. Over the last few years, European and American governments and foundations have begun to explore increased funding for scholarly work on Muslim populations in their countries, framing such projects, at least implicitly, as the study of a social problem. How have Muslim populations adapted, assimilated, resisted, and reformed themselves in non-Muslim environments, and how will they do so in the future? Where do they live, and what are their demographics? Are they similar to previous waves of immigrants, or qualitatively different? How can we help ensure they will not become a danger to their host societies? And at the most basic level, who counts as 'Muslim' (is it a matter of belief, mosque attendance, identification, or descent) in the first place (Leonard 2003)?

Contemporary social theory often defines modernity as a set of techniques for generating particular kinds of intellectual, social, and political order, or even the phenomenon of order itself (Bauman 1990; Foucault 1977; Latour 1993; Mitchell 1988; 2002). Such arguments often revolve around the nation-state as the source and product of an unprecedented type of social and experiential ordering. Arjun Appadurai (2006) has recently extended this literature by examining the intersection of nation-state politics and globalization, looking at the fear that national majority populations often feel about small minority groups. Like Bauman (1990), who traced this fear to the politically productive intellectual ambivalence created by the social category of 'stranger', Appadurai writes that by spoiling the fantasy of categorical purity within the modern nation-state, the existence of quantifiable minorities can act as a focus for violent reaction, especially when those internal minorities are linked with global populations beyond one's borders. 'Given the systemic compromise of national economic sovereignty that is built into the logic of globalization', he writes,

> and given the increasing strain this puts on states to behave as trustees of the interests of a territorially defined and confined 'people', minorities are the major site for displacing the anxieties of many states about their own minority or marginality (real or imagined) in a world of a few megastates, of unruly economic flows and compromised sovereignties. Minorities, in a word, are metaphors and reminders of the betrayal of the classical national project (Appadurai 2006: 43).

When we think about Islam, politics, and modernity, it is insufficient, then, to restrict our attention to obvious cases of 'Muslim politics' in the majority Muslim world (Eickelman & Piscatori 1996), or to the politics of 'real' or even virtual Muslim populations elsewhere. As a 'networked civilization' (Gilmartin 2005), a religious tradition, an act of faith, and a globalized symbol evoking emotions ranging from admiration and desire to dismissal, hostility, and fear, Islam and Muslims are objects of imagination, and this imagination has implications for politics and for experiences of the modern by non-Muslims, even in places where Muslims are nearly absent.

This chapter examines some current controversies regarding teaching and learning about Islam in American public schools, in order to illuminate how Islam as an object of imagination can shape the experience of modernity. Focusing on the federal court case of *Eklund* v. *Byron Union School District* (2003), in which a California family claimed its children's public school was coercing them into Islam, I will describe how parental and community concerns about such teaching have entered the media and the judicial system, and the ways that schools, courts, and activists of various sorts have expressed their understandings of the relationship between knowledge, ritual, and personal commitment.

Appadurai outlines a 'geography of anger' in which majorities fear a 'volatile morphing' whereby majority and minority might switch places. As a preventative measure, majority populations develop 'predatory identities' which seek to destroy the cultural 'other' before 'brute accelerated reproduction or subtler legal or political means' on the part of the minority cause such an inversion to happen (2006: 51, 85). Given this sense of worry, the invisible boundary between Muslim and non-Muslim status becomes an important line of demarcation, and activities normally interpreted as imagination, play, or culturally sanctioned rituals of reversal, such as Halloween or schoolroom make-believe, lose their normal meaning and come to be perceived as potentially earnest expressions of self. In Geertz's idiom, the presumption of a common cultural framework allowing us to distinguish between twitches and winks fails. Becoming or impersonating a Muslim, notorious or not, or engaging in what seems stereotypical Muslim-like behaviour even with 'secular' or consciously parodic purpose, is sometimes interpreted either as crossing a dangerous cultural border or as a psychological prelude to doing so.

In the court case that I analyse here, parents were concerned that children were being proselytized or being made to impersonate Muslims in public school. But as Sullivan (1994; 2005) has shown, judicial and popular understandings of ritual more broadly speak past each other. American courts generally distinguish quite finely between winks and twitches, perceiving secular purposes and effects beneath forms of action and thought which religious activists define much more specifically as sacred. Portions of the religious public, on the other hand, see pedagogical techniques and programmes developed by Christian multiculturalists – meant to teach the values of tolerance and diversity in American society – as attempts by aggressive groups of Islamic militants to hijack schools as platforms for turning the United States into an Islamic nation. The messy politics of modernity, postmodernity, and globalization are clearly not restricted to Muslim societies.

Brazen influence

> Islamist Lawfare is often predatory, filed without a serious expectation of winning, and undertaken as a means to intimidate, demoralize and bankrupt defendants.
>
> Goldstein 2008

> [The development of predatory identities includes] a successful campaign of fear, directed at numerical majorities, which convinces them that they are at risk of destruction by minorities, who know how to use the law (and the entire apparatus of liberal-democratic politics) to advance their special ends.
>
> Appadurai 2006: 58

Harvard-trained medieval historian Daniel Pipes has made his reputation combating 'radical Islam' through his websites, in newspapers, and on television appearances. The intensity of his defence of 'the West' derives perhaps from the fact that he is in agreement with terrorist mastermind Osama bin Laden with regard to the success that such radical Islam enjoys on the world stage. At a late 2001 meeting with supporters in Qandahar, Bin Laden spoke about mass conversions to Islam in Holland and the increase in American interest in Islam resulting from the September 11 attacks: 'I heard someone on Islamic radio who owns a school in America say: "We don't have time to keep up with the demands of those who are asking about Islamic books to learn about Islam". This event made people think [about true Islam] which benefited Islam greatly'.[1] The idea that a cascade of non-believers is likely to convert voluntarily after Muslim military victories recalls contemporary Middle Eastern portrayals of the Prophet Muhammad's victory over the pagan Quraysh at the battle of Badr, after which 'the fence-sitters and fearful among the [pagan tribe of the] Quraysh ... enter[ed] Islam in droves' (al-Duwwa, Sulayman, 'Alish & Rashwan, 1987/8: 82), inspired either by feelings of awe at the divinely guided victory or by fear of the victors.

Pipes, too, sees Islam making strides in the United States. For him, this is not because of true popular interest, but because of a concerted effort by what he terms 'militant Islamic groups' to co-opt popular culture and academia with the goal of turning the

United States into an Islamic nation. 'More ominously yet', he wrote in right-wing activist David Horowitz's on-line journal *FrontPageMagazine*, 'they wish to transform public schools at all levels into venues for spreading Islam' (Pipes 2004). 'Schools and campuses are no exceptions as places where Islam can be victorious', Pipes quotes the Muslim website DawaNet.com as evidence for this fear; 'We should use every opportunity to sensitize non-Muslim peers and school staff to Islam and to establish an environment in which everywhere a non-Muslim turns, he notices Islam portrayed in a positive way, is influenced by it and eventually accepts Islam' (Pipes 2004).

One of the ways such an environment is created is through the actions of local schools and school boards, state departments of education, and commercial textbook publishers. Each of these bodies, according to Pipes and his readers, is subject to pressure from 'a highly successful insidious industry that is extremely well organized, well connected, legally savvy, brazenly influential, and without successful opposition' (White 2005). Examples of Islamic proselytization have multiplied in the blogosphere through the testimony of parents being picked up by various media. In Tulsa, Oklahoma, parents met in a church to oppose a workshop for public school teachers on 'The Arab World and Islam' (KOTV 2004). In Middletown, Ohio, seventh-grade social studies teachers cancelled a class trip to a Cincinnati mosque over parental fears that 'the students would be asked to engage in Muslim rituals while at the mosque', according to school officials (Kershaw-Staley 2004). In Scottsdale, Arizona, a seventh-grade world history text was criticized for pro-Islamic bias, and one parent complained that children in a social studies class were forced to write biographies of Muhammad and listen to 'professional Muslim speakers' who 'brought prayer rugs and taught the children to pray the Muslim way. I also believe', she continued, that 'there were recitations from the Koran and possibly an Islamic "fashion show" ' (White 2005). An unnamed parent alleged that shortly after September 11, children at the local school 'were asked to get on their hands and knees and pray to Allah with the words of Islam [*sic*] prayer'.[2] The folkloric dynamism of these charges as they zoom about the internet, surfacing here and there on conservative websites and blogs, transforms news into archetype and confused hearsay about schoolroom experiences – mixed with heavy doses of parental suspicion and anxiety – into news. One popular narrative quotes a 2002 *Kansas City Star* report on Muslim third-, fourth-, and fifth-grade children from a private Islamic school in Herndon, Va., touring local public schools to demonstrate Muslim crafts and ritual. The story quickly morphed into accusations that a Muslim diversity consultant touring public schools directed young *non*-Muslim students in performing Muslim prayer, seemingly confirming parental fears that Islam can only be 'presented' performatively, through its instantiation in new Muslims.

Probably the most talked-about cases among parents and activists are those involving a particular seventh-grade social studies textbook, Houghton-Mifflin's *Across the centuries* (Cordova *et al.* 1999), and a supplementary curriculum unit called *Islam: a simulation of Islamic history and culture, 610-1100* (Handy 1991). Both were criticized by Pipes in columns in the *New York Post*, the *Jerusalem Post*, and on his blog. *Across the centuries* was criticized for its allegedly apologetic tone and factual distortion, its inclusion of classroom activities meant to identify students with Muslims ('Assume you are a Muslim soldier on your way to conquer Syria in the year A.D. 635. Write three journal entries that reveal your thoughts about Islam, fighting in battle, or life in the desert'), and for allegedly failing to distinguish between Muslim belief and historical fact.

The other curriculum unit, *Islam: a simulation*, was even more problematic. It outlined a three-week curriculum in which

> students adopt a Muslim name ('Abdalla,' 'Karima,' etc.). It has them wear Islamic clothing: for girls this means a long sleeved dress and the head covered by a scarf. Students unwilling to wear Islamic clothes must sit mutely in the back of the class, seemingly punished for remaining Westerners. [The publisher] calls for many Islamic activities: taking off shoes, washing hands, sitting on prayer rugs, and practicing Arabic calligraphy. Students study the Koran, recite from it, design a title page for it, and write verses of it on a banner. They act out Islam's Five Pillars of Faith, including giving zakat (Islamic alms) and go on the pilgrimage to Mecca (Pipes 2002).

Islam: a simulation was written by Terry Handy, a veteran middle school social studies teacher in Pismo Beach, California, and published in 1991 by Interaction Publishers of Carlsbad, California, which specialized in simulation exercises for schools. It was listed by the California Department of Education as a supplemental curriculum unit eligible for adoption in California schools, which, like most of the other fifty states, has adopted social studies standards requiring students to learn about Islam, its prophet, and the everyday significance of its texts and beliefs (California School Boards Association 2004). In late June 2002 the Thomas More Law Center, a conservative Catholic legal foundation, filed a lawsuit on behalf of Jonas Eklund in the US District Court for the Northern District of California to prevent the Byron Union School District from using the simulation (Eklund's son Chase had taken part in the simulation during the autumn of 2001 and his younger child, Samantha, was excused at her parents' request from participation the following year). The court granted a decision in this case to the school district on 5 December 2003. The Eklunds appealed to the Ninth Circuit Court of Appeals, which agreed with the lower court's decision on 17 November 2005. On 2 October 2006 the Supreme Court declined to hear the case during its current session, but certified the American Catholic Lawyers Association to file a brief as *amicus curiae* ('friend of the court', a legal analysis submitted by an individual or institution who is not a direct party to a court case), as the Mountain States Legal Foundation had done in July 2006.

'Try to teach the subject in a non-threatening, secular way'

Islam: a simulation is contained in a 116-page packet outlining five phases of a three-week class simulation. It is designed so teachers can customize the unit, choosing one or more elements to use in class. On the introductory day students take a pre-test, learn about Muslim dress, customs, and history, and break into six 'city groups', representing Cairo, Jerusalem, Medina, Damascus, Baghdad, and Cordoba. Each city group has a caliph, a banker, a secretary, and a number of citizens who, on the subsequent days, compete in exercises labelled 'Caravan Days', 'Oasis Days', and 'Festival Days'. During Caravan Days, cities compete to answer questions on Quiz cards, collect Wisdom cards and dirham scrip, and survive life events ('You failed to offer refreshments to your guest. Lose 1 dirham'; 'While on your last caravan, your herd increased by three camels, five goats, and 12 sheep. Gain 15 dirhams'). During Oasis Days, students learn more about Islamic beliefs, practices, and history, doing simulated activities and role-playing historical caliphs. The simulation builds to Festival Days, during which each city presents a project (art, food, music, or a more traditional presentation about Islam), and ends with the Islamic Bowl, a contest in which each qualifying city chooses contestants for a game testing Islamic knowledge.

According to court records, Chase Eklund's teacher had her students choose Arabic names, and then focused on the 'Oasis Days' elements of the simulation, including having the city groups engage in activities 'analogous to' the five pillars of Islam. The children heard prayers and portions of the Qur'an read aloud in class, recited a line from prayer (e.g. the *basmallah*, 'In the name of God, the Merciful, the Compassionate') on their way out of class, and made group banners featuring the *basmallah* (in Arabic script or in English translation) as analogues to the *shahada*, the Muslim declaration of faith, and *salat*, prayer. Students gave up eating candy or watching television for a day, and did community service projects as analogues to the Ramadan fast and the payment of *zakat*, or alms. As an analogue to the pilgrimage, the children in their city teams competed in a board game called 'Race to Makkah', moving markers around a game board while answering questions about Islam. The simulation's general instructions to classroom teachers remind them of the sensitivities potentially arising from the exercise, and advise them to teach in a 'non-threatening, secular way' (Handy 1991: 6), framing the simulation as a historical and cultural activity rather than a ritual or religious one.

Ritual arbitration

> Students should comprehend the religious ideas that have helped to shape Western and Eastern cultures and civilizations; they should become aware of the influence of religion on lifestyles ... and on the development of ideas. The teacher should assist students to understand religious views that can be quite unfamiliar in the United States. Care should be taken, however, to avoid emphasizing unusual religions or religious practices so that respect for religion will not be undermined.
> California Department of Education 1994, quoted in California Schools Board Association 2004: 21

The case of *Eklund* v. *Byron Union School District* hinges on the special nature of role-playing exercises and whether they are similar enough to religious ritual to trigger a valid claim that the public school is violating the Constitution. The United States Constitution contains two directives regarding religious practice: the Establishment Clause ('Congress shall make no law respecting an establishment of religion') and the Free Exercise clause ('or prohibiting the free exercise thereof'). Recent Supreme Court rulings regarding violations of these constitutional guarantees have identified five principles or tests by which state action may be found to have violated the Constitution. These are the three-part 'Lemon test', set down by Chief Justice Warren Burger in the case of *Lemon* v. *Kurtzman* in 1971, and refinements of the third element of the Lemon test in *Lynch* v. *Donnelly* (1984) and *Lee* v. *Weisman* (1992).[3]

The Lemon test specifies that in order to meet Constitutional requirements, government action must (1) have a secular purpose; (2) not have the primary effect of advancing or inhibiting religion; and (3) not foster excessive government entanglement with religion. In the 1984 *Lynch* case, Sandra Day O'Connor posed the 'entanglement' principle as a matter of 'government endorsement or disapproval of religion', so that a state agency would be in violation of the Constitution if their action 'sends a message to nonadherents that they are outsiders, not full members of the political community, and an accompanying message to adherents that they are insiders, favored members of the political community' (*Lynch* v. *Donnelly* 1984: 16). The Supreme Court's ruling in the *Lee* case developed a supplementary test to O'Connor's endorsement rule, that the government 'may not coerce anyone to support or participate in religion or its exercise' (*Lee* v. *Weisman* 1992: 6).

The *Eklund* plaintiffs argued in District Court that although the state of California is justified in teaching students about the basics of Islamic religion and culture, role-playing games are an improper way of doing so, because the Islam simulation asked students 'to role-play or perform activities that were roughly analogous to each pillar [of Islam]' (*Eklund* v. *Byron* 2003: 8), and that these activities, 'taken as a whole, constitute the practice of Islam' (*Eklund* v. *Byron* 2003: 11). Seventh graders, the plaintiffs argued, 'could reasonably have believed they were practicing the Islam [*sic*] religion, even if in fact they were not, and the students could also have believed that their grade in the class would be based on their willingness to believe the tenets of Islam' (*Eklund* v. *Byron* 2003: 14). In addition, they claimed that certain elements of the Islam simulation included the presentation of Islamic beliefs as matters of historical fact, and that the teacher of Chase's class, (non-Muslim) Brooke Carlin, instructed students to write essays supportive of Islam.

District Court judge Phyllis Hamilton ruled, on the contrary, that neither the facts of the case nor the precedents and principles of law developed over the last thirty years lent support to the plaintiffs' claims. Carlin had not referred to students by their Arabic names, although the students sometimes used the names in a joking manner outside class. When giving students their instructions, she had 'specifically emphasized that the module was merely a role-playing game and that the students would not actually become Muslims through their participation in the module' (*Eklund* v. *Byron* 2003: 3), a point confirmed by students in other sections of the class and not denied by Chase Eklund. When distributing wisdom and quiz cards bearing statements like 'The Holy Qur'an is God's word as revealed to the Prophet Muhammad', she had explained that these were Muslim beliefs rather than historical fact. And Chase himself had done previous role-playing simulations, including a mock Senate in US history and one on medieval Europe in which he dressed as a priest (he had declined to dress in Muslim garb for the Islam simulation). He remembered dressing as a priest, but did not associate it with religion: 'That doesn't have anything really to do with God or anything or anybody that you look up to' (*Eklund* v. *Byron* 2003: 6). He did not believe he had become a senator or a priest through participation in these exercises.

Hamilton's legal analysis of the possible Establishment clause violation centred largely on the extent to which the role-playing activities during the Oasis Days might have been religious, given that 'students were asked to role-play or perform activities that were roughly analogous to each pillar [of Islam]' (*Eklund* v. *Byron* 2003: 10). Whether these activities are impermissible depends both on whether students felt compelled to participate, and on 'an objective review of whether the students were actually practicing a religion' (*Eklund* v. *Byron* 2003: 11). The defendants argued, the plaintiffs' experts admitted, and the judge agreed that the students had not performed the actual five pillars of faith in their class, and that while their activities may have been analogies or 'approximations' of Islamic behaviour, they were not 'actually the Islamic religious rites ... [and that r]ole-playing activities which are not in actuality the practice of a religion do not violate the Establishment Clause' (*Eklund* v. *Byron* 2003: 12-13).

This finding applies even when simulations resemble religious rituals far more closely than did those in *Islam: a simulation*. As the California School Boards Association argued in a brief to the Ninth Circuit Court of Appeals regarding the appeal of *Eklund*, the court had previously found in the 1992 case of *Brown* v. *Woodland* (see below) that

> Some student participatory activity involving school-sponsored ritual may be permissible even under [the Establishment Clause] where the activity is used for secular pedagogical purposes. For example, having children act out a ceremonial American Indian dance for the purpose of exploring and learning about American Indian culture may be permissible even if the dance was religious ritual. Similarly, a reenactment of the Last Supper or a Passover dinner might be permissible if presented for historical or cultural purposes (California Schools Board Association 2004: 11).

What mattered were the intent element of the Lemon test, the context in which such rituals were performed, and the attitude of students. In both the *Brown* and *Eklund* cases, the line was drawn between 'genuine' ritual, on the one hand, and activities that teach 'in an engaging manner', but 'did not occur in a sacred or worshipful manner' (California School Boards Association 2004: 11), and were without 'devotional or religious intent', or with a 'subjective lack of spiritual intent' (*Eklund* v. *Byron* 2003: 13), on the other. Since 'the students subjectively understood the distinction between the simulation and their actual religious faith' (*Eklund* v. *Byron* 2003: 15), there was no Constitutional violation.

Worshipful attitudes

> But learn, at least, your inability to believe, since reason brings you to it, and yet you cannot believe; try then to convince yourself, not by the augmentation of proofs of the existence of God, but by the diminution of your own passions ... [L]earn from those who have been bound like yourself ... these know the road that you wish to follow ... *Follow their course, then, from its beginning; it consisted in doing all things as if they believed in them*, in using holy water, in having masses said, etc. Naturally this will make you believe and stupefy you at the same time.
>
> Blaise Pascal, *The Wager*, emphasis added

The issue of worshipful attitude in the *Eklund* decisions specifies the courts' understanding of ritual. True ritual practice, as opposed to simulation, is practice engaged in with a particular set of mental dispositions (focus, sobriety) and emotional states (humility, love, fear). In 'real' Islamic prayer, of course, as in other traditions (Garrett 1993), intention is a vital element of making prayer valid and effective as a means of communicating with God. This approach to ritual assumes that proper intention and worshipful attitude not only accompany but also precede ritual performance. One enters the performance of ritual once a decision to do so has been made, and the mental state of the worshipper has been adjusted or prepared to provide the internal context for a performance which is then serious or sincere. There are other ways to think about these connections, though. Durkheim's discussion of rituals as activities 'which take rise in the midst of ... assembled groups and which are destined to excite, maintain, or recreate the mental states in these groups' (Durkheim 1965 [1912]: 22) is the most obvious theoretical sanction for Pascal's practical observation that ritual can nurture worshipful mental states rather than result from them. As Saba Mahmood (2005) and Charles Hirschkind (2006) have shown, there are substantial movements in Egypt and elsewhere which conceptualize ritual practice as means for cultivating proper attitudes and mental and emotional states.

This understanding of the connection between ritual and belief is of long standing. In the sixteenth and seventeenth centuries, nonconformist activists and Anglican clergy in England debated the twin issues of public liturgical activity and the ethical status of theatre. Both parties argued, for different purposes, that the mimicry or enactment of roles which did not match the actor's internal state could effectively transform that state. Critics of the theatre argued that acting was dangerous to performers and audiences because such temporary hypocrisy could collapse the gap between an enactment on stage and the performer's own personality, transforming the performer's inner state by bringing it into concert with what it was mimicking. Churchmen used the same theory of influence to argue that private devotion and prayer were insufficient for personal transformation. True piety required not only private prayer but public enactment of standard liturgical forms so that the inner state of worshippers would be brought into concert with the rest of the congregation (Targoff 1997).

The United States Supreme Court's jurisprudence on the religion clauses of the First Amendment has not followed this logic. For the first several decades of its dealing with religion cases, beginning with *Reynolds* v. *United States* in 1879 (a case restricting Mormon polygamy), the Court solved the problem of free exercise simply by distinguishing between religious belief, which was constitutionally protected, and religious action, which could be regulated by statute. The Court implicitly endorsed a Protestant valuation of belief over ritual (Sullivan 1994; 2005; see Smith 1956 [1889]: 16) in which the former was both the necessary core and sufficient expression of religion. While beliefs could not necessarily justify otherwise illegal activity, particular *kinds* of belief were necessary to qualify actions as religious. The *Reynolds* case was cited, for example, by a Texas court ruling in 1903 that local restrictions on alcohol consumption could be enforced against Jews but not Roman Catholics. In the view of the court, in Jewish tradition alcohol was not a sacrament. Even though its use was required at some points in the ritual calendar, the court wrote, '[s]uch use of wine has no symbolical or mystical meaning, and is in no sense for sacramental purposes, but is used on such occasions as a beverage' (quoted in Cookson 2001: 11). Action sanctioned by tradition but not derived from an explicit theological imperative did not count as ritual, because, implicit in the court's logic, legitimate ritual is an expression of pre-existing dogma.

The concerns expressed by some parents and pundits with regard to *Islam: a simulation* play on a very different understanding of the connection between ritual and belief. In a broader cultural context, parental fears of Islamic ritual are not merely the result of a tense world situation and a perceived clash of civilizations symbolized most powerfully by the terrorist attacks of September 11, 2001.[4] Those concerns emerge also from two other assumptions about religious life. Many parents do not merely assume, with the courts, that beliefs generate ritual action, and that ritual action is meaningful only as an expression of belief. Instead, they perceive both speech and ritual as activities with transformative psychological or spiritual effects. Ritual is not merely the enactment of belief, but can be belief's gateway.

Related to this implicit theoretical stance is a widespread substantive set of popular American beliefs about intercourse with demonic forces, and specifically the belief that Islam has a demonic origin. A recent survey by the Council for American Islamic Relations reports that as many as 10 per cent of Americans believe Muslims are pagans who worship a moon god or goddess,[5] a belief energetically disseminated by some Christian activists. In February 2007, for example, a social studies teacher at Enloe High School in Raleigh, North Carolina, invited a speaker from Kamil International Ministries to his ninth-grade social studies class. Kamil Solomon, an Egyptian-born Christian evangelist, distributed pamphlets to students (including at least one Muslim girl) that called the Prophet Muhammad 'demon possessed' and 'inspired by Satan', and said that his 'militant commands and pagan beliefs are contained in the Koran', which is 'the book of Islam that Muhammad claimed was revealed to him by Allah, the moon god of Arabs' (Shimron 2007a; 2007b; 2007c).[6] In Rockland County, New York, in April 2007 a Christian prison chaplain was disciplined for distributing similar literature – a Chick Publications religious tract calling Allah an idol – to inmates. The tracts led to arguments and 'to inmates labeling Muslim detainees devil worshipers' (Clarke 2007). Far from being a fellow, if troubling, monotheism, Islam is portrayed as a heathen belief with Satanic roots.

Folklorist Bill Ellis (2000; 2004) and others have shown that as rumour panics about witchcraft and Satanic ritual abuse spread across the United States during the 1970s and 1980s through churches and professional networks of police, therapists, child welfare specialists, and the mass media, one pervasive theme was the ease with which children and teenagers could be unwittingly drawn into demonic activity. Occult books, not to mention idle experimentation with seemingly harmless witchcraft or New Age rituals such as the ubiquitous ouija board,[7] could easily entrap young people and render them helpless to resist Satanism. Even some law enforcement officers charged with investigating occult rumours came to believe that the 'intense study of resource books and materials by occult sources or practitioners is hazardous ... The unknown realm of the occult beckons with many lures. Study and/or experimentation are to be avoided' (quoted in Ellis 2004: 48-9). Other evangelical Christian groups talk about powerful religious language being 'ingested' by worshippers, or even 'impregnating' them (Coleman 2000: 118, 171), both metaphors for processes that are initiated by acts of will, but which then proceed outside the control of volition to assimilate into or transform the individual's substance. This necessitates that believers take great care of the sorts of language, music, and imagery to which they expose themselves lest they open themselves to spiritual corruption.

The connection between the *Eklund* case and concerns about the occult was highlighted when presiding judge Phyllis Hamilton cited a similar case from a decade earlier. The case of *Brown* v. *Woodland* (1994) centred on parental objections to a children's literature series called *Impressions*, used in California elementary schools. Parents Katherine and Douglas Brown argued that the *Impressions* series contained more than three dozen (out of several thousand) selections from literature describing witchcraft and magical practices and therefore had the effect of 'endors[ing] and sponsor[ing] the religions of Witchcraft and or Neo-Paganism in violation of federal and state constitutional separation of church and state principles' (*Brown* v. *Woodland* 1994: 1). The California School Boards Association, in its *amicus* brief for the *Eklund* appeal, cited *Brown* v. *Woodland* in addition to another case regarding the *Impressions* series, *Fleischfresser* v. *Directors of School District 200* (1994), from the US Seventh Circuit Court of Appeals in Illinois.

The *Brown* and *Fleischfresser* cases both involved the issue of role-play, in this case lesson plans encouraging children 'to prepare and cast chants and spells and to practice being witches' (plaintiffs quoted in *Fleischfresser* v. *Directors* 1994: 3) as part of their engagement with stories about the supernatural. The plaintiffs in *Brown* argued that such activities 'convert neutral reading into sponsorship and promotion of the practice and belief systems of Witchcraft and Neo-Paganism' (*Brown* v. *Woodland* 1994: 11). While both courts agreed that witchcraft and neo-paganism could be considered religious practices, they rejected the plaintiffs' arguments in part because the intent of the exercises was secular (a point to which we will return), the effect of the exercises would have been negligible in the context of the entire curriculum, even from the standpoint of an impressionable child, and elements of witchcraft and neo-paganism are so much part of American popular culture that their use in a literature curriculum did not represent excessive state entanglement with religion.

As Benjamin Soares (2006) has shown in the case of Mali, and John Bowen (1993) in Indonesia, it is precisely the widespread nature of such pagan practices and ideas that proves most troublesome to pious activists living in states which are officially 'secular' but which cannot avoid involvement in religious life. In the context of the broad availability of communications media, such activists can use their skills and energy to express the concerns of ordinary people who face challenges to their beliefs and values in the public sphere (Soares 2006). In the American context, the use of the *Impressions* literature series was upheld despite ritual elements that the court admitted could be part of some religious tradition somewhere, perhaps even the identifiably real but minority religions of witchcraft or neo-paganism. But merely because governmental activity 'happens to coincide or harmonize with the tenets of some or all religions' (a finding from *Harris v. McRae* in 1980, quoted in *Brown v. Woodland* 1994: 11), this does not automatically result in an Establishment Clause violation. The courts ruled that the secular intent of *Impressions* rested not only on its reflection of the cultural diversity of North American society (*Brown v. Woodland* 1994: 16) and its teaching of the value of tolerance by encompassing many cultural traditions (*Fleischfresser v. Directors* 1994: 8), but especially through its uses of enchantment.

According to the court, this enchantment is not the literal phenomenon of Christian parental fears – an entrapment into occultism and damnation – but a mind-broadening door into modern consciousness through an intense but temporary engagement that results in the development of creativity, imagination, and psychological flexibility.

> [The literature series] invokes mystery and imagination associated with folklore to promote learning ... Religions also invoke mystery and imagination for their own special purposes. However, the convergence of religious themes with the outcroppings of mystery and imagination contained in *Impressions* does not afford a constitutional basis for circumscribing the teaching tools available to educators (*Brown v. Woodland* 1994: 17).

Judges on the Seventh Circuit Court of Appeals in Illinois elaborated on this point:

> [T]his 'religion' that is allegedly being established seems for all the world like a collection of exercises in 'make-believe' designed to develop and encourage the use of imagination and reading skills in children ... The purpose of the series, stated by the publisher ... is that the inclusion of a variety of stories serves to stimulate a child's senses, imagination, intellect, and emotions; according to the publisher, this is the best way to build reading skills. This reading series includes works of C.S. Lewis, A.A. Milne, Dr. Seuss, Ray Bradbury, L. Frank Baum, Maurice Sendak and other noted authors of fiction. Further, these works, and so many others that are part of any elementary classroom experience have one important characteristic in common; they all involve fantasy and make-believe to a significant degree. The parents would have us believe that the inclusion of these works in an elementary school curriculum represents the impermissible establishment of pagan religion. We do not agree. After all, what would become of elementary education ... without works such as these and scores ... of others that serve to expand the minds of young children and develop their sense of creativity? With that off our chest, we can now properly dispose of the parents' claim within the structure of the Lemon test (*Fleischfresser v. Directors* 1994: 6).

Fantasy and make-believe, according to this extra-legal aside, are 'skills ... fundamental to children of this age, and it is critical that the [schools] select the best tools available to them to teach these skills' (*Fleischfresser* v. *Directors* 1994: 8). It is possible to read these cases as translations into legal idioms of different interpretations of the spiritual and psychological power of ritual, rather than merely as adjudications of the abstract principal of state sponsorship. The court's evaluation differs from that of the parents in that it sees enchantment as a path to the development of a flexible consciousness, while parents see it as linked, always, with a specific content that both narrows and misleads.

Magical thinking and modernity

That children in the United States are expected to learn the skills of fantasy and make-believe as a matter of course, while the children of Manus (Mead 1932) and other 'traditional' cultures might not, is one of the key features of the idea of modernity. If the category of 'stranger' disrupts the ordering power of the nation-state's fundamental opposition between friend and enemy (Bauman 1990), it is the undecidability of the stranger's intentions, rather than lack of knowledge about his or her beliefs, that proves most perplexing. 'The commitment the stranger declares cannot be trusted' (Bauman 1990: 150) precisely because one's imagination has been primed to appreciate his or her difference. Half a century ago, sociologist Daniel Lerner, in his classic articulation of modernization theory, *The passing of traditional society*, wrote:

> The model of behavior developed by modern society is characterized by empathy, a high capacity for rearranging the self-system on short notice ... [T]he interdependent sectors of modern society require widespread participation. This in turn requires an expansive and adaptive self-system, ready to incorporate new roles and to identify personal values with public issues. This is why modernization of any society has involved the great characterological transformation we call psychic mobility (Lerner 1958: 51).

Empathy, the ability to imagine oneself in another's place, is a central psychological feature in this reading of modernity, as it allows the modern personality to imagine and accomplish self-directed change and to predict, appreciate, and use the perceptions, understandings, and goals of others. Classroom simulations try to develop this sort of understanding in a more or less literal way through the temporary, restricted, and shallow re-enactment of other lifeways. The goal, for Lerner, was a psychic flexibility that would allow personal change and transformation within the context of social and economic development. For contemporary educators, the goal is both socio-economic and moral: to encourage an understanding of cultural diversity and promote tolerance in the context of an irreducibly multicultural society and encompassing 'global village'.

But as literature scholar Stephen Greenblatt notes in an argument about the way this mobile personality served the European colonial project that began in the sixteenth century, '[w]hat is essential' in this Western sense of empathy

> is the Europeans' ability again and again to insinuate themselves into the preexisting political, religious, even psychic structures of the natives and to turn those structures to their advantage ... There are periods and cultures in which the ability to insert oneself into the consciousness of another is of relatively slight importance, ... others in which it is a major preoccupation, the object of cultivation and fear. Professor Lerner is right to insist that this ability is a characteristically (though not exclusively) Western mode ... he misleads only in insisting ... that it is an act of imaginative generosity, a sympathetic appreciation of the situation of the other fellow ... [W]e must understand that he is speaking of the exercise of ... power, power that is creative as well as destructive, but that is scarcely ever wholly disinterested or benign (Greenblatt 1980: 227-8).

Such power depends on

> the ability and willingness to play a role, to transform oneself, if only for a brief period and with mental reservations, into another. This necessitates the acceptance of disguise, the ability to effect a divorce ... between the tongue and the heart. Such role-playing in turn depends upon the transformation of another's reality into a manipulable fiction (Greenblatt 1980: 228).

This is the use of make-believe 'as foundation of an all-too-seriously serious reality', which Taussig (1993: 255) sees as a fundamental element of human experience central to the process of creating cultural 'others'. Recent proposals by US government agencies, consultants, and private organizations to respond to the threat of globalized radical Islam through a public diplomacy offensive, seeking to encourage particular forms of Islamic thought and practice (Benard 2004; Kaplan 2005; Mahmood 2006; Rabasa, Benard, Schwartz & Sickle 2007), derive in part from a confidence that we can rearrange the theology and devotional practices of others by imagining and supporting alternative Islams, often Islams developed by thinkers whose own psychic flexibility derives from modern forms of education and match our own or that of our modernist ancestors (Starrett 2008).

In *Eklund* v. *Byron*, the 'other's' reality is Islam, and its manipulability as fiction is simultaneously the goal of one non-Muslim party and the fear of the other. From the perspective of contemporary evangelical culture, Islam as a demonic and proselytizing reality cannot be manipulated, even in fictional form, without spiritual danger. Anyone encouraging such practice in the classroom is a *de facto* ally of Islamist radicals, a popular reaction that led one schoolteacher involved in a controversy over teaching about Islam to remark ruefully that in the public consciousness he had been suddenly transformed from 'a Methodist boy from the deserts of California ... into a pro-Muslim fundamentalist multiculturalist activist' (pers. comm., 28 February 2007).

Added to this cultural concern is the more strictly legal question of the boundaries and uses of ritual in secular contexts. Is an analogue to ritual action ritual itself? Is it part of a devotional and therefore illegitimate ritual whose aim is 'learning Islam', or part of a secular and therefore legitimate schoolroom ritual whose aim is 'learning about Islam'? And does it make a difference in our multicultural society precisely whom the targets of these exercises are? Can a Muslim student be expected to simulate 'his or her own culture' in the context of schoolroom lessons? The Council on Islamic Education (CIE), one of the allegedly 'militant Islamic groups' that Daniel Pipes has accused of pressuring textbook publishers and school districts to use their power to indoctrinate children in Islam, has itself criticized the use of role-playing exercises in public schools.[8] The CIE advances two main reasons for cautioning against such exercises, both drawn from guidelines developed by a non-profit organization called The First Amendment Center and endorsed by almost twenty American religious and educational groups (Haynes 1999). First, according to CIE,

> [s]imulating acts of worship or mimicking the language of beliefs and personal identity can trivialize deeply held ideas and spiritual experiences. It is not necessary to inhabit another's religious beliefs in order to learn about differing belief patterns. ... Second, such role-playing activities simulate conforming to a particular religion by following some or all of its practices. As such, these activities violate ... the principles that study of religion must be academic and not devotional, that teaching about religion must not seek to conform students to a religion, and that the teaching neither denigrates or promotes any religions or religion per se. ... To see how inappropriate such role-playing activities are,

one need only ponder the possibility that a student who practices the religion in question is present in the class. How could they perform the 'simulation'?[9]

Such simulations are deployed more often than we might think, though, as Muslim Student Associations sponsor Ramadan 'Fast-a-Thons' on college campuses, raising consciousness and resources by having non-Muslim students sign up to fast for a day during Ramadan in return for community or corporate donations of food or money to local charities (600 students signed up for the 2006 Fast-a-Thon at Indiana University in Bloomington, and thirty at Texas State University in San Marcos). On a number of college and even high school campuses, non-Muslim women – with the encouragement of local Muslim organizations and individuals as well as their non-Muslim social studies teachers – have donned *hijab*, or modest dress, for short periods of time to investigate the everyday discrimination, anxiety, and hostility that veiled women attract in the United States. The objectified form of exotic ritual has multiple uses.

Conclusions

Social conflict is not something that happens when, out of weakness, indefiniteness, obsolescence, or neglect, cultural forms cease to operate, but rather something which happens when, like burlesqued winks, such forms are pressed by unusual situations or unusual intentions to operate in unusual ways.

Geertz 1973: 28

The Council on Islamic Education's concerns about burlesqued winks at Islam are matched by the concerns of some Christian activists about those same winks as rehearsal. At least three theories of ritual action are at stake in *Eklund* and related cases. In the first, ritual is a coercive tool to distance children from their parents' religious heritage. As noted above, for some Protestants this theory is informed by a theological conception of demon-inspired writing and ritual which draws people into intercourse with dark spirits and entraps them. The Council on Islamic Education and others like the lawyers of the Thomas More Law Center and the American Catholic Lawyers Association may be informed by a less suspicious but more widespread view of ritual as a central element of specific religious traditions that helps bind the congregant to the past, the present, and the future community of worship. Engaging in the rituals of a tradition to which one does not acknowledge membership or commitment is evidence of inauthenticity and must be the result of misunderstanding, coercion, hypocrisy, or evil intent.

The third theory of ritual is that of teachers and the courts, for whom some limited types of coercion – and even the performance of rituals acknowledged as sacred to particular traditions, as long at they are approached with 'secular' intent – are legitimate for the sake of learning, a particular kind of psychological transformation which is assumed not to affect the student's relationship to family social identities or spiritual loyalties. Ritual and ritual-like action are legally troublesome only if approached with a particular set of cognitive or emotional orientations. But much of the contemporary anthropology of ritual takes a different view. Humphrey and Laidlaw (1994) have argued, like Smith (1956 [1889]) and Rappaport (1983), that action belonging to the abstract category of 'ritual' is independent of the intentions or understandings of its participants, and that engagement in ritualized action is a kind of 'performative think- ing' that demonstrates a particular kind of commitment to, or even the creation of,

entities outside the self (Houseman 2005). To expand on this analysis, it is worth
pointing out that these entities might be anything: an idea, a person, a deity, an
institution, a kinship group, a tradition, a social relationship.

From this perspective, the difference between ritual and the 'simulation' of ritual
becomes clearer. If ritual is a culturally meaningful act in Geertz's sense (even if not
defined by the mental state or intention of any particular actor), then its simulation is
not a meaningless act, but rather an act which is meaningful relative to a different set
of entities, entities potentially unspecified in the ritual's own manifest content. In this
case, the enactment is relative to the values of tolerance, cosmopolitanism, and diversity, or to the very modernist attitude that Lerner attributed to developed societies. In
a more specific sense, these are not rituals of Islam, but rituals relative to Islam as a
member of the category of 'world religions' rather than merely the national religion of
the Arabs (Masuzawa 2005) or one of the 'unusual religions or religious practices' that
the California Department of Education feared might undermine respect for religion as
such (California School Boards Association 2004: 21). Schoolroom rituals are also
meaningful relative to traditions of pedagogy charged with developing imagination
and creativity 'for their own sake' as taken-for-granted elements of psychological well-
being. And finally, they are practical responses to the difficulty of teaching history to
middle grade students, whose teachers assume that the participatory nature of dramatic or ritual enactments holds their attention long enough to slide 'secular' information into their brains. Like other daily rituals, they help define the relationship
between student and teacher.

In thinking through 'the dark side of globalization', Appadurai noted that one of the
many uncertainties common in the modern world

> is about whether a particular person really is what he or she claims or appears to be or has historically
> been ... [L]ocal and regional forms of cultural fundamentalism may be seen as part of an emerging
> repertoire of efforts to produce previously unrequired levels of certainty about social identity [and]
> values (2006: 6-7; see also Bauman 1990; 1991).

Absent or much attenuated in such fundamentalisms – whether religious or secular –
is the ability to contextualize public representations of identity in complex or nuanced
ways. Absent also is an appreciation that the depth of one's discomfort with the
identities of Others might be more severe the closer they are to one's own (Harrison
2002). While Appadurai's analytical framework attaches the adjective 'predatory' to
majority populations seeking to halt the growth and influence of minorities, anti-
Muslim activists in the United States attach it to the phenomenon of Muslim civil and
legal engagement (Goldstein 2008).

For Geertz, the chief difficulty in understanding people of other cultures is 'a lack of
familiarity with the imaginative universes within which their acts are signs' (1973: 13).
Like Lerner, he thinks of the modern consciousness as one in which a flexible generosity
of spirit prompts us to seek a morally engaged conversation with others aimed at 'the
enlargement of the universe of human discourse' (1973: 14). Greenblatt and Taussig
might reply that the issue of cultural gulfs is partly a matter of the different degrees
of power people have to choose which imaginative universe is to be the framework
in which given actions are to be interpreted.[10] Unlike non-Muslim projects to
reform Islam, schoolroom simulations and Muslim 'ritual outreach' activities like
Fast-a-Thons evoke imaginative universes of religious ritual, but do so with properly

court-sanctioned secular intent, seeking neither to represent nor to create 'sacred and worshipful' orientations. They may even act as buffers between the understandings and interests of Muslims and non-Muslims, preventing either from engaging too directly or explicitly with assumptions and experiences underpinning the imaginative universes of the other.

Ritual simulation, being something that anyone might do, interferes with the certainty about identity that Appadurai and Bauman identify as one of the urgent desires of a modern, mobile world. For some communities concerned about the politics of Islam, the experience of modernity is one in which it is possible to believe that their governing agencies and educational institutions are collaborating with Muslim minorities to convert children to Islam in the interest of 'secularism', 'tolerance', or 'multiculturalism.' As the twenty-first century proceeds, we can hope that these experiences and these perceptions of an insidious politics of enchantment do not result in the development of further predatory identities.

NOTES

[1] 'It is above all the media said. Some of them said that in Holland, at one of the centers, the number of people who accepted Islam during the days that followed the [September 11] operations were more than the people who accepted Islam in the last eleven years' (Osama bin Laden, from transcript at *http:// archives.cnn.com/2001/US/12/13/tape.transcript/*, accessed 29 January 2009).

[2] *http://www.blessedcause.org/coverup.htm*, accessed 29 January 2009.

[3] *Lemon* v. *Kurtzman* concerned the constitutionality of providing state funds and services to students and employees of parochial schools; *Lynch* v. *Donnelly* centred on the issue of whether municipalities could display publicly funded religious symbols as part of holiday displays.

[4] Several times since that date, Muslims praying in public areas such as malls or airports in the United States have triggered reports to local or federal authorities of suspicious activity, the assumption being that would-be martyrs pray before conducting suicide attacks.

[5] See, for example, *http://www.biblebelievers.org.au/moongod.htm* and *http://www.chick.com/information/ religions/islam/allah2.asp*, both accessed 29 January 2009.

[6] See *http://www.kimo4jesus.org/modules.php?name=Content&pa=showpage&pid=16* and *http:// www.kimo4jesus.org/modules.php?name=Content&pa=showpage&pid=26*, both accessed 29 January 2009.

[7] The ouija board (implicated in the demonic possession in William Friedkin's 1973 film *The Exorcist*) is a divination game in which two players place their fingers on a flat marker which moves across a board printed with the letters of the alphabet. Participants ask the board questions, and the spelled-out answers are taken to be the work of spiritual forces. For more details, see Ellis (2000).

[8] See *http://www.cie.org/ItemDetail.aspx?id=N&m_id=52&item_id=113&cat_id=99*, accessed 29 January 2009.

[9] As previous note.

[10] Misconstrual may be a tactical decision, as when pundits at Pipes' website Campus Watch and related publications launched an effort in November 2006 to discredit University of Pennsylvania president Amy Gutmann by posting noisy denunciations of her actions at an annual Halloween party at her official residence. Like the parents of the trick-or-treater dressed as Osama bin Laden, Gutmann was criticized as unpatriotic and morally insensitive for having posed for photographs with a number of students dressed in costume, one of whom, an engineering student of Middle Eastern heritage, was dressed as a Muslim 'martyr' complete with replica rifle and suicide belt (*http://www.campus-watch.org/article/id/2941*, accessed 29 January 2009).

LEGAL CASES CITED

All cases can be consulted through the Lexis/Nexis database.
Brown v. *Woodland Joint Unified School District* 1994. Ninth Circuit Court of Appeals.
Eklund v. *Byron Union School District* 2003. United States District Court for the Northern District of California.
Eklund v. *Byron Union School District* 2005. Ninth Circuit Court of Appeals.

Fleischfresser et al. v. *Directors of School District 200* 1994. Seventh Circuit Court of Appeals.
Harris v. *McRae* 1980. Supreme Court of the United States.
Lee v. *Weisman* 1992. Supreme Court of the United States.
Lemon et al. v. *Kurtzman, et al.* 1971. Supreme Court of the United States.
Lynch v. *Donnelly et al.* 1984. Supreme Court of the United States.
Reynolds v. *United States* 1878. Supreme Court of the United States.

REFERENCES

APPADURAI, A. 2006. *Fear of small numbers: an essay on the geography of anger*. Durham, N.C.: Duke University Press.
BAUMAN, Z. 1990. Modernity and ambivalence. In *Global culture: nationalism globalization and modernity* (ed.) M. Featherstone, 143-70. London: Sage.
——— 1991. *Modernity and ambivalence*. Ithaca, N.Y.: Cornell University Press.
BENARD, C. 2004. *Civil democratic Islam: partners, resources, and strategies*. Santa Monica, Calif.: Rand Corporation.
BOWEN, J. 1993. *Muslims through discourse: religion and ritual in Gayo society*. Princeton: University Press.
CALIFORNIA DEPARTMENT OF EDUCATION 1994. *Handbook on the rights and responsibilities of school personnel and students in the areas of providing moral, civic and ethical education, teaching about religion, promoting responsible attitudes and behaviors and preventing and responding to hate violence*. Sacramento.
CALIFORNIA SCHOOL BOARDS ASSOCIATION 2004. Amici curiae brief to the US Court of Appeals, 9th Circuit, in the case of *Eklund* v. *Byron Union School District*.
CLARKE, S. 2007. Rockland jail suspends chaplain over anti-Islam booklets. *The Journal News*, 13 April (available on-line: *http://www.cair-ny.com/HomePage/Community/NewsList/newsDetails/Params/news/1532/prevstruct/970/default.aspx*, accessed 29 January 2009).
COLEMAN, S. 2000. *The globalisation of charismatic Christianity: spreading the gospel of prosperity*. Cambridge: University Press.
COOKSON, C. 2001. *Regulating religion: the courts and the free exercise clause*. New York: Oxford University Press.
CORDOVA, J.M., J.J. KLOR DE ALVA, G.B. NASH, F. NG, C.L. SALTER, L.E. WILSON & K.K. WIXSON 1999. *Across the centuries*. Boston: Houghton Mifflin.
DURKHEIM, É. 1965 [1912]. *The elementary forms of the religious life* (trans. J.W. Swain). New York: Free Press.
al-DUWWA, M. al-SAYYID, M.'A. SULAYMAN, M.S. as-DIN 'ALISH & S.'A. al-KARIM RASHWAN 1987/8. *Al-Tarbiya al-Islamiyya*. Cairo: Al-Jihaz Al-Markazi lil-Kutub Al-Jami'iyya wa al-Madrasiyya wa al-Wasa'il al-Ta'limiyya.
EICKELMAN, D.F. & J. PISCATORI 1996. *Muslim politics*. Princeton: University Press.
ELLIS, B. 2000. *Raising the Devil: Satanism, new religions, and the media*. Lexington: University Press of Kentucky.
——— 2004. *Lucifer ascending: the occult in folklore and popular culture*. Lexington: University Press of Kentucky.
FOUCAULT, M. 1977. *Discipline and punish* (trans. A. Sheridan). New York: Pantheon.
GARRETT, C. 1993. The rhetoric of supplication: prayer theory in seventeenth-century England. *Renaissance Quarterly* **46**, 328-57.
GEERTZ, C. 1973. Thick description: toward an interpretive theory of culture. In *The interpretation of cultures*, C. Geertz, 3-32. New York: Basic Books.
GILMARTIN, D. 2005. A networked civilization? In *Muslim networks from hajj to hip hop* (eds) m. cooke & B.B. Lawrence, 51-68. Chapel Hill: University of North Carolina Press.
GOLDSTEIN, B. 2008. Welcome to 'lawfare' – a new type of jihad (available on-line: *http://www.campuswatch.org/article/id/4995*, accessed 29 January 2009).
GREENBLATT, S. 1980. *Renaissance self-fashioning*. Chicago: University Press.
HANDY, T. 1991. *Islam: a simulation of Islamic history and culture, 610-1100*. Carlsbad, Calif.: Interaction.
HARRISON, S. 2002. The politics of resemblance: ethnicity, trademarks, headhunting. *Journal of the Royal Anthropological Institute* (N.S.) **8**, 211-32.
HAYNES, C. 1999. *A teacher's guide to religion in the public schools*. Nashville, Tenn.: First Amendment Center.
HIRSCHKIND, C. 2006. *The ethical soundscape: cassette sermons and Islamic counterpublics*. New York: Columbia University Press.
HOUSEMAN, M. 2005. The red and the black: a practical experiment for thinking about ritual. In *Ritual in its own right* (eds) D. Handelman & G. Lindquist, 75-97. New York: Berghahn.

HUMPHREY, C. & J. LAIDLAW 1994. *The archetypal actions of ritual: a theory of ritual illustrated by the Jain rite of worship.* Oxford: Clarendon.

KAPLAN, D.E. 2005. Hearts, minds, and dollars. *US News and World Report* **23**, April (available on-line: *http://www.usnews.com/usnews/news/articles/050425/25roots.htm*, accessed 27 January 2009).

KERSHAW-STALEY, T. 2004. Mosque trip yanked. *Middletown Journal*, 26 February (summary available on-line: *http://www.pluralism.org/news/article.php?id=6154*, accessed 29 January 2009).

KOTV 2004. Tulsa parents express concern over teacher workshop on Islam (partial reprint available on-line: *http://www.jihadwatch.org/dhimmiwatch/archives/003649.php*, accessed 29 January 2009).

LATOUR, B. 1993. *We have never been modern* (trans. C. Porter). Cambridge, Mass.: Harvard University Press.

LEONARD, K. 2003. *Muslims in the United States: the state of research.* New York: Russell Sage Foundation.

LERNER, D. 1958. *The passing of traditional society: modernizing the Middle East.* New York: Free Press.

MAHMOOD, S. 2005. *Politics of piety: the Islamic revival and the feminist subject.* Princeton: University Press.

——— 2006. Secularism, hermeneutics, and empire: the politics of Islamic reformation. *Public Culture* **18**, 323-47.

MASUZAWA, T. 2005. *The invention of world religions.* Chicago: University Press.

MEAD, M. 1932. An investigation of the thought of primitive children, with special reference to animism. *Journal of the Royal Anthropological Institute of Great Britain and Ireland* **62**, 173-90.

MITCHELL, T. 1988. *Colonising Egypt.* Cambridge: University Press.

——— 2002. *Rule of experts: Egypt, techno-politics, modernity.* Berkeley: University of California Press.

PIPES, D. 2002. Become a Muslim warrior. *The Jerusalem Post*, **3** July (available on-line: *http://www.danielpipes.org/article/430*, accessed 29 January 2009).

——— 2004. Spreading Islam in American public schools. *FrontPageMagazine.com*, 24 November (available on-line: *http://www.danielpipes.org/article/2236*, accessed 29 January 2009).

RABASA, A., C. BENARD, L.H. SCHWARTZ & P. SICKLE 2007. *Building moderate Muslim networks.* Santa Monica, Calif.: Rand Corporation.

RAPPAPORT, R. 1983. The obvious aspects of ritual. In *Ecology, meaning, and religion*, R. Rappaport, 173-222. Berkeley: North Atlantic Books.

SHIMRON, Y. 2007a. E-mail thanks enemy of Islam: teacher seems to bless evangelism. *Raleigh News & Observer*, 27 February (available on-line: *www.newsobserver.com/105/v-print/story/547751.html*, accessed 29 January 2009).

——— 2007b. Enloe students questioned: former students say teacher suspended this week often talked about Christianity. *Raleigh News & Observer*, 2 March (available on-line: *http://www.newsobserver.com/102/v-print/story/548787.html*, accessed 29 January 2009).

——— 2007c. Schools forbid selling religion: teacher relocated after Enloe episode. *Raleigh News & Observer*, 24 May (available on-line: *http://www.newsobserver.com/news/v-print/story/578088.html*, accessed 29 January 2009).

SMITH, W.R. 1956 [1889]. *The religion of the Semites.* New York: Meridian.

SOARES, B. 2006. Islam in Mali in the neoliberal era. *African Affairs* **105**, 77-95.

STARRETT, G. 2008. When theory is data: coming to terms with 'culture' as a way of life. In *Explaining culture scientifically* (ed.) M.J. Brown, 253-74. Seattle: University of Washington Press.

SULLIVAN, W. 1994. *Paying the words extra: religious discourse in the Supreme Court of the United States.* Cambridge, Mass.: Harvard University Press.

——— 2005. *The impossibility of religious freedom.* Princeton: University Press.

TARGOFF, R. 1997. The performance of prayer: sincerity and theatricality in early modern England. *Representations* **60**, 49-69.

TAUSSIG, M. 1993. *Mimesis and alterity: a particular history of the senses.* New York: Routledge.

WHITE, J. 2005. Islamic indoctrination in Scottsdale, Arizona public school. Reader comment on Pipes 2004, posted 27 February (available on-line: *http://www.danielpipes.org/comments/20546*, accessed 29 January 2009).

Index